THE ONE YEAR® DEVOS 4 SPORTS FANS

JOHN & KATHY HILLMAN WITH **JESSE FLOREA**

TYNDALE HOUSE PUBLISHERS, INC., WHEATON, ILLINOIS

Visit Tyndale's exciting Web site at www.tyndale.com

The One Year is a registered trademark of Tyndale House Publishers, Inc.

Designed by Dean H. Renninger

Library of Congress Cataloging-in-Publication Data

Hillman, John, date.
   The one year devos for sport fans / John and Kathy Hillman with Jesse Florea.
     p. cm.
   Includes index.
   ISBN 0-8423-8711-0 (sc)
   1. Devotional calendars. 2. Sports spectators—Religious life. I. Hillman, Kathy. II. Florea, Jesse, date.
III. Title.
BV4810.H55 2004
242'.2—dc22   2004009718

Printed in the United States of America.

08   07   06   05   04
5   4   3   2   1

JAN
UARY

You will
keep him in
perfect peace,
whose mind is
stayed on You,
because he
trusts in You.

ISAIAH 26:3, NKJV

FEW COLLEGE FOOTBALL FANS expected a highly successful 2000 season from the University of Oklahoma. While they had won the 1999 Independence Bowl, the team had gone the five previous years without a bowl appearance and had endured three losing seasons.

But the Sooners proved the experts wrong by taking an undefeated record into the 2001 Orange Bowl, where they faced Florida State for the national championship.

Playing the nation's toughest schedule, OU rose to the top in the polls with successive victories over Texas, Kansas State, and Nebraska. A second victory over KSU in the Big 12 title game brought the Sooners to a perfect 12–0 record. Although Oklahoma stood as the nation's only undefeated team, many figured perennial power Florida State would win and claim No. 1 bragging rights for the 2000 season.

Despite the high-powered offenses of both teams, defense reigned in the contest. Oklahoma led 3–0 at halftime on the strength of a 27-yard Tim Duncan field goal. The Sooners upped their lead to 6–0 in the third quarter when Duncan kicked a second field goal from 42 yards.

In the fourth quarter, OU's defense created a turnover, leading to the team's only touchdown. Linebacker Rocky Calmus stripped the ball from Florida State quarterback Chris Weinke, and safety Roy Williams recovered the fumble deep in Seminole territory. Two plays later, tailback Quentin Griffin scored from the 10-yard line and Oklahoma led 13–0.

FSU avoided the shutout with a last-minute safety, but Oklahoma's 13–2 victory gave the Sooners a perfect 13–0 record and their seventh national championship.

EXTRA POINT

< < < < < < < < < < < < < < < < < < <

Complete perfection in any aspect of life is impossible, whether it's school, job, relationships, or athletics. And while Oklahoma didn't play every game perfectly, the Sooners finished with a perfect record. They trusted their coaches and kept their minds steadfastly focused on their national championship goal.

No one on earth, except Jesus, has ever lived every moment of life perfectly. And while God does not promise us perfection when we trust in him, he does grant us perfect peace if we focus our mind on him.

GOAL! *Make at least one New Year's resolution that will you help you experience perfect peace. Write it down.*

Ask God to help keep you focused on him throughout the year.

CAN YOU IMAGINE a football defense so good that it doesn't give up a point all season? Well, in 1937, Duke University had that kind of defense.

The Blue Devils opened the year by defeating Virginia Tech 18–0. Then Duke blanked Davidson, Colgate, Georgia Tech, Wake Forest, North Carolina, Syracuse, North Carolina State, and Pittsburgh to tally an amazing nine-straight run of shutouts!

Duke's perfect record coupled with its perfect defense earned the school a berth in the Rose Bowl against the University of Southern California Trojans.

The teams battled fiercely through three quarters, but Duke went ahead 3–0 in the fourth on Tony Ruffa's 23-yard field goal. With the game winding down, USC took over on offense, 61 yards away from the Blue Devils' goal line.

During the drive, USC assistant coach Joe Wilensky telephoned head coach Howard Jones from the press box and suggested that fourth-string quarterback Doyle Nave be sent into the contest. Assuming his entire staff backed the call, Jones sent Nave into the huddle along with Al Krueger—his favorite, yet seldom used, receiver.

The duo immediately brought the sluggish Trojan offense to life. Three straight passes from Nave to Krueger netted 13, 9, and –2 yards. With only 41 seconds remaining, the substitute quarterback found his fellow reserve in the end zone for an 18-yard touchdown. The only scoring play Duke allowed all year gave USC a 7–3 victory.

EXTRA POINT < < < < < < < < < < < < < < < < < < < < < < What unlikely heroes! Imagine sitting on the bench in a bowl game listed fourth on the depth chart. Surely Nave and Krueger never thought they would play unless the Trojans suffered a lot of injuries. But the call came.

The two turned defeat into victory and went from overlooked to exalted. Why? They remained willing and ready to be used by the coach.

In the Bible, Jesus says we need to be ready to serve him at all times. Nobody knows when he will return. So as a member of his team, always be prepared to get into the game.

GOAL! *Think of a time when you got to do something because you were willing and ready. Ask the heavenly Father to help you be prepared to hear and answer his call.*

> You must be ready all the time, for the Son of Man will come when least expected.
> LUKE 12:40

02 JAN

In the morning,
O Lord, you
hear my voice;
in the morning
I lay my
requests
before you
and wait in
expectation.

PSALM 5:3, NIV

WHEN IT COMES TO COMPETING, you'd think that the

athlete with most experience would have the edge—especially if the sport involves racing at speeds over 65 mph on a high-performance snowmobile. But at the 2002 Winter X Games, T. J. Gulla proved that's not always the case.

Racing in the X Games hillcross competition for the first time, Gulla brought home the gold. The hillcross event is a snowmobile race that takes a mere 45 seconds to complete. Not only is this race fast, it's all uphill!

While Gulla was certainly no hillcross pro, he wasn't a stranger to snowmobiling. He had raced in the snocross event many times. But after finishing 23rd in that event at the X Games, he hoped to redeem himself in hillcross.

With only one race under his belt, Gulla faced hillcross legend Carl Kuster—who was going for his third-straight X Games championship in the event. Up until the finals, Kuster had won every hillcross race he'd entered and was anxiously awaiting another victory. This time it was for the prestigious X Games gold medal.

As the green flag went up, Gulla was the first off the starting line. It didn't take long for him to realize that a medal was in his grasp, and he grinded his way up the mountain. Gulla's quick start earned him a huge upset and an unexpected gold.

EXTRA POINT < < < < < < < < < < < < < < < < < < <

In the hillcross competition, experience is important, but a quick jump off the starting blocks can make a big difference. T. J. Gulla timed his start perfectly and won a highly sought-after X Games gold medal.

Just like getting a good start can bring victory in a race, getting a good start can also bring victory in a day. Beginning the day by reading the Bible and praying can help you accomplish victories you never thought possible!

GOAL! *Before you begin your day at school or jump into the weekend, get a good start by spending some time with God. Do you have challenges in your day? List a few of them:*

_____

_____

_____

_____

Ask God to give you strength as you face those daily challenges.

HAVING 12 PLAYERS on the field in a football game rarely goes unnoticed, because two officials carry the responsibility for counting the men on offense while two others count the defensive players. But in the 1969 Orange Bowl, Kansas linebacker Rick Abernathy nearly led his team to victory as the 12th man.

The only Jayhawks football team to win a Big Eight conference title led Penn State 14–7 late in the fourth quarter. However, with just over a minute remaining, Nittany Lions quarterback Chuck Burkhart completed a 47-yard pass to Bob Campbell, setting up first-and-goal at the Kansas 3-yard line.

Kansas coach Pepper Rodgers called for his goal-line defense and substituted two tackles for two linebackers. In the confusion, Abernathy's replacement failed to inform the linebacker to leave the huddle, and Kansas played with a 12-man defense.

Surprisingly, officials overlooked the extra defender for three plays. Penn State twice handed the ball to fullback Tom Cherry, but Abernathy stopped him both times for no gain. With only 15 seconds left to play, Burkhart bootlegged around the left end for the tying touchdown.

Rather than settle for a tie, Penn State coach Joe Paterno opted for a two-point conversion. Burkhart rolled right, attempting a pass to Campbell, but the Kansas defense knocked the ball away.

As the Jayhawks celebrated, they didn't notice that official Foster Grose had flagged Kansas for illegal participation. Given a second chance, Campbell bolted into the end zone and Penn State emerged with a 15–14 victory.

EXTRA POINT < < < < < < < < < < < < < < < < < < < < < < < Abernathy and the Kansas coaches didn't intend to break the rules. But a miscommunication caused Abernathy to be on the field when he shouldn't have been. The officials almost overlooked the error that would have given Kansas the Orange Bowl trophy.

In life, we often don't intend to sin or break God's rules. We make an accidental mistake, or someone causes us to mess up. Occasionally no one finds out, but we can never hide from God. He always throws the penalty flag, and we always pay the price.

GOAL! *Watch a football game in person or on television. Imagine you are the referee or umpire, and count the offensive players. Did you miss any? If you ask him to, God will forgive your accidental—as well as your intentional—sins.*

O God, You know my foolishness; and my sins are not hidden from You.

PSALM 69:5, NKJV

04 JAN

His great
works are too
marvelous to
understand.
He performs
miracles
without
number.

JOB 9:10

MICHAEL JORDAN WILL BE remembered as one of the all-time best players in the National Basketball Association. And when he returned from retirement in 2001 to play for the Washington Wizards, he brought renewed excitement to a lackluster team. Fans could again watch the all-star soar and score, and when his former Chicago Bulls teammates came calling, they witnessed a record-setting performance.

Midway through the 2001–02 season, the holder of six NBA championship rings proved he could still fill up a scorebook. Averaging over 24 points a game, Jordan scored 51 and 45 points in the two contests prior to the game against the Bulls.

The Wizards struck early against Chicago, erupting to a 32–18 first-quarter lead. Then Jordan took charge of the offense, netting 19 of Washington's 25 second-quarter points.

With 5:28 remaining before halftime, Ron Artest fouled Jordan, and the 6-foot-6-inch guard calmly sank both free throws. The second gave the ex-Bull 30,000 career points. He joined Kareem Abdul-Jabbar, Wilt Chamberlain, and Karl Malone as the only players to achieve that feat.

EXTRA POINT < < < < < < < < < < < < < < < < < < < < Michael Jordan may be the most admired athlete in the world. If not, he's certainly one of the most famous. Many consider him the finest basketball player ever. For more than 20 years, Jordan performed miraculous wonders on the basketball court.

As a college freshman in 1982, he scored the winning bucket for the University of North Carolina against Georgetown in the NCAA championship. Jordan led the United States to a gold medal in the 1984 Olympic Games in Los Angeles and added another Summer Games gold in 1992 in Barcelona, Spain.

As incredible as Jordan's career was, someday someone will surpass him. We will be able to count more points and see better defense and scoring ability from another star.

But no one surpasses God. We will never understand his wonders or count his miracles.

GOAL! *Read about Michael Jordan or watch one of his highlight videos. Think about his achievements. Then consider the awesomeness of God—who created each of us and gave everyone on earth specific gifts— and praise him.*

PLAYING THINGS SMART and not taking unnecessary risks can often reward an athlete. American figure skater Todd Eldredge was proof of this fact in the 1998 United States championships.

The 26-year-old performer faced criticism for never attempting a quadruple jump in competition. Seeking his fifth U.S. title, the son of a Cape Cod commercial fisherman unveiled the spectacular maneuver for the first time. He completed the four revolutions successfully but leaned awkwardly on his landing and fell to the ice early in his routine. Despite the fall, the audience cheered.

Showing his veteran experience, Todd recovered with grace and style. He completed a triple axel flawlessly. With music from the movie *Gettysburg* playing in the background, the skater hit six triple jumps and exhibited his characteristic perfect spins.

Eldredge's chief competitor, Virginia native Michael Weiss, attempted two quads. Although Weiss two-footed both jumps as well as a triple axel and a triple flip, five other clean jumps landed the 21-year-old the runner-up spot and a berth on the 1998 Olympic team.

Seven of the judges awarded Eldredge first place, and all gave him solid marks of 5.8s and 5.9s, ensuring his fifth United States title and another shot at Olympic gold.

So be careful how you live, not as fools but as those who are wise.
EPHESIANS 5:15

EXTRA POINT One fall in figure skating can be forgiven. Two mistakes usually cost the athlete big points. Todd Eldredge knew that. When he faltered on the quad, he decided to do his best on safer jumps and attempt perfection on less risky moves. He wanted the U.S. championship. But more than that, he wanted to make the Olympic team with a top-three finish.

The apostle Paul reminds us to be wise and not make foolish decisions. Eldredge's choice to be careful paid off, and he stood atop the medal stand.

GOAL! *Try to jump and turn around as many times as you can in the air. Did you make it all the way around once? twice? Praise God that he gives us the ability to act wisely.*

For you have
been my hope,
O Sovereign
Lord,
my confidence
since my youth.

PSALM 71:5, NIV

AGE OFTEN DOESN'T MATTER in athletics. It's talent that shines through. That was certainly the case in 1978 when Brown University hosted the first international swimming meet held solely for women.

More than 100 swimmers representing the United States, Belgium, Canada, Great Britain, Italy, Norway, Sweden, the former West Germany, and the former Soviet Union converged in Providence, Rhode Island, for the history-making competition.

Tracy Caulkins, a 14-year-old from Nashville, Tennessee, dominated the field from the outset. On the first day, she broke the American record in the 200-yard breaststroke with a time of 2:16.47. In the race, Caulkins edged out 13-year-old Soviet Julia Bogdanova, who had beaten her twice the previous summer. Later that same day, the Tennessee native broke another record in the 200-yard individual medley at 2:00.27.

But the teenage swimmer wasn't finished. The following day, Caulkins set a new mark in the 400-yard medley, clocking in at 4:16.75. She also led the United States team to a gold medal in the 400-yard medley relay.

Only one event marred an otherwise perfect performance. In the 100-yard breaststroke, Caulkins placed second to Bogdanova at 1:04.46, compared to the Soviet swimmer's 1:03.20.

EXTRA POINT < < < < < < < < < < < < < < < < < < < < < < < Tracy Caulkins possessed athletic ability. She hoped to do well in the first international women's swimming meet.

But hope wasn't enough. Caulkins trained hard. She worked on the breaststroke, the freestyle, the butterfly, and the backstroke. She spent hours in the pool practicing turns, race starts, and proper stroke mechanics. All the while, she built her hope into confidence. She knew she had the potential to win. She knew she was ready. Then she made it happen.

Hope in the Bible isn't merely wishful thinking. It doesn't consist of hoping it will rain or hoping to do well. Instead, biblical hope carries the meaning of confident expectation. We can confidently count on that kind of hope.

That's the hope we have in God, Creator of the universe. If he says it, he'll make it happen. If he promises, he'll keep the promise. From youth to old age, we can have absolute confidence if we put our hope in God.

GOAL! *Count the number of times in a day that you say or hear the word hope. How was the word used? Praise God for his confident hope.*

TRAILING THE BUFFALO BILLS by one point with only 16 seconds left in the game, the Tennessee Titans needed a miracle to keep their Super Bowl aspirations alive in the 2000 American Football Conference championship game.

With the slimmest glimmer of hope, Tennessee head coach Jeff Fisher reached deep into the playbook for a "gadget" kickoff return play called "Home Run Throw Back." It called for tight end Frank Wycheck to get the ball and then throw it across the field.

As expected, Buffalo kicked short to prevent a runback, and Lorenzo Neal fielded the pigskin on the bounce. He handed off to Wycheck, who then fired it from sideline to sideline to a waiting Kevin Dyson. With blockers leading the way, Dyson bolted 75 yards down the sideline for a game-winning touchdown that stunned the Bills.

But after the play, the officiating crew huddled. Buffalo claimed Wycheck's pass traveled forward rather than backward as is required of a lateral. The crew called a time-out to look at the video.

Referee Phil Luckett reviewed replays for almost five minutes before judging them inconclusive and allowing the touchdown to stand. Sportswriters nicknamed the unusual play "The Music City Miracle," and Tennessee went on to play in the Super Bowl.

> For God will bring every deed into judgment, including every hidden thing, whether it is good or evil.
>
> ECCLESIASTES 12:14, NIV

EXTRA POINT

< < < < < < < < < < < < < < < < < < < <

The outcome of that playoff game came down to one issue: judgment. The official's judgment call awarded the touchdown—and the game—to the Tennessee Titans.

The outcome of many life situations comes down to that same issue: judgment. We often talk about people as having good or bad judgment because they make good or bad choices.

Through prayer, reading the Bible, and talking with knowledgeable Christians, we learn to judge good from evil and to make wise decisions. That's what God desires.

GOAL! *Think about football's instant-replay rule. Do you think it's a good idea? Would you like to have an instant-replay machine to help you make good decisions in life? God wants to help you develop good judgment. All you have to do is ask him.*

08 JAN

ROMANS 12:11

SERVE THE LORD ENTHUSIASTICALLY.

NEVER BE LAZY IN YOUR WORK, BUT

TIGER WOODS CLOSED OUT the 1999 Professional Golf Association season with four straight tournament victories. When the 2000 PGA competition began, Woods continued his winning streak.

Following victories in the National Car Rental Classic, the Tour Championship, the American Express Championship, and the World Cup of Golf, the 24-year-old traveled to Hawaii for the Mercedes Championship. Tied after three days, Woods and Ernie Els matched each other stroke for stroke in the final round.

When Woods took a lead on the 10th hole, Els responded with a birdie on 11. On the final hole, a 633-yarder, Woods appeared to gain the upper hand by reaching the green in two shots. But using his 3 wood, Els guided his ball closer to the pin. Both golfers carded eagles on No. 18 to remain tied at 276 after four rounds.

Going to sudden death, Woods and Els recorded birdies on the first playoff hole. On the next hole, Woods sank a 40-foot downhill putt to edge his rival for the title. With the championship, he became the first PGA player to win five tournaments consecutively since Ben Hogan accomplished the feat in 1953.

EXTRA POINT < < < < < < < < < < < < < < < < < < < < < < Five in a row. Amazing!

Tiger Woods could have let down a little after his third or fourth win. He could have gotten tired. Traveling across the Pacific Ocean to Hawaii and fighting the time change could have made for a good excuse. But he maintained his zeal and enthusiastic devotion to his sport. He kept his fervor and emotional intensity throughout the contest and into the playoff.

When we begin a task in life, it's easy to start off strong. We're excited and give our all. After a while though, we let up some. We coast. We don't work quite as hard as we could or should.

In the Bible Paul reminds us that we must never lose our zeal for serving God. We should be enthusiastically devoted to all the Lord wants us to do . . . no matter what.

GOAL! *Ask the Father to lead you to do a simple service for him. It might be running errands for an elderly person or writing a letter to someone in the military.*

Be sure to complete the task with as much zeal as when you started.

09 JAN

AN INTIMIDATING COURSE can psych out even the best athletes. And the ski superpipe at the 2003 X Games Global Championships was the biggest, steepest pipe that even veteran competitors had ever seen. Sound scary?

Not for Sarah Burke. She wasn't fazed by Whistler Blackcomb Resort's mammoth superpipe in British Columbia. Even after she crashed hard in a practice run while attempting a 720 the day before the finals, Burke came back and attacked the pipe with more huge air during the championships.

Fans were surprised to see Burke walking and absolutely shocked to see her dominate the largest pipe ever built for this type of competition. In spite of the painful crash the day before, this Midland, Ontario, native was the first woman to ever land a 720 in competition. Her determination and refusal to be overcome by fear gave her the win—and the respect of fans and fellow competitors.

EXTRA POINT < < < < < < < < < < < < < < < < < < < < A brutal crash can be enough to discourage any progressive freestyle skier. Sarah Burke could have looked back at her fall the day before and shied away from giving her all. But she chose to look ahead at the competition at hand. She didn't let a past mistake hinder her ability to perform when she needed to most.

Making a mistake during sports can be hard, but making mistakes in life because of sin can be much more discouraging. If there was anyone who could have let past mistakes get him down, it was the apostle Paul. Before Paul came to know Christ personally, he was spiritually dead. He hated Jesus so much that he imprisoned and even killed Christians.

Instead of letting the past get him down, Paul confessed his sin to God and followed him. The Lord canceled Paul's debt of sin and made him a new creation. God used Paul's life in amazing ways—he even used Paul to write much of the New Testament.

GOAL! *Is there a sin in your life that's holding you back from obeying God? If you confess it right now and ask him for strength, you'll have the courage to move forward with his help. God wants to do great things in your life!*

When you were spiritually dead because of your sins and because you were not free from the power of your sinful self, God made you alive with Christ, and he forgave all our sins. He canceled the debt, which listed all the rules we failed to follow. He took away that record with its rules and nailed it to the cross.

COLOSSIANS 2:13-14, NCV

GREATNESS IS HARD to maintain, especially in football. Injuries, free agency, and salary-cap issues cause teams to lose key players and eventually fade into mediocrity. In 1999, the Dallas Cowboys discovered their days of Super Bowl glory had passed.

Dallas, a three-time Super Bowl champion in the '90s, hosted the Arizona Cardinals in the first round of the NFL playoffs. Unlike the Cowboys, the Cardinals hadn't won a postseason contest since defeating the Philadelphia Eagles for the 1947 NFL championship.

As the game unfolded, Arizona played like seasoned veterans, and Dallas looked like newcomers. In the first three minutes, the Cardinals put points on the scoreboard with a 12-yard touchdown pass from Jake Plummer to Adrian Murrell. And just before halftime, the visitors kicked a field goal.

Arizona added to its lead early in the third quarter as Plummer and Larry Centers connected on a touchdown to make it 17–0.

Troy Aikman attempted to pass the Cowboys back into contention, but the quarterback finished the contest with 22 completions in 49 attempts for only 191 yards and 3 interceptions.

Dallas did get on the scoreboard with a late touchdown pass to Billy Davis, but Arizona collected its second playoff win in franchise history with a 20–7 triumph.

> Turn us back to You, O Lord, and we will be restored; renew our days as of old.
>
> LAMENTATIONS 5:21, NKJV

EXTRA POINT

‹ ‹

The Cowboys were the team to beat in the 1990s. Every time Dallas took the field, the athletes   and everyone else—knew they could, should, and probably would win.

Then it happened. The Cowboys slowly lost their glory.

The same thing can happen to us. We can start thinking we're unbeatable and drift away from God. If we aren't tapped into God through Bible study, prayer, and worship, our spiritual life can lose its vibrancy. We start to miss the excitement we had when we were walking with God every day. That's when we need to turn back to him.

GOAL! *Think about the time you felt strongest in your relationship with God. What were you doing during those "glory days"? Ask God to help you always stay connected to him.*

All you have made will praise you, O Lord; your saints will extol you.

PSALM 145:10, NIV

SINCE THE TEAM'S FORMATION in 1966, the New Orleans Saints have experienced a lot of frustration and little jubilation. But in the 2000 NFL playoffs, the franchise found reason to celebrate.

New Orleans, the NFC West divisional champion, faced the defending Super Bowl champion St. Louis Rams at the Superdome in the first round of the playoffs. The teams had just met in the regular season finale with St. Louis claiming a 26–21 victory. The odds of New Orleans exacting revenge appeared bleak, since starting quarterback Jeff Blake and running back Ricky Williams were injured.

True to form, the Rams took an early lead on a 17-yard touchdown pass from Kurt Warner to Isaac Bruce.

But then the Saints erupted for 31 straight points as Aaron Brooks threw scoring passes of 12, 10, 49, and 16 yards, and Doug Brien kicked a 33-yard field goal. Willie Jackson, who caught six passes for 142 yards in the contest, snared three touchdown receptions.

Although the 31–7 lead seemed insurmountable, St. Louis attempted a fourth-quarter comeback. Warner tossed two touchdown passes and scored another on a 5-yard scamper, narrowing the margin to 31–28.

With under a minute remaining, the Rams forced a New Orleans punt, but Az-Zahir Hakim botched the fair catch, and the Saints recovered the fumble. Brooks took a knee three times to run out the clock, and New Orleans captured its first playoff victory in the team's 34-year history.

The entire city of New Orleans celebrated. Their Saints had finally won in the postseason.

EXTRA POINT < < < < < < < < < < < < < < < < < < < < For the die-hard Saints supporters, victory after so many years tasted especially sweet. It's easy to get excited when our favorite pro team wins.

Many of us enjoy cheering at college games too. High school, middle school, and even youth league contests bring us to our feet after a great play.

But there's one who deserves our praise even more. We should constantly extol God for his greatness, yet we often find it easier to cheer for our favorite athlete. The Lord is the greatest of all time. And he's great every moment of every day of every year—for now and forever.

GOAL! *Write a prayer of praise to God.*

_____

_____

_____

WAYNE GRETZKY PUT POINTS on the board at a mind-boggling pace during his 20-year National Hockey League career. And at the midpoint of the 1997–98 season, when the *Hockey News* honored Gretzky as the greatest player in NHL history, he shone like the star he was.

With the New York Rangers and the Toronto Maple Leafs struggling to remain in the playoff chase, Madison Square Garden was packed to watch the "Great One" compete on the ice and receive his award. The veteran accepted the honor, acknowledging that greats such as Bobby Orr and Gordie Howe deserved recognition.

As the game unfolded, both teams played with intensity. The Rangers scored first as Pat LaFontaine tallied with an assist from Gretzky. Tied at 1–1 in the second period, New York went ahead on a goal by Niklas Sundstrom, set up by Gretzky's pass from behind the net.

The Rangers collected their final goal just over two minutes later on a power play. Adam Graves netted the puck by one-timing a Gretzky pass. New York held on for a 3–2 win, thanks to three Gretzky assists.

EXTRA POINT < < < < < < < < < < < < < < < < < < < < Wayne Gretzky dreamed his whole life of being the greatest hockey player of all time. His league-leading 2,857 points on 1,963 assists, and 894 goals in 1,487 games help make the case that he achieved that goal.

Notice that Gretzky had more than twice as many assists as goals. Could he have scored more? Probably. But Gretzky looked to his teammates and wanted to make them better. And it was his unselfishness on the ice that led to his greatness.

God wants us to think more about others than ourselves too. When we have God's Spirit inside us, we live with unselfishness and humility. We see others through the Father's eyes. We become the best, maybe not in the way the world defines greatness, but in the way our Lord does.

GOAL! *Look at a sports page in the newspaper or flip through a sports magazine. Note the athletes in the headlines. Do they think more about their own statistics or about their team's success? Praise God for his Spirit that helps us stay away from sin and live more like him.*

> So I advise you to live according to your new life in the Holy Spirit. Then you won't be doing what your sinful nature craves.
> GALATIANS 5:16

DURING HER OUTSTANDING SWIMMING career, Jenny Thompson claimed eight Olympic gold medals in relay events. But in the 1998 World Swimming Championships, the American found a way to shine on her own.

The 25-year-old swimmer began the meet on a high note, capturing first place in the 100-meter freestyle. Her 54.95 time edged out Slovakia's Martina Moracova (55.09) and China's Shan Ying (55.10) for the gold.

Two days later, Thompson excelled in her specialty: the relays. Along with Kristy Kowal, Lea Maurer, and Amy Van Dyken, she won the 400-meter freestyle relay gold medal, setting an American record of 4:01.93 in the process.

But Thompson saved her greatest performance for last. The next day in the 100-meter butterfly prelims, she established a meet record of 58.91, breaking the old mark of 58.98 set by Liu Limin in 1994.

In the finals, Thompson swam even faster. She shattered her own record with a time of 58.46.

EXTRA POINT < < < < < < < < < < < < < < < < < < < < <
Swimming or running on a relay team means being part of a group. But unless each person carries his or her load, the team loses.

In a loss, it's easy to point fingers at the slowest person or the one who didn't meet the coach's time goal in the race. We blame them for the loss. Or if we're the slowest—even if we did our best—we blame ourselves.

The Bible says we shouldn't compare ourselves to other people. Instead, we should test ourselves against God's standard of excellence. We should carry the load that God has assigned to us without worrying about what he asks from someone else.

The Lord expects us to do this in sports . . . and in life.

GOAL! *Think of a time you compared yourself to another person. Did you compare well or did you fall short? How did it make you feel? Inadequate? Prideful? Ask the Father to help you look only at your own actions.*

WHEN THE GAME'S ON THE LINE, winning teams have a knack for rising to the occasion. The Dallas Cowboys did just that in the 1996 National Football Conference championship.

Dallas, looking for its third Super Bowl appearance in four years, hosted the Green Bay Packers at Texas Stadium.

The Pack opened the scoring on a 46-yard field goal following a blocked punt. And after a back-and-forth first half, the Cowboys entered the second half ahead 24–17, thanks to a late 1-yard scoring plunge by Emmitt Smith.

The third quarter belonged to the Packers, however. A 37-yard field goal and a 1-yard touchdown pass from Brett Favre to Robert Brooks brought Green Bay a 27–24 edge.

In the fourth quarter, the home team called on its dependable tailback to carry the load. Smith capped a 90-yard drive with a 5-yard touchdown run. Less than two minutes later, Larry Brown put Dallas back on offense with a 28-yard interception and return.

Following a 36-yard pass to Michael Irvin, Smith scored his third touchdown on a 16-yard jaunt. The NFL's leading rusher finished the day with 150 yards on 35 carries, and the Cowboys advanced to Super Bowl XXX with a 38–27 victory.

EXTRA POINT

For many years, Emmitt Smith anchored the Dallas Cowboys' offense. Teammates, coaches, and fans knew that as long as Emmitt could run, they had hope of winning any game.

Have you ever noticed how some Christians solidly anchor their lives to God? God strengthens those people and helps them become an anchor for others. They show consistent confidence. They never give up. They understand that the future remains secure and firm. Their hope is contagious.

That's the way the writer of Hebrews encourages us all to be. Our secure hope of salvation and eternal life in Jesus should always be our anchor.

GOAL! *Think about the purpose and importance of anchors. Write down some ideas below.*

_____

_____

Thank God for being your anchor.

So God has given us both his promise and his oath. These two things are unchangeable because it is impossible for God to lie. Therefore, we who have fled to him for refuge can take new courage, for we can hold on to his promise with confidence. This confidence is like a strong and trustworthy anchor for our souls.

HEBREWS 6:18-19

Why should we,
mere humans,
complain
when we are
punished for
our sins?
Instead, let
us test and
examine our
ways. Let us
turn again in
repentance to
the Lord.

LAMENTATIONS

3:39-40

NOTHING FRUSTRATES a top-ranked tennis player more than losing an important first-round match before a hometown crowd. But in the 2002 Australian Open, Lleyton Hewitt compounded his failure with petty gripes.

The 20-year-old native of Adelaide, Australia, had risen to the No. 1 spot in the world rankings prior to the 2002 season. His fellow Aussies hoped Hewitt could claim the Open title for the host country for the first time since 1976.

But two weeks prior to the tournament, Lleyton contracted chicken pox. Although it posed only a minor inconvenience, the illness sapped his strength. In the first round, Hewitt drew Spain's Alberto Martin. Initially it appeared as if Hewitt would handle the 39th-ranked player easily, as he won the first set 6–1.

Martin rallied, however, by keeping the ball in play for long stretches and wearing down his physically weakened opponent. The Spaniard won the next two sets 6–1, 6–4 as Hewitt committed three unforced errors for every winning shot.

With the decisive fourth set tied 6–6, the match went into a tiebreaker. Leading 5–4, Martin asked the umpire for a time-out due to cramping in his legs. Following three minutes of treatment, he took the next two points and captured a four-set victory.

After the match, Hewitt complained that although the time-out was legal, his opponent should have waited until the game break.

EXTRA POINT < < < < < < < < < < < < < < < < < < < < < Did Martin have an outstanding game plan? Yes. Was his plan of wearing down his weakened opponent effective? Yes. Was the official following the rules when he awarded the time-out to Martin? Yes. Should Hewitt have complained about the umpire's ruling? No.

Nobody likes to lose. Sometimes we want to make excuses and complain instead of congratulating our opponent or examining why we lost. The fact is, maybe we deserved to lose. Perhaps we didn't work hard enough or were weakened by injury or illness.

The truth is, there are consequences for our actions. When we don't follow the coach's plan, we can lose games. Just like when we don't follow God's rules, we must accept the consequences.

GOAL! *Think of a time you were punished for something you did or said. Did you complain? Instead of complaining, ask God to help you accept the consequences and turn back to him.*

CARDING A ROUND OF GOLF under 60 strokes is nearly unthinkable. Every shot must be perfect—a golfer must score under par on more than half the holes. But in 1999, David Duval not only recorded a 59, but he did it when the stakes were high.

Duval trailed Fred Funk by seven strokes as the Bob Hope Chrysler Classic headed into the final day. He got off to a strong start, making five birdies on the front nine.

But on the back nine, Duval shot even better. The golfer collected six birdies. Steve Pate had already passed Funk as Duval headed into the final hole, ready to challenge Pate for the lead.

On the par-5, 543-yard 18th hole, Duval's tee shot carried 325 yards. Selecting a 5 iron for his second shot, Duval placed the ball on the green, six feet away from the pin. With the pressure mounting, he sank the short putt for an eagle and a final-round score of 59.

Watching from the clubhouse, Duval waited for Pate to finish his round. Needing a birdie to force a playoff, Pate's 18-foot putt hit the edge of the cup and lipped out. Duval claimed the championship with a five-day total of 334, 26-under-par. He also joined Al Geiberger and Chip Beck as the only three men to record a 59 in professional golf competition.

> Glorious and majestic are his deeds, and his righteousness endures forever.
>
> PSALM 111:3, NIV

EXTRA POINT < < < < < < < < < < < < < < < < < < < < < < David Duval's 59 will forever be etched in the record books. But fans and athletes eventually forget most things that happen in professional, collegiate, and high school sports. Even record-setting performances will be broken and replaced. People remember only the truly rare accomplishments.

Of course, some things do last forever. God's handiwork through creation endures as a testimony to his greatness. The Creator's six days of forming the universe and everything in it stand out as an amazing accomplishment. God's special feats stand the test of time.

GOAL! *Online or in a sports encyclopedia, review records in your favorite sport. How many marks will likely stand for more than five years? ten years? twenty years? forever? God wants to help make your life a rare accomplishment for him.*

17 JAN

Therefore do
not be unwise,
but understand
what the will
of the Lord is.

EPHESIANS
5:17, NKJV

BEING FOOLISH CAN CAUSE PROBLEMS in life and

in sports. In the 1987 NFL playoffs, the New York Jets paid the price for an unwise—and easily avoided—penalty.

Despite a lackluster offensive performance, the Jets led the Cleveland Browns 20–10 with just over four minutes remaining in the game. The situation appeared hopeless for the Browns. Cleveland quarterback Bernie Kosar faced second-and-24 at the Browns 18 yard line, and a fierce pass rush forced an incompletion. But Jets defensive lineman Mark Gastineau blasted Kosar after he released the ball, and the referee penalized New York for roughing the passer.

Given new life, the Browns signal caller completed six of nine passes on the drive, and Kevin Mack scored from a yard away with just under two minutes to play, making the score 20–17.

Less than a minute later, Cleveland forced a New York punt and took over on its own 33.

A penalty and a 37-yard completion took the Browns to the New York 15, and Mark Moseley kicked a 22-yard field goal with seven ticks on the clock, tying the game 20–20. Both teams struggled in overtime with neither squad scoring in the first 15-minute period.

In the second overtime, Cleveland worked its ground game and moved the ball to the Jets 9-yard line. The Browns called on Moseley again, and his boot sailed true for a 23–20 victory in a game that lasted four hours and five minutes.

EXTRA POINT < < < < < < < < < < < < < < < < < < < <

Television commentators pointed to Mark Gastineau's penalty as the turning point in the game. Early in their football careers, all defensive linemen are taught not to hit the quarterback after he gets rid of the ball. Had Gastineau followed the rules and his coach's instruction, his team would likely have won the game. And this wasn't an ordinary game. This was the playoffs.

In the Bible, Paul encourages believers in Jesus not to act foolishly. Instead, we should understand what God wants us to do—and then do it. Foolishness almost always has negative consequences. Following God's will for your life also has consequences, but they are pretty great ones . . . like peace and joy.

GOAL! *Think of a time when you did something or saw something foolish at an athletic contest. What were the consequences? God is ready to help you be wise in all that you do. You just have to ask for his help.*

DURING THE EARLY 1970S, the University of California at Los Angeles men's basketball team seemed unstoppable. The Bruins didn't lose a game for nearly three years as they won 88 straight contests.

But on January 19, 1974, Notre Dame proved to be a tough foe. With a national television audience watching, the second-ranked Fighting Irish hosted No. 1 UCLA.

The visitors, who had collected seven consecutive national titles, shot 70 percent from the field in the first half and took a 43–34 lead into the locker room.

In the second half, the team from South Bend slowly narrowed the gap but still trailed 70–59 with 3:32 remaining. Notre Dame coach Digger Phelps instructed his players to press, and the Bruins committed five straight turnovers that the Irish converted into baskets. With 21 seconds left to play, Dwight Clay completed Notre Dame's incredible comeback, hitting a jumper from the corner and putting the Irish up 71–70.

UCLA called a time-out to set up a possible winning shot, but Tommy Curtis misfired on a 25-foot jumper. Dave Myers attempted a tip-in that went awry, and the Irish knocked the ball out of bounds with six ticks left on the clock.

Bill Walton of the Bruins took the inbounds pass, but his 12-footer failed to fall. Two more Bruins rebound shots missed the hoop, and the buzzer sounded. Notre Dame had stopped the UCLA streak.

> The Lord is good, a refuge in times of trouble.
> He cares for those who trust in him.
>
> NAHUM 1:7, NIV

EXTRA POINT

When we're on a winning streak, it's easy to trust in ourselves. We believe in our intelligence, our athleticism, or our knowledge. We think we can't fail.

The same holds true in life. When all seems to be going well, we often trust in ourselves, holding a high opinion of our gifts and abilities. But then it happens. We fail. Things stop going right. Only when we trust in God can we rise and stand firm. Nothing and no one but him deserves our love and faith.

GOAL! *Go to the library or search the Internet to learn more about UCLA coach John Wooden, who guided Bruins teams to ten NCAA men's basketball titles between 1964 and 1975. Even more than Wooden's team trusted his coaching, we can thank God for the faith we have in his heavenly guidance.*

Brothers, stop thinking like children. In regard to evil be infants, but in your thinking be adults.

1 CORINTHIANS 14:20, NIV

WHEN YOUNG ATHLETES COMPETE against more experienced competitors with a strong reputation, judges tend to favor the older athlete. But in 1996, Michelle Kwan transformed herself from a child prodigy into a world-class contender in the judges' eyes.

Although only 14 at the time, the Torrance, California, native had placed fourth in the World Figure Skating Championships in 1995. Her coach, Frank Carroll, believed she placed lower than she should have because she appeared too childlike to the judges.

The following year at the United States Figure Skating competition, Michelle unveiled a new look. She wore her hair in a bun rather than a ponytail and accentuated her features with heavier makeup. Even her costuming and routine reflected a more sophisticated and mature skater.

Her new look helped, and Michelle's precision and athleticism clinched the gold. She landed seven triple jumps including a triple-toe-loop combination and two tough triple lutzes. Her only falter occurred late in the program when she failed to complete a planned double axel.

All nine judges awarded Kwan first place, and seven gave her marks of 5.9 out of 6.0 for artistic expression. In capturing the American figure-skating crown at age 15, she became the youngest champion since Peggy Fleming achieved the feat in 1964.

EXTRA POINT < < < < < < < < < < < < < < < < < < < < < < < Michelle and her coach rejoiced when the judges stopped thinking of the skater as a child and began marking her as an adult. She needed to be viewed as a mature competitor to top the medal stand.

Michelle Kwan discovered the mark of an adult isn't just age. It's how a person thinks and acts. The apostle Paul understood that. He encouraged Christians to think and act like adults no matter what their age. However, he commanded followers of God to be as innocent as babies when it came to doing wrong.

GOAL! *Do you have any childish things holding back your relationship with Jesus Christ? Try to identify and overcome childish thinking. Ask God to keep you innocent from evil and to help you be an adult Christian throughout your life.*

TODAY, NASCAR POWERS past most sports with its popularity and fanatical fans. But until the 1979 Daytona 500, auto racing found most of its supporters in the South. That year CBS broadcast the "Great American Race" live. It marked the first time a Winston Cup race was on TV from start to finish.

Dale Earnhardt made his first start at Daytona, but legendary drivers Cale Yarborough, Donnie Allison, Bobby Allison, A. J. Foyt, Richard Petty, and Darrell Waltrip made history.

Heading into the final lap, Donnie Allison held a slight lead over Yarborough. On the Superstretch, Yarborough went low to slingshot past Donnie. Not about to let Yarborough make one of his textbook passes, Donnie steered low to block. The two cars banged fenders and crashed into the outside wall at turn three before sliding down into the infield.

Meanwhile, Foyt, Petty, and Waltrip watched the action from about a half lap back. Foyt eased up when he saw the caution flag, allowing Petty and Waltrip to dust him. Petty hung on in the final couple of turns to claim his sixth Daytona 500 victory.

Even though the race was decided, the highlights continued. Yarborough and Donnie Allison jumped out of their cars and started pushing each other. Soon Bobby Allison joined the fray as national TV cameras caught the fight live.

EXTRA POINT < < < < < < < < < < < < < < < < < < < < What is it about fights that makes everybody stop and watch? Have you seen a fight at school where students gathered around the combatants and egged them on? The fight between Cale Yarborough and the Allison brothers during the first televised NASCAR race caught the nation's attention.

While humans seem to like to watch people fight, the Bible isn't so big on the idea. As Christians we're encouraged not to fight. Instead we should try to live at peace with all people. With God in our life, we can have peace in our heart. And that contentment should be evident to everybody.

GOAL! *If somebody tried to pick a fight with you, what would you do? Before a conflict arises, decide to have the courage to walk away. Ask God to give you the wisdom to live at peace with all people.*

> Make every effort to live in peace with all men and to be holy; without holiness no one will see the Lord.
> HEBREWS 12:14, NIV

FOLLOWING AN ALL-PRO QUARTERBACK with four Super Bowl rings creates problems for his successor. Fans naturally compare the new guy to his successful predecessor. And everybody expects the team to continue its winning ways.

For years San Francisco's Steve Young lived in the shadow of Joe Montana, but in Super Bowl XXIX in 1995, Young proved he was a great quarterback in his own right.

Experts pegged the San Francisco 49ers as overwhelming favorites against the San Diego Chargers. As expected, the NFC champions dominated from the outset.

Taking the opening kickoff, San Francisco moved 59 yards in only three plays as Young connected with Jerry Rice on a 44-yard scoring pass to tally the quickest touchdown in Super Bowl history.

After a three-and-out Charger series, Young directed his offense to another quick six. The quarterback hit Ricky Watters with a 51-yard touchdown reception on the fourth play of the drive, and San Francisco led 14–0. Twice more in the first half, Young threw touchdown passes—a 5-yard toss to William Floyd and an 8-yarder to Watters. At halftime, the 49ers entered the dressing room with a 28–10 lead.

San Diego never recovered. Young continued the offensive onslaught and finished the game with 325 yards passing, completing 24-of-36 with six touchdowns and no interceptions. For his role in the 49–26 victory, Young was selected as Super Bowl MVP.

EXTRA POINT < < < < < < < < < < < < < < < < < < It's tough in any aspect of life, particularly athletics, to follow a successful person. We measure this year's teacher against last year's. We weigh the latest president's achievements against those of previous leaders. Family members naturally compare younger sisters and brothers with their older siblings. Others size up sons and daughters against their mom and dad.

While we don't want to be exactly like someone else, we do want to imitate the good qualities of others. We can learn from people who came before us. The writer of Hebrews challenges us to work hard and imitate the faith and patience of past Christians.

GOAL! *Write down some people in the Bible who have traits you want to imitate.*

Person: **Trait:**

_____   _____

_____   _____

Ask God to help you imitate their good qualities and their faith.

WE DO NOT WANT YOU TO BECOME LAZY, BUT TO IMITATE THOSE WHO THROUGH FAITH AND PATIENCE INHERIT WHAT HAS BEEN PROMISED. HEBREWS 6:12, NIV

> We are pressed on every side by troubles, but we are not crushed and broken. We are perplexed, but we don't give up and quit. We are hunted down, but God never abandons us. We get knocked down, but we get up again and keep going.
>
> 2 CORINTHIANS 4:8-9

FOR NASCAR LEGEND Dale Earnhardt, it appeared that the 12th time at the Daytona 500 would be memorable.

In 1990, Earnhardt's famous No. 3 black Chevrolet paced the field in more than 150 laps of the 200-lap race. And Earnhardt was in front during the last lap. With less than a mile to go and victory within his grasp, Earnhardt's car ran over a sharp piece of bellhousing from another vehicle, which slashed his back tire. Amazingly, Dale kept his car from hitting the wall, but he could no longer run at the speeds necessary to win.

Earnhardt's misfortune opened the door for Derrike Cope. Driving in just his third Daytona, Cope saw Earnhardt veer off course. Cope kept focused on the track and found himself in the lead with two turns to go. With Terry Labonte and Bill Elliott breathing down his bumper, Cope took the checkered flag in one of the greatest upsets in motorsports history. It was Cope's first top-five finish—let alone victory—in his 72 races on the NASCAR tour.

EXTRA POINT < < < < < < < < < < < < < < < < < < < < Dale Earnhardt's misfortune turned out to be Derrike Cope's big break. Everybody favored the hard-driving Earnhardt to win NASCAR's biggest race, but a freak blown tire took him out of contention. His No. 3 car had been the class of the field before the cut tire took him out.

Sometimes bad breaks hit our lives. We run over something unexpected that keeps us from achieving what we had hoped. It's not because we did something wrong; it just happens. We find ourselves surprised and unable to cope. During those times, God sticks close to us and helps us get back on our feet. While we may experience setbacks, God helps us overcome in the long run.

GOAL! *Can you think of any bad breaks or mishaps that have happened to you on the athletic field or in real life? Write down one or two:*

_____

_____

How did you overcome those misfortunes? Looking back, do you see God's hand in your situation? Thank God that he's always with you during life's trying times.

IF YOU'RE A BIG FAN of watching pistons in an engine, you're bound to love freestyle moguls. Since being introduced into the Winter Olympics in the 1990s, the moguls have amazed audience members and television viewers. And maybe one of the most knee-knocking performances of all time was turned in by American Jonny Moseley in the 1998 Nagano Games.

Mogul skiers earn points in three areas. Fifty percent of the score is derived from the quality of the skiing. Athletes must navigate a 300-yard heavily moguled course using aggressive, controlled turns. The knees bounce up and down together, the upper body remains calm, and the arms plant the poles in preparation for the next turn. Any fall or loss of form spells disaster. Twenty-five percent of the score is based on two jumps—going big and sticking the landing means huge points. The final 25 percent is earned by how fast the athlete makes it down the course.

In Nagano, Japan, Moseley put all of those elements together in an unbeatable performance. Not only did he pump his way down the mountain with precision turns, but his 360 Mute Grab amazed even the announcers and outclassed the competition.

Moseley's gold medal was the first one for the United States in Nagano. And it set the tone for more U.S. skiing success.

EXTRA POINT < < < < < < < < < < < < < < < < < < < < < < <

Jonny Moseley's 360 Mute Grab was a trick nobody had ever seen. By combining a cross-skied helicopter from skiing with a snowboarding grab, Moseley took moguls to a new level and assured himself of the gold. Innovation and creativity marked Moseley's skiing career.

God desires for Christians to show that same creativity. He wants us to stand out. God doesn't want you to follow the crowd or be like people in the world. He asks you to be transformed—not copy someone else. Every person reacts differently to God's Word. So be innovative with how you live your faith.

GOAL! *Are you bored in Sunday school or church? It's okay to admit it. But don't stay tuned out. Come up with fresh ideas to bring excitement into your church. You may also want to share your ideas with a youth leader. Be creative!*

> Don't copy the behavior and customs of this world, but let God transform you into a new person by changing the way you think. Then you will know what God wants you to do, and you will know how good and pleasing and perfect his will really is.
>
> ROMANS 12:2

Count it all
joy when
you fall into
various trials,
knowing that
the testing
of your faith
produces
patience.

JAMES 1:2-3, NKJV

THE DENVER BRONCOS had never fared well in the Super Bowl until 1998. Until that point, they stood at 0–4 in football's biggest game. Quarterback John Elway, Denver's signal caller in three of the defeats, bore much of the burden. But in Super Bowl XXXII, the 37-year-old field general showed the Green Bay Packers his last-minute comeback skills.

Oddsmakers favored the Pack by almost two touchdowns, primarily on the strength of three-time NFL Most Valuable Player Brett Favre. And Favre looked impressive in the game's first possession, connecting with Antonio Freeman for a 22-yard touchdown pass. However, Denver battled back to tie the game in the first quarter.

Both teams had difficulty gaining the upper hand. With the score knotted 24–24, Denver took over on the Packers 49-yard line with 3:27 left to play in the game, setting up some last-minute Elway heroics.

A pass to Terrell Davis picked up 2 yards with an additional 15 tacked on for a face mask penalty. Elway then completed another pass to Howard Griffith for 23 yards, and Davis swept left for 17, setting up Denver at the Green Bay 1-yard line. Davis put the Broncos in front, 31–24, with his third touchdown, plunging into the end zone with 1:45 remaining.

Green Bay drove to the Denver 31 with 32 seconds still on the clock. But linebacker John Mobley batted away Favre's fourth-down pass to clinch the Broncos victory and end Denver's Super Bowl frustrations.

EXTRA POINT < < < < < < < < < < < < < < < < < < John Elway faced years of trials on the football field and in life, but he persevered. No signal caller was hit more often than Elway during his playing years. And when asked how he felt after winning the Super Bowl, the great quarterback said it was better than he could have imagined.

When life brings tests and trials, God helps us persevere. He gives us the strength to persist and keep going in spite of difficulties. And when we do, the heavenly Father gives us that special feeling of his joy.

GOAL! *Imagine always coming in second. Would you keep trying to be the best, or would you give up? Praise God for the joy he gives when you persevere.*

NATIONAL HOCKEY LEAGUE All-Star teams primarily play offense in their annual showcase. But with the Winter Olympics looming, defense played a decisive role in the 2002 contest.

Since 1998, these elite hockey squads have been divided by birthplace. Players born in the United States and Canada form the North American team, and those from other countries comprise the World team. In four contests, the World team had only collected a single victory.

After two periods in the 2002 game, the North American squad led 5–3. Mario Lemieux tied Wayne Gretzky's record with his 13th All-Star goal in the second period, while Eric Daze of the Chicago Blackhawks netted two goals and added an assist.

But in the third period, World coach Scotty Bowman inserted an all-Russian lineup to push for the win. Sergei Fedorov tied the game with three minutes left to play in regulation, and Markus Naslund slapped the puck into the net for the go-ahead goal a minute later. Tampa Bay's goalie, Nikolai Khabibulin, aided the World team comeback by stopping 20 American and Canadian third-period shots on goal.

In the final seconds, the North Americans pulled their goalie in a desperate attempt to tie. But the World team twice guided the puck into an unguarded net to cement an 8–5 triumph.

EXTRA POINT < < < < < < < < < < < < < < < < < < < All-Star games in any sport carry the reputation of lots of fun and very little work. After all, the players don't regularly practice or play together. Fans pay to see stars score, not to watch low-scoring contests.

But those at the 2002 hockey game saw players work hard for victory. The Russians demonstrated defensive strength and determination en route to their win for the World team.

Working hard and being strong both physically and mentally often yields success in the rink, on the field, or on the court. Working hard at following God and being strong in faith brings success in the Christian life too.

GOAL! *Make a list of five things you believe are worth working for in sports, in your family, or in life.*

Now choose one to concentrate on. Plan how you can work hard to become successful. Ask God to be with you as you work to meet your goal.

"Be strong, all you people of the land," declares the Lord, "and work. For I am with you," declares the Lord Almighty.

HAGGAI 2:4, NIV

26 JAN

Give all your worries and cares to God, for he cares about what happens to you.

1 PETER 5:7

WHEN PERSONAL PROBLEMS and poor decisions forced Jennifer Capriati off the women's tennis tour at age 17, many believed she would never return to championship form. But in the 2001 Australian Open, the 24-year-old American proved she could still play at a top level.

Few expected the tournament's 12th seed to last past the early rounds. But Jennifer showed heart as she played each match. Capriati surprised everyone by eliminating four-time titleholder Monica Seles 5–7, 6–4, 6–3 in the quarterfinals and defeating defending champion Lindsay Davenport 6–3, 6–4 to reach the finals.

Capriati faced three-time champion Martina Hingis in the title match and dominated her opponent from the outset. After only 12 minutes of play, she led the first set 4–0, eventually winning it 6–4.

In the second set, the Florida native played even stronger. Hingis's double fault in game five put Capriati in front by a service break, 3–2. The American's serve, a weakness in the past, remained strong, leading to a 6–3 win.

On match point, Capriati closed out the victory by slamming a backhand down the line. The one-time child superstar celebrated her first Grand Slam championship by embracing Stefano, her father and coach.

EXTRA POINT < < < < < < < < < < < < < < < < < < < In 1990, Jennifer Capriati took the tennis world by storm. That year the 14-year-old became the youngest player ever to win a Wimbledon match, the youngest to reach the semifinals of the French Open, and the youngest ever to be seeded in a Grand Slam tournament. For the next two years, she continued to reach "youngest ever" milestones.

Then problems struck this talented teen. Too much pressure caused her to make bad decisions. But Jennifer eventually overcame her troubles. She began winning at an age when many tennis stars consider retiring. Jennifer turned things around when she stopped worrying about other things and concentrated on tennis.

What bothers you? Do problems or pressures eat away at your insides? Have you ever been so worried you felt sick to your stomach? Trust God with your worries, because he cares for you.

GOAL! *Discuss with your parents or a trusted Christian friend the difference between damaging worry and healthy concern. Praise God that we can always give our problems to him.*

NO TWO TEAMS HAVE MET more often in football's biggest game than the Dallas Cowboys and the Pittsburgh Steelers. In Super Bowl XXX on January 28, 1996, these teams clashed for the third time.

While Pittsburgh had won the previous two matchups, the Steelers trailed 13–7 at halftime. Dallas added to its lead midway through the third quarter when cornerback Larry Brown intercepted quarterback Neil O'Donnell's errant pass. Returning the ball to the 18-yard line, the Cowboys capitalized on the mistake with Emmitt Smith scoring from the 1.

But the Steelers kept battling. Answering the Cowboys' score with a field goal and a touchdown, the Steelers cut the margin to 20–17.

And with 4:15 remaining in the game, Pittsburgh went on offense on its own 32-yard line. But on the second play of the do-or-die drive, O'Donnell underthrew his receiver. Brown broke perfectly on the ball and grabbed his second interception, taking the ball 33 yards to the Steelers 6-yard line. Two plays later, Smith scored from 4 yards out and secured a 27–17 Super Bowl win.

EXTRA POINT < < < < < < < < < < < < < < < < < < < < < < For Larry Brown's opportune interceptions, he was named the game's MVP—only the fifth defensive player to win the award. The honor capped a bittersweet season for Brown. Enduring criticism for penalties and defensive lapses, the 12th-round pick out of Texas Christian nearly lost his starting spot.

Winning this award energized Brown's career, just like winning the game energized the Cowboys.

God loves it when we win awards. He wants us to use the talents he gives us to claim the prize. And when we win, we should thank God for the good and perfect gifts that he gives each one of us.

GOAL! *You can find information about football's MVPs at the library or by searching the Super Bowl Web site. Always remember you're an MVP to the heavenly Father. That's an awesome reason to thank him.*

> Whatever is good and perfect comes to us from God above, who created all heaven's lights. Unlike them, he never changes or casts shifting shadows.
>
> JAMES 1:17

28 JAN

> Then Jesus said, "Come to me, all of you who are weary and carry heavy burdens, and I will give you rest."
>
> MATTHEW 11:28

PLAYING A TENNIS MATCH

under the broiling sun tests anyone's limits. In the 2002 Australian Open, Jennifer Capriati showed her determination to defeat both the elements and her opponent.

For the second straight year, the Florida native faced Martina Hingis in the tournament final. Unlike their previous encounter, the Swiss player dominated the American early in the match.

After trailing 5–1 in the first set, Capriati rallied but still lost 1–6. The three-time Australian Open champion continued to overwhelm Capriati in set two, taking a 4–0 lead.

Capriati again fought back and fended off three match points to close the margin to 5–6. She won the next game to force a tiebreaker. Then, facing another match point at 6–7, the defending champion won three straight points to claim the second set 9–7.

Hard-fought points from the baseline and the 95-degree heat left both players exhausted after the second-set tiebreaker. They agreed to take a ten-minute break before resuming play, and the pair lay in the training room covered in ice packs.

The rest proved more beneficial to Capriati than to Hingis. After the duo traded early service breaks, Capriati won five straight games to take the third set 6–2 and win her second straight Australian championship.

EXTRA POINT < < < < < < < < < < < < < < < < < < < <

Weather can be a factor in athletic contests. The winner must successfully overcome both an opponent and nature. Sun, snow, rain, heat, and cold may make an athlete weary and ready to give up.

In the Australian Open, a compassionate official let the women take a break. Rest, shade, and cool water revived and refreshed them—especially Jennifer Capriati.

Jesus knows we get tired. As God living in human form, he felt what it was like to battle the heat as he walked from town to town. And Jesus wants to give us comfort. Just like a cool drink and shade can revive us on a hot day, Jesus can refresh your life by giving you perfect rest.

GOAL! *Next time you're playing, working, or competing in the hot sun, take a break to grab a drink. Pay careful attention to how you feel as you gulp down that reviving beverage. Then praise God for his refreshing love.*

SUPER BOWL XXXIII pitted the defending champion Denver Broncos against the upstart Atlanta Falcons. Although emotion favored the newcomers, the veteran team from Colorado knew when and how to adjust its game plan, while the Georgia squad's ideas didn't end up leading to success.

Trailing 7–3 in the second quarter, the Falcons intercepted a John Elway pass at the Denver 35-yard line for the game's first turnover. Three plays later, Atlanta faced fourth-and-one. Coach Dan Reeves elected to go for the first down rather than kick a field goal, but the gamble failed. Keith Traylor tackled Jamal Anderson for a two yard loss to give the ball back to the Broncos.

Denver went up 10–3 on a 26-yard Jason Elam field goal. On Atlanta's next possession, Morten Andersen missed his 26-yard attempt. The next play turned the tide in Denver's favor.

Studying a photo taken earlier, Mike Shanahan's offensive coordinator Gary Kubiak noticed that the Falcons' safeties bit on a play fake to running back Terrell Davis. The assistant coach inserted a play Denver hadn't used since midseason.

Kubiak called for wide receiver Rod Smith to run a deep post route rather than a curl. Elway faked to Davis, then threw a perfect spiral to Smith. He caught the ball in stride at the Atlanta 43 and coasted into the end zone, putting the Broncos in front 17–3.

Interceptions on two consecutive drives in the fourth quarter set up touchdowns for Denver, and the lead proved insurmountable. Denver cruised to a 34–19 victory and back-to-back Super Bowl wins.

EXTRA POINT

< < < < < < < < < < < < < < < < < < <

During the game, the Falcons moved inside the Broncos 30-yard line seven times. Interceptions, missed field goals, and turnovers on downs doomed Atlanta. The Falcons' plans to score points and put the ball in the end zone never worked out. But Denver's idea to implement an infrequently used play worked perfectly.

In the Old Testament, Job had a special relationship with God. He knew God could do whatever he wanted—that all of God's ideas worked out exactly how he planned. God's plans still are flawless today.

GOAL! *Think about how Atlanta might have changed their plans to win. Then think of some areas in your life that need changing.*
Ask God to help you come up with a plan to make those things happen.

Job replied to the Lord: "I know that you can do anything, and no one can stop you." JOB 42:1-2

30 JAN

> We have come to share in Christ if we hold firmly till the end the confidence we had at first.
>
> HEBREWS 3:14, NIV

A TENNIS MATCH ISN'T OVER until the final point of the final game of the final set. While this might sound obvious, Lindsay Davenport almost learned this lesson the hard way in the 2000 Australian Open.

The No. 2 seed had blitzed through her preliminary rounds without dropping a single set. The American faced Martina Hingis, the defending three-time champion, in the finals at Melbourne Park. Davenport began her match against Hingis with confidence. After 45 minutes of play, the California native had won the first set 6–1, held a 5–1 in the second, and was up 30–15 in the game. Davenport needed only two points to capture the Grand Slam event.

Unexpectedly, however, things went awry. Davenport lost the game when she netted a backhand, failed to return a Hingis overhand, and misfired on another backhand. Hingis held serve to make the score 5–3, then broke her opponent's serve to trail by a single game. Davenport's four errors in the next game brought the set to a 5–5 tie.

But the 23-year-old former Olympic gold medalist regained her confidence. Two spectacular shots—a vicious backhand down the line and a volley—gave Davenport a 6–5 lead.

With the pressure on, Davenport's Swiss adversary faltered. She double faulted on the first point, then hit two shots long and one wide, giving Davenport her third Grand Slam title.

EXTRA POINT < < < < < < < < < < < < < < < < < < < < Somewhere in the middle of the seventh game of the second set, Davenport's confidence faded. She lost her concentration and almost lost the set. But Davenport found her focus again just as Hingis lost hers. In the end, Davenport won.

The Bible reminds us to hold on to our confidence in God from the day we accept Christ as our Savior until the end of our life. Some Bible translators use the word *faith* for confidence. In other words, we must keep the faith from beginning to end!

GOAL! *Identify things that take your mind off of Christ and cause your faith in him to fade. Ask God for firm faith and confidence in him each moment of every day.*

Oh, magnify
the Lord with
me, and let us
exalt His name
together.

PSALM 34:3, NKJV

SINCE BEING INTRODUCED as an Olympic sport in 1998, snowboarding has become one of the most thrilling events in the Winter Games. In the 2002 Salt Lake City Games, United States fans had plenty of reasons to cheer.

In the halfpipe, snowboarders cruise back and forth across the snow, soaring high into the air as they pull various grabs, spins, and airs. The course typically runs 110 meters with sides three to four meters high and banked at 85 degrees. Judges award points based on standard technique, rotation, height, landing, and technical value with 50 as the maximum score.

A rule change from 1998 allowed greater creative expression. Rather than a combined score of the two runs, only the better of the two efforts counted.

Four Americans, led by 1998 bronze medalist Ross Powers, made the 12-man final competition. Powers, who finished ninth in qualifying, nailed his first run with a series of twists and flips for a 46.1 score. Danny Kass, a 19-year-old New Jersey native, followed with a 42.5.

But after both runs were complete, Powers's score remained on top for the gold. Kass claimed the silver. Another American, Jarret "J. J." Thomas improved to 42.1 on his second attempt and took the bronze.

The 1-2-3 American finish marked the first time any country had captured all three medals in a Winter Games event since the United States accomplished the feat in men's figure skating in 1956.

EXTRA POINT

< < < < < < < < < < < < < < < < < <

Together Ross Powers, Danny Kass, and J. J. Thomas exalted their country. What a glorious sight for Americans to see not one, not two, but three flags bearing the Stars and Stripes raised during the medal ceremony. Tears welled in the winners' eyes as the "Star-Spangled Banner" played.

But as great as it is for an athlete to bring glory to his or her country, it's far greater to glorify God. The psalmist reminds us to exalt God's name together with other believers. Individual worship brings joy to the Father and to the worshipper. Singing praises and lifting up God's name with two, three, or more people helps us feel closer to God and to fellow believers.

GOAL! *Each day, plan an individual worship time with the Lord. Every week, share worship with a church or Christian group. It's important to praise God and exalt his name, both individually and together.*

SKI RACERS WHO HIT the slopes first seldom win. But in the 1998 Winter Olympics, Picabo Street discovered an early start isn't always a bad thing.

The flamboyant skier captured a surprising downhill silver medal in the 1994 Lillehammer Olympics. However, a severe fall in a World Cup race left the American bruised and suffering from severe headaches leading into the 1998 Games.

Qualification for the Olympic Super G (a combination of downhill and giant slalom with long, sweeping, high-speed turns) is based on World Cup standings. Since the event utilizes only a single run, positioning often affects final placements.

Picabo's mediocre World Cup showing forced her to the second starting spot in the field. The favorites chose later starts, believing the course would get icier and faster.

But on race day, the sun broke through a clear blue sky. Instead of hardening, the course softened. In her No. 2 spot, Street sped down the course, clocking a 1:18.02 to capture a surprising gold medal.

Austria's Michaela Dorfmeister completed her run only .01 behind Picabo. Street's close friend, Alexandra Meissnitzer, recorded a 1:18.09. The three medalists finished within .07 of each other—the closest grouping in Olympic skiing history.

> Very early in the morning, while it was still dark, Jesus got up, left the house and went off to a solitary place, where he prayed.
>
> MARK 1:35, NIV

EXTRA POINT < < < < < < < < < < < < < < < < < < < < Competing early paid off for Picabo Street. She set the pace on a harder course. Others had to risk speeds too fast for the softening snow.

Maybe you've heard the expression "Save the best for last." In sports, athletes normally want to be toward the end of the competition so they can see what mark they have to beat.

But in life, we often gain by getting up early and tackling the tasks we've been given. The book of Mark notes that Jesus woke up early to pray. As our ultimate role model, Jesus set the best example for us to follow. He got a head start. And God wants us to get a head start for him too.

GOAL! *Here's a question for you: Would you rather go first or last in a competition? Why? Ask God to help you get an early start when he calls.*

Our beloved Barnabas and Paul . . . have risked their lives for the sake of our Lord Jesus Christ.

ACTS 15:25-26

PROFESSIONAL FOOTBALL TEAMS seldom take risks

in the late stages of a tie game. Fearing the repercussions of a bad play, most teams prefer to move to overtime.

But in Super Bowl XXXVI on February 3, 2002, the New England Patriots defied logic and went for the last-second victory.

The Patriots squared off against the St. Louis Rams at the Superdome in New Orleans. Oddsmakers favored the Rams by two touchdowns, and St. Louis looked tough early, scoring a 50-yard field goal midway through the first quarter.

Employing extra defensive backs to thwart Kurt Warner's passing, the Patriots forced an interception early in the second quarter. Ty Law picked off the errant throw and returned it 47 yards for a score, giving New England a 7–3 lead. The underdogs upped their margin to 14–3 just before halftime with an 8-yard touchdown pass from Tom Brady to David Patten.

Down 17–3 in the fourth quarter, St. Louis rallied. Warner ran in from two yards out to make the score 17–10. With 1:30 left to play, Warner connected with Ricky Proehl for a 26-yard touchdown to knot the game at 17–17.

But Brady and Coach Bill Belichick refused to wait for overtime. Brady moved New England 53 yards in nine plays, giving Adam Vinatieri a field goal opportunity with seven seconds remaining. The 48-yard kick cleared the uprights with room to spare, and the Patriots triumphed 20–17.

EXTRA POINT < < < < < < < < < < < < < < < < < < < <

Tom Brady won MVP honors. He took huge risks with a hurry-up offense in the waning moments of the Super Bowl. An interception could have meant defeat. A blocked field goal could have been run back for a score. But the risk paid off.

In the Bible, the apostle Paul and Barnabas are commended for risking their lives for God. On numerous occasions, Paul put his life on the line to spread God's Good News.

We may never be called on to risk our lives for Christ. But the heavenly Father does call on us to take risks as we tell others about him and follow his will for our lives.

GOAL! Think of someone you know who isn't a Christian. Write down his or her name:

_____

Will you ask God to help you risk sharing what the Lord has done for you?

RECORDS ARE MADE to be broken. In the 2002 Olympic Games, speed skater Derek Parra discovered a record might last only minutes.

At first glance, the 31-year-old American seemed unlikely to achieve the world's fastest time in the 5,000-meter race. The former inline skater, who converted to ice in 1997, had never finished above 14th in World Cup competition. His only fame had come in the opening ceremonies when he joined seven other athletes carrying the World Trade Center flag into Rice-Eccles Stadium in Salt Lake City.

But the Utah Olympic Oval proved to be a speedy track. At 4,675 feet above sea level, the high-altitude–hardened ice, the dry air, and the low pressure made records fall.

Prior to his competition, Parra downed a package of Fig Newton cookies—his favorite treat. The combination of fast ice and figs proved successful for the Home Depot employee. Shaving almost 15 seconds off his personal best, Derek finished the course in 6:17.98, eclipsing the world mark of 6:18.72.

But gold-medal favorite Jochem Uytdehaage had yet to compete. Taking advantage of the conditions, the Dutch skater blazed the 5,000 meters in 6:14.66, claiming first place and the record.

Although Parra held the world record for less than 30 minutes, his time won second place. His silver medal marked the first time an American had placed in the men's 5,000 meters since Eric Heiden won the gold in 1980.

> Don't be afraid, for I am with you. Do not be dismayed, for I am your God. I will strengthen you. I will help you. I will uphold you with my victorious right hand.
>
> ISAIAH 41:10

EXTRA POINT

< < < < < < < < < < < < < < < < < < <

No one gave Derek Parra much of a chance for a medal in 5,000-meter speed skating. But the American didn't let anyone intimidate him. He showed no fear. He focused on his own race. Eating his trademark snack gave Derek a feeling of peace, a boost of energy, and the strength for an outstanding performance.

God wants to strengthen his followers—and we don't even have to eat a snack. God told the prophet Isaiah not to be afraid or confused. His strength would get his people through their troubles. With God, they would overcome.

GOAL! *Do you have a special psych-up food? Try a Fig Newton and think of Derek Parra's silver medal. Thank God that he's in charge, so we don't need to be afraid.*

04 FEB

Jesus looked at them intently and said, "Humanly speaking, it is impossible. But with God everything is possible."

MATTHEW 19:26

IMAGINE SCREAMING DOWN an icy hill riding on a set of steel blades. Cowbells ring. People scream. The world whips past in a blur.

Bobsledders don't have to imagine. They hop in their Plexiglas vehicles and zoom down a mountain of ice all the time. And some of the best bobsledders in the 2002 Winter Olympics turned out to be a squad of Americans.

Many believed that German and Swiss bobsled teams would dominate and that it would be impossible for the United States to earn a medal. But with two heats remaining on the competition's final day, the team, captained by Texan Todd Hays, led the field by .09 seconds. A second American team with five-time Olympian Brian Shimer at the head appeared out of the running in fifth place.

In the third Olympic heat, the Germans took over first place, Hays' squad faltered, and Shimer's team moved into medal contention. As the final heat began, a cold front dropped the temperature 20 degrees.

The 39-year-old Shimer and his teammates, Mike Kohn, Doug Sharp, and Dan Steele, turned in the heat's fastest time at 47.23 seconds. Hays, along with Randy Jones, Bill Schuffenhauer, and Garrett Hines pulled a 47.33 to remain in second place, ensuring the United States of both the silver and the bronze. It marked the first time since 1956 that Americans had claimed a bobsled medal.

EXTRA POINT < < < < < < < < < < < < < < < < < < < < < "Unimaginable!" "Impossible!" Reporters used the words to describe the American medal performances. But the unimaginable happened, and the impossible became possible.

Jesus knew that with his Father, the improbable and impossible become possible. One day while Jesus walked the earth, a rich young man asked him how to have eternal life. When Jesus told him to give his possessions to the poor, the man went sadly away.

Christ then explained to his disciples that it's easier for a camel to go through the eye of a needle than for a rich man to get to heaven. But he added that with God all things are possible.

GOAL! *Read the story of the rich young ruler in Matthew 19:16-26. Praise God that with him all things are possible.*

MANY EXPERTS BELIEVED NFL quarterback Trent Dilfer didn't have the skills to take a team to the top. For six years he labored with the Tampa Bay Buccaneers, until they turned him loose.

But in Super Bowl XXXV, Dilfer returned to Tampa and proved he was a winner.

Before the 2001 season, Dilfer signed as a free agent with the Baltimore Ravens. Led by a defense that allowed the fewest points ever in a 16-game season, the Ravens faced the New York Giants for NFL supremacy at Tampa's Raymond James Stadium.

Midway through the first quarter, Dilfer opened the scoring by connecting with Brandon Stokley for a 38-yard touchdown pass. In the second period, the Raven signal caller hit a second long pass—a 44-yarder to Qadry Ismail—setting up a 47-yard field goal. With the two scores, Baltimore led New York 10–0 at the half.

The Ravens broke open the contest in the third quarter when Duane Starks intercepted a Kerry Collins pass and bolted 49 yards for a score. On the ensuing kickoff, New York's Ron Dixon scampered 97 yards for a touchdown, but seconds later Baltimore's Jermaine Lewis matched the scoring effort with an 84-yard return.

While holding the Giants to 149 yards total offense, the Ravens scored another touchdown and field goal for a 34–7 victory.

> Go home to your family and tell them how much the Lord has done for you, and how he has had mercy on you.
>
> MARK 5:19, NIV

EXTRA POINT < < < < < < < < < < < < < < < < < < < < < Trent Dilfer probably felt comfortable in Tampa and the stadium he had played in for so many years. He knew the locker room. His familiarity extended to every inch of the turf. Fans who loved him as a Buccaneer welcomed him home as a Raven.

Sometimes Christians face uncertainty about how they will be received when they tell their family and friends about God. We find witnessing to strangers far easier than to our "home team."

But Jesus commands us to go home and tell all he has done for us. God wants our earthly homecomings to be times we spread his love and share about the blessings he has brought to our lives.

GOAL! *Think about how far you would travel to tell a family member or friend what Christ has done for you. Will you be a witness for him, especially to those closest to you? God is right there to help you.*

06 FEB

God blesses you
who weep now,
for the time
will come when
you will laugh
with joy.

LUKE 6:21

BEING ON THE WORLD STAGE can sometimes cause athletes to melt under the pressure. But Hiroyasu Shimizu stayed cool as ice to bring glory to himself and Japan at the 1998 Nagano Games.

The 23-year-old speed skater took up the sport at age three. Eventually coaching duties fell to his father, Hitoshi, but the elder Shimizu died of cancer when Hiroyasu was only 17.

Despite losing his coach and parent, the Japanese skater continued to improve. In 1996, he set the world record in the 500 meters with a time of 35.39.

On the final day of the 500-meter Olympic competition, the quest for the gold intensified. Canada's Jeremy Wotherspoon moved from seventh to first place by clocking a 35.80.

Shimizu skated in the final pair of the day. Bolstered by the Japanese crowd, including Crown Prince Naruhito and Crown Princess Masako, the racer broke his own Olympic record with a time of 35.59 seconds.

Tears of joy cascaded down Hiroyasu's face as he completed a victory lap. Fans snatched up thousands of newspapers that declared Shimizu a national hero, and television stations replayed the race over and over.

EXTRA POINT < < < < < < < < < < < < < < < < < < < <
This gold-medal athlete deserved to cry through the victory lap and on the medal stand. Tears reflect great emotion, both sadness and happiness. Surely Hiroyasu cried happy tears over his medal-winning performance. But those tears also showed his sadness because his father-coach wasn't there to share the gold.

People frequently say, "Big boys don't cry." The Olympics show another picture. And the Bible speaks differently too. Tears of sadness often lead to joy. Joy frequently results in wonderful tears. After all, God made our emotions. When we cry or when we laugh, we're reflecting the fullness of God.

GOAL! *Think of the last time you cried. Was it because of pain, sadness, happiness, or sorrow? Praise God for turning tears into joyful laughter.*

MAJOR LEAGUE BASEBALL OWNERS banned African-American ballplayers from the league in the beginning of the 20th century. But in 1947, the barrier came tumbling down.

Two years earlier, on August 28, 1945, Brooklyn Dodgers general manager Branch Rickey signed Jackie Robinson off the roster of the Kansas City Monarchs, one of America's top Negro League teams. Rickey believed the Georgia native, who grew up in California and played football at UCLA, possessed the intelligence, skill, and demeanor to integrate baseball. Robinson spent 1946 with the Dodgers' top minor league club in Montreal.

Brooklyn manager Leo Durocher named Jackie the starting first baseman for the Dodgers as spring training concluded in 1947. In the season's opening game, the Dodgers hosted the Boston Braves. More than 26,000 fans passed through the Ebbets Field turnstiles to watch the 28-year-old rookie start at first base.

Although Robinson went hitless in three official at bats, his blazing speed turned a routine play into a Dodgers victory. With Eddie Stanky on first, Robinson bunted. Braves first baseman Earl Torgeson fielded the ball and made a wild throw, allowing Robinson to reach base and advancing Robinson and Stanky to second and third. Both players scored on Pete Reiser's double to claim a 5–3 victory.

That season, Jackie Robinson played in more games than any other Dodger. He hit .297 and tied for the team lead in homers. He doubled the number of stolen bases of any other competitor in the league with 29. Baseball honored him as Rookie of the Year, an award later named for him.

EXTRA POINT < < < < < < < < < < < < < < < < < < < < < < < Jackie Robinson broke the baseball color barrier before President Harry S. Truman integrated the armed services, or the famous Brown vs. Board of Education Supreme Court decision integrated public schools. The choices made by Rickey, Durocher, and Robinson were right, but they weren't easy.

Prejudiced whites hurled abuses at Jackie and the rest of team. Opponents threatened to boycott the Dodgers. But in the end, the team's courageous stand united Negro League baseball with the previously all-white American and National Leagues.

The heavenly Father loves every person of every race. There's no room for color barriers in his kingdom.

GOAL! *Search the Internet for information about Jackie Robinson and Black History Month. Thank God for courageous people who do what's right. Ask God to show you any prejudices in your heart; then ask him to help you overcome them.*

For he himself is our peace, who has made the two one and has destroyed the barrier, the dividing wall of hostility.
EPHESIANS 2:14, NIV

God is a judge who is perfectly fair. He is angry with the wicked every day.

PSALM 7:11

OLYMPIC EVENTS BASED on judges' marks rather than time or distance often lead to differences of opinion. In the 2002 Games, pairs figure skating created a debate unparalleled in Olympic history.

Canadians Jamie Sale and David Pelletier, the reigning world champions, performed a flawless free skate using music from *Love Story.* Pelletier stretched out full-length and kissed the ice at the end of their awesome program. As the pair bowed to every corner of the arena, the crowd voiced its enthusiastic approval and waved hundreds of Canadian flags.

But applause turned to boos when the judges awarded the Canadians their lowest scores ever for the breathtaking program. Even with the low scores, the pair stood on top of the leaderboard.

The duo's strongest competition, Russia's Yelena Berezhnaya and Anton Sikharulidze, led after the short program but did not appear to match the Canadians in either technical merit or presentation in the free skate. Anton faltered in landing a double axel–double toe loop.

But as the judges announced the scoring, the crowd gasped. Berezhnaya and Sikharulidze received nothing lower than 5.7 for technical merit. Presentation generated all 5.8s and 5.9s. The Russian couple edged out the Canadians for the gold, running the string of Russian victories in pairs to 11.

A closer look at the scores showed judges from the United States, Canada, Germany, and Japan ranked the Canadian pair first, while Russia, Poland, China, Ukraine, and France opted for the Russians. Newspaper articles carried such words as "Gold medal performance wins silver," and "Judges steal gold medal."

Several days later the French judge admitted coercion. The International Olympic Committee investigated and eventually ruled both teams should be awarded gold medals.

EXTRA POINT < < < < < < < < < < < < < < < < < < < < < Following the ice dance original program, the IOC held a second medal ceremony for the pairs. Both teams stood atop the podium. Both flags rose. Both national anthems played.

Yelena and Anton graciously smiled and posed with Jamie and David as hundreds of cameras flashed. Justice prevailed for the Canadians.

Judges usually try to be objective. But they're human. They have prejudices. They make mistakes. A few even take bribes or broker deals. Only God judges perfectly fairly.

GOAL! *Have you ever had a judgment call go against you? Did it cost you a victory? Maybe you shouted, "That's not fair!" But you can praise God for his justice.*

THE COMEBACK ABILITY of Tiger Woods almost defies imagination. At the 2000 Pebble Beach National Pro-Am, the golfer emerged with another thrilling tournament victory.

After three rounds, Woods trailed the leader, Matt Gogel, by five strokes. On the final day of competition, the margin widened to seven with only seven holes remaining.

Without warning, however, Gogel faltered and Woods caught fire as he sank unbelievable shot after shot. Almost 100 yards from the green on hole 15, he launched the ball high into the dull gray sky. It fell about four feet from the pin and spun back to drop in for an eagle. Birdies followed on 16 and 18, giving Woods an 8-under 64 for the day.

With Woods in the clubhouse, Gogel could have forced a playoff with a birdie on the final hole. But his ten-foot putt slid left past the cup.

Shocked by his fall from the top, Gogel missed his comeback and took another bogey, falling into a second-place tie with Vijay Singh. Woods's 17th career PGA victory brought his incredible string to six straight, tying Ben Hogan's mark set in 1948.

> I work very hard at this, as I depend on Christ's mighty power that works within me.
> COLOSSIANS 1:29

EXTRA POINT

< < < < < < < < < < < < < < < < < < < <

Power and energy hallmark Tiger Woods's professional golf career. Though he makes the sport look easy, he labors daily. He practices driving, chipping, and putting. He spends hours perfecting his game.

For Woods, golf isn't just fun. It's a job that demands his full attention. His love of the game fuels his drive to win.

Power and energy should hallmark our Christian service, too. Just like Tiger Woods is an example to other golfers, the apostle Paul should be an example to us. We should spend hours making our lives more like Jesus Christ's.

For us, telling others about our Savior shouldn't be a game. It should be a lifestyle that demands constant attention. And our love for God should fuel our desire to witness to others and serve him.

GOAL! *Go to a driving range or play a round of mini golf. Concentrate hard and try to do your best. Ask God to help you put all your energy into serving him, just like the apostle Paul did.*

VONETTA FLOWERS DREAMED of making the 2000 Summer Olympics team. But after two knee operations and ankle surgery, she discovered God had alternate Olympic plans.

Flowers, a former track star at the University of Alabama–Birmingham, took up bobsledding when she failed to land a spot on the U.S. track team. Just months prior to the 2002 Salt Lake City Winter Games, Jill Bakken selected the 28-year-old athlete as her brakewoman for the two-woman bobsled event.

While Flowers may have made the team, nobody expected her to earn a medal. Experts rated the combo of Jean Racine and Gea Johnson as America's best hope to overcome the Germans' long domination of the sport.

The weekend prior to the race, Racine approached Flowers about switching teams. But the Alabama native refused, preferring to remain loyal and compete with her original partner.

Flowers positioned her team well on its first run, getting off a 5.31-second start. Bakken then guided their sled to a clocking of 48.81, which was .29 seconds faster than the German team of Sandra Prokoff and Ulrike Holzner.

On their second run, the underdog Americans bettered the Germans once again, posting a 48.95 compared to their rivals' 48.96. With their combined time of 1:37.76, Flowers and Bakken claimed the gold—and the first bobsled medal for the United States since 1956.

At the same time, Flowers became the first African-American athlete to capture a Winter Olympics gold.

EXTRA POINT < < < < < < < < < < < < < < < < < < < < Vonetta Flowers could have decided to change bobsled teams to gain a better chance at a medal. But she chose loyalty over victory and received her heart's desire anyway. Shouts of joy greeted her as her country's banner rose and the "Star-Spangled Banner" played.

The psalmist wrote a song that asked God to give us the desire of our heart and success in our plans. That's what God wants for us, too, if our hearts beat with his. Then we will all shout in victory.

GOAL! *What is your heart's desire? Write down some plans you have for the future:*

_____

_____

_____

Ask God to make his desires and your plans a gold-medal match.

MAY HE GRANT
YOUR HEART'S DESIRE
AND FULFILL ALL YOUR PLANS.
MAY WE SHOUT FOR JOY WHEN WE
HEAR OF YOUR VICTORY, FLYING BANNERS
TO HONOR OUR GOD.

MAY THE LORD ANSWER ALL YOUR PRAYERS.

PSALM 20:4-5

TO COINCIDE WITH ITS 50TH ANNIVERSARY,

the National Basketball Association honored the league's 50 all-time greatest players at the annual All-Star game in 1997.

With living legends such as Bill Russell, Wilt Chamberlain, Larry Bird, and Julius Erving looking on, the West All-Stars opened a 53–30 lead with just under six minutes to play in the second quarter. But the East closed out the half with a 27–7 run, narrowing the margin to 60–57.

During halftime ceremonies, the NBA presented its former stars to the crowd of 20,562. All the athletes flashed broad smiles, and many beamed with unbounded joy, unashamedly revealing that they considered this moment one of the most memorable in their life.

Fueled by the adulation heaped upon their predecessors, the East All-Stars continued their torrid pace. Holding the West scoreless, Vin Baker opened the second half with two straight dunks, and Glen Rice followed with three consecutive three-pointers. The 40–7 run spanning halftime put the East Conference in front, 70–60.

Now in command, the East kept its opponent at bay and held on for a 132–120 victory. Rice, who scored 20 points in the third quarter, claimed the MVP award, and Michael Jordan posted the first triple-double in an All-Star game with 14 points, 11 rebounds, and 11 assists.

EXTRA POINT

< < < < < < < < < < < < < < < < < < < < <

Some athletes deserve praise from the media, from fans, from coaches, and from teammates. They possess great talent that they use well. They become stars. In basketball, those top 50 stars of 50 years deserve adoration.

But God is the greatest star of all time in all things. He alone deserves to be worshipped.

GOAL! Make a list of athletes who deserve your praise. Include the reason why you believe they're worthy.

Athlete: **Praiseworthy characteristic:**

_____   _____

_____   _____

Then make a list of people you know personally who deserve your praise. They may be teachers, firefighters, ministers, or family members.

Name: **Praiseworthy characteristic:**

_____   _____

_____   _____

Remember God deserves praise most of all.

CHRIS WITTY EARNED A SILVER and a bronze medal in speed skating at the 1998 Winter Olympics. She hoped to complete her medal collection with a gold at the 2002 Games. But a bout with mononucleosis a month prior to competition threatened to keep her away from the victory stand entirely.

Because of this contagious disease, which strikes people who are run-down, training became almost impossible. On some days, mono left Witty so weak she was unable to get out of bed. Even when skating was possible, Witty's practice sessions amounted to little more than warm-ups.

The illness contributed to a 14th-place finish in the 500 meters. After performing poorly in the 500, the Wisconsin native almost decided not to compete in the 1,000-meter event.

But on race day, Witty stepped onto the ice with Catriona Le May Doan, the two-time Olympic 500-meter gold medalist from Canada. Although not considered a medal contender in the 1,000, the Canadian always opened strong.

Witty felt fatigued before her race but settled down and followed closely behind Le May Doan until the final turn. Despite having achy legs, she passed the Canadian in the home stretch. To her shock, Witty clocked a 1:13.83—a new world's record.

EXTRA POINT < < < < < < < < < < < < < < < < < < Athletes expect to face injuries during their careers. They often fight through pain to train and compete. But unexpected illness can knock an athlete off her feet at inopportune times. For Chris Witty, mononucleosis brought weakness and pain. The flu-like symptoms could be cured only with rest. While she rested, she trained as best she could and ended up winning the gold.

Every day people get sick. The psalmist knew that. He asked God for the healing that only the heavenly Father can bring.

GOAL! *Help yourself to stay healthy this winter by washing your hands often, drinking lots of fluid, and getting plenty of rest. Ask God to heal those who are sick and to help them patiently rest.*

Have compassion on me, Lord, for I am weak. Heal me, Lord, for my body is in agony.

PSALM 6:2

13 FEB

Our Redeemer, whose name is the Lord Almighty, is the Holy One of Israel.

ISAIAH 47:4

NOTHING HURTS MORE than letting down your team. In the 1998 Nagano Olympics, Masahiko Harada redeemed his poor performance from the previous Games.

At the 1994 Lillehammer Olympics, the Japanese ski-jump team led the 120-meter event with one jump remaining. Harada, who soared 122 meters in his first run, needed 110 meters to clinch the gold for his country.

But when he landed, Harada's effort measured just 97.5, the worst leap of anybody on the top eight teams. Japan fell to second place, and Germany claimed the gold.

Four years later, Harada appeared jinxed again. In the 90-meter individual competition, he led after the first jump but faltered on his second and dropped to fifth. Although Harada later captured bronze in the 120-meter individual event, the pain of performing poorly in his native country brought sadness to the constantly smiling athlete.

A final opportunity for redemption came in the 120-meter team competition. Once more, Harada's first attempt, a paltry 79.5 meters, dropped the Japanese from first to fourth. But down to his last chance, Harada rallied.

Speeding down the runway like one of his country's bullet trains, he sailed through the sky and landed at 137 meters. His leap tied the world record, and Japan's final jumper clinched the gold for the team.

EXTRA POINT < < < < < < < < < < < < < < < < < < < < < Masahiko Harada redeemed himself by overcoming his poor jumps under pressure. His spectacular performance didn't just keep the Japanese from losing—it caused them to win.

Unlike Harada, many people never experience redemption. Redemption involves regaining something lost, fulfilling a promise, or compensating for an action. Sometimes we can't redeem ourselves. If our debt is too great, someone else must help us.

That's the way it is with the debt of sin. We could never make up for all the poor decisions we make. No matter how *good* we are, it's impossible to make ourselves *righteous*. But Jesus came to redeem us.

His perfect life, his death on the cross, and his victory over the grave allow us to know him and live with him forever in heaven.

GOAL! *Think of examples of redemption. You might include a kicker making a winning field goal after missing an extra point. Thank God for Jesus, our Redeemer.*

AN UNDEFEATED WORLD CHAMPIONSHIP season

and a gold medal in the previous Olympics gave the United States women's hockey team an air of confidence heading into Salt Lake City for the 2002 Winter Games.

Early on it appeared as if the Americans had plenty of reason to be confident as they advanced through the competition to the gold medal game. Riding a 35-game winning streak, Team USA hoped to defeat Canada, America's old nemesis and toughest opponent, for the second straight time and hold on to bragging rights.

But Team Canada took the lead less than two minutes into the gold-medal game with Caroline Ouellette scoring. The United States tied the game early in the second period on Kane King's power play, but Canada regained the lead a few minutes later as Hayley Wickenheiser scored off the rush.

With only a second remaining in period two, Jayna Hefford made the victory-clinching goal for the Canadians. Taking a fumbled clearing pass, she broke unabated toward the net and fired the puck past American goalie Sara DeCosta.

The United States narrowed the gap to 3–2 early in the third period on a power-play goal by Karyn Bye. But with goalie Kim St. Pierre stopping 25 of the 27 American shots, Team Canada captured the 2002 gold medal.

EXTRA POINT
< < < < < < < < < < < < < < < < < < < <

What happened to the USA hockey team? Were they as good as the Canadians? Did they play as hard? Yes, the teams both played hard and were fairly equal in talent. Perhaps the American women felt overconfident, and the Canadian women had more reasons to win.

In athletics, confidence often plays a role in victory. But overconfidence can also be a factor in defeat.

In the Bible, the apostle Paul had plenty of reason to boast, but he chose not to. Instead he let his words and actions do the talking. God wants us to be confident in our talents and abilities. But he doesn't want us to be cocky and overconfident.

GOAL! *Praise God for the confidence we have in him. Ask him to provide you with healthy confidence and to allow your actions—not your mouth—to do the talking.*

Though I might desire to boast, I will not be a fool; for I will speak the truth. But I refrain, lest anyone should think of me above what he sees me to be or hears from me.

2 CORINTHIANS 12:6, NKJV

---

15 FEB

> For the wages of sin is death, but the gift of God is eternal life in Christ Jesus our Lord.
>
> ROMANS 6:23, NKJV

TO EXCEL AS A DOWNHILL SKIER, an athlete must always be on the brink of disaster. And disaster almost struck Hermann Maier during the downhill in the 1998 Nagano Olympics.

The Austrian skier attempted to turn left on an icy bend during his run. But his skis glossed over the snow, and Maier flew off the course, traveling more than 70 mph. The high winds, which had forced the run to be altered before the race, carried him into the air and made his body look like a plastic grocery sack blowing along the ground.

The "Hermanator," as fans called him, tumbled over and over like a rag doll before some orange safety netting caught him over 50 yards from the accident site.

As Maier lay still in the snow, many assumed he was dead. But suddenly, the gold-medal favorite stood up and walked away. Hermann had suffered only minor injuries to his shoulder and knee. And thousands soon watched as Maier transformed into a surprising survivor.

Despite the pain, he returned to the slopes within days. Showing no ill effects from the dangerous accident, Maier captured gold medals in both the Super G and the giant slalom.

EXTRA POINT < < < < < < < < < < < < < < < < < < < < < <

Some sports carry significant risks. Each time a skier straps on his boards or a NASCAR driver gets behind the wheel, he or she faces serious injury or death.

But the greatest risk in life isn't physical death. It's death without Jesus. And unlike spending a lot of money on safety equipment, assurance of eternal safety is free for us. Christ already paid the price on the cross.

What we have to do is to confess our wrongs, ask Jesus to forgive us, and put our trust in him as Savior. Eternal life is ours for the asking.

GOAL! *If you don't already know you'll live forever in heaven, will you pray to God now? You can say something like, "Dear God, please forgive me. I know I'm a sinner. I believe Jesus died and rose from the dead so I could be forgiven of my sins. Thank you for allowing me to have a personal relationship with you. Amen."*

Thank God for his free gift of forgiveness.

FRIENDS CAN HELP ATHLETES accomplish bigger and

better things. Casey FitzRandolph and Kip Carpenter discovered that as they squared off against each other in the 500-meter speed-skating finals at the 2002 Olympics.

In his first 500-meter run, FitzRandolph led the field with an Olympic-record time of 34.42 seconds. But 1998 gold-medal winner and world-record holder Hiroyasu Shimizu of Japan loomed as a formidable challenger. Shimizu boldly predicted he would break his own world record of 34.32.

After racing on Monday morning, the two Americans spent the afternoon engaged in FitzRandolph's favorite pastime—watching televised hunting and fishing programs. The outdoorsy show enabled both men to relax and prepare for the following day.

Shimizu raced in the next-to-last heat in the final runs. But instead of breaking the record, he clocked 34.65, giving him a total of 1:09.26. FitzRandolph needed a 34.84 on his final run to capture the gold, and Carpenter required a 34.58.

Somewhat shaky at the start, FitzRandolph hit a pylon and wobbled momentarily. However, he recovered and finished at 34.81, winning the gold. His friend Kip Carpenter came in at 34.79, claiming the bronze.

For the first time since 1980, an American earned a medal in the 500 meters, and the one-three finish marked the best United States effort in the event since 1952.

> Perfume and incense bring joy to the heart, and the pleasantness of one's friend springs from his earnest counsel.
>
> PROVERBS 27:9, NIV

EXTRA POINT
< < < < < < < < < < < < < < < < < < <

FitzRandolph and Carpenter's friendship probably helped them relax and perform well at the Olympics. Spending time with a friend makes life richer. Playing on an athletic team with a friend or training with one helps the sport become even more fun. When friends do their best to compete fairly and encourage each other, the relationship grows stronger.

Often athletes don't join a team or begin training as friends. The bond develops over time. Days, weeks, months, and sometimes years spent together working hard and sharing dreams strengthen the connection.

The Bible uses the word *friend* or *friends* more than 150 times. Friendships should be treasured as one of God's greatest gifts.

GOAL! *Think of special friends you've made in athletics. Let them know how they've helped you. If you don't have a friend on your team or in your sport, work on developing relationships. Praise God for his gift of friends.*

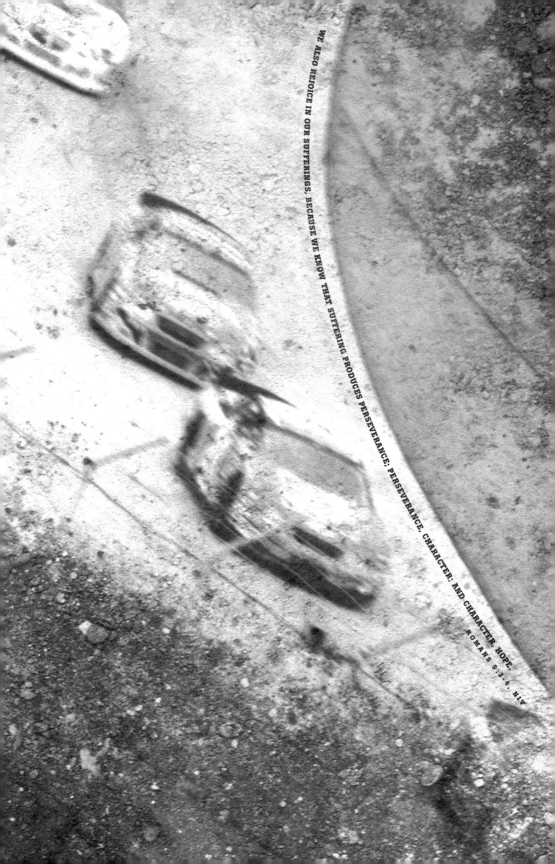

WE ALSO REJOICE IN OUR SUFFERINGS, BECAUSE WE KNOW THAT SUFFERING PRODUCES PERSEVERANCE; PERSEVERANCE, CHARACTER; AND CHARACTER, HOPE.

ROMANS 5:3-4, NIV

CAN YOU IMAGINE *STARTING* the football season with the Super Bowl? No way! Right? But every February the NASCAR season begins with its most important race. Called the "Super Bowl of stock-car racing," the Daytona 500 kicks off the year in grand style.

For 20 years, NASCAR legend Dale Earnhardt tried to win the Daytona 500. But a cut tire, an empty gas tank, a missing lug nut, and a myriad of other mishaps had kept him out of the winner's circle. And although he'd won 30 races on the Daytona International Speedway, he'd never walked away with NASCAR's top prize . . . until the 1998 race.

That year Earnhardt led for 107 laps, including the last 60, to take the title. He passed teammate Mike Skinner on lap 140 and led a pack of the leaders to a quick pit stop on lap 175 when a caution flag went up. Earnhardt made it out of the pits first. When the caution flag went down, only 12 laps remained. That's when Jeremy Mayfield, Rusty Wallace, Jeff Gordon, and Bobby Labonte pushed Earnhardt to the brink.

First Mayfield and Wallace filled Earnhardt's rearview mirror for five laps. Then Gordon, the 1997 Daytona winner, pushed his way into third. A dropped cylinder forced Gordon out, and Labonte took his place. When a caution flag appeared with one lap to go, Earnhardt gunned his No. 3 Chevrolet to the line. He edged Labonte for the victory, and Mayfield settled for third.

EXTRA POINT < < < < < < < < < < < < < < < < < < < < < <
Dale Earnhardt never gave up the hope of winning the Daytona 500. Although he suffered 20 years of defeat in NASCAR's biggest race, he stayed determined. And his average speed of 172.712 mph was the third fastest of all time.

The Lord wants us to keep going during difficult times too. We'll definitely suffer setbacks as Christians. But by persevering, we'll develop character and become more like Christ.

GOAL! *Which feels better: winning something without trying or tasting victory after lots of hard work and practice? Hard-fought victories feel great because you know your effort was rewarded. God will help you persevere during difficult times if you ask him to.*

18 FEB

Do not follow the crowd in doing wrong.

EXODUS 23:2, NIV

SHORT TRACK SPEED SKATING can look a lot like a rugby match. With five skaters racing on a 111-meter oval, spills and collisions frequently occur. In the 2002 Olympics, Australia's Steven Bradbury discovered that keeping his distance from the pack sometimes pays dividends.

The 1000-meter event featured American Apolo Anton Ohno, whom many considered a favorite to claim four gold medals. In the finals, Ohno led going into the final turn.

Jockeying for position, 1998 silver medalist Jiajun Li of China engaged in a light, one-armed shoving match with Ohno. Without warning, Canada's Mathieu Turcotte and Korea's Hyun-Soo Ahn became entangled with the two leaders. In an instant, all four skaters sprawled across the ice.

Bradbury, the weakest competitor of the five, trailed the others by several meters. Never focusing on his fallen competitors, he skated past the heap of humanity and crossed the finish line for the gold medal with a time of 1:29.109.

Ohno managed to escape from the pile and staggered to the line for the silver. Turcotte also scrambled to his feet and claimed the bronze. Judges disqualified Li from the race for impeding the progress of his rivals.

EXTRA POINT < < < < < < < < < < < < < < < < < < < < Steven Bradbury didn't intentionally keep his distance from the other skaters. He didn't want a wide gap, but he couldn't quite keep up. Yet Steven kept skating his best. He wasn't part of the crowd, and that paid off with a gold medal.

In life, often it's best not to be part of the crowd. When the crowd stumbles and falls because of unwise choices and questionable actions, keeping a wide space pays off. God wants us to follow his way, not the crowd's way. Like Steven Bradbury, sometimes we need to keep our distance.

GOAL! *Think about areas where your faith in Jesus Christ distances you from other people. Maybe you've decided not to drink, smoke, or become sexually active, while a lot of your friends have. Ask God to help you know when to stay away from the crowd.*

SOMETIMES OLYMPIC ATHLETES face the choice to play it safe and earn a lesser medal or to go all out in the quest for the gold. In the 2002 Salt Lake City snowboarding competition, Kelly Clark left it all on the halfpipe.

The 18-year-old American stood securely in second place after her first run. But Clark wasn't feeling great. Several days earlier in practice, she had fallen and injured her tailbone. Medication and physical therapy brought some relief, but the deep bruise caused nagging pain. Before her second attempt, she contemplated holding back and being content with the silver, since only the best run actually counted.

Despite her injury, Clark's competitive nature wouldn't allow her to do anything but go big. Fueled by adrenaline, she attacked the halfpipe with determination—she wanted that gold.

With rock music blasting, the Mount Snow, Vermont, native stunned the judges with her amplitude and acrobatics. The five-member panel awarded her a combined score of 47.9 out of a possible 50.

France's Doriane Vidal, the leader prior to Clark's run, watched her performance with a combination of dismay and admiration. Before the results flashed on the board, Vidal knew Clark had taken the gold. She deserved it. Clark's tremendous performance brought the United States its first championship in the Salt Lake City Games.

> God has chosen the foolish things of the world to put to shame the wise, and God has chosen the weak things of the world to put to shame the things which are mighty.
>
> 1 CORINTHIANS 1:27, NKJV

EXTRA POINT
< < < < < < < < < < < < < < < < < < < <

Some might have thought Kelly Clark foolish for competing in the Olympics with her injury. Once she'd clinched the silver, others could have considered her foolish for fighting through pain to gain the gold. But her wisdom and competitive drive pushed her to victory.

The Bible talks about God using seemingly foolish things to overcome what most people believe to be wise. God's wisdom is often viewed as foolish. He said the first will be last and that you should serve if you want to lead. God wants every Christian to follow his wisdom.

GOAL! *With a friend or family member, think of some statements from the Bible that sound foolish at first, such as "The last will be first, and the first will be last" (Matthew 20:16, NIV) or "Whoever wants to become great among you must be your servant" (Matthew 20:26, NIV). Find the wisdom in those statements. Praise God for the wisdom he gives.*

20 FEB

A fool gives full vent to his anger, but a wise man keeps himself under control.

PROVERBS
29:11, NIV

A PITCHER WITH GOOD CONTROL makes life hard on

opposing batters. In a 1998 high school game, Erik Thompson struck out a heap of batters when he pitched with near perfection.

The sophomore from Pine Forest High School in Pensacola, Florida, stepped on the mound for his first varsity starting assignment. Whatever nervousness Thompson felt before the game quickly dissipated as he struck out the first nine batters he faced.

After giving up a single to right field, Thompson stayed in control and continued to throw strike after strike. Relying primarily on his fastball, he whiffed another 11 batters before allowing a second single to right field.

Since high school baseball games last just seven innings, Thompson needed only one out to complete the game. Before it could be recorded, however, the runner stole second and scored on an error. Despite giving up the run, Thompson fanned the final batter and tallied all 21 outs in the contest via strikeouts.

Pine Forest won the game 9–1, with Thompson providing the bulk of the offense himself. He collected three hits in four at bats, including a triple and a home run.

Surprisingly, Thompson's 21 strikeouts didn't set a national high school record. In 1986, Brett Jennings of Lingleville, Texas, recorded 24 Ks in a seven-inning game. (Since batters can reach base on a third-strike passed ball or wild pitch, it's possible to strike out more than 21 batters in a game.)

EXTRA POINT < < < < < < < < < < < < < < < < < < < <

An excellent pitcher maintains control of his throws, whether fastball, curve, slider, or changeup. Errors by teammates, taunts by opponents, and close calls by umpires don't make him angry or cause him to lose his cool. Erik Thompson had control, refusing to let the two hits bother him.

God wants us to keep that kind of control in every aspect of our life. Words said in anger cause permanent damage. Actions spurred by wrath result in regret. But self-control produces success.

GOAL! *Picture some baseball games you've watched or played. How did the players handle adversity? Did they show anger, or did they exercise control? What about you? Ask God to help you control your anger.*

MIDORI ITO COMPLETED the first triple axel by a woman in international figure-skating competition in 1989. Her phenomenal athletic feat, however, was not repeated in the 1992 Winter Olympic Games.

During the weeks before the competition, newspapers and magazines hyped the event as the battle between "polish and power." Athletic skaters such as Ito and America's Tonya Harding appeared on the verge of dominating the sport and pushing more artistic performers like Kristi Yamaguchi for the gold.

But Yamaguchi led the field after the short program. And in the long program, the native of Fremont, California, skated first in the final group of performers.

While performing a triple toe loop, Yamaguchi's hand touched the ice. The mistake resulted in a more conservative routine, with the substitution of a double rather than the planned triple salchow.

Backstage with her coach, 20-year-old Yamaguchi watched as Midori fell on her triple axel attempt. Fellow Americans Harding and Nancy Kerrigan also took spills, leaving the Californian as the leader despite her subdued performance. In the final voting, seven of the nine judges awarded Yamaguchi the gold medal.

Ito claimed the silver but felt shamed by her error on the ice. She publicly apologized to her native Japan for not winning first place. Recognizing her courage, humility, and athleticism, her country gave Ito the honor of lighting the Olympic Cauldron at the 1998 Nagano Games.

> Blessed are they whose transgressions are forgiven, whose sins are covered.
>
> ROMANS 4:7, NIV

EXTRA POINT

< < < < < < < < < < < < < < < < < < < <

In America, athletes seldom apologize—at least publicly. They may say something to a coach or to teammates, but not usually on television or in print.

Although Midori Ito didn't even do anything sinful, she still felt that apologizing was the right thing to do. And her nation turned her humble, tearful words into joy. They gave her the ultimate athletic honor. They handed her the torch to light the Olympic flame.

God wants us to apologize when we need to—when we're wrong, when we say something we shouldn't, when we hurt another person, or when we don't do our best. The apology frees us to move forward with greater joy.

GOAL! *Have you done something to someone that deserves an apology? If so, it's time to make things right. Apologize to God for the wrongs you've done and ask his forgiveness.*

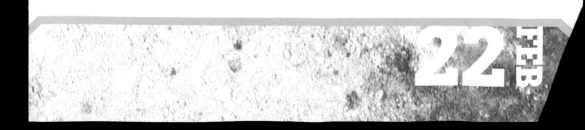

22 FEB

A wise son makes a glad father, but a foolish son is the grief of his mother.

PROVERBS 10:1, NKJV

SKELETON IS A WILD-LOOKING SPORT, which athletes may have to be a little crazed to compete in. In the unique event, participants race 50 yards down a frozen track, plop stomach-down on a sled resembling a cafeteria tray, and navigate 15 treacherous curves while traveling nearly 80 mph only three inches above the ice.

After skeleton was taken out of the Winter Olympics in 1948, the International Olympic Committee approved the sledding sport for the 2002 Games. The decision granted American Jim Shea Jr. the opportunity to become the first third-generation Olympian.

Shea's Olympic roots run deep. In 1932, his grandfather, Jack, captured gold medals in the 500- and 1,500-meter speed-skating competitions. His father, Jim Sr., participated in three cross-country skiing events in 1964. Together the three were asked to carry the Olympic torch into the stadium. However, Jack tragically died at age 91 in an automobile accident a month prior to the 2002 Games.

But Jim Jr. faced more than the loss of his grandfather. After capturing the 1999 World Cup title, he battled a circulatory problem in his left leg. With surgery looming for Shea, most experts rated his teammates Lincoln DeWitt and Chris Soule as America's best medal hopes.

But Shea refused to yield to his injury and attacked the 4,380-foot course with determination. The American posted the best qualifying time but trailed Austria's Martin Rettl for first place in the finals.

As the final racer in the final run, Jim knew the time to beat: 1:42.01. Wearing a photograph of his grandfather inside his helmet, Shea crossed the finish line at 1:41.96 to claim the gold.

EXTRA POINT < < < < < < < < < < < < < < < < < < < < < < <
What a special moment! Unfortunately, Jack Shea missed saluting his grandson on the medal podium where he had stood 70 years earlier. But Jim Jr. and Jim Sr. held the family's first Olympian in their hearts.

God made families for us to enjoy, cherish, and remember. Parents and grandparents have the wonderful opportunity to set an example for their children and grandchildren. And children and grandchildren have the ability to emulate the previous generations and bring joy to their family.

GOAL! *Take time to visit with older family members. Listen to their stories. Record significant family events, and take a multigenerational picture together. Thank the heavenly Father for your earthly family.*

COMPETITORS MUST FOLLOW the rules—even rules they're not totally aware of—if they want to end up in the winner's circle. That fact proved to be true at the 2002 Daytona 500.

The 200-lap race went under a caution flag with just a handful of laps to go. The race was restarted at lap 195 with front-runners Jeff Gordon and Sterling Marlin battling for first place. Marlin went low on the track to pass Gordon, but Gordon blocked him and tangled with Marlin's car. Gordon spun out, and Marlin's fender was damaged in the collision. At the same time, another accident forced the race to go under the caution flag with Marlin in the lead. Soon the red flag went up and the high-powered machines came to a stop on the Daytona International Speedway as the accident was cleaned up.

With the race halted, Marlin jumped out of his window, ran around his car, and started pulling his fender away from his right front tire. NASCAR officials quickly ordered Marlin back into his vehicle. Then they forced him to start behind all the other cars in the lead lap because NASCAR rules state that cars can't be worked on during a red flag.

Marlin's goof meant he finished eighth, while Ward Burton benefited from Marlin's mistake to win his first Daytona 500. Burton's victory also marked the first time a Virginian had claimed NASCAR's most prestigious race.

> I am the Lord your God; follow my decrees and be careful to keep my laws.
>
> EZEKIEL 20:19, NIV

EXTRA POINT

< < < < < < < < < < < < < < < < < < < < < <

Sterling Marlin said he wasn't aware of the red-flag rule when he tried to fix his car, but he still suffered the consequences. Every sport has rules to keep the athletes under control and competing on a level playing field. Without any rules, sports would be chaotic. Society has laws to maintain public tranquility as well.

God also has laws. We won't lose a game if we break them, and we probably won't go to jail for messing up on some of them. But not following God's laws will mess up our relationship with Jesus Christ. Failing to follow God's laws is called sin. Sin separates us from God. The cool thing is that when we break God's laws we can ask for forgiveness and God will forget we messed up in the first place.

GOAL! *Commit to reading the Bible to learn God's rules. Then ask him to give you the wisdom to keep his laws.*

24 FEB

Samuel said,
"Although you
were once
small in your
own eyes, did
you not become
the head of the
tribes of Israel?
The Lord
anointed you
king over
Israel."
1 SAMUEL
15:17, NIV

THE NBA SLAM-DUNK COMPETITION continues to make highlight reels year after year as players get more creative with their high-flying antics. But perhaps no dunk contest will ever be as memorable as the 1986 showdown between Spud Webb and Dominique Wilkins.

At first glance, everybody would've favored Wilkins in the finals. Standing 6-feet-7-inches and nicknamed the "human highlight film," Wilkins was the defending champion in the NBA showcase event in spectators' minds. Webb, on the other hand, appeared like a child compared to the imposing Wilkins. At 5-foot-7 and 133 pounds, Webb didn't send shivers of fear down his opponents' spine. However, his 48-inch vertical jump and unique dunks brought the judges and fans to their feet.

Webb, who had been dunking a basketball on a ten-foot hoop since his teen years when he was just 4-foot-11, scored perfect 50s on his first two dunks in the finals. One of those slams started at half-court as Webb lofted the ball high in the air toward the rim. Sprinting after the ball, Webb leaped into the air, caught the ball on a bounce, and reverse slammed it through the hoop.

Although Wilkins matched Webb with a perfect 50 on his first dunk in the finals, Webb's consistency and amazing dunks helped this little man walk away with the title.

EXTRA POINT < < < < < < < < < < < < < < < < < < < <

Spud Webb was truly an unlikely winner of a contest created for NBA giants. But his fearlessness and jumping ability took him to the top.

God often uses little people to do great things. Just because you're young doesn't mean others can't look up to you. Leadership has nothing to do with size or even age. It involves setting an example and then influencing others. A leader fearlessly goes ahead of the group.

In the Old Testament, Samuel reminded Saul that he once seemed small. Then God chose Saul to be king and used him to lead the Israelites.

Smallness doesn't matter to God, because his power can make anybody great.

GOAL! *Look over the roster of your favorite NBA team. Consider leadership ability and height. Do they match? Ask God to use you and develop you as a leader.*

LEARNING FROM PAST MISTAKES can make any athlete—and any person—better. In 1994 at the Lillehammer Games, American skier Tommy Moe put his past behind him to surprise the world and win an Olympic gold medal.

Eight years before the Olympics, the U.S. national ski team had kicked a 16-year-old Moe off the squad for violating training rules. Angered by his son's lax attitude, Moe's father, an Alaskan building contractor, forced the teenager to spend the next summer working 12 hours a day on a remote Aleutian Island construction site. The humbling and difficult experience intensified the teen's desire to become a world-class competitor.

Moe changed his ways and started working hard.

Despite achieving success on the junior circuit, Moe had no chance of a medal in the downhill, according to *Sports Illustrated*. The magazine categorized the entire men's team as "a lead-footed snowplow brigade."

On race day, Moe followed Norway's Kjetil Andre Aamodt. The local favorite blistered the course in 1:45.79, three-tenths of a second faster than any earlier competitor.

The 23-year-old American took to the course and trailed Aamodt by a slim margin at the midway point. Spurred by his opponent's strong showing, Moe sped down the slope and crossed the finish line at 1:45.75, becoming only the second United States skier to claim gold in an Olympic downhill.

EXTRA POINT < < < < < < < < < < < < < < < < < < < < < < < No one doubted that Tommy Moe possessed talent. Skiing wasn't his problem. His attitude was. He chose not to follow his coach's command. Instead, the young man opted to go his own way. Moe's way led to difficulty and defeat. When he listened to his coach and his father, the skier's path turned to gold and glory.

The prophet Jeremiah applied that same principle to life. If we walk in God's way and obey our heavenly Father, life will go well. Jeremiah didn't mean that we will escape disappointment. But we will live well on God's path.

GOAL! *Think of a time when a coach or parent gave you some good advice or showed you a helpful tip. How did it help you perform? Did you do better and have success? Ask God to guide you to walk in his way.*

> This is what I commanded them, saying, "Obey My voice, and I will be your God, and you shall be My people. And walk in all the ways that I have commanded you, that it may be well with you."
>
> JEREMIAH 7:23, NKJV

26 FEB

Jesus answered
them, "Healthy
people don't
need a doctor—
sick people do."

LUKE 5:31

OLYMPIC ATHLETES NATURALLY WANT to go for the gold. But in the 2002 Winter Games, Chris Klug's bronze in the men's snowboarding parallel giant slalom looked golden. Klug couldn't have been happier with his medal . . . he was just happy to be alive.

Less than a year and a half before the Games, Klug, suffering from a rare degenerative condition, received a liver transplant that saved his life. And less than two months after surgery, Klug was back on the slopes.

Despite his hard work, Klug wasn't a favorite in Salt Lake City. He barely made it past the first round by defeating Jerome Sylvestre of Canada by .05 seconds. (Competitors in parallel giant slalom race side by side on their snowboards through a series of gates. The athlete with the lowest combined time in two head-to-head races moves on.) And in the quarterfinals, Klug trailed Germany's Walter Feichter by .75 seconds after the first run. But in the second race, Feichter fell and Klug continued.

Klug finally lost in the semis to eventual gold-medalist Philipp Schoch of Switzerland. Richard Richardsson of Sweden earned the silver.

EXTRA POINT < < < < < < < < < < < < < < < < < < < Doctors did an amazing thing for Chris Klug on July 28, 2000. By giving him a new liver, they allowed him to extend his life and follow his dreams. And he made his dreams come true by bringing home a medal in the 2002 Winter Olympics.

Klug said he felt fortunate to be alive—to be given a second chance at life. When Jesus Christ walked the earth, he healed lots of sick people. He wanted to give everybody a second chance at life, even people society didn't think had a good chance of surviving. When the religious leaders asked Jesus why he spent time with hurting people, the Savior matter-of-factly answered that sick people need a doctor; healthy people don't.

GOAL! *Can you think of any sick people around you? Maybe they don't need a new liver like Chris Klug. Perhaps they're caught up in drugs or sex or damaging relationships. Sickness comes in a lot of forms. Thank Jesus that he can heal any sickness. Pray for your friends, tell them about the Great Physician, and watch God work.*

PLAYERS ARE SUPPOSED to respect their coaches. And oftentimes, through hard work and extra effort, coaches develop respect for their athletes.

A special relationship between University of Connecticut coach Geno Auriemma and basketball player Nykesha Sales made for a unique start to a basketball game in 1998.

Sales, the 21-year-old senior forward, tore her Achilles tendon against Notre Dame just prior to the Huskies' season finale against Villanova. At the time, Sales had scored 2,176 career points, one less than UConn's record holder, Kerry Bascom-Poliquim.

The situation appeared hopeless. Sales, a deserving player, wouldn't break the record. Then Coach Auriemma spoke with his friend, Harry Perretta, Villanova's coach. Geno proposed letting Sales score an uncontested basket to open the game. The Huskies would then allow Villanova to score. In theory, the competition would begin 2–2 rather than 0–0.

Perretta agreed. Auriemma also approached both schools' athletic directors, presidents, and the Big East commissioner. He requested approval from Bascom-Poliquim. Everyone gave the go-ahead.

The contest began with Connecticut's Paige Sauer tipping the ball to guard Rita Williams, who handed it to Sales. Although hobbling, Nykesha dribbled toward the basket and banked a shot off the glass and through the net. The UConn players then stepped aside to allow Villanova's basket as Sales left the court as the all-time scoring leader for Connecticut.

EXTRA POINT < < < < < < < < < < < < < < < < < < < < < < Nykesha Sales put her heart into UConn basketball. It seemed a shame that she wouldn't hold the all-time scoring record. Her coach wanted to help her achieve that well-deserved goal. Auriemma examined the alternatives. His upright character dictated that he involve everyone in his plan. His integrity allowed nothing less.

And it worked. Sales got the record honestly, and the coach and the university maintained their integrity.

Integrity pleases God. True integrity involves more than simple honesty. It means upright character with sound judgment and no hint of wrongdoing.

In the Bible, David understood that he had not always acted honestly. But at the end of his life, the great king prayed the dedication prayer at his son Solomon's coronation. In his words to God, King David acknowledged the importance of integrity.

> I know, my God, that you examine our hearts and rejoice when you find integrity there.
>
> 1 CHRONICLES 29:17

GOAL! *Have you watched or played for a coach with integrity? If so, what specific situations demonstrated the quality?*

Ask God to help you have integrity.

28 FEB

MAR-CH.

GOLF DEPENDS ON PLAYERS to be honest about enforcing the rules and penalizing themselves when needed. But as Paul Azinger learned, even unintentional violations can bring swift punishment.

On opening day of the 1981 Doral-Ryder Open, Azinger signed and turned in a scorecard reflecting a 3-under-par 69. But an observant fan watching on USA Network caught the golfer in a rule violation for removing loose impediments from the course.

The incident occurred on the 18th hole. While taking his stance for a wedge shot out of a shallow water hazard, Azinger kicked away several rocks. Golf rules call for a self-assessed, two-stroke penalty for the act. But without thinking, the PGA veteran naturally did it to set up his swing.

The television viewer from Colorado called PGA officials the following day to point out the violation. Tournament director Mike Shea reviewed the videotape. He agreed that Azinger broke Rule 13-4c. Under PGA guidelines, a scorecard indicating a score lower than actually tallied results in automatic disqualification.

After Azinger completed his second round—a 65, which left him one stroke behind the leader—officials informed him of their decision. He appealed by telephone to PGA commissioner Deane Beman, but golf's top authority conceded that the rule had been breached.

EXTRA POINT < < < < < < < < < < < < < < < < < < < < < No player or official on the course caught Paul Azinger's error. The gallery didn't notice either. But a fan many miles away carefully watched the broadcast. He knew the rules. He understood the honesty demanded in the game of golf. So he made the phone call. The highest officials of the sport considered the situation and disqualified Azinger.

As Christians, we know that God looks down on us. He always knows what we do. But we should also remember that no matter what we do or where we go, other people watch us too. They notice our actions. As representatives of Christ on earth, we need to watch our actions too.

GOAL! *Think about a time you broke a rule. How did you respond? Would you have acted differently if someone had been watching? Ask God to help you remember that someone is always watching.*

The Lord looks down from heaven and sees the whole human race. From his throne he observes all who live on the earth. He made their hearts, so he understands everything they do.

PSALM 33:13-15

01 MAR

But many who
are first will be
last, and many
who are last
will be first.

MATTHEW

19:30, NIV

NO ONE EVER IMAGINED a 900 could be done on a skateboard in real life. Sure, it had been accomplished on the video game screen in Tony Hawk's Pro Skater. But landing on a halfpipe after spinning around two and a half times? Come on!

That's just what Hawk fans must have thought during the 1999 Summer X Games "Best Trick" competition. As the world's top skaters displayed amazing grinds, kick flips, indies, and a host of new tricks that hadn't been given cool names yet, Hawk made it a night to remember.

Originally, organizers planned for the competition to be held within a specific time limit, but once Hawk started going after the 900, time no longer mattered. All eyes watched as with each attempt, he got closer and closer to hitting his landing. Skateboarding legends such as Andy Macdonald, Bob Burnquist, and Bucky Lasek all banged their boards on the ramp cheering for Tony Hawk.

Hawk was determined. The look on his face showed sheer focus and desire. On his 11th attempt, he nailed it. The Hawk soared high above the coping, spun two and a half times, and landed the first ever 900 during a skateboard vert competition.

EXTRA POINT < < < < < < < < < < < < < < < < < < < Isn't it awesome to be the first one to do something no one else has ever done before? That night, Tony Hawk said it was the best day of his life! After the successful trick, the fans went wild and rushed to congratulate Hawk, carrying him off the ramp on their shoulders.

In the sports world, the first to accomplish a feat is always held in high honor, but God's kingdom is much different. The Lord said that the first would be last. God doesn't want us to focus on ourselves but on others. His desire for us is that we live our life in service to others just like Christ was a servant to us by dying on the cross for our sins.

GOAL! *Try something: The next time you're in a line, go to the back and think about being a servant. Try to look for ways to put others first in your life this week. Remember that God rewards a servant's heart!*

LISTENING TO WISE ADVICE is a good idea in sports . . . and in life. Edward Fryatt learned this lesson at the 2000 Doral-Ryder Open.

After carding an opening round 75, Fryatt tried to work out some kinks on the practice green. While the 28-year-old rookie took a few extra shots, fellow PGA member David Frost detected a flaw in his grip. Taking Frost's advice, Fryatt noticed a marked difference the next day.

The Las Vegas native sank a birdie in the opening holes and discovered newfound confidence. Suddenly, every shot seemed to go exactly where the golfer intended it.

Fryatt recorded a second birdie on hole 4 by sinking a 20-foot putt. Birdie putts of 40 and 25 feet followed on 5 and 6. Two short putts of three and six feet resulted in birdies on 7 and 8. A 25-footer on the par-3 No. 9 gave the first-year pro a 29 for the front nine, tying the tournament record set by Tom Kite in 1974 and 1979.

Two more birdies went on Fryatt's scorecard when he sank 12- and 15-foot putts on 10 and 11. But the string snapped when he recorded a par on the 12th hole. His eight consecutive birdies tied a PGA record shared by Dewey Arnett, Fuzzy Zoeller, and Bob Goalby.

Unaware of his accomplishment, Fryatt finished with a 62. Although his score rose to 71 in round three and 66 on day four, the young pro wound up with a four-day total of 274 to tie for ninth place.

> Listen to advice and accept instruction, and in the end you will be wise.
> PROVERBS 19:20, NIV

EXTRA POINT
< < < < < < < < < < < < < < < < < < < <

Veteran David Frost gave rookie Edward Fryatt excellent advice and timely instruction. Edward listened and learned. That decision made Fryatt a very wise golfer.

In life God gives us many chances for learning. His Word provides sound instruction from cover to cover. Pastors, Sunday school teachers, and mature Christians provide good advice. Spiritual books, movies, and music also teach wonderful lessons and help us grow. If we listen to the advice and accept the instruction, we too will become wise.

GOAL! *If you play a sport, ask your coach for extra instruction. Listen to the advice, and put the lesson to practice. If you're not involved in athletics, ask for advice in another area of your life. Praise God for providing good advice and sound instruction.*

03 MAR

Let us fix our
eyes on Jesus,
the author
and perfecter
of our faith,
who for the joy
set before him
endured the
cross, scorning
its shame,
and sat down
at the right
hand of the
throne of God.

HEBREWS
12:2, NIV

IF THE IDEA OF SOARING 40 feet into the air, twisting around as you flip over and over, and landing on your feet is enough to put shivers up your spine, then join the club. About the only way that sounds remotely possible is if you could do it into a swimming pool.

But freestyle aerialists perform those amazing stunts under *truly* chilling conditions—in the snow. And in the 1998 Nagano Winter Olympics, a couple of American ski jumpers brought home gold medals.

First, Nikki Stone claimed top honors by dominating the women's competition from the start. She opened with a back full double full, where she flew off the launching ramp, pulled a triple-twisting double somersault, and nailed the landing. Her score of 98.15 was the highest of the day. Stone chose to perform a lay tuck full, or single twisting triple somersault, for her second jump and tallied 94.85 points to clinch the gold.

Not to be outdone, Stone's teammate and training partner Eric Bergoust earned gold on the men's side with a world record–breaking score of 255.64. And just like Stone, Bergoust set the tone. His 133.05 on his full double full full, or triple-twisting triple back somersault, was the highest score ever for a single jump. Bergoust followed up by landing a double full full full (that's three back somersaults with four twists) to score 122.59 points—and an Olympic gold.

EXTRA POINT < < < < < < < < < < < < < < < < < < < < < < Nikki Stone and Eric Bergoust pushed the limit in their sport. By perfectly completing the toughest tricks, they won the Olympic gold and brought honor to their country.

Just imagine trying to land on your feet after completing four twists and three back somersaults (let alone landing on skis). If Bergoust and Stone didn't keep their eyes on their target—the ground—they could have been seriously injured.

As Christians we should follow their example. We should always keep our eyes on the target—Jesus Christ. No matter how much our life is spinning out of control, by keeping our eyes on Christ, we can land on our feet.

GOAL! *Think of times you crashed and burned because you weren't focused on Christ. Now remember situations when you kept your eyes on God and succeeded. Ask God to help you always keep your eyes on him.*

YOU MAY NOT RECOGNIZE Steve Cook's name. But no other

American Olympian won more medals during 2002 than Cook. At the 2002 Paralympics in Salt Lake City, Cook skied away with four silver medals in cross-country—not bad for a guy with one and a half legs.

Cook lost the lower part of his right leg in a farming accident in Montana when he was 17. But instead of feeling sorry for himself, he became even more determined to do something exceptional with his life. He made the U.S. Paralympic cycling team and competed in the 1996 Summer Games in Atlanta, where he placed in the top ten. Cook improved at the 1998 Winter Games in Nagano, Japan, as he took fifth in the 10K cross-country event.

But in 2002, Cook showed that hard work, determination, and humility can overcome any obstacle. Skiing for the United States in his hometown of Salt Lake City, Cook claimed silver in the 5K, 10K, 20K, and the 12.5K relay. That's a long way to ski for anybody, let alone for a guy who lost part of his leg.

EXTRA POINT < < < < < < < < < < < < < < < < < < < <

After his amazing performance in the 2002 Paralympics, Steve Cook wasn't plastered across billboards or doing television interviews. Instead he went back to work at a bike shop. And that's okay with him—Cook's not looking for fame. He just wants to be an example to others. Cook, who wasn't much of an athlete before his accident, hopes his medals encourage other people with disabilities to get involved in sports. Plus, he wants the U.S. cross-country ski team to see that it's possible to beat Norwegians and Russians in a sport those countries have dominated for years.

With determination, Steve overcame his injury. And our heavenly Father wants us to overcome any obstacle we might face in life. In the New Testament, the apostle John wrote that if we believe Jesus is the Son of God, we can overcome the world's challenges.

Who is it that overcomes the world? Only he who believes that Jesus is the Son of God.
1 JOHN 5:5, NIV

GOAL! *Do the world's pressures ever feel like a 40-foot-thick brick wall? God doesn't want you to give up or give in. By believing in his Son, you can overcome anything. Just try it!*

05 MAR

WHEN TIMES ARE GOOD,
BE HAPPY; WHEN TIMES
ARE BAD,
CONSIDER:
GOD
HAS
MADE
THE
ONE
AS WELL AS
THE
OTHER.

ECCLESIASTES 7:14, NIV

GETTING THE BALL through the hoop is the goal of basketball. But it's often easier said than done. In the 2001 Colonial Athletic Association tournament final, George Mason and the University of North Carolina–Wilmington staged one of the worst shooting performances of all time.

Neither team could find its shooting range. Things were so bad in the first half that nobody scored for more than six minutes. At halftime UNC–Wilmington led the Patriots 19–17.

The poor shooting continued in the second half. The Seahawks suffered through another scoreless stretch of eight minutes, falling behind 34–33 on Patriots Erik Herring's three-pointer with 3:27 remaining. With the lead, George Mason's defense stiffened and shut out UNC–Wilmington the rest of the way.

Patriot Tremaine Price connected on a free throw with 24.8 seconds left to play, giving the Seahawks one final chance. Brett Blizzard took the inbound pass and threw to Barron Thelmon with seven ticks left on the clock. His desperation shot bounced off the glass.

George Mason escaped with a 35–33 win, the second-lowest combined score in NCAA history since the shot clock came into play. The Patriots hit 14-of-48 field goal attempts for a 29 percent average, while the Seahawks matched 29 percent with 11-for-39 shooting.

EXTRA POINT < < < < < < < < < < < < < < < < < < < < < Both George Mason and UNC-Wilmington played ugly basketball. Absolutely nothing fell right. Although both teams put forth a maximum effort, shots wouldn't go in; passes went awry.

Of course, George Mason coach Jim Larranaga felt a bit gratified after the game. The victory advanced his team to the NCAA tournament. Plus, the Patriots' entire season hadn't been that bad. The team averaged 71 points a game.

We all experience good and bad times, whether in athletics or in everyday life. Sometimes everything goes right. Other times, nothing seems to go well. The Bible tells us that when times are good, we should be happy. But when they're not, we should still praise God. He makes both good and bad for his purposes.

GOAL! *Shoot some hoops. How many did you make? Did you hit two out of four? If so, your percentage was better than George Mason and UNC–Wilmington in their 2001 tournament game. Thank God for good days. Ask him to help you through the bad ones.*

You must
worship Christ
as Lord of your
life. And if you
are asked about
your Christian
hope, always
be ready to
explain it.
1 PETER 3:15

BASKETBALL TEAMS DON'T EXPECT to lose when

they surge to a 28-point first-half lead. But as the Phoenix Suns discovered, no lead is safe if you're not prepared.

The Suns hosted the Sacramento Kings in the teams' third encounter of the 2000–01 season. After losing the first two games, Phoenix wanted revenge. The Suns felt confident, knowing how well they usually played on their home court. An avid crowd of 19,023 packed the America West Arena to witness the contest.

Rooted on by the hometown fans, Phoenix totally dominated. The Suns built a 60–32 lead with a little over three minutes remaining before halftime. At the intermission, the Suns held a 64–40 edge.

Ashamed of their lackluster performance, the Kings regrouped. They opened the third quarter with a 12–0 run. The stunned Suns were outscored 30–9 during the period. Although Phoenix still led 73–70, apprehension grew on the bench and in the stands.

A 10–2 run to open the final quarter put Sacramento up 82–77. The Kings extended the lead to as many as 17 points before winning 100–89.

EXTRA POINT < < < < < < < < < < < < < < < < < < < <

How could the Suns collapse and let the Kings come back on them at home? In athletics, the team on top must watch and be prepared. Otherwise an opponent can catch up and take control.

As followers of Jesus Christ, we should be prepared to talk about our relationship with him at any time. You never know when somebody will ask a question about your faith or when God will give you an opportunity to speak about him. Christians must always be prepared to share about Jesus Christ in a respectful way.

GOAL! *If you knew a pro scout would be coming to your game sometime during the season but you didn't know when, would you make sure you were ready? How would you prepare? Ask God to help you be prepared to share about him.*

A GAME'S NOT OVER till it's over. Nowhere is that statement truer than in college basketball's annual March Madness tournament. And in 1995, UCLA point guard Tyus Edney's refusal to give up gave his team an unbelievable victory.

The Bruins entered the tournament as the No. 1 seed, but in the second round a gritty Missouri Tigers squad looked to knock off the higher-ranked team. Matching UCLA basket for basket, the Tigers took a 74–73 lead with 4.8 seconds remaining as Julian Winfield wheeled inside for two points.

UCLA quickly called a time-out to set up a play. With 94 feet—the distance of the basketball court in Boise, Idaho—separating the Bruins from victory, coach Jim Harrick knew exactly what to do. He put the ball in the hands of his 5-foot-10-inch, 152-pound point guard, Edney, and told him to score. The Bruins had worked on a drill in practice where a player dribbled full court against a defender and tried to score in six seconds, so Edney knew he could do it.

Edney grabbed the inbound pass, weaved through Tigers defenders, leaped up near the basket, and lofted a half-hook, half-layup over a 6-foot-9 Missouri forward. The ball banked neatly off the backboard and swished through the basket as the buzzer sounded. UCLA won 75–74.

EXTRA POINT < < < < < < < < < < < < < < < < < < < < Tyus Edney's shot ranks as one of the best moments in NCAA basketball history. His determination to win not only gave UCLA the victory over the Tigers but also helped his team win the national championship that year.

God wants us to show that same kind of determination in sharing his Good News with others. Sometimes it may feel like none of our friends want to hear about God. It would be easy for us to lose heart and give up. But the Bible tells us to never give up. God gave us the ministry of sharing his love with the world—and that's worth fighting for.

GOAL! *Next time you get discouraged about your faith, think about Tyus Edney's amazing shot. He didn't give up hope, and neither should you. Ask God to help you share his love with the people around you.*

> Since God in his mercy has given us this wonderful ministry, we never give up.
>
> 2 CORINTHIANS 4:1

Though you soar as high as eagles and build your nest among the stars, I will bring you crashing down. I, the Lord, have spoken!

OBADIAH 1:4

HOW TOUGH HAS IT BECOME to place in men's halfpipe competitions? Just ask Olympic medal winners Danny Kass and J. J. Thomas. About a year after standing second and third at the Salt Lake City Games, they were on the outside looking in at the 2003 U.S. Open Snowboarding Championships.

With a new head-to-head format, riders squared off in two runs to see who would advance. Because both runs counted toward the overall score, any false move meant disaster. No one was surprised when Olympic gold medalist Ross Powers cruised into the final three, but Daniel Franck and Kazuhiro Kokubo shocked some people with their placement.

Franck took to the halfpipe first, but binding troubles kept him from finishing the run. That left the door open for Powers, and he blasted through it. Ross started with a 22-foot backside air and a 20-foot frontside air. By the time he was done, Ross had stuck a McTwist, a frontside 900, a backside 360, a switch McTwist, and a cab 720. Kokubo, who was just 14, touched his hand down on his final trick in the first run and trailed Powers.

Powers again went big on his second run by adding another two to three feet of amplitude to every trick. His cab 900 capped off a stellar run. On Kokubo's final attempt, he raised the bar to unparalleled levels. Launching into the pipe with the two biggest airs of the day, the teen hit a 29-foot McTwist and a 15-foot 900. But he couldn't overcome his first-run deficit, and Powers took home his second U.S. Open halfpipe title.

EXTRA POINT < < < < < < < < < < < < < < < < < < < Snowboarders just keep going higher and higher in the men's halfpipe. Soaring 30 feet above the pipe, their amplitude is amazing. But no matter how high they fly, they always come back to the ground.

In the Old Testament, the prophet Obadiah recorded God's words to some high-flying people. The Edomites lived in the mountains and built houses out of rock. They began feeling proud of themselves as their confidence soared, and they treated God's people badly. But God said he would bring them down. God always humbles the proud.

GOAL! *Do you know people who think they're better than everybody else? Perhaps you're one of them. Ask God to keep you grounded—not puffed up with pride.*

SELDOM DO BOYS COMPETE against men in professional sports. But in the 2001 Honda Classic, Ty Tryon proved his maturity and poise on the golf course.

The 16-year-old sophomore at Dr. Phillips High School in Orlando, Florida, played his way into the PGA tournament with a series of amateur victories. When the time came to compete with the pros, the 2000 PGA Junior champion played the Heron Bay course like a seasoned veteran.

Tryon finished his first round with a 67, just two shots behind leader Jesper Parnevik. After connecting for three straight birdies on day two, he struggled with strong winds on the back nine. Tryon endured three bogeys plus a double bogey and carded a 73 for his second round.

The grandson of a three-time New York State amateur champion improved his game on Saturday and Sunday. In round three, Tryon shot a 70, amazing the crowd with a birdie shot from the bunker on the final hole.

On Sunday, Tryon recorded five birdies on the first ten holes but cooled off to card a 68. He finished the four-day event 10-under-par and tied for 37th place. By qualifying for the final rounds of the PGA event, he became the youngest player to achieve the feat since Bob Panasik in the 1957 Canadian Open.

> Don't let anyone look down on you because you are young, but set an example for the believers in speech, in life, in love, in faith and in purity.
>
> 1 TIMOTHY 4:12, NIV

EXTRA POINT < < < < < < < < < < < < < < < < < < < < < < < < No one really thought that Tryon could make the cut in a professional tournament. After all, playing with the pros is tough enough. But he did make the cut, and he played beyond his years.

Tryon was an example to the other golfers with his actions and enthusiasm. He didn't back away from the challenge. Instead, he used his God-given ability to excel against athletes more than twice his age. And those he beat no longer viewed him as only a boy.

GOAL! *What are some of your God-given abilities?*

Think of some ways you can use them for God. Let your words and actions be an example to the adults around you.

10 MAR

The mountains will melt under Him, and the valleys will split like wax before the fire, like waters poured down a steep place.

MICAH 1:4, NKJV

SNOWMOBILES AREN'T the only motorized vehicles that thunder across the frozen white stuff at the Winter X Games. The Moto X Big Air competition pits motorcycle's best athletes riding, jumping, and sliding in the snow. Landing a knobby-wheeled motorcycle in the snow is hard enough, but at the 2003 X Games in Aspen, Colorado, warm temperatures forced the riders to compete in the slush.

The conditions made it difficult for Caleb Wyatt, Mike Metzger, and Nate Adams to pull their signature backflips on these powerful machines. Wyatt, the first rider ever to land a backflip, didn't stick any of his three attempts in the finals but still ended up with the bronze medal. Metzger, however, made the backflip look as easy as getting sunburned at high altitude. His no-footer backflip off the steep 50-foot kicker in his second run locked up 93.33 points and the gold medal. One attempt later, Metzger threw a McFritz—a trick he created a week before competition—where he does a nac-nac, one-handed foot grab, whipped. The stunt may sound impressive, but when Metzger soared 50 feet over a clear, blue Rocky Mountain sky, it was jaw-dropping.

Dayne Kinnaird surprised everybody by finishing second without even trying a backflip. (Adams came up short on three tries and didn't make the podium.) Kinnaird's combination tricks brought high scores from the judges. In fact, his turntable—a one-handed barhop where both legs swing out like a double can, capped with a heel click—garnered 92 points and a solid second.

EXTRA POINT < < < < < < < < < < < < < < < < < < < <

A bright sun and warm temperatures made things difficult during the Moto X Big Air competition at the 2003 X Games. But Mike Metzger overcame the melting snow to go home with gold.

While the most powerful celestial body in our solar system—the sun—can heat things up, nothing created can compare to God's power. The prophet Micah wrote that when the Lord comes, the mountains—not just the snow—will melt away. His power is so great that rock turns to running water in his presence.

GOAL! *Think about powerful motorcycles or the power of the sun. Now ponder God's mind-boggling power and praise him for it. He's awesome!*

THE 2003 U.S. OPEN WOMEN'S halfpipe champion-ships showcased some of the best snowboarding ever. After watching the finals, experts felt that any of the runs would have brought home the gold at the 2002 Olympics. Blowing away anything that was thrown at the 2002 Olympics, these women showed how far their sport had progressed. And possibly nobody is doing more for the sport than Gretchen Bleiler.

Bleiler began the Open by facing off against Olympic gold medalist Kelly Clark. Clark rode well, but Bleiler pulled a combination of tricks that left no doubt in the judges'—or audience's—mind about who was moving on.

The finals pitted Bleiler against two-time Open champ Natasha Zurek and 15-year-old Hannah Teter. Bleiler started things with a frenzy by ripping a crippler 540, frontside 720, backside 720, cab 720, and another crippler. Zurek showed her championship form with nifty airs, a McTwist, and a crippler 720. Then the teen displayed her high-energy moves by sticking a 540, 720, and the only 900 in the finals. But in the end, nothing was good enough to catch Bleiler. Zurek took second, while Teter claimed third.

EXTRA POINT < < < < < < < < < < < < < < < < < < < < < < Gretchen Bleiler continued her hot streak by winning the 2003 U.S. Open women's halfpipe. Throughout much of the 2002–03 snowboarding season, it was hard to find a rider hotter than Bleiler.

Isn't it great to be on a hot streak? You feel like you can't lose. Everything seems to go your way. You pull one victory after another from the ashes of defeat. Your confidence soars.

The apostle John wrote in Revelation about how God likes Christians who are hot on fire for him. God also understands if people are cold toward heavenly things. However, God dislikes people who are neither cold nor hot toward him.

GOAL! *Have you noticed in church how some people are on fire for God, while others want nothing to do with him? And there are those who are hot one minute and cold the next. Then there are those who sort of ride the fence, not caring one way or the other. They might say they're Christians, but their words and actions don't show it—which can actually hurt God's kingdom. Ask God to keep you from that kind of lukewarm faith.*

> I know your deeds, that you are neither cold nor hot. I wish you were either one or the other!
>
> REVELATION 3:15, NIV

As for God, His way is perfect; the word of the Lord is proven; He is a shield to all who trust in Him.

PSALM 18:30, NKJV

YOU'VE PROBABLY HEARD the saying "Practice makes perfect." But what happens when you have a perfect practice? During a 2000 spring training game, the Boston Red Sox found out.

Boston hosted the Toronto Blue Jays at its spring training facility in Fort Myers, Florida. Red Sox ace Pedro Martinez opened the game for three innings of work. Just like clockwork, the Nicaragua native retired the nine batters he faced, striking out six.

Boston manager Jimy Williams followed Martinez with a string of relievers, each working only one or two innings. Fernando De La Cruz pitched two innings and allowed no hits or walks, and no one reached base on an error. Dan Smith, Rheal Cormier, and Rich Garces all hurled one inning, each coaxing his three batters into outs.

While the pitchers cruised, Nomar Garciaparra looked equally impressive at the plate. Nomar homered and drove in four runs in the contest, and Boston held a 5–0 lead.

Heading into the top of the ninth, only catcher Joe Sidall fully realized the pitchers had combined for a perfect game. After Alberto Castillo struck out to end the affair, Sidall pumped his arm in the air and ran out to the mound to greet Boston's final hurler, Rod Beck. Joe pointed to the outfield scoreboard, reflecting 12 zeroes in a row—no hits, no runs, and no errors for the game.

EXTRA POINT < < < < < < < < < < < < < < < < < < < < < Perfection. Wow! The six men pitched flawless baseball. But nobody really noticed. Only the guy shielded behind the catcher's mask and chest protector realized the amazing feat. And even then, the perfection didn't count because it was just a practice game.

Many times God might feel that way too. He's always perfect, but a lot of people don't notice. They take his creation and mercy for granted. And it's not just people who don't believe in him who don't pay attention. Christians often overlook God too—that is, until we need him. At those times, God's perfect love and understanding allow us to find peace and comfort in him.

GOAL! *Have you ever seen a perfect game in Little League, high school, college, or professional baseball? If you have, how did you feel? Were you amazed? Praise God for his amazing perfection.*

THE SPORTS WORLD HAS WITNESSED many remarkable comebacks from physical injury. But in 2000, Sean Elliott of the San Antonio Spurs returned to the court following an amazing gift.

On August 16, 1999, Elliott underwent a kidney transplant after being diagnosed with a disease that prevents the kidneys from properly filtering waste from the blood. Fortunately, his brother Noel provided a suitable match.

Virtually everyone but Sean considered his NBA career over. At first, he walked cautiously. Then he gradually worked up to light training. By February 2000, he began full-scale practice with his teammates.

The forward returned to the starting lineup when the Spurs hosted the Atlanta Hawks on March 14. In the first few minutes, the crowd of 27,000 hushed as Elliott collided with Dikembe Mutombo but cheered as he bounced back to his feet.

Another roar erupted when Elliott drove past Roshown McLeod for a right-handed slam dunk. In his first appearance since the transplant surgery, the 1989 third pick in the NBA draft played 12 minutes, scored two points, grabbed a rebound, and collected an assist. Elliott played the rest of that season and one more before accepting a job as a television commentator.

> Heal the sick, raise the dead, cure those with leprosy, and cast out demons. Give as freely as you have received!
>
> MATTHEW 10:8

EXTRA POINT < < < < < < < < < < < < < < < < < < < < < Sean Elliott became a basketball-playing miracle. First his doctors had to locate the right kidney. The odds of finding a matching donor for a kidney transplant are one in four from a sibling and one in 1,000 for the general population. Then he had to survive the surgery and start the rehabilitation process. But Elliott didn't stop there; he continued to train and got back into the NBA!

God enables doctors to transplant kidneys and other organs to those who would die without them. After all, he's in the life-saving business. When Jesus walked the earth, he sent his disciples out to heal the sick.

GOAL! *Think about ways you can help people who are sick. You could bring cheer to the hospital, take a neighbor some soup, or pray for someone who's ill.*

Praise God for his healing powers and for giving doctors medical breakthroughs like organ transplants.

14 MAR

> For God has not given us a spirit of fear, but of power and of love and of a sound mind.
>
> 2 TIMOTHY 1:7, NKJV

DESPITE NOT HAVING THE BIGGEST or fastest team, Princeton University always proves to be a rugged foe in the NCAA basketball tournament. From 1989 to 1992, the Tigers lost their four opening round games by a total of just 15 points. And in 1996, Princeton's disciplined attack helped them emerge victorious.

Retiring coach Pete Carril's squad drew a formidable opponent in defending national champion UCLA. At first, the Bruins adjusted to Princeton's slow-paced offense and led 16–9 with just under seven minutes remaining before halftime. But the Tigers closed with a fury, putting together a 9–3 run and making the score 19–18 at the break.

Although they trailed 41–34 late in the second half, Princeton stuck with their game plan—tough defense and patient offense. Sydney Johnson nailed a three-pointer and Steve Goodrich canned a layup to cut the margin to two. Another Johnson layup with less than three minutes left to play tied the score at 41–41.

While Princeton's offense started to click, UCLA's faltered. With just over a minute left in the game, the Bruins failed to capitalize on a Tigers intentional foul as they missed both free throws and the shot following their subsequent possession.

Only 21 seconds remained in the tie game when Princeton called a time-out to set a play. Goodrich caught the inbound pass at the high post, and Gabe Lewullis faked to go outside. The freshman forward then cut inside past UCLA's Charles O'Bannon, took a bounce pass from Goodrich, and made a layup over Kris Johnson with 3.9 seconds left on the clock.

UCLA went down in defeat 43–41 when Toby Bailey missed a last-second shot from the baseline.

EXTRA POINT ‹ Princeton rarely has the most talented athletes. But the Tigers always play with confidence, power, and discipline. They're not afraid to compete against the bigger, tougher schools. Sometimes they win; sometimes they don't. But they always draw the respect of their opponents.

The apostle Paul wrote letters to his young pastor friend, Timothy. He advised Timothy to preach and pastor with confidence, power, and self-discipline. God wants us to develop those qualities, too.

GOAL! *When the NCAA tournament brackets come out, look at the low-seeded teams. Guess which ones will engineer upsets. Examine their confidence and self-discipline. Ask God to help you become confident and self-disciplined too.*

SOME PLAYERS AND COACHES stay in sports far past their prime. But in 1975, legendary UCLA coach John Wooden picked the perfect time to step aside.

UCLA faced the University of Louisville in the NCAA basketball tournament semifinals. At the end of regulation, the teams were deadlocked 65–65. With a minute remaining in overtime, the Bruins trailed 74–71. But then Dave Myers hit two free throws, bringing them just one point behind Louisville.

Then Cardinals coach Denny Crum made a brave move, pulling his leading scorer Allen Murphy and inserting Terry Howard. He gave Howard, a sure-handed guard, strict instructions to keep the ball away from UCLA.

However, at the 13-second mark, Howard drew a foul. The ball handler missed the free throw, and the Bruins rebounded. After calling a time-out, UCLA brought the ball downcourt. Bruins center Rich Washington slid from the high post and snared a pass from Jim Spillane. With four seconds left to play, his soft seven-foot jumper sailed through the hoop, giving UCLA a 75–74 win. During the celebration, Coach Wooden announced that the championship game two days later would be his last.

> Unless you are faithful in small matters, you won't be faithful in large ones. If you cheat even a little, you won't be honest with greater responsibilities.
>
> LUKE 16:10

EXTRA POINT < < < < < < < < < < < < < < < < < < < < John Wooden coached basketball for 40 years—from 1932 to 1943 in high schools, from 1946 to 1948 at Indiana State, and from 1948 to 1975 at UCLA. On the day Wooden retired, the Bruins claimed their tenth national championship with him at the helm. Two other times, the Bruins reached the tournament Final Four.

As a player, John led his high school team to a state championship. A three-time collegiate All-American at Purdue, "The Indiana Rubber Man" captained the team to a national championship. What a record!

Coach Wooden was a master of details. From teaching his players how to properly put on their socks to instructing them about the offense, Wooden knew his players had to master the small things before they went on to bigger matters.

The same thing is true in our relationship with Christ. God wants us to learn the little things before he trusts us with more. If we can't be trusted in small matters, we'll never be able to take on greater responsibility.

GOAL! *Think of some small details in your life that you need to take care of.*

Ask God to help you follow through on the little things so you can earn the benefits of being trusted with more.

16 MAR

Enter through
the narrow
gate. For wide
is the gate and
broad is the
road that leads
to destruction,
and many enter
through it.
But small is
the gate and
narrow the
road that leads
to life, and only
a few find it.

MATTHEW
7:13-14, NIV

IT'S SAID THAT BASEBALL is a game of inches. But that's not the only sport that can boast that fact. At the 2003 Carolina Dodge Dealers 400, the race came down to a few inches. Just three *inches* gave Ricky Craven the victory over Kurt Busch in the 400-*mile* race.

Busch, who had battled from the back of the pack, appeared to have a victory at Darlington, South Carolina, wrapped up. But power steering problems in Busch's final laps gave Craven a small opportunity. Craven pulled onto Busch's bumper with four laps to go and the shoot-out was on.

No stranger to tight victories, Craven stayed behind Busch until he pulled alongside him coming out of the final turn. The two drivers banged doors all the way to the checkered flag in one of best endings in NASCAR history. A photo finish revealed that Craven won by a mere three inches. His .002-second margin of victory was the smallest ever since NASCAR instituted the electronic timing system in 1993.

For the race, Craven led for only one lap—the last one. Busch settled for second, and Dave Blaney came in a career-high third.

EXTRA POINT < < < < < < < < < < < < < < < < < < < < < < < What a close finish! Ricky Craven's narrow victory made auto-racing history and thrilled the fans at Darlington Raceway. Tight finishes always excite a crowd more than a blowout does. Most people would rather see a close finish than a large gap at the end.

It's the same way in God's kingdom: narrow is better than wide. In Matthew, the first book of the New Testament, Jesus tells us to take the narrow path. Few people find it, but the reward for those on the narrow path is life. The crowded broad road leads to destruction.

GOAL! *Do you ever find yourself following the crowd? Sometimes it's easy to get caught up doing the popular thing. But Jesus says to take the narrow road. You may not have as many friends, but your eternal rewards will make it worth it. Will you accept the challenge and ask God to help you walk the narrow path?*

MARCH MADNESS EARNED ITS NAME for a reason. Crazy upsets and thrilling finishes always highlight this annual NCAA basketball championship. And maybe one of the most memorable upsets occurred in 1996 when Valparaiso University took on the University of Mississippi.

The 13th-seeded Crusaders earned their bid by winning the Mid-Continent Conference tournament, so many believed they had little chance against fourth-seeded Ole Miss. But the underdogs played an aggressive zone defense, forcing Mississippi out of its inside-game and making the Rebels shoot from the perimeter.

The score at halftime read 38–34 in favor of Ole Miss, and the contest remained close throughout the second half. Leading 69–67 with 4.3 seconds remaining, Mississippi's Ansu Sesay drew a foul and could have clinched a Rebel victory. But Sesay missed both chances.

Following a time-out, Valparaiso's Jamie Sykes inbounded the ball under the Ole Miss basket. He rifled a pass beyond midcourt to Bill Jenkins, who quickly tossed to Bryce Drew, son of Crusader head coach Homer Drew, on the right wing.

Off balance and leaning away from the basket, Drew threw up a shot from well behind the three-point line. Miraculously, it swished through the net at the buzzer, giving Valparaiso a 70–69 victory.

> "We must celebrate with a feast, for this son of mine was dead and has now returned to life. He was lost, but now he is found." So the party began.
>
> LUKE 15:23-24

EXTRA POINT < < < < < < < < < < < < < < < < < < < < < Winning is fun. Victors deserve to celebrate. But the joy multiplies when several family members play or coach on the same team. The family feels doubly bonded—through sports and through blood. The Drews experienced that extraordinary victory together.

Jesus tells the story of another father and son celebrating in the New Testament. When the father's prodigal son returns home after making a bunch of bad decisions, the father welcomes him back and throws a huge celebration. In the same way, Jesus celebrates when his children who have wandered off through poor choices return to him and ask for forgiveness.

GOAL! *Think of some times when your family celebrates. Now imagine the party that occurs in heaven when somebody prays to enter God's family. Praise God for the joy of those family celebrations.*

Be devoted to one another in brotherly love. Honor one another above yourselves.

ROMANS 12:10, NIV

CAN YOU IMAGINE any greater thrill than running onto the field at a Super Bowl as thousands of fans—and millions of people watching on television—cheer? You sprint through the tunnel and dash past cheerleaders. Colored smoke rises into the air. You raise your finger to the sky and hear your name announced over the loudspeakers. The feeling must be awesome.

But before Super Bowl XXXVI in New Orleans, the New England Patriots decided not to take part in the traditional individual player introductions. After the St. Louis Rams announced each member of their offense with a lot of fanfare, the Patriots stepped on the field as one unit. The Pats ran onto the turf with starters, benchwarmers, Pro Bowlers, and scout-teamers all mixed together. Nobody was singled out. Nobody was given a higher status. With their actions, the Patriots' message was clear: We made it here as a team, and we're going to win or lose as a team.

And that's exactly what they did. With a stingy defense and timely offense, the Patriots shocked the Rams 20–17 in one of the biggest Super Bowl upsets in history.

EXTRA POINT < < < < < < < < < < < < < < < < < < < < < In sports, we should remember to treat our teammates with brotherly love. We should honor them above ourselves. By putting team first and playing as a unified force, the New England Patriots did the unthinkable and won the Super Bowl.

In a way, the church is God's "team" on earth. A popular saying states that a team is only as strong as its weakest member. Can you think of anybody at church or a Christian friend who could use a little strengthening? Your efforts to help him or her could build up God's team.

The apostle Paul wrote to the church in Rome urging them to treat one another with genuine love and to honor others over themselves. That way, as a team, the church can spread the gospel to win the world for Christ.

GOAL! *Think of some practical ways to honor others:*

_____

_____

_____

You might write notes or speak encouraging words. Use your creativity to decide what to do, and then follow through on it. Ask God to help you love other people.

UNLIKE MANY SPORTS, golf observes strict rules of conduct. Fans must remain silent until a shot has been taken. When Annika Sorenstam carded her record-breaking round in 2001, the suspense and silence electrified the air.

The 30-year-old Swedish golfer began her surge in the second round of the Standard Register Ping tournament on the front nine. Red-hot from the start, Sorenstam recorded birdies on the first eight holes before making par on No. 9.

Her hot streak continued on the second nine with four straight birdies to go 12-under-par. As the golfer made her way down the Moon Valley Country Club course, the gallery kept growing with the sense that history might soon be made.

On the par 5, No. 17, Sorenstam drove straight down the middle and reached the green on the fly with a long iron shot. With a dove's coo the only audible sound, Annika peered at her 20-foot eagle putt, paced off the distance, and rolled the ball to within eight inches of the hole. When she tapped in for her 13th birdie, the crowd erupted in celebration.

Sorenstam parred the final hole for a 13-under-par 59, the first ever recorded in LPGA history. She joined an elite group that includes the PGA's Al Geiberger, Chip Beck, and David Duval as the only golfers to break 60 in a professional tournament.

> But the Lord is in His holy temple. Let all the earth keep silence before Him.
>
> HABAKKUK 2:20, NKJV

EXTRA POINT < < < < < < < < < < < < < < < < < < < < Golfers need silence to do their best. The gallery respects that quietness, partly because of the rules and partly because of their awe for professional golfers. Annika Sorenstam benefited from that silence.

We all need times of silence to think, to pray, and to listen. Habakkuk wrote that we should be silent before our holy God. Certainly, the heavenly Father loves to hear our songs of worship. But he also treasures our silent times with him.

GOAL! *Focus on being quiet for at least three minutes as you think about the awesomeness of God. Listen to his still voice speaking to you. Praise God with your silence.*

20 MAR

He raises the poor from the dust and lifts the needy from the ash heap; he seats them with princes and has them inherit a throne of honor.

1 SAMUEL 2:8, NIV

YEVGENY PLUSHCHENKO GREW UP under harsh conditions in St. Petersburg, Russia. But in 2001, he found riches at the World Figure Skating Championships.

The ancient rink where Plushchenko trained couldn't even afford to repair its Zamboni. The skating surface contained ruts and chips, making it difficult to work on routines. In addition, the heating system rarely functioned, forcing the teenager to don three layers of jackets and pants. The Russian's family struggled as well. They lived in a one-room apartment, sharing a bathroom with other families down the hall.

But Plushchenko's endurance reaped dividends. After a disappointing free skate the prior year, he refocused for the 2001 championships. During his training, the 18-year-old found inspiration from his memories of watching Viktor Petrenko on television.

When Plushchenko took the ice, the skater immediately engrossed the crowd with an amazing program. Using various musical pieces, including the television theme from *The Addams Family*, Yevgeny jumped and spun with precision and flair. The jumps included his unique quadruple toe loop–triple toe loop–double loop combination and eight additional triples. He highlighted spins with a Biellmann maneuver, placing his leg behind his head as he twisted on the ice.

At the performance's conclusion, spectators shouted for perfect 6.0s. Although no judge gave a perfect score, 5.9s abounded as Plushchenko easily claimed his first world title.

EXTRA POINT < < < < < < < < < < < < < < < < < < < < Competing on the international skating scene takes years of practice and lots of cash. Yevgeny Plushchenko had the time, but his family and city didn't have money for the facilities and coaches available to most top skaters. But somehow Plushchenko managed to rise above his surroundings.

From his poor and needy St. Petersburg beginnings, Yevgeny Plushchenko ascended to skating's princely throne—the world championship. Athletics became a way out of difficult circumstances for him and many others.

In the Bible a woman asked God to help her out of difficult circumstances. Hannah didn't have children at a time in history when a woman's status depended on sons and daughters. But God answered her prayers. He gave her a son named Samuel, who became a godly leader.

GOAL! *Imagine living in the Plushchenkos' cramped apartment and training on the crumbling ice rink. Picture yourself overcoming such obstacles. God will help you overcome your own challenges in life. All you have to do is ask him.*

GREAT PLAYERS REACH for something extra and play beyond their physical abilities in big games. In the 2001 NCAA women's basketball tournament, Jackie Stiles exhibited her greatness to the entire nation.

For most of her collegiate career, Stiles remained virtually unknown. Playing at Southwest Missouri State in the Missouri Valley Conference generated little national attention. But in the NCAA subregional, fans began to notice the small-town girl from Claflin, Kansas. The Lady Bears edged out Rutgers 60–53 on the Scarlet Knights' home court to earn Southwest Missouri a spot at the West Regional in Spokane, Washington. Stiles, the all-time NCAA scoring leader, paced the Lady Bears with 32 points against Rutgers.

In the regional opener, the Lady Bears faced top seeded Duke. After the tip-off, however, the Blue Devils witnessed the 5-foot-8-inch guard's dazzling display of soft jumpers, spin moves, and fearless drives.

Trailing by 12 early in the contest, the Lady Bears cut the deficit to 42–36 at the half. In the second half, Southwest Missouri opened with a 12–2 run and took command midway through the period, outscoring Duke 22–10 during the final 8:11 to down the Blue Devils 81–71.

Stiles, who scored only 16 points in the first half, fueled the offense in the second by hitting 13-of-22 field goals and 10-of-13 free throws. Her 41-point outburst ranked fourth highest in NCAA women's tournament history.

> Now glory be to God! By his mighty power at work within us, he is able to accomplish infinitely more than we would ever dare to ask or hope.
>
> EPHESIANS 3:20

EXTRA POINT

< < < < < < < < < < < < < < < < < < < < <

Most casual women's college basketball fans had never heard of Jackie Stiles. The player grew up in a small town in a small state and played for a small school in a small conference.

But the athlete gave every ounce of her strength and talent to her team and university. Some might say she played above her ability, and her team won because of her amazing scoring.

Likewise, some Christians use all their strength and talents to serve God. They see God work through them and accomplish amazing things. The heavenly Father rewards them with the power to do more than they expected.

GOAL! *Describe someone you know who has been used by God beyond his or her natural ability. You may think of someone at church, on a sports team, or in your family.*

Person: _____

What he or she did: _____

Give God the glory for the person and all he or she does.

God is our refuge and strength, an ever-present help in trouble. Therefore we will not fear, though the earth give way and the mountains fall into the heart of the sea.

PSALM 46:1-2, NIV

TAKING ON AN OPPONENT with a string of seven straight national championships can cause any team to panic. But in the 1974 NCAA basketball tournament, North Carolina State refused to back away.

Playing in Greensboro, North Carolina, the Wolfpack faced longtime powerhouse UCLA in the semifinals. Almost 16,000 fans packed the Greensboro Coliseum hoping for an NC State upset.

The first half ended on a dramatic note as UCLA's Dave Meyers hurled in a 40-foot desperation shot to tie the contest 35–35.

Early in the second half, the Bruins burst to an 11-point lead, but NC State used a 10–0 run to close the margin and tie the game 65–65 at the end of regulation.

The first overtime saw each team trade early baskets, and the five minutes ended with a score of 67–67. UCLA went up quickly by seven in the second OT, and the Wolfpack appeared finished with only 3:27 left to play.

But North Carolina State refused to panic and used an intercepted UCLA pass, missed Bruin shots, and excellent ballhanding by 5-foot-6-inch guard Monte Towe to close with a 13–3 spurt. In the Wolfpack's final stretch, David Thompson poured in six points, Tommy Burleson added three, and Towe scored four in the 80–77 win. UCLA's amazing winning streak had ended.

EXTRA POINT < < < < < < < < < < < < < < < < < < < In NCAA history, most experts consider the UCLA teams of the 1960s and 1970s the greatest basketball dynasty of all time. Certainly their seven consecutive national championships have never been equaled.

The Bruins, like their mascot, brought fear to every opponent, but NC State controlled that fear. In the second overtime, in spite of falling behind, the Wolfpack came back to win.

Fear strikes the heart of every person at some time in life. God holds the secret to overcoming fear. King David knew the key: Trust in the Lord. Give him your fear. You may still feel afraid, but you won't panic. You'll control that fear and tap into God's power to move forward.

GOAL! *What do you fear? Name three things that make you uneasy.*

_____

_____

_____

Ask God to help you control your fears.

TO DO WELL IN SNOWBOARDING slopestyle events, riders have to be able to make the most of the terrain. Competitions include rails, gaps, and huge launch ramps. At the 2003 X Games, Shaun White dressed like a mountain bandit and rode away with gold.

White, decked out in a huge red bandanna that covered his face, put together the two highest–scoring runs to claim the top prize. In the finals, the 16-year-old pulled a frontside 720 stale over the 57-foot channel gap, a neatly timed 50-50 slide to frontside nose-press up and down the A-frame rail, and a cab 900 stale off the big booter. White's smooth, style-perfect landings and technical mastery earned a score of 95 from the judges and wrapped up first place.

But while White's clothing and scores grabbed headlines, several other riders put together notable runs. Jussi Oksanen's first run in the finals included a frontside 720, a buttered switch backside 720, and a massive 720 that he landed near the bottom of the transition. Scoring 93 points, Oksanen took silver. The bronze medal went to first-year X Gamer Jimi Tomer. The rookie put together a rodeo 720, backflip, frontside 180 tail grab over the channel, a frontside 900, and some technical rail work to score 91 points.

> Obey God because you are his children. Don't slip back into your old ways of doing evil; you didn't know any better then.
>
> 1 PETER 1:14

EXTRA POINT

< < < < < < < < < < < < < < < < < < < < < Big, twisting, flipping air is just part of slopestyle snowboarding. Massive slides over metal rails often separate the winners from the losers. Shaun White's 50-50 to frontside nose-press showed off his amazing balance, skill, and creativity. That slide may have been the difference in winning gold.

But there's an area of our lives where we don't want to slide at all—and that's in our Christian walk. The Bible warns us not to slip and slide into old habits. When we become Christians, we should obey God as his children. Backsliding into old habits is easy. But the disciple Peter writes that we shouldn't do it. Before Jesus came into our lives, we didn't know any better. But once we know Christ, we should do whatever we can to solidly follow him.

GOAL! *Do you have any old habits that are easy to slide into? Decide on one that you will work on changing.*

Tell God you want to overcome that habit with his help.

And they sang a new song: "You are worthy to take the scroll and to open its seals, because you were slain, and with your blood you purchased men for God from every tribe and language and people and nation."

REVELATION 5:9, NIV

NEWLY FORMED TEAMS rarely win the championship. But in its second year of existence, the women's hockey team at the University of Minnesota–Duluth proved to be more than a bunch of raw rookies.

When coach Shannon Miller organized the Bulldogs squad, she went after the best talent available, even if it required crossing seas. Miller signed not only American players but also Canadians, Finns, Swedes, and Swiss.

In the team's first year of competition, Minnesota–Duluth achieved remarkable success, finishing fourth in the national tournament sponsored by USA Hockey. The following year women's hockey gained status as an NCAA sport.

Harvard, Dartmouth, St. Lawrence, and UMD filled the brackets for the first Frozen Four. The Bulldogs, a heavy underdog, advanced to the title game against the St. Lawrence Saints with a 6–3 win over Harvard.

The Saints took an early 1–0 lead in the finals, but Minnesota–Duluth tied the game on Jenny Hempel's goal. At the break, Coach Miller encouraged her team to be more physical, and the Bulldogs dominated the rest of the way, outshooting St. Lawrence 13–2 in the second period.

Swedish Olympian Maria Rooth and Finnish Olympian Hanne Sikio scored second-period goals, giving the Bulldogs a commanding lead. Canadian Laurie Alexander boosted the margin to 4–1 on a third-period power play. Minnesota–Duluth held on for a 4–2 victory and garnered the first ever NCAA women's hockey title.

EXTRA POINT < < < < < < < < < < < < < < < < < < < < The Minnesota team's international flavor paid off. Miller couldn't really recruit the top Americans because they had already committed to other universities. But she could gather the best from other nations. They welcomed the opportunity to go to college and take to the ice.

God has gathered the nations in our country. The world has come to the United States. More than 100 languages can be heard in homes throughout our largest cities.

Jesus Christ died for people from every nation and every language and welcomes them into his kingdom. He wants us to welcome them too.

GOAL! *Are there people from other countries in your neighborhood, at your school, or on your favorite sports team? If so, learn more about their nation and culture. Befriend them if you can. Praise the God of all nations.*

ON RARE OCCASIONS, a player enters a zone where every move results in perfection. In the 1992 NCAA basketball tournament, Duke University's Christian Laettner achieved a perfect ten.

The Blue Devils, looking for their fifth straight Final Four appearance, faced the University of Kentucky in the East Regional finals. Duke led by ten points with seven and a half minutes remaining. But Kentucky fought back and tied the game 93–93 with 33.6 seconds left to play. Bobby Hurley missed a ten-footer with three seconds on the clock, sending the contest to overtime.

Both teams, weary from a combination of high-octane offense and pressing defense, fought down to the wire. Kentucky's Sean Woods sank a driving bank shot over Laettner, giving the Wildcats a 103–102 lead with 2.2 ticks showing on the scoreboard.

Duke called a time-out and coach Mike Krzyzewski diagrammed a play. As instructed, Grant Hill threw the ball 77 feet to Laettner, who was standing near the free-throw line. The play called for the All-American to work for an open shot. If he was guarded too closely, Laettner was to pass off quickly to Thomas Hill or Hurley.

Fighting off two defenders, the 6-11 center caught the pass, took one dribble, faked right, pivoted left, and drilled a 17-footer at the buzzer. In the 104–103 overtime triumph, Laettner played 43 minutes, connecting on 10-of-10 field goals and 10-of-10 free throws.

> And the disciples were first called Christians in Antioch.
> ACTS 11:26, NKJV

EXTRA POINT

< < < < < < < < < < < < < < < < < < < <

During Laettner's playing days at Duke, broadcasters kept noting how unusual it was for a "Christian" to be playing for the Blue Devils.

People notice names. During Bible times, names seemed even more important. To know a person's name meant to know that person well. Names also carried specific meanings: Abigail—father's joy; Michael—who is like God; John—God is gracious; Naomi—pleasant; Ethan—firmness; Esther—star.

In Antioch, the followers of Christ came to be called Christians, forever associating them and us with Jesus Christ.

GOAL! *Search the Internet or use a reference book to learn the meaning of your name. Write it down.*

My name: _____

Meaning: _____

Look up the names of some friends and family members. Do you fit the meaning of your name? Do your friends? Ask God to help you live up to the name Christian.

BREAKING A WORLD RECORD is cause for celebration. But after Ian Thorpe set a new mark in the 800-meter freestyle on March 27, 2001, he didn't party at all. Instead the Australian swimmer went to bed early, because another race awaited him.

Swimming the event competitively for the first time at the Australian national championship, the 18-year-old Sydney native broke the 800-meter mark held by fellow countryman Kieren Perkins. The triple Olympic gold-medal winner shaved more than four seconds off the record while marking a 7:41.59.

By getting to bed early, Thorpe wisely saved his strength for the 200 meters, a long sprint swim requiring both speed and stamina. To prepare, Thorpe followed his usual training routine, watched a bit of television, and fell asleep.

The strict regime paid off the next day. Thorpe bolted to an early lead and finished three body lengths ahead of his nearest competitor to shatter the world record with a time of 1:44.69. The clocking knocked .65 seconds off the old mark held by Pieter van den Hoogenband of the Netherlands.

The 200-meter victory also provided Thorpe with a small measure of redemption. At the 2000 Sydney Olympics, van den Hoogenband set the world record while Thorpe claimed the silver.

EXTRA POINT < < < < < < < < < < < < < < < < < < < Ian Thorpe might have been tempted to go out with his friends to celebrate such an incredible victory after the 800 freestyle. He deserved to enjoy himself. But the athlete proved smarter than that. He knew the importance of sleep. Thorpe realized that his body, even though young and in great condition, could compete best when rested.

God created sleep to sustain our body and energize our mind. Sometimes we're tempted to sleep too little. The general rule is one hour of sleep for every two hours awake. Sleeping less than six hours a night can seriously impair your judgment and performance.

GOAL! *For a week, keep track of how many hours you sleep. If it's not enough, find a way to sleep more. Thank God for renewing your body and mind through sleep and rest.*

I LAY DOWN AND SLEPT; I AWOKE, FOR THE LORD SUSTAINED ME.

PSALM 3:5 , NKJV

"Come now,
let us argue
this out," says
the Lord. "No
matter how
deep the stain
of your sins,
I can remove
it. I can make
you as clean as
freshly fallen
snow. Even if
you are stained
as red as
crimson, I can
make you as
white as wool."

ISAIAH 1:18

WEATHER CAN WREAK HAVOC on snowboarding competitions. Resorts, after all, choose their location based on large snowfalls. Yet a huge storm snuffed out the women's snowboard slopestyle finals at the 2003 X Games in Aspen, Colorado.

The day started out nice enough, but shortly into the first of two runs, gigantic snowflakes began falling from the sky. Soon the course turned to mush. The women were able to complete their first runs, but two inches of snow and zero visibility caused officials to cancel the second run.

With only one score deciding the last event at the X Games, Janna Meyen took home the gold. The 2002 silver medalist climbed to first by stomping a backside 360 with an indy grab. Then Meyen nailed a backside 360 off the big ramp to tally 92 points. Hana Beaman benefited by going early in the competition, and her lean grab frontside 360 followed by a backside 360 proved to be good enough for 87.33 points and second place. Lindsey Jacobellis went big over the transfer gap and landed a backside 360 to take home the bronze. Although these women were happy with their medal and big prize money, they all felt bad for winning under the circumstances.

EXTRA POINT < < < < < < < < < < < < < < < < < < < < Snowboarding relies on mass quantities of snow. Duh, right? But the snowstorm in Aspen interfered with the women's slopestyle finals at the 2003 X Games.

While that snowstorm proved to be a downer as it blanketed the mountain and made competing impossible, most people love the look of new-fallen snow. Everything appears calm, peaceful, and beautiful after a big snowstorm. The Bible says that God makes our life as clean as new snow. Can you imagine anything more pure? That's the miracle of Jesus. He takes our red-stained, sinful life and makes it clean and beautiful.

GOAL! *Some people feel their life is too stained with sin for God to clean. But no mistake is so bad that God can't fix it. Praise God for his cleansing powers.*

BASEBALL HAS LONG BEEN KNOWN as America's pastime. But in 2000, the National League took the sport to the other side of the sea.

The Chicago Cubs and the New York Mets agreed to open the season at Japan's Tokyo Dome, even though United States television viewers would need to tune in before dawn to watch. A full house of 55,000 turned out to witness the first regular season baseball game played outside of North America.

Cultural variations provided the only major differences between this game and an American contest. Fans ate sushi with chopsticks and munched on broiled eel and rice balls—rather than chomping on hot dogs and pretzels. Instead of the president of the United States watching from a box seat, Crown Prince Naruhito and Princess Masako sat in the Royal Box.

The Cubs opened with a run in the first on Damon Buford's RBI-single. New York's Darryl Hamilton matched it in the third with a sacrifice fly. Chicago took the lead in the fifth after a single and three straight walks to Sammy Sosa, Henry Rodriguez, and Shane Andrews.

Andrews homered off Dennis Cook in the seventh, putting the Cubs up 4–1, and Mark Grace parked another in the eighth. Mets catcher Mike Piazza connected on a two-run home run in the bottom of the inning, but Chicago held on to win 5–3.

> Then Peter replied, "I see very clearly that God doesn't show partiality. In every nation he accepts those who fear him and do what is right."
> ACTS 10:34-35

EXTRA POINT < < < < < < < < < < < < < < < < < < < How exciting to play a familiar game in a faraway place. How fun to watch players from across the ocean. The experience proved rewarding for both the American teams and the Japanese fans. The cultures discovered common ground.

God made every person, every nation, every culture. He accepts all people into his family who believe in him. And he guides us as we relate to each other wherever and whenever we meet.

GOAL! *Taste food from another culture—sushi or rice balls if you can. Try to use chopsticks. How do you think people from other nations feel about eating hot dogs and pretzels? Ask God to help you appreciate other cultures and to live your life as a witness for him to them.*

29 MAR

Make the most of every opportunity for doing good in these evil days.

EPHESIANS 5:16

ATHLETES SHOW THEIR RESPECT for a sport by learning its history. And today's pro skateboarders can be grateful for a group of restless surfers known as the Z-Boys.

This group of young surfers hung out in the mid-1970s. They longed for a sport they could have fun with even when the California waves weren't too great. They turned to "sidewalk surfing"—known today, of course, as skateboarding.

Skateboarding originated in the 1930s when kids attached wooden boards to their metal roller skates. But it didn't gain widespread popularity because many people felt it was too dangerous. The Z-Boys brought it back to life as they invented new tricks that no one had ever seen before. Tony Alva, one of the leaders of the pack, almost single-handedly invented vertical skating when he started riding in empty swimming pools.

The Z-Boys got their name from the Zephyr Surf Shop, which provided custom-made surfboards for them to ride. eBay wasn't around back then, so skateboards were hard to find. But that didn't hinder the Z-Boys. They were creative and made their own, even sawing off roller skates for wheels. Little did they know that skateboarding would soon become one of the country's favorite alternative sports.

EXTRA POINT < < < < < < < < < < < < < < < < < < < < < The Z-Boys loved to surf so much that they couldn't live without it. They were determined to surf even without water. What a revolutionary idea!

The Z-Boys took advantage of their passion to surf and came up with something totally new. In the same way, God wants us to take advantage of the opportunities that he gives us. Every day God gives us chances to witness to friends, to serve someone in need, or simply to glorify him by making good decisions. As we follow God and take advantage of the opportunities he gives us, we will see that he will do new things in our life and in the life of those around us.

GOAL! *What motivated the Z-Boys to reinvent skateboarding? How can you be motivated to serve God? Ask him today to help you find creative ways to serve him and to take advantage of every opportunity that comes your way.*

REAL LIFE CAN SOMETIMES IMITATE motion pictures, especially in the realm of sports. In the 2001 NCAA women's basketball title game, Notre Dame's Ruth Riley relived a scene from her favorite film.

Two Indiana institutions—Notre Dame and Purdue—squared off in the championship. The Fighting Irish started slowly and fell behind 19–7, but Notre Dame narrowed the gap to six at halftime.

The Fighting Irish continued to battle in the second half, and when Alicia Ratay nailed a three-pointer the score was tied 62–62 with 4:02 remaining. Not about to give up the lead, the Boilermakers regained a 66–64 edge with a little more than a minute to play.

Riley tied the contest 66–66 at the 1:01 mark. Then on defense the 6-foot-4-inch post rebounded Shereka Wright's missed shot, enabling the Irish to set up a game-winning play.

With the clock winding down, Notre Dame fed the ball inside to Riley. Fouled by Wright, Riley went to the line for two shots. Recalling the scene from the movie *Hoosiers* where two free throws decided a state high school championship, Riley sank the first. Following a Boilermakers time-out, she canned the second as well.

Purdue's Katie Douglas missed an 18-foot shot at the buzzer, giving the Irish a 68–66 triumph and its first national basketball title. Riley, named the tournament MVP, scored 28 points, grabbed 13 rebounds, and blocked 7 shots in the contest.

EXTRA POINT < < < < < < < < < < < < < < < < < < < < < <
Ruth Riley followed the instruction of her coach during the championship game. But more than that, she remembered the example of the players and of Coach Norman Dale in the movie *Hoosiers*. She imitated their basketball skills and faith in their abilities. And Riley brought home victory.

The writer of Hebrews instructs us to remember Christian leaders who have taught us in the past. We must look at the outcome of their life and imitate their belief and faith. Then we will have victory in life.

GOAL! *Think about leaders in your life. Perhaps they include a parent, a coach, a teacher, or a youth pastor. Consider their positive leadership qualities. Thank God for leaders worth imitating.*

Remember your leaders, who spoke the word of God to you. Consider the outcome of their way of life and imitate their faith.
HEBREWS 13:7, NIV

31 MAR

FOR MORE THAN 50 YEARS, the magazine *Sports Illustrated* has distinguished itself as one of the best-written sports publications. But in 1985, a tongue-in-cheek article made some readers laugh and other fans look foolish.

In the April 1 issue, noted sportswriter George Plimpton profiled Hayden "Sidd" Finch, a spring-training wonder in the New York Mets organization. The author quoted a number of Mets sources in the story, including pitching coach Mel Stottlemyre, manager Dave Johnson, and minor league manager Bob Schaefer.

Finch's life story appeared incredulous. Raised in an English orphanage, he was adopted by archaeologist Francis Whyte-Finch, who later died in an airplane crash in Nepal. After briefly attending Harvard, Finch studied in Tibet where he mastered "siddhi," a technique of body-mind control, which enabled him to throw a 168-mph fastball. Debating whether to pursue a career in baseball or as a French horn player, Finch agreed to inform the Mets of his decision by April 1.

Sports Illustrated received more than 2,000 letters, mostly from curious Mets fans. On April 14, the magazine admitted the story was simply a well-written hoax.

Plimpton hinted at the joke in the subheading that read, "He's a pitcher, part yogi and part recluse. Impressively liberated from our opulent lifestyle, Sidd's deciding about yoga—and his future in baseball." The first letters of each word formed the phrase, "Happy April Fool's Day."

EXTRA POINT < < < < < < < < < < < < < < < < < < < < Die-hard sports fans trust *Sports Illustrated* for truthful reporting. George Plimpton's reputation as a serious writer with a no-nonsense style made the story more credible. But even *SI* and Plimpton enjoyed the harmless joke.

If Mets fans hadn't been so frustrated with losing, they wouldn't have believed Sidd Finch existed. In the end, though, everyone had a good laugh.

Many people think of Christianity as a serious, no-nonsense way of life. Some believe we can't have fun. But the Bible describes life with God as happy and joyful. Even Solomon, considered the world's wisest man, said there's a time to laugh.

GOAL! *Plan a fun activity or tell a story or joke to your family or friends to make them laugh. Thank God for laughter.*

There is a time for everything, and a season for every activity under heaven . . . a time to weep and a time to laugh, a time to mourn and a time to dance.
ECCLESIASTES
0.1, 4, NIV

01 APR

So why do you condemn another Christian? Why do you look down on another Christian? Remember, each of us will stand personally before the judgment seat of God.

ROMANS 14:10

THE BEST TRICK SKATEBOARD competition at the 2003

Gravity Games looked more like a Saturday afternoon at a crowded skate park than a battle between top riders. Twenty competitors tried hitting their biggest tricks on two different sections of the street course in Cleveland, Ohio, as seven judges took in the whole chaotic scene.

The first part had competitors fighting for space on numerous rails and transfers. After 20 minutes of grinds, kickflips, and gnarly crashes, riders spent another 20 minutes trying to impress the judges on two miniramps, a quarter-pipe, a cutout wall, and a flat rail on top of a backwall box. Needless to say, riders took it up a notch with their creativity and technical skills in the second part of the competition.

Brazil's Daniel Vieira appeared to have a lock on first by knocking out a switch frontside flip, switch hardflip, and a backside nollie heelflip. Then he pulled a 360 flip drop off the center gap. But late entry Chris Haslam, who didn't skate in the street finals, brought out a frontside boardslide to kickflip that stunned the crowd. He also ripped off a 360 varial flip over the center gap and a frontside 270 heelflip, which left little doubt in anybody's mind about who was going home with the gold.

EXTRA POINT < < < < < < < < < < < < < < < < < < <

The skateboarders in the best trick competition obviously wanted to take first place. But with 20 guys going at the same time, they couldn't concentrate on each other. Every rider had to personally challenge himself to yank out his biggest trick in the midst of the pressure. If a skateboarder started comparing himself to his competition, he'd only waste precious time and miss out on an opportunity to wow the judges.

As Christians, God wants us to do the same thing—focus on our own actions. If we start comparing ourselves to others, two things may happen:

No. 1: We'll see people not living for God and start feeling high and mighty.

No. 2: We'll see others walking more closely with Jesus and begin feeling like a failure.

God doesn't want either of those things to happen. He desires that we focus on our own relationship with him.

GOAL! *Do you ever think, I'm doing a better job living for God than that person? It's okay to admit it. Ask God to help you focus on him and his will for your life instead of comparing yourself to others.*

CHANGING COACHES always creates a tricky situation, especially in midseason. But in 1989, newly appointed University of Michigan basketball coach Steve Fisher took his team all the way.

Former Wolverines coach Bill Frieder accepted a post at Arizona State on the eve of the NCAA tournament, and Michigan athletic director Bo Schembechler banished him from the playoffs. Schembechler then appointed Fisher, Frieder's assistant, to head the program during March Madness.

But the move affected the team very little. Michigan rolled through the NCAA tournament, averaging over 90 points per game before reaching the Final Four. Following an 83–81 decision over Illinois, the Wolverines faced the Seton Hall Pirates for the championship.

The Pirates trailed 51–39 midway through the second half but streaked to a 71–71 tie at the end of regulation on the strength of John Morton's 20 second-half points.

In the overtime period, Seton Hall led 79–76 with 1:17 remaining, but Terry Mills connected on a turnaround jumper 20 seconds later to bring Michigan to within one.

Working the shot clock down, Morton missed a short jumper with 11 seconds left, and Michigan's Rumeal Robinson blazed down the court with the ball. Seton Hall's Gerald Greene fouled, and Robinson hit two free throws with three seconds showing on the clock. The Wolverines won 80–79 to earn their first national basketball crown.

EXTRA POINT < < < < < < < < < < < < < < < < < < < < < < Steve Fisher proved he could lead the team when it counted. But Bill Frieder still deserves a lot of credit. Good coaches develop well-prepared, highly motivated players who know what to do whether the coach is there or not. Great coaches also mentor assistants who can take their place without the team suffering.

The same should be true of Christian leaders. They should develop well-prepared, highly motivated believers who know how to minister and witness whether the leader is there or not. Great Christian leaders train and mentor assistants to take their place.

The story of Moses helping Joshua take over as leader of the Israelites is a perfect example of what God wants to happen in spiritual leadership.

GOAL! *Observe midseason changes in basketball coaches and baseball managers. How did each team perform after the change? Praise God for Christian leaders who prepare others to take their place.*

Now Joshua son of Nun was filled with the spirit of wisdom because Moses had laid his hands on him. So the Israelites listened to him and did what the Lord had commanded Moses.
DEUTERONOMY 34:9, NIV

03 APR

But God, who is
rich in mercy,
because of
His great love
with which
He loved us,
even when we
were dead in
trespasses,
made us alive
together with
Christ (by grace
you have been
saved).
EPHESIANS
2:4-5, NKJV

GOT CUPS? If so, you've got a sport . . . seriously.

The sport of cup stacking is growing around the world. More than one million kids compete in this activity that demands lightning-fast reflexes and precise hand-eye coordination.

Still don't think it's a sport? Well, just imagine sitting in front of 12 specially designed plastic cups. You've got a stack of three, a stack of six, and another stack of three. You start by building a pyramid of three cups, then of six cups, and another of three cups. Then you tear them all down. Next, you up-stack two pyramids of six cups each. After tearing those down, you build a ten-cup pyramid with a cup on each side. Finally, you down-stack the pyramid and end up with the cups in the same way you started. Sounds easy, right?

Now try doing that in 7.43 seconds. Seems impossible, but a teenage girl from Denver, Colorado, did it. Emily Fox set the world record at the 2002 Rocky Mountain Cup Stacking Championships. And when her hands start moving you think she's on fast-forward.

Fox says stacking cups has helped her in more ways than just developing quick hands—which also help her in playing basketball. You see, cup stacking has a couple of key rules.

No. 1: You finish what you start.

No. 2: You fix your fumbles.

EXTRA POINT
< < < < < < < < < < < < < < < < < < < < < < Life, just like cup stacking, is filled with fumbles. Things don't always go your way. (Maybe you've noticed that?) Sometimes you mess up and everything seems to fall apart—especially when you're too busy or trying to go too fast.

If you fail to fix your mistakes in cup stacking, your time doesn't count. The sport demands perfection. And when it's not done perfectly, you must fix it before it counts.

God's the same way. To live with him in heaven, we have to be perfect. Of course, we never will be. We're human. Our lives are filled with fumbles. The cool part is that God fixes our fumbles when we have a relationship with Jesus Christ.

GOAL! Think about some of the ways you consistently mess up. Do you ever lie, act disrespectfully to your parents, or cheat on assignments? You can decide to fix your fumbles. Ask Jesus for forgiveness, and then ask the person you wronged to forgive you as well.

BEING TOO ANXIOUS for a hit is never good for a batter. Boston's Hideo Nomo took advantage of the Baltimore Orioles' overanxiousness to turn in a hitless performance in 2001.

The 1995 National League Rookie of the Year joined the Red Sox as a free agent following the 2000 season and drew the starting assignment for Boston's second game of the year. With a mixture of his trademark hesitation delivery, baffling off-speed pitches, and high heat, Nomo handcuffed Baltimore from the outset.

Baseball commissioner Bud Selig's directive to major league umpires to call higher strikes contributed to the Japanese pitcher's success.

Although Nomo walked three and Cal Ripken reached on third baseman Shea Hillenbrand's error in the second inning, the Orioles went hitless through eight frames. With one out in the ninth, second baseman Mike Lansing saved Nomo's pitching masterpiece by catching Mike Bordick's soft looper to center with a backhanded, tumbling snag. Two pitches later, Delino DeShields flied out to left for the game's final out, giving the Red Sox a 3–0 win.

Brian Daubach provided all the offense by blasting two home runs—a two-run shot in the second and a solo effort in the eighth.

In pitching his second major league no-hitter, Nomo joined Cy Young, Jim Bunning, and Nolan Ryan as the only pitchers to hurl no-hitters in both leagues. The 32-year-old pitcher also no-hit the Colorado Rockies on September 17, 1996.

EXTRA POINT < < < < < < < < < < < < < < < < < < < < < Hideo Nomo's performance not only brought anxiety to the Oriole batters, his no-hitter put butterflies in the stomach of his own teammates and fans. But with great thanksgiving, Nomo joined the exclusive two-league–no-hit club.

We can also experience anxiety in everyday life. We too feel those butterfly wings when we face tense situations and problems. How do we get those butterflies to fly away?

Paul told the Philippian Christians how to control their anxiety: Pray. And his advice still works today. With thanksgiving, we can present our requests to God.

GOAL! *Think about times you feel butterflies inside during athletic contests and in life. Pray and give your anxieties to the Lord.*

> Do not be anxious about anything, but in everything, by prayer and petition, with thanksgiving, present your requests to God.
>
> PHILIPPIANS 4:6, NIV

05 APR

MORE AND MORE PROFESSIONAL basketball teams are looking overseas for top talent. In the 2002 NBA draft, the Houston Rockets used the first overall pick to select Yao Ming from China.

Standing 7-feet-5-inches and weighing nearly 300 pounds, Ming was one of the most highly anticipated players to join the NBA. In the Olympics and during the China Basketball Association (CBA) season, Ming showed the talent to be a difference-maker in the NBA. In the 2001–02 CBA season, he averaged 32.4 points per game, 19 rebounds, and 4.8 blocked shots. Ming's dominating presence in the middle helped the Shanghai Sharks win their first CBA championship.

After the Rockets negotiated with the Sharks and with the Chinese government to get Ming on the team, he quickly made his mark as a rookie. He was a unanimous selection to the All-Rookie team. Plus, he averaged 13.5 points a game—even scoring 30 against Dallas—and grabbed 8.2 rebounds for Houston during the 2002–03 season.

As the young 7-and-a-half-footer continues to become stronger and adjusts to playing against NBA competition, he'll improve into the all-star that everybody expects him to become.

EXTRA POINT < < < < < < < < < < < < < < < < < <
Outstanding athletes hail from around the globe. But most who turn pro find the biggest money in the West. The promise of an extraordinarily tall and potentially dominating basketball player sent the Houston Rockets after Yao Ming. The promise of a high salary and global influence may have brought Ming to the United States.

East and West met successfully with Ming's arrival in Houston. He played well and gained popularity in spite of the language difference. His quiet style and fun personality endeared him to fans around the world. And the language of basketball—with its baskets, free throws, and fouls—proved universal.

God's language transcends east, west, north, and south. His language overcomes all barriers and needs no translation. His language is love.

GOAL! Review the roster of your favorite pro team. Note any international players. Ask God to help you express God's love to people you meet from other countries.

NO GOLF TOURNAMENT RIVALS the Masters for beauty, tradition, and prestige. Much of the credit for the tournament's elevation from sporting event to cultural icon belongs to Gene Sarazen, who stroked the "shot heard 'round the world."

Born Eugenio Saraceni, the sixth-grade dropout Americanized his name to sound more like a golfer. By electing to play in a series of South American exhibitions, Sarazen missed the first Masters held in 1934. In the second annual affair, the Harrison, New York, native trailed Craig Wood by three strokes on the final day.

With Wood already in the clubhouse at 282, "Squire" (a nickname Sarazen acquired from owning a farm in Brookfield, New York) stood 220 yards from the pin on the par-5 15th hole. A small creek guarded the front of the green. Any approach required clearing the water if the golfer hoped to break par. After consulting with his caddie, Sarazen decided to go for broke and hit a 4 wood. The ball landed on the green and slowly rolled into the hole for a double eagle—golf's rarest shot.

Sarazen held par on the remaining three holes and tied Wood. Rules called for a 36-hole playoff the following day to determine the winner. Sarazen bettered Wood 144 to 149 in the extra affair to take home the victory.

EXTRA POINT

< < < < < < < < < < < < < < < < < < < < <

Sarazen put his hope in one shot. The ball soared over the creek like an eagle, ran strong and sure across the green, and dropped into the hole. One swing in one moment etched the golfer forever in the pages of Masters history.

The prophet Isaiah knew about hope and strength. He watched eagles soar through the sky and wrote a beautiful verse comparing those who put their hope in the Lord with these magnificent birds.

Just like scoring an eagle in golf gives us a jolt of energy, tapping into God's strength helps us stay strong in the long haul.

GOAL! *Search the Internet or look in an encyclopedia to learn more about eagles. Praise God for examples in nature of the strength, courage, and freedom he gives.*

Those who hope in the Lord will renew their strength. They will soar on wings like eagles; they will run and not grow weary, they will walk and not be faint.

ISAIAH 40:31, NIV

07 APR

CONSISTENT TRAINING leads to success. Lance Armstrong proves that. By winning the Tour de France—the most grueling bicycle race in the world—six times in a row from 1999 to 2004, he's established himself as one of the fittest athletes in the world.

But being in great physical shape didn't happen by accident. Lance trains hard to be able to push himself up the mountains in France. He sometimes works out seven days in a row. Check out these stats from Lance's Web site:

TUESDAY: Four hours of high cadence on all hills, 95 to100 revolutions per minute (rpm), stay in saddle on hills, low cadence on flat terrain—60–65 rpm. Heart rate 135 to 140 on flat terrain.

WEDNESDAY: Weight workout in morning. Afternoon, two hours of cadence high, 95-plus rpm, stay seated on hills but include two to three uphill sprints of eight seconds each with maximum effort.

THURSDAY: Same as Tuesday.

FRIDAY: Same as Wednesday.

SATURDAY: Three-hour group ride with no heart rate ceiling or cadence; ride as hard as you like!

SUNDAY: Four hours with six four-minute muscle tension intervals at 50 to 55 rpm. Max effort for each interval. Six minutes recovery between.

MONDAY: Same as Friday and Wednesday.

TUESDAY: Day off.

EXTRA POINT < < < < < < < < < < < < < < < < < < <
Wow! No wonder Lance Armstrong's legs look like they were chiseled out of granite. His work ethic is second to none, making him the best cyclist in the world. By consistently training, Lance stays in top shape.

Sometimes in life we aren't consistent with our Christian faith. We follow God in spurts. We read through the Bible. We attend church camp. We take a mission trip or help with Vacation Bible School. Then we take a break. God never wants us to take a break from our Christian life. The heavenly Father desires that we walk consistently with him.

GOAL! *Read about King Jotham in 2 Chronicles 27:1-9. Why did he grow powerful? Thank the Lord for the power he gives when we walk consistently with him.*

SO JOTHAM BECAME MIGHTY, BECAUSE HE PREPARED HIS WAYS BEFORE THE LORD HIS GOD.

2 CHRONICLES 27:6, NKJV

At that time
the Spirit of the
Lord will come
upon you with
power, and you
will prophesy
with them. You
will be changed
into a different
person. After
these signs
take place, do
whatever you
think is best,
for God will
be with you.

1 SAMUEL 10:6-7

FOR 14 YEARS JOHN SMOLTZ dominated batters as a starting pitcher for the Atlanta Braves. His 14 playoff and World Series wins give him more postseason victories than any other pitcher in major league history. And his 163 wins, including 24 in 1996 when he won the National League Cy Young Award, aren't too bad either.

But at the end of the 2001 season, Smoltz's role on the team changed. After he returned from elbow surgery in 2000 and battled through setbacks in 2001, the Braves put Smoltz in the bull pen. He converted 10 of 11 save opportunities in 2001. And even when his arm felt 100 percent in 2002, the Braves kept him as their closer—a decision Smoltz wasn't too happy about. He didn't want to be a closer; he wanted to start.

Atlanta told Smoltz he could help the team more coming out of the bull pen, and eventually he accepted and excelled in his new role. In 2002 he set a National League record with 55 saves. And from May 29, 2002, to May 25, 2003, the Braves didn't lose a game in which Smoltz appeared.

"You may have asked me five years ago what I was going to do, and I had everything planned out—none of which included two surgeries, being a closer, or even preaching the gospel to so many different people," Smoltz says. "I can tell you that nothing that I wished or planned for has happened, and it's all turned out for the best."

EXTRA POINT < < < < < < < < < < < < < < < < < < < < <
John Smoltz became a closer to help his team. He didn't want to at first, but God blessed him in his new role.

In life our roles sometimes change, for better or worse. In the Bible, God told Samuel to anoint Saul king of Israel. Saul was like a different person. Although his reign included many mistakes when he didn't fully obey God, he did grow from a frightened man to a powerful king. God knows that our roles change from time to time, but he promises that no matter what task he gives—he will be with us when we follow him.

GOAL! *Talk to a coach about the change in his or her role from player to teacher. Ask God to help you accept and deal with your changing roles in life.*

THE EMOTIONS OF THE FINAL GAME of the season can run from intense to lackadaisical—depending on what's on the line. When the Detroit Red Wings visited the Colorado Avalanche to conclude the 2000 campaign, the results were surprising.

How we thank God, who gives us victory over sin and death through Jesus Christ our Lord!
1 CORINTHIANS 15:57

Fierce competition, continual action, and constant checking usually highlighted the encounters between the two perennial Stanley Cup contenders. But with a playoff spot clinched, Detroit benched most of its starters. The Avalanche, well rested from claiming a playoff spot early, elected to play the regulars at home.

The Red Wings' halfhearted effort readily manifested itself. The players skated tentatively and exhibited little emotion or enthusiasm. Game officials never whistled either team for an infraction, the first NHL game without a penalty since the Montreal Canadiens visited the Buffalo Sabres on February 17, 1980—more than 20 years beforehand.

On defense, the difference in talent caused the Avalanche to dominate. Allowing the Red Wings only two shots compared to its own 15, Colorado jumped to a 2–0 lead on goals by Milan Hejduk and Serge Aubin. Detroit narrowed the gap to 2–1 on Brendan Shanahan's 41st goal of the season, but backup goalie Ken Wregget allowed Alex Tanguay a third-period score. The Red Wings fell 3–2 as Stacy Roest netted a last-second goal.

EXTRA POINT < < < < < < < < < < < < < < < < < < < < Many thought the Red Wings were the better team because they won the Stanley Cup in 1997 and 1998. But they approached the ice with subdued intensity. To Coach Scotty Bowman, the battle made no difference. The Avalanche secured the victory because Coach Bob Hartley relied on his starting stars and the team played at home before fans that cared.

While God doesn't care too much if you win or lose every game (sure, he wants you to do well), he does care very much that you gain victory over sin. And there's only one way to do that: through Jesus Christ. Jesus gives you the victory over death just for believing in him. Jesus' sacrifice helps you win the most important victory of all—even more important than a season finale.

GOAL! *Watch a sporting event in which the outcome has no bearing on final season standings. Notice the players' and coaches' attitude. Praise God that his Son has already won the greatest battle in your life.*

10 APR

Be sure to stay busy and plant a variety of crops, for you never know which will grow—perhaps they all will.

ECCLESIASTES

11:6

WHEN TWO TOP PITCHERS are up against each other, the face-off can make for a fast and lively game. And if both players are performing at their peak, winning or losing often comes down to the slightest mistake.

In April 2001, the Arizona Diamondbacks hosted the Los Angeles Dodgers with Curt Schilling squaring off against Kevin Brown. From the outset, both hurled with deadly accuracy. Neither walked a batter, and Brown allowed only three hits. Schilling fared even better, giving up just two singles after retiring the first 15 men he faced.

But in the fourth inning, Los Angeles first baseman Eric Karros dropped Tony Womack's bunt attempt. After reaching first base, Womack raced to third on Jay Bell's single and scored when Luis Gonzalez hit into a double play for the Diamondbacks' first run. Later, Gonzalez crushed a solo home run 428 feet to center field.

Despite the lapses, Brown threw only 88 pitches in the contest, 65 of them strikes. His counterpart and the winning pitcher, Schilling, delivered 93 pitches, 73 going for strikes. The game itself lasted only one hour and 55 minutes as the Diamondbacks won 2–0.

EXTRA POINT < < < < < < < < < < < < < < < < < < < < Both Curt Schilling and Kevin Brown tried hard. Both pitchers did well. Both succeeded in throwing strikes. Both deserved to win. But only one could add the victory to his season's stats. Only one could succeed.

The writer of Ecclesiastes knew that many things in our life have an equal chance of succeeding or failing, and we cannot know which is which. He used the example of planting seeds in the morning and then working at other tasks in the evening. The farmer could not be certain whether the seeds would grow or if his other work would succeed. Therefore, to be sure of success, he had to work hard at all he did all day long. And so should we. Because we never know, maybe God will bless all our efforts and we'll be doubly successful.

GOAL! *Interview people you would consider successful. Ask if they've always succeeded at everything they've done. Praise God for the ability to work hard and succeed.*

WINNING ONE OF GOLF'S four major tournaments isn't easy. A player must have his A-game going to win the Masters, U.S. Open, British Open, or PGA Championship. But in 1998, it was Mark O'Meara's patience that helped bring him a well-deserved Masters victory.

Wait for the Lord; be strong and take heart and wait for the Lord.

PSALM 27:14, NIV

The 41-year-old golfer had participated in 56 major championships without a single triumph. As he neared completion of his final round at Augusta National, it appeared the string would run to 57.

David Duval and Fred Couples battled fiercely for the top. Through eight holes on the final day, Couples led by five. Six holes later, however, Duval moved in front by two. Couples pulled even with an eagle on 15 as Duval three-putted the 16th for bogey.

Their neck and neck struggle set the stage for O'Meara's remarkable finish. Both Couples and Duval missed birdie putts on 17. On the same hole, however, O'Meara chipped to within seven feet and dropped his putt to tie the other golfers with a birdie.

With the score knotted, a playoff seemed unavoidable. Duval couldn't nail a 20-foot birdie opportunity at 18 and finished 8-under at 280. Couples also fell victim to No. 18 by driving into a bunker and barely salvaging par.

Meanwhile, O'Meara curled in his 20-foot birdie putt on the final hole. The shot gave him the lead for the only time in the tournament at 9-under-par.

EXTRA POINT

< < < < < < < < < < < < < < < < < < < <

Mark O'Meara finally won the Masters after his 15th try, the most for any first-time champion. Later in July, he won the British Open, becoming the oldest player to win two major tournaments in the same year. Though he had won some professional tournaments, O'Meara waited 18 years to claim a major.

The golfer could have lost heart. He could have become impatient and left the tour. But Mark O'Meara didn't. His patience served him well.

Ask people what character quality is their greatest struggle, and many will say patience. We dislike standing in line. We look at our watch as we nuke popcorn. We flip the TV remote during commercials. We grow weary during a long sermon.

King David of the Bible must have struggled with patience too. When life became difficult, he sang psalms of waiting.

GOAL! *Try to catch yourself in impatient habits such as looking at the clock or sighing when it's someone else's turn. Commit to changing those reactions. Ask God for patience.*

12 APR

> And let us
> consider how
> we may spur
> one another
> on toward
> love and
> good deeds.
>
> HEBREWS
> 10:24, NIV

TRACK MEET OFFICIALS sometimes schedule a race not to determine a winner, but to spur on a record-setting performance. In the 2001 New York Road Runners Club Challenge, the stage was set in the 5,000 meters for Marla Runyan.

Organizers put together a field of four. Three runners would set a fast pace in the early going, and then Marla would try to set a record.

British native Danielle Thornal led the pack through the first eight laps on the 200-meter indoor track. Next Thornal dropped back and Alisa Harvey took over the lead. After 11 laps, Thornal, Harvey, and Gladys Prieur, the other runner, dropped out of the race and left Runyan to run alone.

The race's rapid opening gave the former San Diego State racer the spark she needed. Despite having no other competition for the last 14 laps, Marla pushed herself to the limit. Sensing a record in the making, the crowd urged Runyan to sprint the final 200 meters. She bolted toward the finish line, completing the final lap in 31.5 seconds.

Runyan, who finished eighth in the 1,500 meters at the 2000 Sydney Games, completed the course in 15:07.33, shattering Lynn Jennings' American record of 15:22.64. Runyan's time also represented the sixth-best mark of all time.

EXTRA POINT

< < < < < < < < < < < < < < < < < < < <

Track stars seldom run their best when they compete alone or in a slow field. Runners need to be pushed to get better. They need solid competition to break records. They need others to ensure success.

The writer of Hebrews understood the importance of other Christians in our life. Encouragement from friends and family inspires confidence in our abilities to love and perform good deeds. Compliments for completing acts of kindness spur us on to do more.

We can make a difference, not just in what we do, but more importantly, in what we inspire others to do. That's how the Lord planned it.

GOAL! *Ask God to help you choose someone or several people who need spurring on in their sport. Write down their names.*

_____

_____

Encourage them in athletics and inspire them in their Christian life as well.

EXTREME SPORTS GET THAT NAME for a reason . . . they earn it. For years in freestyle motocross, competitors were happy flying 70 feet off jumps, twisting the bike in the air, letting go of the handlebars and floating above the machine, and clicking their heels together in every which way. But that wasn't extreme enough for Carey Hart, so at the 2000 Gravity Games, he pushed the sport to a new level by attempting a backflip.

Hart was the first person to try a backflip in competition on a motorcycle 125cc or larger. Although the force of the landing knocked Hart from his ride, the Providence, Rhode Island, crowd and Hart's fellow competitors came to their feet and cheered. From that point, the race was on to be the first person to nail and ride away from a backflip. And about a year and half later, Caleb Wyatt became the first man to complete the trick on a bike that big when he rode his 2002 Honda CR 250 into the record books—although it almost killed him.

During his first attempt to hit the trick in 2001, Wyatt came off his motorcycle in midair. He hit the ground first and then the bike landed on his head! If it hadn't been for a good helmet and a soft landing surface, Wyatt would have died. But the extreme athlete didn't give up and finally landed the trick in the spring of 2002 on a dirt ramp in Clamis, California. It took him six attempts and several bad spills, but on Wyatt's sixth try—with a crew filming *Road to the X Games*—he controlled the rotating bike and stuck a picture-perfect landing.

EXTRA POINT < < < < < < < < < < < < < < < < < < < < < < Having a metal motorcycle that weighs hundreds of pounds land on your head would have been enough to scare away a lot of people, but not Caleb Wyatt. He weighed the risks, planned the jump, and didn't give up until he completed a backflip on his motorcycle . . . and he did it safely.

The writer of Proverbs encourages us to listen to God's wisdom to stay safe. God may ask you to do some pretty dangerous things, but if you follow his will, he'll keep you safe.

GOAL! *Read through the Bible to find some of God's wisdom on staying safe—but remain ready to take risks for him.*

But all who listen to me will live in peace and safety, unafraid of harm.

PROVERBS 1:33

14 APR

Meanwhile, as
young Samuel
grew taller, he
also continued
to gain favor
with the Lord
and with the
people.

1 SAMUEL 2:26

AFTER TIGER WOODS shocked the golf world with his first Masters victory in 1997, he requested that the traditional green jacket be tailored several sizes larger than he wore. Following the 2002 event, observers realized the golfing superstar had made a wise decision.

The 2002 tournament witnessed three of the soggiest days in Augusta National history. Rain interrupted the second round, forcing 26 holes to be played on Saturday. At the end of the marathon day, Woods and U.S. Open champion Retief Goosen were tied for the lead at 205.

But on Sunday, the weather turned perfect. The sun shone, the azaleas glowed, and the fairways shimmered. But for some reason, only Woods took advantage of the serene scene.

Woods gained three strokes on Goosen in the first three holes of Sunday's round and never let go of his lead. Although he shot only a 1-under-par 71, the PGA's five top-ranked golfers behind Woods combined for rounds totaling 9-over.

Woods claimed his third Masters title by finishing 12-under-par and became the first golfer to garner back-to-back crowns on the fabled course since Nick Faldo won in 1989 and 1990. The 26-year-old also earned the distinction of becoming the youngest golfer to win seven major tournaments, joining the elite group of Bobby Jones, Gene Sarazen, Sam Snead, and Arnold Palmer.

EXTRA POINT < < < < < < < < < < < < < < < < < < < < <
Masters' tradition provides a custom-tailored jacket for each winner. But most people don't know that the coveted clothing stays in Augusta. Champions wear their prized suit coat during the week's events. And each champion gets only one green jacket made for him. The first custom coat remains the only one worn for a lifetime, regardless of later titles.

The 21-year-old Tiger Woods understood in 1997 that he would grow stronger and larger. He also felt certain he could take the Augusta National course again and again. He was right. A jacket tailored to his 1997 body would never have fit his 2002 frame.

Like Tiger Woods, God intends that we grow. But his plan includes more than physical stature. He wants us to grow spiritually, too.

GOAL! *Chart your physical growth over the last several years. Think about your spiritual growth. Which has changed more? Ask God to help you continue to grow in his favor.*

DOING WHAT YOUR COACH says isn't always easy. In Super Bowl XXXII, Terrell Davis followed his coach's advice although he was in tremendous pain.

The Denver Broncos running back entered the NFL's biggest game on a roll. He had led the AFC in rushing during the regular season with 1,750 yards and added 100-plus-yard performances in each playoff game leading up to the finale against Green Bay.

And early in the game, it appeared as if Davis would continue his domination. After the Packers took a 7–0 lead, Davis led the Broncos on a 58-yard drive to knot things at 7–7 in the first quarter. But during the opening 15 minutes—in which Davis rushed for 64 yards—he got jolted on a tackle and blacked out for a moment. He went to the sidelines suffering from a huge migraine headache and poor vision.

Davis didn't play almost the entire second quarter. But when the Broncos drove deep into Green Bay territory, Denver coach Mike Shanahan called on Davis to enter the game. Davis told his coach he couldn't see, but Shanahan insisted, saying Davis would only be a decoy and didn't need to be able to see. Terrell strapped on his helmet and ran onto the field. Despite terrible pain and blurred vision, he faked taking a handoff from quarterback John Elway and ran into the line. With the Packers defense keying on Davis, Elway kept the ball and ran into the end zone for a 14–7 Broncos lead. During halftime, Davis received medical attention and returned to the game. He ended up rushing for 157 yards and two more touchdowns, and he was named the game's Most Valuable Player in Denver's 31–24 win.

> Obey your spiritual leaders and do what they say. Their work is to watch over your souls, and they know they are accountable to God.
>
> HEBREWS 13:17

EXTRA POINT

< < < < < < < < < < < < < < < < < < < < < < < < <

Can you imagine playing professional football without being able to see? Terrell Davis battled migraine headaches throughout his football career. But when his coach needed him, Davis did what he was told.

God wants us to react the same way when people in authority over us ask us to do something. Their requests won't always be painless or easy, but we need to obey anyway.

GOAL!

Have you ever felt that your parents or teachers ask too much from you? It's a normal feeling, but try to honor God as you obey the authority figures in your life.

A wise teacher's words spur students to action and emphasize important truths.

ECCLESIASTES 12:11

NO ATHLETE ACHIEVES SUCCESS without good instruction. In the 1995 Masters, Ben Crenshaw displayed the lessons taught to him by his golf instructor, Harvey Penick.

The day before the prestigious tournament opened, Crenshaw flew to Austin, Texas, to attend 90-year-old Penick's funeral. Penick coached the University of Texas golf team from 1931 to 1963, winning 22 Southwest Conference titles. Although Ben played for the Longhorns after Harvey retired, Penick still served as Crenshaw's teacher and mentor. His golf instruction manual, *Harvey Penick's Little Red Book,* remained on the *New York Times* best-seller list for 54 weeks.

Crenshaw played the Augusta National with intense emotion after the loss of his coach and friend. He began his final round tied for the lead but moved to the top with a birdie on Sunday's second hole. On the treacherous 16th—a par-3, 170-yarder—Crenshaw stroked a perfect 6 iron shot, leaving the ball five feet from the pin. Using Penick's advice to putt with "dead aim," he nailed the birdie. The ex-UT golfer followed with another birdie on 17, set up by a terrific sand wedge shot that landed ten feet from the hole.

After closing his round with a four-day total of 274 and edging out Davis Love III by a single stroke for the green jacket, Crenshaw bent over and sobbed. He explained the emotion, stating that he played this Masters with 15 clubs rather than the PGA-allowed 14. His 15th was Harvey Penick.

EXTRA POINT < < < < < < < < < < < < < < < < < < < <

Athletes are sometimes blessed by caring, competent, and dedicated coaches who teach by words and example. Ben Crenshaw understood the role Harvey Penick played in his success in golf and in life. And Crenshaw let his coach know how much he admired him. During the Masters, Crenshaw especially missed the mentor who for many years had been a phone call away.

Occasionally during our lives, God blesses us with teachers like Penick. When the Lord gives us such men and women, we should let them know what they mean to us.

GOAL! *If you've been blessed with a wonderful coach, teacher, or parent, make sure that person knows how you feel. Call or write your thanks. Praise God for wise teachers.*

BASEBALL TEAM MARKETERS spend hours developing promotions to entice fans to the stadium. Bat day, bobble-head doll prizes, and team hat giveaways often help attendance soar. But the Toronto Blue Jays' "Hot Dog Blaster" promotion proved not to be such a great idea.

The Anaheim Angels visited the Toronto SkyDome early in the 2000 season. In the second game of the series, the club planned to shoot cooked, wrapped franks into the crowd.

However, the apparatus was never properly tested. Instead of producing wieners in a bun, it caused the hot dogs to explode into tiny bits while airborne. Cries echoed throughout the stands from frustrated fans, who were being assaulted by scraps of meat descending from the sky. Despite the protests, operators continually fired franks into the crowd throughout the game.

The action on the field did little to improve the disgruntled disposition of those watching. With the bases loaded and the Angels leading 1–0 in the fourth, Adam Kennedy drove Frank Castillo's pitch over the right-field fence for a grand slam.

One inning later, the 24-year-old second baseman tripled to right center, plating another three runs. He capped off his night with an RBI-single in the ninth and tied an Anaheim single-game RBI record with eight. Although the Angels gave up six runs in the bottom of the ninth, they held on to win 16–10.

Because of the Lord's great love we are not consumed, for his compassions never fail.

LAMENTATIONS 3:22, NIV

EXTRA POINT

< < < < < < < < < < < < < < < < < < < <

What a night for Toronto fans! They surely spelled *attendance* at that game F-R-U-S-T-R-A-T-I-O-N and D-I-S-A-P-P-O-I-N-T-M-E-N-T. Imagine driving to the ballpark expecting free supper and a decent game, but leaving with food-stained clothes and an embarrassing loss. Sometimes in sports and in life, expectations far exceed reality.

Surely God often feels the same about the humans he created. He desires obedience and effort. We offer sin and avoidance. But because of our heavenly Father's compassion, we aren't destroyed by our mistakes. God's love saves us again and again.

GOAL! *Prepare hot dogs for your family. As you eat them, recall the disappointed Toronto fans. Ask God's forgiveness when you disappoint him.*

18 APR

NEW SPORTS SEEM TO POP UP all the time. With the creation of every new sport, more and more athletes get the chance to showcase their skills. And while Aleisha Cline may have had some previous notoriety, she certainly made a name for herself in the Skier X competition at the X Games.

From 1999 to 2002, Cline won the wild-looking event three out of four years. Skier X pits athletes together racing down a mountain. However, unlike many skiing events, racers compete at the same time to see who reaches the finish line first. With multiple athletes jockeying for position on the jumps, bumps, and tight turns, the audience can expect a lot of excitement . . . and a few spills.

At the 2002 X Games, Cline showed she possessed all the skills to remain at the top of the sport. Everybody already knew she wasn't afraid of skiing fast. Cline earned an Olympic berth in the 1992 Winter Games in speed skiing. Her clocking of 135 mph ranked her as the fastest in North America and the second fastest in the world. However, she gave up the sport in 1994. With the women's Skier X event added to the X Games in 1999, Cline found her niche and won the competition's first gold medal.

Then in the 2002 competition, Cline demonstrated her patience and high-flying abilities to win top honors again. Without an early gap to shoot, Cline stayed in the back of the pack. But by the fourth hit, she flew into the lead. Cline never looked back and won her third Skier X gold.

EXTRA POINT < < < < < < < < < < < < < < < < < < < < < Aleisha Cline's fearless attitude makes her great in both speed skiing and Skier X. She zooms down the mountain, seemingly without a care in the world.

God wants us to show that same fearlessness in serving others. Because God loves us, we have nothing to fear. His love should drive away all our fears.

GOAL! *Think about God's amazing love. He loved you so much that he sent his Son to die for your sins. As you get opportunities to serve others and show them God's love, remember his love and sacrifice for you.*

THERE'S MORE TO MOTORSPORTS than cars and

motorcycles . . . high-horsepower trucks also zoom around racetracks. The Craftsman Truck Series packs fans into racing venues all over North America. And Rick Crawford's victory in the 2003 Florida Dodge Dealers 250 showed why so many people are excited about this sport.

With average speeds exceeding 127 mph at the Daytona International Speedway, Robert Pressley appeared to have claimed the victory when he passed Crawford in the final lap. But Crawford stayed on Pressley's bumper and caught him in the last turn. Pressley went high to block, so Crawford went low. At the same time, Travis Kvapil pulled next to the two other trucks and it became a three-way race to the finish line. Every driver pushed his truck to the max as the vehicles cruised inches away from each other.

Crawford proved to have a little extra under the hood as he passed the checkered flag first—just .027 seconds ahead of Kvapil. Pressley settled for third. For Crawford, it was his first victory in five years and his only one during the 2003 season.

EXTRA POINT

< < < < < < < < < < < < < < < < < < < < < <

Rick Crawford hadn't finished first in 120 consecutive races. When Robert Pressley passed him with just two turns to go, he could've easily given up hope. But Crawford knew his truck was running well and believed he was a good driver. He stuck with Pressley and beat him at the finish.

As Christians we have certain beliefs that we need to stand up for as well: God created the world; Jesus died for our sins; Jesus is God's Son. The list could go on and on. When these beliefs are challenged, we should show courage and stand up. If we do, God will give us victory in the end.

GOAL! *What are some things you believe? Write them down.*

_____

_____

_____

Trust God and expect him to give you the courage to stand strong for your beliefs.

Be on guard. Stand true to what you believe. Be courageous. Be strong.
1 CORINTHIANS 16:13

20 APR

PRIDE

GOES BEFORE
DESTRUCTION,
AND A HAUGHTY
SPIRIT BEFORE A

FALL.

PROVERBS 16:18, NKJV

SEVERAL LEAGUES, including the United States Football League (USFL) and the World League of American Football (WLAF), have attempted unsuccessfully to provide professional football to fans in the spring. And in 2001, the Xtreme Football League (XFL) met a similar fate.

The NBC network and the World Wrestling Federation (WWF) formed the XFL to attract young male television viewers on Saturday evenings. The league employed more spectacle than sport, however, focusing on anti-NFL bluster, screaming announcers, and in-your-face player nicknames. Organizers changed rules—such as no fair catches—to add excitement. The league saw some initial success, but the ratings quickly plummeted.

The XFL survived until the title game matching the Los Angeles Xtreme against the San Francisco Demons. Only 24,153 witnessed the contest in the 90,000-seat Los Angeles Coliseum.

Ex-NFL quarterback turned insurance agent Tommy Maddox led the Xtreme to a 38–6 rout over the Demons. Maddox, the 1992 first-round draft pick of the Denver Broncos, completed 16 of 28 passes for 210 yards and two touchdowns in the contest.

The Xtreme's kicker, Jose Cortez, a former roofer from Oregon, kicked four field goals—including a 50-yarder! Reggie Durden returned a punt 71 yards for a touchdown to highlight the otherwise dull affair. For their efforts, the winning team split one million dollars 45 ways, working out to $22,222 per player. Three weeks later, the league disbanded.

EXTRA POINT < < < < < < < < < < < < < < < < < < < < NBC hyped the new Xtreme Football League. When the proud peacock network lost its NFL television contract to CBS, it decided to spend around $100 million to help start a new league. The ratings fell and so did NBC's credibility with many serious sports fans. Xtreme pride led to an Xtreme downfall.

The writer of Proverbs knew pride can be a problem in life, too. The dictionary gives several definitions of the word. Sometimes pride can mean a proper sense of worth or something we're rightly proud of, like our country or working hard to get good grades. Those things aren't a problem.

Destructive pride develops from an extreme sense of superiority, including arrogance and conceit. God wants us to steer clear of that.

GOAL! *Think of athletes who possess pride that involves a healthy sense of worth. Then think of some who exhibit arrogance, conceit, and false superiority. Ask God to help you always show the right kind of pride.*

The Lord
hates cheating,
but he delights
in honesty.

PROVERBS 11:1

WINNING A LONG-DISTANCE RACE requires hours of

training and dedication. In the 1980 Boston Marathon, Rosie Ruiz decided to take a shortcut to victory.

The 23-year-old Havana-born New Yorker qualified for the 84th running in Boston by participating in the New York City Marathon and posting a time of 2:56.39. In the Patriot's Day race, she started with the pack and soon disappeared among the hundreds of participants.

As the 26-mile–385-yard run concluded, Ruiz suddenly appeared near the leaders. Incredibly, she finished first among all female participants, recording the third fastest women's marathon time in history at 2:31.56. Race officials immediately whisked her to the winner's podium and placed a laurel wreath on her head.

But questions soon arose concerning her achievement. Other top runners could not remember Ruiz passing them and believed Canada's Jacqueline Gareau had led for most of the race. Still photographs and videotapes revealed no trace of the New Yorker in competition.

Two Harvard students later testified that they saw Ruiz enter the race from the crowd approximately one-half mile before the Boston Marathon finish line. Susan Morrow, a New York photographer, corroborated the findings by admitting seeing Ruiz take a subway during the running of the New York City event.

Despite having no positive evidence of fraud and no admission of guilt, race officials stripped Ruiz of the gold medal eight days later and declared Gareau the winner.

EXTRA POINT < < < < < < < < < < < < < < < < < < < <

What a way to win! Rosie smiled with the traditional laurel wreath resting on her head. Cheating obviously didn't bother her. She chose to ride the subway instead of run the course. But the victory soon turned to shame as her "winning strategy" became known.

God knows that shortcuts and cheating are tempting. Some people spend hours figuring out how to gain an advantage—legally or illegally—on the track, the court, the field, or the diamond. We long for the sweet taste of success, and sometimes we don't care how we get it. But the Bible reminds us how God feels about cheaters.

GOAL! *Explore the Internet for examples of fraud in sports, in business, and in life. Note the consequences. Ask God to help you always be honest in all areas of your life.*

NOTHING EXCITES BASEBALL PLAYERS and fans like a grand slam home run. And watching the same player hit two in the same inning seems almost unimaginable.

But in 1999, the St. Louis Cardinals visited the Los Angeles Dodgers with Fernando Tatis batting cleanup. Normally Eric Davis batted fourth for the Cards; however, a Davis injury caused Cardinal manager Tony LaRussa to move the third baseman into the cleanup spot.

The Dodgers took an early 2–0 lead, but in the top of the third, after two singles and a hit batsman, the bases were loaded for Tatis with no outs. After Los Angeles pitcher Chan Ho Park fell behind 2–0, Tatis blasted a fastball 450 feet into the left-field bull pen for a grand slam.

Park continued to struggle in the third, and the Cardinals kept pecking away. Three more runs crossed the plate for St. Louis, and Tatis returned to the plate, facing Park again with the bases loaded and two outs. Tatis worked the count to 3-1 then hammered Park's next pitch into the left-center pavilion for his second grand slam of the inning.

Only nine other players in baseball's history had slugged two bases-loaded home runs in a single game, and none had ever achieved the feat in just one inning. With his grand slam blast, Tatis also set a record for RBIs in a single inning, breaking the old mark of six.

> After Job had prayed for his friends, the Lord made him prosperous again and gave him twice as much as he had before.
>
> JOB 42:10, NIV

EXTRA POINT

< < < < < < < < < < < < < < < < < < < <

Fernando Tatis hadn't batted cleanup until Davis's injury. Tony LaRussa looked like a genius when his third baseman twice parked grand slams over the fence.

In the Bible, Job also experienced a "twice" blessing. The Lord first allowed Satan to test the obedient and faithful Job, and the man lost everything but his wife and his life. But when Job remained true to God and prayed for the friends who turned on him, the heavenly Father gave him twice as much as he had lost.

GOAL! *Read the list in Job 42:12-17 of all that the Lord restored to Job. Praise God for the blessings he gives us.*

23 APR

Encourage each
other and build
each other up,
just as you are
already doing.

1 THESSALONIANS
5:11

NOTHING INSPIRES an athlete's performance more than the confidence of family or teammates. David Robinson, "the Admiral," enjoyed the luxury of both as he pursued the NBA single-season scoring title in 1994.

With one game remaining, the San Antonio Spurs center trailed Shaquille O'Neal by three points in the race. San Antonio closed out the season on the road against the Los Angeles Clippers, while O'Neal's team, the Orlando Magic, hosted the New Jersey Nets.

Although the contest meant nothing in the NBA playoff pairings, it represented a special opportunity for the former Navy All-American.

Robinson tallied the first 18 Spurs points, but a stern Clipper defense held the 7-footer to six in the second quarter. Bolstered by his team's confidence, the Admiral rolled in the third period, racking up 19 points. With teammates continuing to feed him the ball, Robinson netted another 28 points in the fourth quarter—totaling 71 points in a 112–97 Spurs victory.

The San Antonio post joined Wilt Chamberlain, David Thompson, and Elgin Baylor as the only NBA players to score more than 70 points in a game. Later that day when O'Neal connected for 32 points, Robinson claimed the scoring crown.

EXTRA POINT < < < < < < < < < < < < < < < < < < < David Robinson not only inspired the confidence of his family and teammates, he also gained confidence from them. The supportive Spurs dished ball after ball to Robinson, sure he could take the title and doing what they could to help him to earn the honor. Robinson's teammates encouraged him to play his best.

God also wants us to encourage other Christians—after all, we're all on his team. It's a boost when others encourage us in life. We feel like we can accomplish anything when others show confidence in us.

GOAL! Decide which statement is more true for you:
- "Others have more confidence in me than I have in myself."
- "I have more confidence in myself than others have in me."

Praise God for friends and family who encourage us.

COMING FROM BEHIND is hard in any sport. The extra energy to make up a deficit taxes both the mind and the body. But the Pittsburgh Penguins persevered in a 1996 marathon hockey game.

Trailing the Washington Capitals 2–1 in their playoff series, the Penguins went on the road to even things up.

However, Washington took a 2–0 lead on power play goals by Michal Pivonka and Peter Bondra in the first and second periods. The comeback prospects appeared even more grim for Pittsburgh in the final seconds of the second period when superstar forward Mario Lemieux received an ejection for punching Todd Krygier.

The Penguins did pick up a goal on Jaromir Jagr's second-period tally. Then Pittsburgh tied the contest on a power play goal by Petr Nedved with 12 minutes left. At the end of regulation, Washington and Pittsburgh remained tied at 2–2.

Neither team scored in the first overtime or the second . . . or the third. Both goalies—Ken Wregget for the Penguins and Olaf Kolzig for the Capitals—stopped shot after shot. In the second overtime, Wregget saved Pittsburgh from defeat by snaring Joe Juneua's penalty shot awarded because Chris Tamer knocked the net from its moorings.

As the fourth overtime neared its conclusion, Jim Johnson entered Washington's penalty box for hooking. Pittsburgh took advantage of the shorthanded situation, and Nedved scored with 44.6 seconds remaining to give the Penguins a 3–2 victory in the third-longest playoff game in NHL history.

EXTRA POINT < < < < < < < < < < < < < < < < < < < < < The skaters on both teams must have been extremely tired at the end of what turned out to be nearly two whole games. Most likely their sore muscles ached, their dehydrated body felt thirsty, and their legs barely held up. Yet both teams persevered. They kept doing the best they could until Pittsburgh finally emerged victorious.

The writer of Hebrews understood the need to persevere in life. Sometimes being a Christian and doing what's right seems hard. Our "ministering muscles" ache. Our dehydrated spirit needs nourishment. Our godly attitude barely holds up. But if we ask, the heavenly Father helps us persevere so that we can receive all that he has promised.

GOAL! *Write your own definition of perseverance.*
Perseverance means _____

_____

_____

Praise God for his perseverance with you. Ask the Lord to help you persevere for him.

You need to persevere so that when you have done the will of God, you will receive what he has promised.

HEBREWS 10:36, NIV

25 APR

Forget the
former things;
do not dwell
on the past.

ISAIAH 43:18, NIV

EXPANSION FRANCHISES often struggle early in their existence. It took nine years for the Minnesota Timberwolves to record the team's first National Basketball Association playoff victory.

In 1998, Minnesota squeaked into the postseason with a 45–37 record to finish seventh in the Western Conference. With its mediocre record, few considered the club a championship contender. And drawing the No. 2 seed, the Seattle Supersonics, in the first round did little to inspire confidence.

The first contest in Seattle ended how most expected: with Minnesota going down 108–83. The loss dropped the Timberwolves' postseason record to 0–5, and prospects for a first playoff victory appeared bleak.

Game two, however, saw a different Minnesota team. Taking a 28–20 first-quarter lead, the T-Wolves never allowed Seattle to dominate. With the score tied 86–86, Michael Williams fed Kevin Garnett for a layup. Following a miss by Seattle's Detlef Schrempf, Stephon Marbury grabbed the loose ball and drove for another layup, giving the Timberwolves a four-point margin with 1:42 remaining.

The Supersonics closed the gap to 92–90 with 15.2 seconds to play, but Minnesota hit four free throws in the closing moments and held on to a 98–93 win.

EXTRA POINT < < < < < < < < < < < < < < < < < < < < < The Minnesota Timberwolves overcame a lot of past frustration with that win. After years without a playoff victory, the T-Wolves forgot about their history and strove to make a new, more successful future.

Sometimes in our life, we need to put away the past. The heavenly Father gives us memories for our enjoyment and education, but he doesn't want us to dwell there. In the Old Testament, the Lord told Isaiah to get ready for a new beginning. He was going to make a pathway for his people to come to him.

GOAL! *Do you know Christ as your Savior? If not, admit your sins and put your trust in Christ, who died for you. A simple prayer is all it takes. If you already serve God, do your friends and family members know Jesus? If not, ask God to help them start a new life with him.*

ORGANIZED BASEBALL around the world recognized Babe Ruth as the game's greatest living player on a Sunday afternoon in 1947. The ceremonies centered at Yankee Stadium, often called "the House That Ruth Built."

More than 58,000 fans filled the legendary facility where Ruth led the Bronx Bombers to four world championships from 1920 to 1934. Cardinal Francis Spellman prayed to open the pregame ceremonies that were broadcast to every major and minor league baseball stadium in the United States. The commissioner of baseball, along with the presidents of the American and National Leagues, made brief remarks before turning the microphone over to the Babe.

With his voice rasping due to throat cancer, Ruth spoke only a few words. He thanked those in attendance and said how much baseball meant to him and to the youth of America. Babe then retired to a box seat and watched the game.

When Ruth came to the Yankees from the Boston Red Sox in 1920, the team's attendance soared. A year later, the Yankees bought land in the Bronx to build their own stadium (they had been sharing the Polo Grounds with the New York Giants). Yankee Stadium opened on April 18, 1923, as baseball's first triple-decked structure.

From its opening to the end of the 2003 season, Yankee Stadium has hosted 33 World Series and has witnessed the home team claim 26 world titles.

EXTRA POINT < < < < < < < < < < < < < < < < < < < < Sometimes one athlete causes so much interest that he or she becomes almost bigger than the game. Babe Ruth did for the Yankees and Major League Baseball in the 1920s what Michael Jordan did for basketball and what Tiger Woods has done for golf in recent years.

Because of Ruth's tremendous skill and popularity, the Yankees built Yankee Stadium. The ballpark known as "the House That Ruth Built" has come to also be known as "the Home of Champions" because of all the world titles the Yankees have won.

As Christians we have the opportunity to go to "the Home of *the* Champion" every week. Jesus' victory over death makes him the greatest winner of all time. And all over the world, we can go into his "stadium"—the church—to worship and cheer for him.

GOAL! *Plan to attend a church service this week. Think about the holiness of God's house. Praise him that he's in our midst whenever we get together with other Christians to worship him.*

> For where two or three are gathered together in My name, I am there in the midst of them.
> MATTHEW 18:20, NKJV

27 APR

> The Lord does not look at the things man looks at. Man looks at the outward appearance, but the Lord looks at the heart.
>
> 1 SAMUEL 16:7, NIV

WHEN MOST PEOPLE THINK skateboarding, they think of Tony Hawk or Andy Macdonald. But don't be surprised if eventually the first name that will pop into a person's head is Ryan Sheckler.

Sheckler, the youngest competitor at the 2003 Gravity Games, surprised everybody—including three-time reigning champ Eric Koston—when he brought home the gold . . . and a check for $23,000. That'll buy a lot of video games and candy for the 13-year-old. Of course, he'd better stay away from the sticky stuff, because it'll ruin the work of his braces.

Out of the gate, it was obvious that it was Sheckler's day. The teen sensation led after the first round and never relinquished the lead. In fact, he just kept building on it. In his third and final run, Ryan coolly busted off a backside lipslide to a kickflip 180 alley-oop. Plus, he soared on a couple of lofty transfers over the midsection.

Koston, a pregame favorite, had to settle for fourth. Veteran competitor Rick McCrank, who's 14 years older than Sheckler, took second. And Chris Senn, the oldest skater in the competition, finished third.

EXTRA POINT < < < < < < < < < < < < < < < < < < < Athletes just seem to get better at a younger age these days. Ryan Sheckler was less than half the age of many of his competitors, but he performed like a veteran under pressure. His focused concentration and fluid combinations impressed the judges and the crowd as he brought home the gold.

In God's eyes, age doesn't matter. He looks at the heart. He cares about our spiritual maturity, not how many candles we blew out on our last birthday cake. Have you noticed how some teens make better decisions and act more maturely than some adults? It's true. You can be a gold-medal performer for God right now. Why wait?

GOAL! *Some teens use their age as an excuse to make poor decisions or to act wild. Commit to acting older than your age. Dedicate yourself to being a mature Christian and having a heart for God. Ask him to help you.*

MOST SPRINT RELAY TEAMS spend hours practicing handoffs and honing their timing to split-second precision. But when an extremely talented relay team forms at the last minute, surprising results can occur.

In the 2000 Penn Relays, the United States competed against squads from Africa, Asia, and the Caribbean. Just prior to the running of the women's 4 x 200, American coaches decided LaTasha Jenkins, LaTasha Colander Richardson, Nanceen Perry, and Marion Jones would comprise the United States Blue team. Once selected, the quartet decided to go all out for the world record in spite of their inexperience at handing the baton to each other.

With a crowd of 45,203 packing the stands at the Philadelphia track, Jenkins bolted to an early lead. After Colander Richardson took the baton, the margin increased. By the time Perry finished the third leg, the Americans owned a commanding lead.

Jones, who would later capture three gold medals in the 2000 Olympics, received the baton and blazed around the curve. As spectators chanted, "USA! USA!" the track star crossed the finish line in a time of 1:27.46. The Americans' clocking shattered the 20-year-old world record of 1:28.15.

The coaches saw the potential of this dream team. Then the women's swift legs, strong lungs, and sure hands combined for the win. They saw the time and exclaimed, "We did it!"

> You may say to yourself, "My power and the strength of my hands have produced this wealth for me." But remember the Lord your God, for it is he who gives you the ability to produce wealth.
> DEUTERONOMY 8:17-18, NIV

EXTRA POINT

< < < < < < < < < < < < < < < < < < <

We love it when we win in athletics, score high on a test, earn an honor, or simply hear the words "You did a great job." When we do, it's easy to think, *I did that!* But we forget that while our ability may have earned the prize, God gave us that ability.

Moses warned the Israelites to never forget that their achievements came from the Lord. And we shouldn't forget either.

GOAL! *Write down some of your special abilities.*

_____

_____

_____

Remember to thank him for giving you those skills.

29 APR

In everything you do, stay away from complaining and arguing.

PHILIPPIANS 2:14

THE GAME OF BASEBALL has long been known for its heated discussions after a close call. But as pitcher David Cone learned in 1990, arguing is best reserved for when time has been called.

The New York Mets visited the Atlanta Braves at Fulton County Stadium. In the fourth inning, with the Braves leading 2–1, Atlanta had runners on first and second with two outs when Mark Lemke came up against Cone. Lemke quickly tapped a slow roller to the first-base side of the field.

Mets second baseman Gregg Jeffries and first baseman Mike Marshall converged on the ball. Jeffries reached it and tossed it underhand to Cone, who was running toward first. The New York pitcher attempted to brush the base with his foot as he glided by, but umpire Charlie Williams called Lemke safe.

Cone became livid and followed Williams up the first-base foul line, protesting the call. In the meantime, the Atlanta runners continued rounding the bases. Mets catcher Mackey Sasser yelled for Cone to throw the ball home, but his cries went unheeded. The Braves scored two runs on the play before time was called. The official scorer chalked up the runs to "player indifference."

Cone stayed in the game but exited after allowing a two-run homer to Jeff Treadway in the fifth, and the Braves won 7–4.

EXTRA POINT < < < < < < < < < < < < < < < < < < < < < What useless and costly arguing. David Cone took his head out of the game when he took his protest down the line. Most likely he knew his complaint would be useless. Umpires almost never reverse calls. But Cone kept yelling anyway, costing his team two runs and a chance to get back in the game.

In the Bible, we learn that a wise person doesn't argue when it's pointless. But sometimes we're not wise. We get angry and argue when we know it won't make a difference. We focus on protesting a relatively insignificant action while the greater issue passes us by. God wants us to avoid arguing and speak valuable words.

GOAL! *This week, try to avoid arguing. Instead, concentrate on speaking positive words. Ask God for help.*

MAY

Similarly, if anyone competes as an athlete, he does not receive the victor's crown unless he competes according to the rules.

2 TIMOTHY 2:5, NIV

MOST SPORTS HAVE a vast rule book that governs the sport and covers tons of different situations. But baseball also has a bevy of unwritten rules. Seattle center fielder Mike Cameron showed his understanding of one of those rules in 2002.

The Seattle Mariners journeyed to Chicago for a series against the White Sox. In the top of the first, Cameron and Bret Boone earned a spot in baseball's record book. During a ten-run Mariners outburst, the teammates twice blasted back-to-back home runs. But Cameron's power display continued. He added a solo shot in the third inning and his fourth home run with two out in the fifth.

The fifth-inning homer tied the center fielder with 12 other major leaguers who had accomplished the feat of hitting four round-trippers in a single game. When they realized a record was within reach, a majority of the 12,891 folks in attendance switched their loyalties from the White Sox to Cameron and his quest for the home-run record. A chorus of boos reverberated through Comiskey Park in the seventh when pitcher Mike Porzio plunked the Seattle outfielder in the thigh.

One last opportunity awaited Cameron in the ninth. The count went to 3-0, and Porzio delivered a belt-high fastball that the 2001 Gold Glover took for strike one. After fouling off a pitch, Cameron belted a drive to deep right center, but Jeff Liefer snared the ball with a running, backhanded catch at the warning track.

EXTRA POINT < < < < < < < < < < < < < < < < < < < < < Why, some fans wondered, did Cameron not swing at the fat pitch down the middle on the 3-0 count? Baseball experts knew the reason. An unwritten rule says a player doesn't swing at a 3-0 pitch during a blowout, and Seattle was winning 15–4. The unwritten rule gives the opposing pitcher a small break in a bad situation.

Sometimes we think of the Bible as a rule book. While God's Word does contain rules like the Ten Commandments, it also provides principles, kind of like unwritten rules, such as treating others with kindness, fairness, friendliness, and mercy . . . to name just a few.

GOAL! *Identify some other unwritten rules in baseball or another sport. If you get stuck, ask a coach or a friend. Now come up with two or three good unwritten rules for life.*

Ask God to help you stick not just to his rule book but to his unwritten rules as well.

RAIN DELAYS CAN BE ANNOYING. Athletes don't know when their contest will begin; they may get fidgety and restless. But in the 1999 City of Hope Myrtle Beach Classic, golfer Rachel Hetherington waited patiently to rise to the top.

In Thursday's opening round, the 27-year-old Australian shot a 69, leaving her one shot off the pace. But eight inches of rain forced both Friday's and Saturday's rounds to be canceled—the first time the LPGA had reduced a tournament from 72 to 36 holes in 18 years.

On Sunday, Hetherington started slowly, taking a bogey on the first hole. But four straight birdies propelled her into the lead.

The backstretch, however, played a different tune. Consecutive bogeys on 11 and 12 left Hetherington two strokes behind Leta Lindley. Then birdies at 13 and 15, as well as difficult saves of par on 17 and 18, helped her finish with a 4-under-par 68.

Thinking her competitors would pass or tie her, Hetherington waited in the clubhouse for more than an hour. But every golfer faltered in the clutch. Lindley lipped a 5-foot par putt on 18 that would have forced a playoff. Fellow Australian Karrie Webb missed birdie putts on 17 and 18, and Helen Alfredsson drove into the rough on the final hole to settle for a par. The trio finished in a tie for second as Hetherington captured her third LPGA title.

> Be patient, then, brothers, until the Lord's coming. See how the farmer waits for the land to yield its valuable crop and how patient he is for the autumn and spring rains.
> JAMES 5:7, NIV

EXTRA POINT < < < < < < < < < < < < < < < < < < < < < < While she sat in the clubhouse, Rachel probably understood how farmers feel waiting for their crops. Every moment would have seemed like an eternity. But eventually, she saw the leaderboard and knew the title and $101,250 belonged to her.

In the Bible, James offers practical advice on waiting. When Christians of his day grew impatient, he reminded them to follow the example of farmers, who can't make rains come sooner or a plant grow faster. If they hurry the harvest by reaping early, they ruin or diminish the crop. When we grow impatient, we too can benefit by remembering James's words about farmers.

GOAL! *Buy some flowers for your mother or another female relative. Think about the gardener who grew the flowers needing to be patient before the plants turned into something beautiful. Ask God to help you be more patient.*

02 MAY

God will
strengthen you
with his own
great power so
that you will
not give up
when troubles
come, but you
will be patient.

COLOSSIANS
1:11, NCV

GOLD MEDALS WERE HARD to come by for the United States at the 2002 Mountain Bike World Championships. In a winner-gets-all-the-cash format, the world's best mountain bikers gave maximum effort to earn a little green to go along with the brown mud being kicked up by their knobby tires. Only Brian Lopes claimed gold for the United States in four-cross—an event that replaced dual slalom for the first time at the championships.

Four-cross (4X) matches four riders on a steep, short course (usually about three football fields long). The first rider to navigate the sharp turns, big jumps, and other pitfalls wins. Obviously not an event for the timid, this race requires competitors to be aggressive in order to be successful. One bump, wreck, or misstep spells defeat, as the race takes just minutes to complete.

Under sunny skies in Kaprun, Austria, the stage was set for a great showdown. Kaprun is known for two things: (1) a huge hydroelectric plant that supplies electricity to much of Europe and (2) awesome mountain-biking terrain. With perfect weather and a perfect course, Lopes rode his Fox/GT-sponsored bike to the gold. Teammate Eric Carter took bronze in the same event.

EXTRA POINT < < < < < < < < < < < < < < < < < < < <
Brian Lopes's victory in 4X juiced up the U.S. mountain biking team. His win provided the team with a lot of energy and excitement. But Lopes wasn't the only machine creating a stir at the World Championships. The Kaprun hydroelectric facility churned out energy for all of Europe as fans were electrified by the performances of the top mountain bikers in the world.

As Christians, we're tied into a power source that's infinitely stronger than the Kaprun hydroelectric station—and that Source is the one who created the rivers and mountains that allowed the station to be built in the first place. We often don't think about it, but God is the supreme Power Source.

GOAL! *What energizes you? Is it winning? The thrill of victory can pump you up. But after the jolt of excitement, there's always a letdown. With God, there is no letdown. His energy is limitless. His power is supreme. Ask God to allow you to tap into his power.*

THOUSANDS UPON THOUSANDS of runs have been scored in Major League Baseball's history. But in 1975, Bob Watson tallied a historic run.

During the 1975 off-season, statisticians calculated baseball's one millionth run would be plated in late April or early May. Seiko Watch Corporation joined the promotion of the notable event and sponsored scoreboards across the country reflecting the countdown.

A Saturday rainout forced the Houston Astros and San Francisco Giants to schedule a Sunday doubleheader. In the first game's second inning, Astros first baseman Bob Watson walked on four pitches. Jose Cruz followed with a second walk, and catcher Milt May stepped to the plate.

With May standing in the box and Watson on second, the run counter clicked down to one. Almost instantaneously, the catcher belted a home run, and the first baseman began jogging home. When he reached third, Houston teammates in the bull pen urged Bob to sprint home and ensure his spot in baseball history. Watson reached the plate with baseball's one-millionth run a second and a half before Cincinnati's Dave Concepcion, who homered at virtually the same time as May during a game in a different part of the country.

Baseball Hall of Fame officials stopped the game and dug up the historic home plate. They also requested May's bat and Watson's shoes, retrieved the home run ball from a fan, and placed the items in a special spot in Cooperstown, New York.

If you see your brother's donkey or his ox fallen on the road, do not ignore it. Help him get it to its feet.
DEUTERONOMY 22:4, NIV

EXTRA POINTS < < < < < < < < < < < < < < < < < < < < < < < Bob Watson experienced one of baseball's golden moments and will forever be remembered in that sport's Hall of Fame. He didn't make Cooperstown because of his years as an outstanding player. He made history because of his teammates' encouragement. If his friends hadn't helped him, somebody else probably would've taken the honor.

In the Old Testament, Moses talked about helping the people around him Just like Watson's teammates did everything they could to help him earn a once-in-a-lifetime honor, God wants you to help your friends when they need it. Don't walk away when God gives you the chance to assist your friends.

GOAL! *Describe an achievement in your life that you accomplished completely alone. If you can't think of one, you're normal. Now think of something you achieved because of help from friends, teammates, or family members.*

Praise God for help and encouragement from others.

04 MAY

HAVE YOU NEVER HEARD   OR   UNDERSTOOD?

DON'T YOU KNOW

THAT THE LORD IS

THE EVERLASTING GOD,

THE CREATOR OF ALL THE EARTH?

HE NEVER GROWS FAINT

OR WEARY.

ISAIAH 40:28

LONG OVERTIME GAMES tire out even the best athletes. In the

2000 National Hockey League playoffs, the Philadelphia Flyers and the Pittsburgh Penguins played to the brink of exhaustion.

The Flyers journeyed to Pittsburgh, attempting to even the best-of-seven series at two games apiece. But the Penguins took a 1–0 lead about two minutes into the game on Alexei Kovalev's slap shot from the high slot.

Philadelphia tightened defensively and didn't allow another Penguins goal. Then early in the third period, Daymond Langhow won a face-off in Penguins territory. The puck flew to Eric Desjardins, whose slap shot missed. But John LeClair redirected it into the net, tying the score at 1–1.

Neither team scored again before regulation time elapsed, and the contest went into overtime. Minute by minute, the players grew more weary, but no one could force the puck into the net. The Flyers and the Penguins played four full overtime periods with the scoreboard stuck at 1–1.

An unlikely hero emerged in the fifth extra period. Philadelphia's Keith Primeau, who had scored only seven goals in his 78 playoff games, carried the puck along the right wing boards. After putting a move on defenseman Darius Kasparaitis, he powered a wrist shot past goalie Ron Tugnutt to give the Flyers a 2–1 overtime win in the NHL's third-longest playoff game in history.

EXTRA POINT < < < < < < < < < < < < < < < < < < < < <

Even the Penguins probably breathed a sigh of relief when the game finally ended. Philadelphia likely won because Primeau knew where he planned to skate, and Kasparaitis's legs felt too tired to move quickly.

In life, we often grow tired. Our body needs rest and rejuvenation. Our mind becomes weary. When we reach exhaustion, others can't depend on us, and we can't depend on ourselves. We need recreation and relaxation.

God, on the other hand, never grows tired. He never becomes weary. The Lord is always ready to hear and help when we call.

GOAL! *Think of a time you grew so tired you couldn't function well. Thank God for being constantly alert and always available.*

05

You are
awesome,
O God, in your
sanctuary; the
God of Israel
gives power
and strength
to his people.
Praise be
to God!

PSALM 68:35, NIV

ON DAYS WHEN A PITCHER THROWS his best, hitters

complain that the baseball looks as tiny as an aspirin tablet. In 1998, Chicago Cubs pitcher Kerry Wood threw so well it gave the Houston Astros headaches.

The Astros visited Wrigley Field. Wood, a young right-hander making his fifth career start, began the game by striking out the first five batters.

In the second, the Cubs got on the scoreboard following Mark Grace's double and Henry Rodriguez's sacrifice fly. The rookie pitcher continued to dominate—whiffing one Astro in the third, two in the fourth, three in the fifth, and one in the sixth.

With his fastball approaching 100 mph and his breaking balls crossing the plate at unreachable angles, Wood appeared untouchable. Except for Ricky Gutierrez's third-inning single, no Houston player collected a hit.

The Cubs hurler gained even more strength as the game progressed. In both the seventh and the eighth, he struck out the side with 18 Ks through eight innings. Sensing a record-breaking performance, the crowd stood on every pitch, shouting, "Kerry! Kerry!"

In the ninth, Wood fanned pinch hitter Billy Spears on a 1-2 pitch for his seventh straight strikeout. Following Craig Biggio's groundout, the Cub rookie blew a 1-2 pitch by Derek Bell for the final out and his 20th strikeout of the game. Wood's effort tied the major league record set twice by Roger Clemens in 1986 and 1996.

EXTRA POINT < < < < < < < < < < < < < < < < < < < <

Imagine standing in the batter's box watching a baseball come at you at almost 100 miles per hour. *Scary!* Then imagine the ball changing angles at the last second. *Impossible!* Most sportswriters agree that hitting a pitched baseball is one of the most difficult accomplishments in sports.

God gives everybody special abilities. For many professional athletes, God's gifts are on display for everybody to see. Kerry Wood certainly showed off his talents in striking out 20 batters in one game.

The next time we witness an amazing athletic performance or do something pretty impressive ourselves, let's not forget where our power comes from.

GOAL! *The next time you ride in a car going 50 miles per hour, think of throwing a baseball twice that fast. Thank God for the many gifts he gives people.*

THE BOSTON CELTICS dominated the National Basketball Association for many years, winning a league-best 16 championships from 1957 to 1986. The Charlotte Hornets, on the other hand, didn't even become a team until 1988. But in the 1993 playoffs, Charlotte showed Boston that the "old" powers in basketball had passed away.

Down 2–1 in the opening round of the playoffs, the Celtics journeyed to North Carolina hoping to bring the series back to Boston for a fifth and deciding contest. But the Hornets kept Boston at bay and led by 19 points as the third quarter drew to a close.

The old Celtics spirit rekindled in the final 12 minutes. Boston mounted a tremendous comeback, taking a 103–102 lead with 42.7 seconds remaining. As the clock ticked down to 24.9 seconds, Charlotte appeared to give the game away when Kendall Gill missed a 16-footer and Boston's Robert Parish grabbed the rebound. But an official called Celtics Rick Fox for a ten-second backcourt violation, and the Hornets received one last opportunity.

Larry Johnson zeroed in on Xavier McDaniel. Johnson worked for a shot in the lane, but failed to connect with eight seconds left to play. The ball caromed out of bounds, and officials ruled that possession still belonged to Charlotte with the scoreboard showing 3.3 seconds. Given new life, Alonzo Mourning took the inbound pass from Dell Curry and nailed a 17-footer from the baseline, and the Hornets advanced to the next round with a 104–103 victory.

EXTRA POINT < < < < < < < < < < < < < < < < < < < < Dynasties come and go in sports. A strong team can turn into a weak squad in no time. The Celtics couldn't believe they lost to the upstart Hornets. But they did. Despite their long history, the team changed from champions to chumps. Of course, Charlotte felt surprised and elated. The old had gone. The new had come.

In the Bible, the apostle Paul writes to the Corinthian Christians about old and new. Accepting Christ as our Lord and Savior makes us different people. Our history is wiped away. We put aside our old selfish, sinful selves. We become a new creation in Christ.

GOAL! *Name some historically successful, consistently winning sports teams like the Celtics that have become mediocre. Why do you think this happened? Praise God for the new life he gives us when we pray to accept him. Thank him for turning us from chumps into champions.*

> If anyone is in Christ, he is a new creation; the old has gone, the new has come!
>
> 2 CORINTHIANS 5:17, NIV

07 MAY

POWER RULES IN MOST SPORTS.

But in 1973, Bobby Riggs showed that a slowdown tennis match could be devastating.

The 1939 Wimbledon champion garnered great press coverage with his constant put-downs of women's tennis. To back up his claims of male superiority, Riggs helped organize a special match between himself and 1970 Grand Slam winner Margaret Court. The event took place at the San Vicente Country Club, an isolated resort 38 miles northeast of San Diego, California.

The appeal of a 55-year-old man playing a 30-year-old woman caught the public's fancy. Televised worldwide on Mother's Day, the winner-take-all challenge drew more viewers than any tennis tournament in television history.

Riggs, a consummate showman, stole the spotlight from the more reserved Court. After presenting her with a pregame bouquet of roses, he proceeded to neutralize her powerful serve with an array of dinks and sliced ground strokes.

Playing more at the pace of a weekend country clubber than a world-class player, Riggs faulted on only 7 of 41 first serves, while the obviously nervous Court landed her first serve only 18 of 37 times and committed ten service errors. In just 57 minutes, the player 25 years her senior beat Court 6–2, 6–1.

EXTRA POINT

< < < < < < < < < < < < < < < < < < < <

Margaret Court couldn't seem to keep her cool on the court that day. The braggart, showboating Riggs didn't beat her. She beat herself. She let his words and her anger affect her play. She lost a match she should have won.

How many times in life has our anger gotten the better of us? And how many times have we spoken too quickly when we should have listened?

The book of James takes a look at the practical side of life and offers some sound advice. We should talk less, listen more, and keep our anger under control. That's good insight for an athlete or anyone else.

> My dear brothers, take note of this: Everyone should be quick to listen, slow to speak and slow to become angry, for man's anger does not bring about the righteous life that God desires.
>
> JAMES 1:19-20, NIV

GOAL!

Think of a time in sports when you or another player got angry and spoke out when listening would have been better. Write about a time when the same thing happened in a nonathletic life situation.

_____

_____

_____

Ask God to help you control your anger and your tongue.

RAIN MAKES THE GRASS GREEN. But it made fans' and competitors' faces red with frustration at the 2003 Gravity Games Bike Street finals. A steady drizzle turned the Masonite course into a slip-fest. The competitors got in only one run before the weather made riding impossible.

Even though the event was cut short, Dave Mirra, Ryan Nyquist, Steven McCann, and the other riders gave the fans plenty of oohs and aahs.

Mirra rode home with the gold after scoring 94.2 points and standing up all his tricks—something he hadn't done recently. Because the course was already getting a little slick in the first run, Mirra didn't know what to expect. Add to that the fact that he hadn't fared too well in recent street competitions, and he was as surprised as anyone about his placement. Mirra strung together a backwards 360 off the box and a single whip, double whip combination that left spectators slack-jawed. Then he pumped out a wallride to flare—something he'd never done successfully in competition.

Nyquist, a fellow Greenville, North Carolinian, ended up just a point away from gold. His 720 over the box, 540 on the quarterpipe, and flip over the spine were good enough for any highlight film. McCann rounded things out, pulling a 720 turndown along with other technical tricks to score 91 points and take third.

EXTRA POINT < < < < < < < < < < < < < < < < < < < < < < < Bike street competitions are tough enough under perfect conditions. But a slick course can spell disaster. Although fans stayed out in the rain chanting, "We want bike," organizers made the correct decision in calling the event after one run. The safety of the athletes was more important than a few thrills.

Safety is an important issue to God, too. He cares about our health. He watches over us every day. And he saves us from slipping into dangerous situations all the time. Because our heavenly Father controls everything, we'll never know how important he is to our safety. The psalmist knew about God's protection. He described God as our guard who never falls asleep.

GOAL! *Think back on a time when God rescued you from a dangerous situation. Thank him for his never-ending protection.*

He won't let your foot slip. He who watches over you won't get tired.
PSALM 121:3, NIrV

09 MAY

MANY SPORTS CHANGE AND EVOLVE. Until 1980

skydiving looked something like this: Jump out of plane, free-fall, deploy parachute, float gently to ground, repeat. But that year several skydivers experimented by jumping out of a plane holding Styrofoam boogie boards. Lying flat on the board, they'd "air surf" before opening their chutes.

It wasn't long—seven years to be exact—before French skydiver Joel Cruciani leapt from an aircraft with a surfboard strapped to his feet . . . and the sport of skysurfing was born.

Of course, tweaks still had to be made. Jerry Loftis became the first American to skysurf in 1990. Later that year at the first World Freestyle Championships in Texas, each surfer jumped with a cameraflyer, who videotaped the performer's entire routine so judges could easily score the competition from videotape.

The phenomenal speeds, mind-dizzying spins, tight tumbles, and amazing camera angles caught the public's attention as skysurfing started showing up in television commercials and sports shows. At the first X Games in 1995, ten skysurfing teams competed for the top prize, which went to Americans Rob Harris and Joe Jennings.

I am now controlled by the law of the Holy Spirit. That law gives me life because of what Christ Jesus has done. It has set me free from the law of sin that brings death.
ROMANS 8:2, NIrV

EXTRA POINT < < < < < < < < < < < < < < < < < < < <

People have always wanted to fly. Even before parachutes were invented, folks would jump off buildings with wings attached to their arms (definitely not a good idea). Skysurfing may be the closest to flying an athlete will ever get. By standing on the board, skysurfers can slow themselves down and cut across the sky. And by going upside down, these adrenaline junkies can spin and gyrate in ways not possible on the ground. There are few limits in the sky.

As Christians, we also have few limits. A relationship with Jesus frees us from sin and death and allows us to soar. God doesn't want our faith to bog us down and force us to crawl along the ground. Our heavenly Father desires for us to experience what true freedom is in him.

GOAL! *Imagine what it's like to surf through the air—the thrills, the exhilaration, the freedom. Realize that's why Jesus came to earth—to bring all those things into your life. We can thank God that true freedom from sin can only be found in him.*

NO PROFESSIONAL SEEMS TO ENJOY playing golf more than Shigeki Maruyama. But in the 2002 Verizon Byron Nelson Classic, the Japanese player had even more reason to smile.

Maruyama led by three strokes as the tournament entered its final day. Despite maintaining his margin, Maruyama struggled on the back nine with the muggy weather conditions and lack of wind.

After hitting out of a bunker on hole No. 10 and getting an unexpected birdie, he pulled his next drive into the water and needed an outstanding pitch to save a bogey. Maruyama also missed the green on 12 but made an 18-foot putt to record a par. He saved another par on 14 with a 9-footer.

Ben Crane, playing in the group ahead, staged a mini-rally. The 26-year-old rookie carded an eagle on 16, a birdie on 17, and a par on 18 to finish at a 12-under-par.

Maruyama's tee shot on 17 barely cleared the water. But the golfer (nicknamed "the Smilin' Assassin") chipped four feet from the hole to remain two shots ahead. After making a routine par on the final hole, he thrust his arms into the air and bowed to host Byron Nelson. For the day, Maruyama finished with a 68, giving him the tournament title at 14-under-par.

> A happy heart makes the face cheerful, but heartache crushes the spirit.
>
> PROVERBS 15:13, NIV

EXTRA POINT

< < < < < < < < < < < < < < < < < < < <

Some people constantly reflect joy and happiness. Smiles light up their face and reflect on those around them. Shigeki Maruyama always plays golf with a joyous expression. He spreads happiness on television or in person to those watching him. Spectators catch his contagious smile and spirit.

God wants our face to shine with the joy of his love. He wants our smiles to reflect our Lord and his refreshment. We are precious to the Father and to others who see his glory shining through us.

GOAL! *Describe a sports figure who always seems happy. Think of friends or acquaintances who constantly smile. Write down their names.*

_____

_____

Try to discover the source of their joy. Ask God to help you reflect him in your face and in your smile.

Knowing God leads to self-control. Self-control leads to patient endurance, and patient endurance leads to godliness.

2 PETER 1:6

BASEBALL NO-HITTERS are usually considered pitching gems. But in 2001, A. J. Burnett lacked the control that normally results in a no-hitter.

The Florida Marlins went on the road against the San Diego Padres. Burnett, after missing the season's first month with a stress fracture in his toe, drew his second starting assignment of the year. The right-hander, who had never thrown a complete game in his three-year major league career, exhibited characteristic wildness.

But inconsistency with the strike zone caught the opposing Padres off guard. Despite throwing only 65 of 128 pitches for strikes, allowing nine walks and hitting a batter, Burnett proved unhittable. Even though every San Diego regular reached base, the closest any Padre came to chalking up a hit occurred in the seventh

Alex Arias grounded a slow chopper behind the mound that shortstop Alex Gonzalez gloved with a sliding, backhanded stop. His throw went up the first-base line, and Arias attempted to leap over the tag of first baseman Derrek Lee. Despite being on his knees, Lee nicked Arias on the foot for the out.

In San Diego's ninth, Arias lined Burnett's first pitch straight to right fielder Eric Owens for out number one. Pinch hitter Santiago Perez struck out swinging. And Phil Nevin, a second pinch hitter, popped out to Gonzalez to end the game.

The Marlins, who scored two runs on Charles Johnson's two-run double in the third inning and a single run in the fifth, capitalized on the unconventional no-hitter for a 3–0 victory.

EXTRA POINT < < < < < < < < < < < < < < < < < < <
Who would have ever thought A. J. Burnett could throw a no-hitter? His record-setting game included lots of base runners and just over half his balls connecting for strikes. But in baseball, sometimes the lack of control works well.

The same thing can't be said about the Christian life. The Bible is clear: Self-control makes us more like God. Being wild isn't a characteristic for a follower of Jesus.

GOAL! *Think about areas in your life that are still a little wild. What could you do to bring them under control? Ask God to help you know him more, which leads to becoming more like him.*

ANYONE WHO QUALIFIES can play in an open professional golf tournament. That was proved at the 2001 U.S. Women's Open, which included a very young participant.

Morgan Pressel, a 12-year-old from Boca Raton, Florida, entered a 107-player qualifying tournament at Bear Lakes Country Club. The top five finishers in the qualifier earned slots in the prestigious LPGA event. The seventh grader at Omni Middle School started her athletic career as a tennis player, following the lead of her uncle, Aaron Krickstein, a former professional player. But on the advice of her grandfather, the young girl switched to golf.

The preteen, who began swinging a club at age seven, decided to play at Bear Lakes primarily for the experience of competing against top-caliber players. After her initial nervousness wore off, Morgan settled into a solid game. Her uncle Aaron served as her caddy and steadied his niece through the 6,300-yard course.

Through 16 holes, Pressel stood at 4-under-par and appeared to be a lock for an Open spot. Although she bogeyed the final two holes, her 2-under-par 70 made the grade for the 2001 tournament held at Pine Needles Lodge & Golf Club in Southern Pines, North Carolina. At age 12, Morgan became the youngest U.S. Open participant since Beverly Klass qualified at age ten in 1967.

EXTRA POINT < < < < < < < < < < < < < < < < < < < < Few professional sports remain as open to every athlete as the men's and women's U.S. Open. In theory, any player of any age who competes well enough in a qualifying tournament can make the field. Morgan Pressel took advantage of her opportunity.

Although Morgan shot 77 in each of the first two U.S. Open rounds and failed to make the cut, she made history and created a great memory for herself.

Isn't it cool that the U.S. Open is open to anyone? God's love is the same way. Plus, there's no qualifying tournament to get through. The Lord throws open his gates to all who believe and then rejoices when we come in.

GOAL! *Try to find other clubs or teams that are totally open. There aren't a lot. Usually there are tryouts and cuts. Praise God that he's open to anybody joining his team.*

Open for me the gates where the righteous enter, and I will go in and thank the Lord.

PSALM 118:19

> Since we died with Christ, we know we will also share his new life. We are sure of this because Christ rose from the dead, and he will never die again. Death no longer has any power over him. He died once to defeat sin.
>
> ROMANS 6:8-10

MANY PROFESSIONAL SPORTS leagues have come and gone. The American Basketball Association met its demise in 1976, but the final contest provided a glorious ending.

The New York Nets hosted the Denver Nuggets in the ABA championship series. Leading three games to two in the best-of-seven series, the Nets hoped to claim the title and avoid a trip back to Denver.

Despite the home-court advantage, New York trailed 80–58 with five minutes remaining in the third quarter. Desperate for a turnaround, the Nets changed to their "yellow" defense. In that setup, three defenders trapped the ball in the backcourt while two others patrolled the basket to prevent breakaways. The gambling defense rattled the Nuggets, and the Nets closed the gap to 92–78 at the quarter's end.

The pressure continued in the fourth quarter. Point by point, New York chipped away. Finally the Nets took a 106–104 lead with 2:19 left to play. At the 1:29 mark, Denver lost an opportunity to tie with a missed pair of free throws. The Nuggets never recovered, and the Nets captured the ABA's final crown with a 112–106 victory.

Julius Erving led the Nets with 31 points and received the Most Valuable Player award for the series. John Williamson fueled the New York comeback, scoring 24 of his 28 points in the second half.

EXTRA POINT < < < < < < < < < < < < < < < < < < < < < < The ABA may not have been able to make it financially, but the league went out in style with a glorious championship series.

But while the league died, four ABA franchises rose to life again to join the National Basketball Association. The New York Nets, the Denver Nuggets, the Indiana Pacers, and the San Antonio Spurs survived the merger. And many outstanding players transferred into the NBA.

The book of Romans explains how Jesus Christ broke the power of sin and defeated death. When we believe in Christ's death and resurrection, we also have power over death. Our earthly bodies may die, but we will rise again to live forever in heaven with our Savior.

GOAL! *Is there any sin holding back your relationship with Jesus Christ? Confess it and tap into God's power to overcome it. Praise Jesus that he defeated death and gives us power over sin.*

SWIMMING RECORDS have been broken frequently in recent years, although sometimes the difference comes down to only fractions of seconds. But almost 20 years elapsed before a swimmer shaved any time from the women's 200-meter butterfly mark.

The Sydney Aquatic Center's "fast pool," built for the 2000 Games, had proved to be a great place for record-breaking performances with six world marks falling in three days at the previous summer's Pan Pacific Championships. So when the 2000 Australian Olympic trials were held there, the competition was primed for more record-setting races.

Mary T. Meagher's 200-meter butterfly record set in 1981 at Brown Deer, Wisconsin, however, remained at 2:05.96. But Australia's Susie O'Neill, who had gone undefeated in the butterfly since 1994, vowed to take advantage of the opportunity. For the trials, she opted to wear a conventional neck-to-knee swimsuit rather than the newly developed full-length Fastskin to avoid controversy over her time.

At the 50-meter mark, O'Neill clocked 28.51, well inside the 29.53 world-record pace. Her split at 100 meters totaled 1:00.24, still over a second faster than the time needed to set a new mark. Through 150 meters, the 1996 Olympic gold-medal winner maintained a world-record margin. With the crowd of 10,126 roaring to urge her on, O'Neill touched the wall in a time of 2:05.81, breaking the old mark by 0.15 seconds.

Who else has held the oceans in his hand? Who has measured off the heavens with his fingers? Who else knows the weight of the earth or has weighed out the mountains and the hills?
ISAIAH 40:12

EXTRA POINT < < < < < < < < < < < < < < < < < < < < Decades-old records offer extra incentives for athletes. Conquering a time no one else has beaten in a generation makes the feat particularly special. And Susie O'Neill didn't want her world mark tainted by excuses of "It wasn't really Susie. It was the new Fastskin." So she chose to compete in a regular suit.

But as glorious as Susie O'Neill's record swim and other athletes' accomplishments are, no one on earth will ever touch God's greatness. He spoke everything into creation—even water for swimming. He scooped out the oceans and lakes. The Lord traced the rivers and streams with his fingers. He is awesome!

GOAL! *Spend time outside enjoying God's world. Go fishing, swimming, or canoeing. Thank him for a glorious creation.*

EVERYBODY LOSES. It's a fact of sports: If you compete, eventually you'll lose. Travis Pastrana learned that at the 2003 Gravity Games. During the first freestyle motocross competition broadcast live on network television, Pastrana didn't take the gold—something he'd done at every other Gravity Games he'd entered. But it wasn't for the lack of trying.

At the end of his first run, Pastrana crashed hard while trying to land a one-handed, one-footed backflip. The defending champ was knocked unconscious for a few moments before he came to and walked into the crowd to greet his fans. Then during a TV interview before his second run, Pastrana still seemed woozy and didn't remember anything about his first attempt. Doctors looked at Pastrana and advised him not to get back on his motorcycle.

Still on the top of the leaderboard with 87.5 despite his crash, Pastrana watched Nate Adams pull a killer run that included two backflips—one was a gigantic trick over the transfer—and a ton of other solid stunts. Nate's score of 91 knocked Pastrana out of first in the most-watched FMX competition of all time.

EXTRA POINT < < < < < < < < < < < < < < < < < < < < By constantly pushing to the next level and taking chances, Travis Pastrana became a legend in freestyle motocross. However, after a head injury, Pastrana showed that he wasn't willing to do something stupid. He followed the doctor's opinion and sat out his second run—even though he knew it might cost him the gold. His long-term health proved more important than short-term glory at the Gravity Games.

In our Christian life, we're often faced with the same decision: Do we make a bad decision for temporary excitement or do the right thing and gain long-term joy? Looking at it that way makes the decision seem easy, but it's a lot more difficult when we're caught in the heat of the moment, such as being offered alcohol or being tempted sexually.

GOAL! *Decide right now where you stand on premarital sex and underage drinking. By setting that choice in stone, you'll be better able to make the right decision when temptation comes. Ask God to give you the strength to do the right thing.*

BUT RUN AWAY
FROM THE EVIL
YOUNG PEOPLE
LIKE TO DO.
TRY HARD
TO LIVE RIGHT
AND TO HAVE
FAITH, LOVE, AND
PEACE, TOGETHER
WITH THOSE WHO
TRUST IN THE
LORD FROM
PURE HEARTS.

2 TIMOTHY 2:22, NCV

Remember the wonders he has done, his miracles, and the judgments he pronounced.

1 CHRONICLES 16:12, NIV

EVERY PROFESSIONAL ATHLETE wants to be remembered in history. In 1998, David Wells made a little history by joining the ranks of only 13 others who had achieved perfection on the mound during the 20th century.

The New York Yankees engaged the Minnesota Twins on a Sunday afternoon at legendary Yankee Stadium. Wells, three days shy of his 35th birthday, drew the starting assignment.

Wells never showed his age or slowed down as the game wore on. With an array of fastballs, changeups, and cutters, he kept every Twins batter off balance. In the seventh, the pitcher went to a 3-2 count on Brent Gates but enticed the second baseman to bounce out to first base. The next hitter, Paul Molitor, worked the count to 3-1 but took a fastball on the corner for a strike. He went down swinging on the next pitch to end the inning.

With 49,820 partisans standing on their feet and holding their breath in the ninth, Wells retired Jon Shave on a fly ball to shallow right for the 25th consecutive out. Javier Valentin struck out swinging, and Pat Meares lofted a short fly ball down the right-field line that Paul O'Neill squeezed for the final out in a 4–0 Yankee triumph. In pitching his perfect masterpiece, Wells threw 120 pitches with 79 counting as strikes.

EXTRA POINT < < < < < < < < < < < < < < < < < < < < < David Wells and his family cherish that May day. His teammates loved being part of David's perfect game. They'll likely talk about it all through their lives. Each one played his role and helped make Wells' special moment possible.

In life, we value memories of athletic accomplishments, team victories, and shared defeats that bond us closer together. We treasure holidays with family, times with friends, and moments with someone special.

King David encouraged God's people to remember the Lord. God showed his power many times to the Israelites in history-making ways.

GOAL! *What are some memories that you cherish? Write a few of them down.*

_____

_____

_____

Share them with a family member, friend, or teammate. Thank God for memories that have value.

CLOSE COMPETITIONS often make for exciting endings. Heading into the skysurfing finals at the 2000 X Games, the top three teams all had a chance for the gold. But in the end, nobody could overcome Stefan Klaus and Brian Rogers.

The team of skysurfer Klaus and cameraflyer Rogers didn't pull the most technical routines. However, their style, their close flying quarters, and their unique moves put them a cut ahead in the judges' eyes.

Coming into the competition, Eric Fradet and Alex Iodice were favored. And they began the final day by putting together an incredibly technical jump to score 97 points. However, a low score on their third-round jump kept them from the top. Valery Rozov and Clif Burch found themselves in the mix as they entered their final attempt just 13 points behind Klaus and Rogers. However, a poor performance cost them a chance at No. 1.

But Klaus and Rogers didn't falter. They ended the competition the same way they'd started it—by turning in the top score. Their average of 95.8 points over six rounds gave them the gold medal and $18,000 in prize money—the largest monetary prize to that date in skysurfing. Rozov and Burch averaged 94.6 to claim the silver, while Fradet and Iodice averaged 94.1 per jump.

EXTRA POINT < < < < < < < < < < < < < < < < < < < <
Consistency was the key for Stefan Klaus and Brian Rogers. By not posting a bad score, they won the gold at the 2000 X Games. Both athletes trusted the other to be in the right place at the right time as they fell to the ground at speeds of more than 100 mph. Tightly packed twists and smooth transitions between tricks demonstrated the hard work the team had put into doing well.

God wants us to show that same kind of teamwork in our Christian life. We need to trust fellow believers and work together to build up God's kingdom.

They started on their journey to serve Jesus Christ. They didn't receive any help from those who aren't believers. So we should welcome people like them. We should work together with them for the truth.

3 JOHN 1:7-8, NIrV

GOAL! *God knows you work best with a friend or as a team. Who are some of your teammates from church or school?*
Thank God for partners who make you more effective for him.

18 MAY

All who heard
him were
amazed at his
understanding
and answers.

LUKE 2:47, NCV

HOW OLD DOES AN ATHLETE have to be to be considered the greatest of all time in his or her sport? Does 16 sound too young? But that's exactly how old Dallas Friday was at the 2003 X Games Wakeboarding competition. Experts already considered Friday the best women's rider of all time, and she proved it again by taking home her second freestyle gold.

The teenager locked up the victory with possibly the cleanest run in X Games history. She combined an air rally, frontside front roll, and a tantrum off the kicker jump to take first. Melissa Marquardt finished second with Emily Copeland earning third.

On the men's side, Danny Harf thrilled the packed crowd at Long Beach Marine Stadium in California by winning his third-straight X Games men's title. Harf's 93.7-point run was highlighted by a perfect 900 combined with a whirlybird 720 off the double-up jump. Parks Bonifay claimed second with 81.1 points, and Daniel Watkins earned third—a point behind Bonifay.

Even with the men pulling big-time moves, the first X Games wakeboarding event held in California truly belonged to the ladies.

EXTRA POINT < < < < < < < < < < < < < < < < < < < < < <
What would it feel like to be called the greatest female wakeboarder of all time with so much of your life ahead of you? Kind of overwhelming, huh? But if you look around, you'll see a lot of teenagers who are among the world's best at their sport. Child prodigies come from around the globe. You see gymnasts, ice skaters, soccer players, and skateboarders claim big-time prizes before they're out of braces. Golfer Tiger Woods first appeared on television when he was three.

Not surprisingly, the Bible tells us that Jesus was a child prodigy. When he visited the temple in Jerusalem as a child, he amazed everybody with his knowledge about God's Word.

GOAL! *What would you like to be known for? Your goal-scoring ability in soccer? Your speed on the ice? Your bone-crunching tackles? Your gracefulness on the court? How about your knowledge of God's Word?*

By studying the Bible every day and memorizing verses, you can follow in Jesus' footsteps and learn things that will benefit you for a lifetime.

ANY TIME AN ATHLETE APPEARS to be putting his desires above team goals, he subjects himself to criticism—especially if his team loses. In the 2001 NBA playoffs, Vince Carter found the public questioning his decision.

The Toronto Raptors and the Philadelphia 76ers took their Eastern Conference semifinal series to the full seven games. The deciding contest was scheduled for a Sunday evening in Philadelphia, the same day as Carter's graduation ceremonies at the University of North Carolina.

Carter, who earned a degree in Afro-American studies, elected to fly in Raptor owner Larry Tanenbaum's private jet to Chapel Hill, North Carolina, and participate in the exercises. Leaving before the commencement address, he arrived back in Philadelphia five hours prior to tip-off.

Other than a bit of early sluggishness, Carter suffered no apparent effects from his quick jet jaunt. Both teams struggled offensively. With 2:34 remaining in the game, the Sixers held an 88–84 lead. The teams then traded misses before Dell Curry nailed a three-pointer for the Raptors that cut the margin to 88–87 with less than a minute to play.

Philly's Allen Iverson and Eric Snow both missed jumpers before Toronto rebounded with 3.6 ticks on the clock. Following a nonshooting foul, Carter hustled from right to left, took the inbound pass, and fired a last-second shot that bounced off the rim at the buzzer. Philadelphia claimed the hard-fought victory and continued in the playoffs.

> Then the people of Ephraim asked Gideon, "Why have you treated us this way? Why didn't you send for us when you first went out to fight the Midianites?" And they argued heatedly with Gideon.
>
> JUDGES 8:1

EXTRA POINT

< < < < < < < < < < < < < < < < < < < < <

In athletics, it's easy to play the blame game. Everyone searches for reasons in a loss. The criticism becomes most vocal when an errant play comes near the end of a game.

Vince Carter saw his college graduation as a once-in-a-lifetime opportunity. Never again could he walk across the stage to receive his diploma. Unfortunately, fans forgot all the missed shots by other players earlier in the game, remembering only Carter's final effort. They criticized him even though nothing could change his decision after the game.

In the Bible, Gideon received his share of criticism. The Ephraimites blamed Gideon for not calling them to fight Midian. Would the outcome have been different? We don't know, but we do know that results don't change after a battle—or game—is over.

GOAL! *Have you ever blamed someone else for your loss? Ask God to keep you from playing the blame game.*

20 MAY

I am the Lord,
I do not change.

MALACHI 3:6, NIrV

WHAT DO YOU GET when you combine snowboarding, surfing, and skateboarding? A severe head injury? Close . . . just kidding. It's actually the sport of mountainboarding.

Mountainboarding began in the 1990s as the popularity of snowboarding and skateboarding skyrocketed. Mountainboards are basically the same size as a snowboard with a few big differences: They have tires, a suspension system, and brakes. The larger surface, bindings, and big wheels allow riders to attack difficult mountain terrain. But you can also find mountainboards on city streets, dirt roads, BMX tracks, and grassy ski slopes. Mountainboarding was first highlighted during the 2000 Summer Gravity Games, but U.S. Olympic Snowboard Team members have trained with these supersized skateboards since 1996.

Of course, you can't have a sport without competition. Mountainboarders compete in boardercross (where at least four racers try to reach the finish line first while navigating a sloping dirt course with jumps, turns, and berms), downhill (where speed and clean, rounded turns are key), and freestyle (where 360s, grabs, and flips earn top honors).

EXTRA POINT < < < < < < < < < < < < < < < < < < < < < When your grandparents were your age, they probably didn't have a lot of choices when it came to athletics. Baseball, football, basketball—the big three—ruled the sporting landscape. But today the choices seem endless.

Mountainboarding takes the best elements of several popular sports and brings them up a notch. The changes made to a mountainboard—especially the hand brake—make it a viable sport for athletes who want to snowboard year-round.

Change is a natural part of life, just like it is in sports. You've probably noticed that few things stay the same. Families can separate. Friends move away. Teachers come in and out of your life. But there is one thing that never changes: God. You can count on him and trust him to be the same loving, caring God forever.

GOAL! *Do you ever feel overwhelmed by change? Change can be good, but it comes in many flavors. Sometimes change hurts. At those times it's good to know that God never changes. You can thank God for being rock solid in your life.*

WHEN A SOCCER TEAM plays as one, it truly becomes a beautiful game. In a 1999 warm-up game for the Women's World Cup, the togetherness of the United States National Team elevated Mia Hamm to new soccer heights.

More than 10,000 fans flocked to Orlando's Citrus Bowl to witness the United States take on Brazil. In the United States' previous exhibition contest against Holland at Chicago's Soldier Field, Hamm tied the international scoring record of 107 goals held by Italy's Elisabetta Vignotto.

As a scoreless first half reached the final seconds, Michelle Akers of the U.S. team lofted the ball to Hamm about 40 yards from Brazil's goal. Hamm nodded the ball to Kristine Lilly, who popped a pass to Cindy Parlow at the top of the penalty box. Parlow shielded her defender away and fed the ball back to Hamm, who cut toward the goal. The former North Carolina All-American evaded her defender and drove the ball through the legs of Brazilian goalkeeper Didi from ten yards away. The United States bench emptied onto the field to congratulate Hamm, who was playing in her 172nd international match.

The Americans maintained their pressure on the Brazilians in the second half. In the 72nd minute, Lilly knocked the ball off her knee and into the net for her 72nd international goal, the sixth highest of all time. The United States scored again with less than three minutes remaining and claimed a 3–0 victory.

Then make me truly happy by agreeing wholeheartedly with each other, loving one another, and working together with one heart and purpose.

PHILIPPIANS 2:2

EXTRA POINT

< < < < < < < < < < < < < < < < < < <

The U.S. National Soccer Team stood united by country and uniform. They also showed chemistry in practice and during games. Each player's ability to know where her teammates would be on the field greatly improved the team's effectiveness.

Great teammates keep sports fun and make success possible. In life, we need other people to enjoy shared moments and reach common goals. Paul knew that. He encouraged the Christians in Philippi to work together.

GOAL! *Write down some qualities of a good teammate.*

_____

_____

How could those same traits help you in your walk with Christ? Praise God for close teammates and friends.

22 MAY

A glorious throne, exalted from the beginning, is the place of our sanctuary.

JEREMIAH 17:12, NIV

NOTHING HELPS A BASEBALL TEAM to victory more than a big first inning. In 1952, the Brooklyn Dodgers erupted for the biggest beginning ever seen in the 20th century.

The Dodgers entertained the Cincinnati Reds at Ebbets Field. After retiring the Reds in the top of the first, the "Boys of Summer" (a nickname bestowed on the Dodgers by author Roger Kahn) came to bat.

Ewell Blackwell, the Reds pitcher, got out the first hitter, Billy Cox, on a grounder to third. But following a walk to Pee Wee Reese, Duke Snider homered. Then Jackie Robinson doubled, Andy Pafko walked, and George Shuba singled. Cincinnati sent Blackwell to the showers, and Bud Byerly came in to pitch.

An attempted double steal resulted in out number two with Pafko thrown out at third. But the offensive onslaught continued as Byerly allowed a walk and five straight singles before being replaced by Herman Wehmeier. The Reds right-hander fared no better, walking Snider, plunking Robinson, and giving up a single to Pafko before being replaced by Frank Smith.

With the score at 10–0, Smith struggled as well. Seven more Dodgers stepped to the plate for three walks, two singles, and a hit batsman before Snider took a curveball for third strike.

At the end of the first inning (which lasted for 59 minutes), Brooklyn had scored 15 runs, collected 10 hits, and sent 21 batters to the plate. The 11,850 spectators sat back and watched the Dodgers cruise to a 19–1 win in the sanctuary of Ebbets Field.

EXTRA POINT < < < < < < < < < < < < < < < < < < < Games that begin in exalted fashion for a team, especially the home team, give fans a glorious experience. Nobody worries about the outcome. No one experiences tension. Everybody relaxes, confident of victory.

When we know Jesus Christ personally, we can live without worry because we have confidence of our victory in the end. God's glorious throne was exalted from the beginning of time. The prophet Jeremiah wrote about that throne as our sanctuary, our resting place, our shelter. Nobody worries there. No one experiences tension. Hallelujah!

GOAL! *Review some baseball box scores in the newspaper. Note particularly the tone set at the beginning of the game. Praise God for his glorious throne.*

BATTING SLUMPS can frustrate players, managers, and fans. But in 2002, Shawn Green overcame his hitting struggles in a record-setting way.

The Los Angeles Dodgers jetted to Milwaukee to face the Brewers. A few days earlier, Dodgers manager Jim Tracy had benched Green after he went 0–18, batting only .231 with three homers.

Put back in the lineup against Milwaukee, the right fielder began the game with a bang. His RBI-double in the first inning gave Los Angeles a 1–0 lead. In the slugger's next three at bats, he tagged Glendon Rusch for a three-run home run in the second and belted solo shots off Brian Mallette in the fourth and fifth.

But the 29-year-old outfielder wasn't finished. After lining a single to center in the eighth, Green batted for a final time in the ninth. Looking for a pitch to drive, Green powered Jose Cabrera's offering 450 feet into the right center field stands for his fourth homer of the evening, tying the major league mark.

In the 16–3 rout, Green not only tied 13 others for the single-game home-run record, he also set a new standard for total bases in a single game. Green's 19 bases coming from the four homers, one double, and one single broke the old record of 18 set by Joe Adcock in 1954.

EXTRA POINT < < < < < < < < < < < < < < < < < < < < < < < Wow! What a way to end the frustration. Shawn Green couldn't have scripted the end of his slump any better if he had been writing a movie. In fact, a director would probably have changed the scene because the truth seemed so unbelievable.

King David suffered through a lot of slumps too. The Old Testament records many of the ups and down in this man's life. But one thing is for sure: David always had a heart for God. He kept trusting, even in the hard times. David is quoted in the New Testament, talking about how faith affects attitude. And we could all learn something from this great king.

GOAL! *Discuss with a friend how living with a positive attitude makes a difference. Pray that God will help you live with enjoyment and satisfaction.*

I know the Lord is always with me. I will not be shaken, for he is right beside me. No wonder my heart is filled with joy, and my mouth shouts his praises! My body rests in hope.

ACTS 2:25-26

At all times, pray by the power of the Spirit. Pray all kinds of prayers. Be watchful, so that you can pray. Always keep on praying for all of God's people.

EPHESIANS 6:18, NIrV

ANY ATHLETE WHO WANTS to play goalie in lacrosse may need to get his head examined. Wearing little padding and facing shots exceeding 100 mph, lacrosse goalies have a difficult chore.

Still, a good goalie makes the difference between winning and losing. That fact was proven during the 2003 NCAA Division I men's lacrosse championships as Virginia goalie Tillman Johnson got on a roll and led his team to the title.

The Cavaliers entered the postseason ranked No. 2 in the nation. After battling through the early rounds, Virginia met top-ranked Johns Hopkins in the finals at M&T Bank Stadium in Baltimore. The Blue Jays had beaten Virginia 8–7 during the regular season, and Johnson made sure the outcome was different this time.

The Cavs got on the board early as their first two shots found the back of the net. And they built a 5–0 edge in the second quarter thanks to three goals by A. J. Shannon. Johns Hopkins narrowed things to 5–3, but Virginia held a 6–4 margin at halftime.

In the second half, Johnson stepped up. With his team ahead 8–5, he made three monster saves early in the fourth. His 13 saves in the game helped the Cavaliers earn a 9–7 victory.

EXTRA POINT < < < < < < < < < < < < < < < < < < < < < < < Many people think lacrosse goalies don't have a prayer trying to stop bouncing, speedy, well-placed shots. But Tillman Johnson shows it's possible. With a career-high 18 stops in the semifinals and 13 saves in the finals, Johnson earned first All-American status and helped Virginia win the national title.

While many of us wouldn't have a prayer trying to guard a lacrosse goal, we can all pray to God. We can share our problems with him, ask for his comfort or just tell him about our day. God cares about all our needs. The Bible tells us to pray all the time about all kinds of things. Because the Holy Spirit is in our life, our prayers have power. But God doesn't want us to pray only for ourselves—he wants us to pray for other Christians as well.

GOAL! *How often do you pray? What do you pray about? Remember to constantly communicate with God.*

TECHNICALLY, A SOCCER GAME lasts only 90 minutes. Referees, however, add extra time at the match's end for stoppage that occurs during the game. In 1999, three extra minutes in the European Club Champions Cup proved to be a historic 180 seconds for Manchester United.

The United Kingdom's premier soccer club had already captured the English Premier League crown and the Football Association Cup. Winning the European Club Champions Cup would represent the equivalent of claiming both the World Series and the Super Bowl to British soccer fans.

In the finals, United's chances of completing the "treble" appeared bleak. With the full 90 minutes played, Bayern Munich led 1–0, and the Union of European Football Associations representatives prepared to make the official presentation to the German club.

But the field official tacked on three minutes to compensate for injury time during the match. In the 91st minute, Manchester's David Beckham kicked from the corner. Substitute Teddy Sheringham picked up the Bayern attempted clearance at the edge of the area and twisted around to send the ball into the corner of the net, tying the score 1–1.

Less than a minute later, Beckham made a second corner kick. Norwegian striker Ole Gunnar Solskjaer pounced on the ball and slammed it into the net from close range. Time ticked away until the referee blew the whistle. Then the more than 30,000 Manchester United faithful at Barcelona's Camp Nou stadium sang in joy, celebrating the 2–1 victory.

> Can all your worries add a single moment to your life? Of course not.
>
> MATTHEW 6:27

EXTRA POINT

< < < < < < < < < < < < < < < < < < < <

In most sports when the clock ticks down to 00:00, the game's over. But soccer officials normally add extra time to make up for substitutions and injuries that occurred during play. So the game isn't necessarily over when it's over. Time can be extended, like it was at the European Club Champions Cup. And Manchester United benefited.

The same can't be said about life. Jesus made it clear when he said that a single moment cannot be added to your life. God has given you a certain amount of time on this planet. Do your best to make the most of it before the clock reads 00:00.

GOAL! *What are some of the things you'd like to accomplish for yourself and God before you go to heaven?*

Praise God for the time he gives you on earth.

26 MAY

COMING BACK from a three-games-to-one deficit in a seven-game playoff is one of the most difficult feats in sports. The pressure is immense as one more loss will end the season for good. But in 2000, the New Jersey Devils surprised the Philadelphia Flyers to advance to the National Hockey League championship series.

New Jersey's Stanley Cup prospects appeared bleak as they trailed the Flyers 3–1. But the Devils rebounded with a 4–1 road win and a 2–1 triumph at home. The two victories forced a seventh and deciding game in Philadelphia.

In the seventh game, New Jersey took the early lead on a first-period power play. Jason Arnott fired a pass from behind the net through the legs of defenseman Chris Therien to Patrik Elias, who shot the puck past goalie Brian Boucher.

The Flyers knotted the contest with 6:01 left in the second period as Rick Tocchet scored. With the third period drawing to a close, the contest appeared to be headed into overtime. But as the time ticked down to less than three minutes, New Jersey's Arnott centered the puck toward the net. Elias lifted the stick of defenseman Dan McGillis in the slot. Sneaking off his check, Elias flipped a shot over Boucher's right shoulder. Philadelphia never regrouped, and New Jersey rode the 2–1 triumph into the Stanley Cup finals.

EXTRA POINT < < < < < < < < < < < < < < < < < < < < < <
Needing only one victory in three games, Philadelphia most likely had no doubt they would play in the Stanley Cup finals. Their fans could taste it. The players could see it. But Philadelphia lost first one, then two, then three games in a row.

In life, like in sports, situations change. What we believe will happen doesn't always happen. What we think should happen sometimes changes.

Solomon is considered the wisest man in the Bible. He wrote several books, including Ecclesiastes. In that book, he reminds us that we can't tell the future. Instead of counting our victories before the final whistle, we need to trust God.

GOAL! *Surely you have dreams and goals for your future. And you should! God has dreams for you too. His dreams go far beyond what you could imagine, but you have to stay close to him to find out what he has planned for you. Ask God to help you accept his choices.*

FOR NEARLY THREE YEARS, Jamie Bestwick missed competing in an X Games bike event. Whether his foot was healing in a boot or his arm was resting in a sling, injuries kept Bestwick—one of the best riders in the world—out of the Games. But Bestwick returned with a bang at the 2003 X Games Global Championships by pulling a new trick out of his bag.

The final event of the Games pitted Team Europe against Team USA in the Bike Vert competition. With the United States already wrapping up the top overall prize at the Men's Ski Superpipe, the riders competed for personal pride and bragging rights. Bestwick earned both with the first ever tailwhip flair pulled in competition—that's where the rider flies off the halfpipe, flairs away from the bike, and spins the entire machine all the way around before catching the pedals with his feet and landing it. It's a got-to-see-it-to-believe-it kind of move, and it easily won Bestwick first place.

Team USA's Kevin Robinson and Dave Mirra took second and third. Robinson's no-handed corkscrew flair, 540, and tailwhip over the elbow garnered him the silver. Mirra hit a good final run by landing a tailwhip 540 and double tailwhip that earned him the bronze.

EXTRA POINT
< < < < < < < < < < < < < < < < < < < < < < Jamie Bestwick didn't just limp back into X Games competition; he returned healthy and with a new arsenal of tricks. For months he had worked on the tailwhip flair, and he pulled it at the perfect time to win gold.

Anyone who doesn't know Jesus Christ limps through life. Without a Savior, no one is complete. The Bible says Jesus brings us back to wholeness through him. The old injuries of sin disappear. God's newness of life takes over. We gain strength and the ability to love through Jesus. And now we have the ability and the command to go out and tell others about him.

GOAL! *Can you think of anything that's different about you since you accepted Jesus into your life? Write these things down.*

_____

_____

_____

Thank God for giving you a new life.

> All this newness of life is from God, who brought us back to himself through what Christ did. And God has given us the task of reconciling people to him.
> 2 CORINTHIANS 5:18

28 MAY

We wait in
hope for the
Lord; he is our
help and our
shield. In him
our hearts
rejoice, for we
trust in his
holy name.

PSALM
33:20-21, NIV

AMERICANS HAVE ALWAYS LOVED the mile race in track, but years have elapsed since the United States fielded a top contender. In 2001, however, hopes renewed as a new miler rose to the forefront.

The 27th annual Prefontaine Classic (named for legendary distance runner Steve Prefontaine) took place on the University of Oregon's Hayward Field in Eugene. Alan Webb, a recent graduate of South Lakes High School in Reston, Virginia, joined a stellar group of Olympians and world-record holders in the mile run.

As the race began, the future University of Michigan runner fell to the back of the 16-man pack. But Webb maintained a solid pace, clocking a 1:58 at the midway point. He moved from last to 12th place during the third lap and passed the 1320-yard mark at 2:58.4, perfect timing to record a sub-four-minute mile.

With Hicham El Guerrouj of Morocco, a four-time world champion and the 2000 Olympic silver medalist in the 1,500 meters, leading the pack, Webb kicked into high gear. He passed six runners in a span of 80 yards over the backstretch of the final lap. With the crowd of 11,211 screaming, Webb sprinted the last 100 yards and finished fifth at 3:53.43, breaking Jim Ryan's American high school record of 3:55.30 set in 1965. El Guerrouj took first place at 3:49.92, the fastest outdoor mile ever run in the States.

EXTRA POINT < < < < < < < < < < < < < < < < < < < < < <
Even though the Olympics now offers competition in the 1,500 meters rather than the mile, tradition dictates its inclusion in many U.S. meets. And for 36 years, America waited for an outstanding miler. Alan Webb proved to be worth the wait. Although he didn't win that day, his record-breaking performance offered hope. An American high schooler could once again run a mile in under four minutes.

Many times in life we find ourselves waiting for something—or someone—to put our hope in. We naturally want to believe in something greater than ourselves.

The psalmist knew who was worth putting our hope in. He knew the wait would be worthwhile because his hope and trust were in the Lord, the almighty God. And we share that sure, secure hope.

GOAL! *Try to walk, jog, or run a mile. Time yourself. How close did you get to four minutes? Keep trying. Ask God to help you wait for the Lord and trust him.*

SEAN ELLIOTT WILL LONG be remembered in San Antonio as a great player with a role in an amazing comeback story. And in 1999, he orchestrated a San Antonio Spurs victory that fans and writers refer to as the "Memorial Day Miracle."

The Spurs hosted the Portland Trailblazers in the second game of the NBA Western Conference finals. With a four-point outburst after halftime, Portland jumped to a 52–34 lead. However, San Antonio countered with a 17–2 run and narrowed the gap to 54–51.

San Antonio could never take the lead but closed the gap to 73–72 with 5:25 left to play. After several baskets by both teams, Damon Stoudamire hit a 17-footer, giving Portland an 84–76 edge at the 1:59 mark.

Elliott, who had lit things up already with four three-pointers, connected on a fifth to cap a 5–0 Spurs run and cut the gap to 84–81. On Portland's next possession, David Robinson stole the ball, and Mario Elie drew a foul. The guard sank both free throws, shrinking the difference to a single point. San Antonio purposely fouled Stoudamire with 12 seconds left to play, and the guard missed the first but canned the second foul shot.

Following a Spurs time-out, Elie passed the ball to Elliott on the right sideline. With his heels hanging near the sideline, Sean fired over a lunging Rasheed Wallace. As 35,260 Alamodome fans rose to their feet, the ball sailed through the hoop with the clock showing 9.9 seconds. Elliott's sixth trey gave the Spurs their only lead of the game and allowed San Antonio to escape with an 86–85 triumph.

> These stones are to be a memorial to the people of Israel forever.
>
> JOSHUA 4:7, NIV

EXTRA POINT < < < < < < < < < < < < < < < < < < < < < < <
What a performance for San Antonio fans to remember on Memorial Day!

This holiday was first observed on May 30, 1868, as a time to remember soldiers who had fought in the Civil War. But after World War I, the holiday broadened to honor all Americans who died fighting for their country.

In the Bible, Joshua knew the importance of remembering. He built a memorial to help the people remember God's deliverance of their nation. The Israelites often stacked up stone pillars as a reminder of God's power and faithfulness.

GOAL! *Think of some appropriate ways to remember those who died fighting for America's freedom. Thank God for their sacrifice. And praise God for the ability to honor others.*

30 MAY

PARKS AND SHANE BONIFAY may have only been 21 and 19 during the 2003 Gravity Games wakeboard finals, but between them they had more than 14 years of professional riding experience. And they showed that experience by topping the podium.

Shane set the tone for these dynamic brothers. With each competitor judged on one double-up hit (caused when the boat turns sharply and creates a gigantic wake), traditional flatwater tricks, and stunts pulled off three obstacles—one 10-foot ramp, a 30-foot super-slider rail, and an A-frame rail—the guys demonstrated just how far this sport has progressed. Shane's frontside batwing, inverted 360, large indy grab, and tootsie roll put him solidly in first with only Parks left to compete. And Shane's ride could've been even better, but he went down on an off-axis backside 360 on his double-up.

Knowing he had to go clean to win, Parks hit every trick in his dynamic run. He threw a frontside board on the A-frame, nailed a half-cab method, and went big on a frontside late 540.

By finishing first and second, the Bonifay brothers accomplished something they'd never done before.

EXTRA POINT < < < < < < < < < < < < < < < < < < < When Shane Bonifay missed his final trick, he was okay with it because he knew only his older brother could beat him. Despite being fierce competitors, the brothers always wished each other the best. And when Parks solidified the victory, Shane was cheering with the rest of the crowd.

The Bible talks a lot about family. God knits families together and wants them to always encourage each other. Of course, reality can be a little different. Older and younger siblings can get on our nerves. And often siblings fight. But God is clear: We should always help our family members. By making our family a priority, we're being a godly example to people around us.

GOAL! *Next time your brother or sister starts bothering you, remember that God wants you to get along and do your best to show love. Thank your heavenly Father for your earthly family.*

If anyone does not provide for his relatives, and especially for his immediate family, he has denied the faith and is worse than an unbeliever.

1 TIMOTHY 5:8, NIV

JUNE

But as for you, be strong and do not give up, for your work will be rewarded.

2 CHRONICLES 15:7, NIV

WINNING THE SEVENTH GAME in an NBA conference series often requires giving total effort for the entire 48 minutes. But in the 1998 Eastern Conference showdown, the Indiana Pacers halted their efforts two minutes short.

The Pacers needed a road victory against the Chicago Bulls to reach their first NBA title series. Despite trailing 48–45 at halftime, Indiana forged ahead 72–69 on a three-point play by Rik Smits with 8:54 remaining in the game. But Chicago, seeking its third straight NBA crown, tied the contest 77–77 almost three minutes later as Steve Kerr completed a three-point play. Scottie Pippen's jumper following an offensive rebound put the Bulls ahead 81–79 at the 4:45 mark.

As the game approached the two-minute mark, Indiana's Antonio Davis converted an offensive rebound into a basket, narrowing the gap to 85–83. But the Pacers never tallied another point.

With the clock winding down, Derrick McKey missed a forced three-pointer for the Pacers, who by then trailed 87–83. Chicago's Ron Harper drew a foul with 8.9 seconds left. His free throw sealed the 88–83 victory and gave the Bulls their third consecutive Eastern Conference title.

EXTRA POINT < < < < < < < < < < < < < < < < < < < The buzzer might as well have gone off for the Pacers with two minutes left. They didn't do anything in clutch time to win the game. Even though Bulls' stars Michael Jordan and Scottie Pippen had off nights with Jordan going 9-for-25 with 28 points and Pippen 6-for-18 for 17 points, the Pacers couldn't capitalize.

Occasionally we fail to capitalize too. Whether in sports, volunteer work, family relationships, or church, sometimes we stop trying. That's not God's plan. He wants us to work until the end and keep trying until the Lord says halt. The Christian life isn't over until God says it is.

GOAL! *Next time you watch a basketball game, note whether each team plays until the final buzzer. See if anybody gives up. Ask God to help you keep trying until life is over.*

AFTER YEARS OF BEING OUTPERFORMED by European and South American powers, the United States had few followers who expected a strong showing from the soccer team at the 2002 World Cup. But as die-hard U.S. fans awakened one morning, the young, brash Americans delivered a surprise.

Since South Korea hosted the 2002 World Cup, the Americans' first round against Portugal—one of the pretournament favorites—kicked off at 5 a.m. eastern time. By the dawn's early light in the United States, the national team opened the scoring in the game's fourth minute following a corner kick by Earnie Stewart. Brian McBride attempted a header into the net that bounced off goalie Vitor Baia's hand. However, John O'Brien knocked the rebound into the back of the net, and the United States took a 1–0 lead.

The Americans extended their margin to 3–0 in the first half. Landon Donovan collected the second goal when his shot from an extreme angle deflected off Jorge Costa's head and sailed past Baia. McBride made the third American goal in the 36th minute with a diving header off a cross from Tony Sanneh.

In the second half, the Portuguese rallied and pulled within one on a United States error. American defender Jeff Agoos, making his World Cup debut at age 34, attempted to clear a cross by Pauleta with his left leg. But instead, he accidentally kicked the ball past his own goalkeeper, Brad Friedel, in minute 71.

Switching to a defensive posture, the Americans kept all but one or two players in their end of the field. Portugal failed to penetrate the tight United States net, and the American nationals won their first World Cup contest since defeating Columbia 2–1 in 1994.

EXTRA POINT < < < < < < < < < < < < < < < < < < < < Soccer faithfuls in the eastern United States set their alarms for 4 or 5 a.m. that day. Avid fans on the West Coast stayed up until two or three in the morning to cheer on their team. And what a totally unexpected victory among the nations!

People rarely set their alarm early by choice. Work, school, or special trips can require that the buzzer go off in the predawn hours. However, some Christians believe it's a good idea to awaken early and start each morning with a quiet time. They begin every day praying to the heavenly Father.

GOAL! *Set your alarm an extra half hour early. Spend the extra time praying, reading the Bible, and praising God. It could make a big difference in your day.*

> Wake up, my soul! Wake up, O harp and lyre! I will waken the dawn with my song.
>
> PSALM 57:8

Put on the full armor of God so that you can take your stand against the devil's schemes.

EPHESIANS 6:11, NIV

GREAT GOLFERS usually play their best in major tournaments. In the 2001 United States Women's Open, Karrie Webb stood high above her challengers.

The 26-year-old Australian entered the tournament's final day at Pine Needles Lodge & Golf Club with a five-stroke lead over South Korea's Se Ri Pak. After Webb posted a 5-under-par 65 on the second day, no one rose to her level.

Paired with Pak for the last round, Webb, the defending U.S. Open champion, continued her peak performance, while her partner struggled. On the seventh hole, she landed a perfect 6 iron, setting up a 15-foot birdie, while Pak overshot the green and took a bogey.

The scenario repeated on the back nine. Webb birdied the final two holes with putts of 45 and 20 feet, finishing the day with a 69. Her four-round tally of 7-under-par brought the Australian the U.S. crown by eight strokes.

Despite missing six fairways and carding a 72, Pak finished second at 1-over-par. Dottie Pepper rallied on the last day to shoot a 69 and take third overall, her best Open showing ever.

With the victory, Webb collected her fourth major title in seven outings. She also earned the distinction of becoming the seventh LPGA member to win back-to-back Open titles.

EXTRA POINT < < < < < < < < < < < < < < < < < < < < < < At some point during a tournament, the winning golfer takes a stand. Karrie Webb decided to concentrate on her game and on nobody else. She stood strong in spite of tough competition and new challengers. That's why she won the U.S. Women's Open.

In life, the time comes when we need to stand up for God and against the devil. Choosing not to gossip, refusing to curse or listen to profanity, and avoiding questionable movies and TV shows takes commitment and power. But with God's strength, we can do it.

GOAL! *Do you remember a time when you didn't take a stand for God? Think about a day you chose to follow the crowd instead of God. Ask the Lord to help you be strong against the devil.*

YOUNG BASEBALL PLAYERS will do almost anything to earn the chance to play in the big leagues. Whether it means hours of practice, tons of weight lifting, or attending numerous camps, any sacrifice would be worth it. But Orlando "El Duque" Hernandez nearly sacrificed his life by riding a flimsy boat through violent seas to make his dream of pitching in the major leagues come true.

The pitcher defected from his native Cuba on the day after Christmas in 1997. He traveled 90 miles to the United States with seven companions on a makeshift raft. The following March, the star hurler of the Cuban national team signed with the New York Yankees.

El Duque opened the 1998 season with the Yankees' Triple-A farm club in Columbus, Ohio. During the season's first two months, he posted a perfect 6–0 record.

Then when Yankee pitcher David Cone got injured, Hernandez got promoted to the majors to fill in. Hernandez took the ball against the Tampa Bay Devil Rays in his first game. Displaying a wide assortment of fastballs, slow curves, and sidearm deliveries, the rookie allowed five hits, walked two, and struck out seven in a 7–1 victory. He ended his first year in the majors with a 12–4 record and returned in 1999 to pitch his best year as a professional by finishing 17–9.

> But I will offer sacrifices to you with songs of praise, and I will fulfill all my vows. For my salvation comes from the Lord alone.
>
> JONAH 2:9

EXTRA POINT < < < < < < < < < < < < < < < < < < < < < < < Orlando Hernandez took a huge risk to get his big break. The rickety raft threatened to disintegrate in the water. He and his friends could have easily lost their lives in the violent ocean waves. But the eight of them made the American shore, and El Duque made an outstanding major league pitcher.

In the Bible, Jonah also faced rough waters. God told him to go to Nineveh to preach against the people's wickedness. Jonah refused to tell Israel's enemy about God and boarded a ship going the other way. His disobedience caused a violent storm, and since Jonah knew he was responsible, he told the sailors to throw him overboard. When they did, the sea calmed. God gave Jonah a second chance, and he went to Nineveh. Jonah preached and the people repented.

GOAL! *Can you imagine telling somebody you don't like about God's Good News? God may ask you to do just that. Praise him that he loves everybody and wants everybody to know him. Will you commit to not run from him?*

> Two people can accomplish more than twice as much as one; they get a better return for their labor.
>
> ECCLESIASTES 4:9

WHAT HAPPENS when you combine the pure athletic talent of skateboarder Tony Hawk and the flawless consistency of Andy Macdonald? Answer: You get one dynamic, gold-medal-winning duo!

Hawk and Macdonald combined efforts in the 1999 Summer X Games vert doubles to take home their third straight gold medal. The fans never wondered which team would come out on top; the only question was: "What will they do next?"

By themselves, these two pro skaters would make any event fun to watch. But as a team, they were simply unstoppable. As in any amazing performance, the stars saved the best for last. Hawk nailed a giant 720 while soaring over Macdonald, who was spinning a 360 indy. This mind-blowing stunt was followed by a board transfer where Hawk—in the middle of a 50-50 grind—jumped onto Macdonald's board to ride out the rest of his slide on top of the halfpipe.

Hawk and Macdonald, both working together with precise timing, gave an amazing performance and rode away with some more hardware.

EXTRA POINT < < < < < < < < < < < < < < < < < < < <
Tony Hawk and Andy Macdonald knew that they had enough talent together to take on anyone. They also knew that talent alone wasn't going to get them to the top. They had to be creative. They had to build on each other's abilities. They had to work together as a team.

Do you think Hawk would have made it far in the vert doubles by himself? Not only would he have been disqualified, he would have missed out on another X Games gold medal.

Just like Hawk needed a friend to help him accomplish his goal, we need friends to help us live out our Christian life. God never intended for us to be alone. He gave us Christian friends at school or church to encourage us and to help us achieve more than we ever could alone. We must work together with our friends to pursue great things for God.

GOAL! *Do you have a best friend who is also a Christian? How can the two of you help each other in your Christian life? You could read a chapter of the Bible together or pray for each other every day. Together you can work as a team for Christ.*

THE NBA'S CONTINUATION RULE (which allows a player

to continue his shooting motion and make a basket after being fouled) generates continual controversy. Referees often have different views of the rule. In 1999, one interpretation allowed the New York Knicks to steal an unexpected victory— at least that's what Indiana Pacer fans thought.

After splitting the first two contests in the Eastern Conference finals, the two teams met again at the Knicks' home, Madison Square Garden. Leading 89–81 with just over three minutes left, the Pacers seemed poised to take a 2–1 advantage in the best-of-seven series.

However, New York went on a 7–0 spurt to pull within one. Indiana's Mark Jackson stopped the run by connecting on two free throws with 11.9 ticks remaining, giving the Pacers a 91–88 margin.

With time expiring, Larry Johnson grabbed an inbound pass intended for Knicks teammate Allan Houston. Standing behind the three-point arc, he made a slight head fake that took defender Antonio Davis into the air. As Johnson dribbled, Davis grabbed Johnson with both hands. At least a half second after the whistle blew, the New York forward let fly a 26-footer that swished through the net. Referee Jess Kersey generously ruled that the points counted. Johnson sank the free throw, completing the improbable four-point play and giving the Knicks a 92–91 victory. The incredible win sent the Garden crowd into pandemonium.

EXTRA POINT < < < < < < < < < < < < < < < < < < < < <

Did New York really steal the game from Indiana? The NBA rules indicate that shooting begins when the player starts the shooting motion and continues until the motion ceases and the athlete returns to "a normal floor position." Rule number 4, section XI also indicates that the interpretation belongs to the official. Did the foul occur before the shot? Most Pacers fans thought so. If so, Johnson should have simply shot three free throws.

But the rule book doesn't begin and end the referee's education. Clinics, articles, and practice help them to know how to make the proper call. One view urges referees in doubt to err on the side of the offense. Obviously, the referee used his judgment, but many fans still saw the game as stolen.

But there isn't room for interpretation in God's rule book. It's clear: "You shall not steal."

GOAL! *Can you think of any time that it might be okay to steal? (It's not fair to say in a baseball game!) Thank God that his rules are clear.*

Jesus wept.

JOHN 11:35, NKJV

ATHLETES OFTEN VIEW tears as a sign of weakness. But in the 1999 French Open, one finalist cried with happiness and excitement, while the other wept with heartache and disappointment.

Five-time champion Steffi Graf faced No. 1 Martina Hingis for the Grand Slam tennis title. Prior to the event, Graf had announced her retirement. The 1999 appearance at Roland Garros would be her last.

Despite a tantrum-induced warning, the 18-year-old Hingis took the first set 6–4 from her 29-year-old German counterpart. But with a 2–0 lead in set two, the Swiss player erupted into a tirade. After stroking a baseline shot long, she stormed over to Graf's side of the court and pointed to a spot she insisted the ball had hit. Umpire Anne Lasserre awarded Graf a penalty point for Hingis's outburst.

Hingis regrouped and moved to within three points of taking the match. But Graf reeled off 23 of the next 26 points, winning the second set 7–5. Feeding her opponent a steady diet of low slice backhands, the German forced Hingis into sloppy strokes. Graf coasted to a 6–2 victory in set three, claiming her 22nd Grand Slam championship.

At the conclusion, Graf wept for joy and called the French Open championship the biggest of her stellar career. Hingis, on the other hand, rushed to her mother in the stands and cried. Only at her mom's insistence did she return to Court Centrale to receive the runner-up plate.

EXTRA POINT < < < < < < < < < < < < < < < < < < < < Steffi Graf concluded her French Open career with a mature attitude and a hard-fought victory. The young Martina Hingis lost her cool—and the match. Her immaturity and poor sportsmanship showed. Graf's tears of joy provided a marked contrast to Hingis's tantrum tears.

Tears represent emotion—whether joy or sorrow, frustration or anger. The Bible talks about Jesus crying. When his friend Lazarus died and Jesus saw Lazarus's sisters, Mary and Martha, and other people crying, God's Son cried too. Then he raised Lazarus from the dead. Jesus turned those tears at a funeral from sadness to gladness.

GOAL! *Think about the last time you cried. What emotions triggered the tears? Thank God for the release tears can bring. And praise him that he knows what it's like to cry.*

WINNING THE TRIPLE CROWN in horse racing is one of the most difficult accomplishments in sports. Since the early 1900s only 11 horses have won the Kentucky Derby, Preakness Stakes, and Belmont Stakes in the same year to claim this honor.

One horse did it in 1919, three accomplished it in the 1930s, and four more won the Triple Crown in the '40s. Then it took 25 years until Secretariat won in 1973. And five years later (after Seattle Slew won the Crown in 1977), Affirmed became the 11th winner of all three races by edging out Alydar in one of the most memorable Belmont races of all time.

With the Kentucky and Preakness already under his belt, Affirmed entered the New York race knowing Alydar would again pose a major threat. That proved to be the case as Alydar took to the front early. But a lot can happen at the 1.5-mile Belmont Stakes. Teenage sensation Steve Cauthen rode Affirmed perfectly, staying near Alydar until the stretch run. That's when these two great horses locked in a back-and-forth battle to the finish line. As 65,000 fans rose to their feet in a huge cacophony of cheering, Affirmed rode into history as he beat Alydar by a nose.

EXTRA POINT < < < < < < < < < < < < < < < < < < < < < < Horse racing has been called the sport of kings. The pageantry, style, and tradition of this sport are hard to match. And winning the Triple Crown stands as the crowning achievement.

The Bible mentions horses on numerous occasions. One of the most notable times comes in Revelation, where it says that Jesus Christ will return to earth riding a white horse. Not only that, but our Savior will be leading an army of heavenly horse riders to conquer Satan. Jesus may have come to earth the first time as a tiny baby to die for our sins. But he'll return the second time as a conquering warrior on a magnificent steed.

GOAL! *Look in the Bible for passages about horses. Notice how many times these animals show up at key moments. Think about Jesus riding out of the sky on a white horse. Praise him that he's victorious in the end!*

I saw heaven standing open. There in front of me was a white horse. Its rider is called Faithful and True. When he judges or makes war, he is always fair. REVELATION 19:11, NIrV

THE LORD REPLIED,

"LOOK AT THE NATIONS AND BE AMAZED!

WATCH AND BE ASTOUNDED AT WHAT I WILL DO!

FOR I AM DOING SOMETHING IN YOUR OWN DAY,

SOMETHING YOU WOULDN'T BELIEVE EVEN IF

SOMEONE TOLD YOU ABOUT IT." HABAKKUK 1:5

NOTHING IS MORE EXCITING in sports than watching an amazing comeback. In the 1999 French Open, Andre Agassi not only stunned the crowd but himself as well with his performance in the finals.

Prior to the tournament Agassi considered withdrawing because of an inflamed tendon in his right arm. But the 29-year-old player fought through the injury to reach the finals against Andrei Medvedev.

In the first two sets, Medvedev dominated with powerful serves and baseline play to win 6–1 and 6–2. In spite of his struggles, Agassi kept his composure, struck the ball aggressively, and continued to improve his speed. His Ukrainian adversary reached break point in set three, but the No. 13 seed saved with a forehand drop volley. Agassi held serve and then broke Medvedev, taking a 6–4 win.

Rejuvenated, Agassi captured sets four and five 6–3 and 6–4 respectively. After Medvedev sailed a forehand long for the match's final point, Agassi threw his racket into the stands and wheeled to face his coach, trainer, and friends. Stunned by his unexpected victory, he sobbed uncontrollably. With the Grand Slam win, he joined Don Budge, Rod Laver, Fred Perry, and Roy Emerson as the only players to capture all four Grand Slams.

EXTRA POINT

< < < < < < < < < < < < < < < < < < < < < <

Even though Andre Agassi had a great professional career before the 1999 French Open—and after it—his injuries nagged, his steps slowed, and his serve lost power that June. Before the tournament, no one—not even Agassi—believed he could capture the title. But the star amazed television viewers, the crowd in the grandstands, and himself by earning the crown.

Sometimes life offers amazing results. Who would have thought that the son of poor farmers would be elected president of the United States? But Lyndon Johnson was. Who could have imagined that the child of immigrants from Jamaica growing up in the south Bronx would become a decorated general and secretary of state? But Colin Powell did. Who would have dreamed that the 12th child of an east Texas sharecropper family would be named president of Brown University? But Ruth Simmons got the job.

God can do anything with anyone with amazing results if we'll just let him.

GOAL! *Find other people who surprised everybody with how they ended up in life. Ask God to do amazing things with your life.*

09 JUN

Then Hezekiah said, "You have now dedicated yourselves to the Lord. Come and bring sacrifices and thank offerings to the temple of the Lord."

2 CHRONICLES 29:31, NIV

WHEN A TEAM DEDICATES a season to a retiring teammate, it risks a lot of people's disappointment. But the Colorado Avalanche watched its dedication to Ray Bourque—one of the best defensemen in NHL history—culminate in the 2001 NHL championship.

The Avalanche advanced to the Stanley Cup finals against the defending champs, the New Jersey Devils. Trailing three games to two, Colorado forced a seventh game back in Denver with a 4–0 road victory.

In the decisive game, Colorado jumped ahead on an early Alex Tanguay goal. The Avs clinched the victory in the second period with two goals. Defenseman Adam Foote started things by banking a clearing pass off the boards to set up a two-on-one break for Joe Sakic and Tanguay. Sakic fired the puck, Devils' goalie Martin Brodeur blocked it, and Tanguay rifled the rebound into a half-empty net.

Four minutes later, New Jersey's Sean O'Donnell drew a high-sticking penalty. The Avalanche capitalized on the power play opportunity as Sakic faked a slap shot from the right face-off circle, then threaded a wrist shot through defenseman Scott Stevens' legs and into the top right corner of the net.

The Devils also scored a second-period power play goal, but goalie Patrick Roy blanked New Jersey the remainder of the game for a 3–1 win.

After NHL officials handed the Stanley Cup to Sakic, the Avalanche captain, he handed it to Bourque for the first victory lap.

EXTRA POINT Ray Bourque's Avalanche teammates grew to love him even though he had played less than two seasons with Colorado. The Boston Bruins traded Ray to give him a shot at a Stanley Cup. And his new team dedicated their season to him. After all, Bourque played 1,826 hockey games, the most ever without winning a championship ring. By the time he won the magical victory, Ray had played 22 seasons, made 19 All-Star teams, and earned the top NHL defenseman honor five times. The veteran deserved his team's dedication.

To *dedicate* means to set apart for a special purpose or as a sign of honor. In the Old Testament book of Chronicles, King Hezekiah cleansed the temple. Then the people dedicated themselves to God as a sign of his honor and their affection for him. We too should dedicate ourselves to the Lord.

GOAL! *Think of some people or things worthy of your dedication. Write down a few.*

Praise the one who is worthy of your honor and affection.

WHEN YOU'RE AT THE TOP, people are always looking to knock you off. That was the case in the women's wakeboard finals at the 2003 Gravity Games.

Fighting choppy water on Lake Erie, Florida boarders Tara Hamilton and Leslie Kent looked to dethrone 2002 champ Emily Copeland-Durham. But the Colorado 20-year-old proved once again that the Rocky Mountain state can turn out more than just great snowboarders and skiers.

On her first pass, Copeland-Durham put together the trifecta by going solid on her heelside tantrum, scarecrow, and heelside back roll. But the Colorado girl saved her best for last. Her second pass featured a nifty KGB (wrapped back roll with a backside 360). She threw another tantrum and nearly grinded the entire length of the super slider. Those big tricks combined with a mixture of rotations, jumps, and consistently solid landings gave Copeland-Durham her second straight Gravity gold. Hamilton settled for her fourth Gravity Games silver.

EXTRA POINT < < < < < < < < < < < < < < < < < < < <
Being the best at something feels great. Everyone looks up to you. But they also want to beat you. Sitting at the top of your sport, activity, or class puts a big target on your chest. That's because everybody wants to be the person who beat you. Sometimes the status can make you perform better. But other times it may make you feel that you want to lose so you don't have to deal with the pressure.

No matter what you do—even if it's something you're not good at—God wants you to try your best. The Bible says we should act like we're performing for God, not ourselves, no matter if it's in a test, an athletic competition, or a job.

GOAL! *Have you ever felt like you wanted to do poorly on purpose? Maybe you've felt too tired to do your best and just wanted to give up. But that's not what God wants. He desires that you make the most out of your talents and work in a way that honors him.*

Whatever you do, work at it with all your heart, as working for the Lord, not for men.
COLOSSIANS 3:23, NIV

A friend loves
at all times.

PROVERBS

17:17, NKJV

FEW THINGS BOND FRIENDSHIP more than sharing in success. In 2000, New Jersey's Patrik Elias and Jason Arnott won a hockey title for an injured friend.

The New Jersey Devils faced the Dallas Stars in the Stanley Cup finals. Leading the series three games to one, the Devils missed an opportunity to capture the crown on their home ice when Dallas claimed a 1–0 triple-overtime victory.

With game six moving to Dallas, the intensity continued. In the first period, New Jersey wing Petr Sykora skated across the blue line and fired a slap shot toward the Stars' goal. An instant later, Dallas defenseman Derian Hatcher leveled him with an elbow, and Sykora fell to the ice, hands outstretched.

Medical staff strapped the Czech player to a stretcher and transported him to a hospital, where a CT scan revealed no serious injuries. When the game resumed, the Devils and the Stars each scored second-period goals. Tied 1–1, the contest went into overtime.

Neither team found the net in the first extra period, but midway through the second, Scott Stevens sent the puck deep. Elias retrieved and blindly made a backhand pass across the goalmouth. It neatly slid to Arnott, who shot it past a defenseless Eddie Belfour for the winning New Jersey score.

At the Stanley Cup presentation, Elias draped Sykora's jersey over his shoulders. Seeing the display of friendship, Devils coach Larry Robinson donned Sykora's uniform for the championship photograph.

EXTRA POINT

< < < < < < < < < < < < < < < < < < < <

After Petr Sykora left the arena, Elias and Arnott vowed to win the Stanley Cup for their friend. And although Sykora missed the winners' picture, he got the next best thing: his uniform with its unique number as part of the photo op.

Following the game, instead of celebrating out on the town, Patrik Elias spent the evening in Petr Sykora's hospital room admiring the Cup. Sykora knew his friends loved him.

The writer of Proverbs describes that kind of friendship. And other stories in the Bible demonstrate a friend's love. Naomi and Ruth, Jonathan and David, and Paul and Timothy all show how a friend loves at all times. We're blessed when God gives us such good friends.

GOAL! *Who are some of your close friends?*
Praise God for good friends who are always there to help.

DURING HIS CAREER, Michael Jordan amazed the basketball world with his incredible shots and fantastic moves. In his final game as a Chicago Bull in 1998, Jordan finished in grand style.

The Bulls faced the Utah Jazz on the road in game six of the NBA championship. Leading three games to two, Chicago would earn its sixth title in the 1990s with a victory that night.

Chicago opened an early nine-point lead, but an injured back forced Scottie Pippen to the locker room, and the momentum shifted. Utah took an 81–79 lead on two Bryon Russell free throws with 3:20 remaining. The Jazz stayed in front until Jordan canned two foul shots, tying the score 83–83 with just under a minute to play.

John Stockton's three-pointer at the 42-second mark put the Jazz up by three, but Jordan nailed another pair of free throws five seconds later to pull the Bulls within one. As the clock ticked down to 20 seconds, the five-time NBA MVP sneaked behind Utah's Karl Malone, swatted the ball away, grabbed the steal, and dribbled upcourt.

With a collective gasp, the 20,000 fans at Utah's Delta Center feared the outcome. Jordan pulled up and let fly a 17-foot jumper with 5.2 seconds left. His shot swished. Utah got one final chance, but its three-pointer bounced off the rim, giving the Bulls an 87–86 victory and their sixth NBA crown.

> But my life is worth nothing unless I use it for doing the work assigned me by the Lord Jesus— the work of telling others the Good News about God's wonderful kindness and love.
>
> ACTS 20:24

EXTRA POINT < < < < < < < < < < < < < < < < < < < < < What a way for Michael Jordan to finish his career with the Bulls! Those who saw the game noticed that Jordan stood for a moment after his last shot with his bent wrist perfectly frozen in the follow-through position. He seemed to want to hold that feeling forever, but his success with the Bulls was over.

The apostle Paul understood about finishing a task. God gave him the job of telling the world about Jesus' gift of salvation. Many call Paul the first missionary. God sends missionaries around the world today. And the Lord calls the rest of us to serve as missionaries where we are.

GOAL! *If you know missionaries in other countries, pray for them. If not, see if your church supports some. Choose a country and pray for all the missionaries who live there. What work does God have planned for you? Pray that he'll show you his will for your life.*

As far as the
east is from
the west, so
far has he
removed our
transgressions
from us.

PSALM 103:12, NIV

MAKING A HUGE MISTAKE in a key situation can haunt an athlete for years. But when Retief Goosen missed a short putt that would have given him the United States Open title in 2001, he quickly regrouped.

In the final round, the 32-year-old South African played in the day's last pairing. He reached the 18th hole in the lead, one stroke ahead of Mark Brooks at 5-under-par. After hitting a solid tee shot in the fairway, he chipped his ball to about ten feet from the pin.

Needing only a par-4 to claim the Open championship, Goosen gently tapped the ball. It rolled to within two feet of the hole. Inexplicably, the golfer hammered his next putt, overshooting the hole by three feet. Instead of winning the championship, Goosen recorded a bogey, leaving him tied with Brooks.

Since the U.S. Open rules require an 18-hole playoff in the case of a tie, the two golfers teed off the following morning. Goosen prepared for the extra day by scheduling a session with sports psychologist Jos Vanstiphout, who advised the European Tour player to think good thoughts and forget the past. Fellow South African golfer Ernie Els wished Goosen the best by writing a note in Afrikaans, their country's native language.

After Brooks took an early lead, Goosen opened up a five-shot margin through 16 holes. His bogey and Brooks's birdie on 17 cut the gap to three, but Goosen saved a bogey with a six-foot putt on the final hole. His playoff round of 70 bettered Brooks by two strokes and brought him the U.S. Open title.

EXTRA POINT < < < < < < < < < < < < < < < < < < < < Retief Goosen could have spent the hours between the tournament's final round and the playoff by mentally beating himself up. Missing a two-foot putt is almost inexcusable to a professional golfer. He could have focused on his past error and what might have been instead of on his future opportunity. But Retief relied on his friends' advice and looked to the future. He captured the crown.

Too many times in life we dwell on past errors and disappointments. We focus so hard on what's gone wrong in our life that we miss future opportunities. But that's not God's way. He's the Father of new beginnings! He forgives and forgets your mistakes, and so should you.

GOAL! *On a separate sheet of paper, write down any past errors or mistakes that still bother you. Now rip up that paper and throw it away to symbolize putting those problems behind you. Ask God to help.*

FOR YEARS, MAURICE GREENE dreamed of breaking the world's 100-meter record. In 1999, his dreams materialized when he concentrated on preparing for races—rather than discussing them—and focused on setting the new mark.

The 24-year-old Kansas City native competed in a meet on the Grand Prix International Circuit in Athens, Greece. Track experts considered the 5-foot-9, 165-pound speedster a likely candidate to break the world record. Only Donovan Bailey, who set the world mark of 9.84 in 1996, and Leroy Burrell, with 9.85 in 1994, had posted faster marks than Greene's personal best of 9.86.

On the hot, windless evening, organizers arranged a special 100-meter event to showcase some of the world's top runners. For Greene, the race had special meaning. He had won the 1997 world outdoor championship on the same track. The Greek venue would also host the 2004 Olympics in the birthplace of track and field.

At the gun, the sprinter bolted down the straightaway. Pursued by Trinidad's Ato Boldon and Canada's Bruny Surin, Greene crossed the finish line in a time of 9.79 seconds, .05 faster than the world record. The difference represented the largest margin of a record-breaking time since electronic timing began in the 1960s. Boldon placed second at 9.86, and Surin finished third with a 9.97.

Preach the Word; be prepared in season and out of season; correct, rebuke and encourage—with great patience and careful instruction.
2 TIMOTHY 4:2, NIV

EXTRA POINT < < < < < < < < < < < < < < < < < < < < < < Maurice Greene worked hard for the win. He prepared to do his best. The sprinter made sacrifices, including moving from his hometown of Kansas City to Los Angeles. He left Al Hobson, the coach he'd had since age eight, to train under UCLA assistant coach John Smith. Maurice found a running partner in Ato Boldon and began weight training. And Greene's preparation made a difference.

Too many times we wing it in sports and in life. We don't practice. We don't work hard. We don't sacrifice. We don't prepare. And then we're surprised when we don't do well. The apostle Paul knew that preparation was the key to success. He instructed followers of Jesus Christ to be ready all the time to tell others about their Lord.

GOAL! *Think of an upcoming race, game, activity, assignment, or event that you need to prepare for. Plan how you will get ready. Ask God to help you always be prepared.*

> Do nothing out of selfish ambition or vain conceit, but in humility consider others better than yourselves.
>
> PHILIPPIANS 2:3, NIV

GEORGE MIKAN, Wilt Chamberlain, and Kareem Abdul-Jabbar brought the Los Angeles Lakers 11 NBA championships with their outstanding play at center. And recently Lakers fans have cheered Shaquille O'Neal in the middle. This big man helped the franchise add three more championships in the beginning of the 21st century—the first in 2000.

Leading three games to two, the Lakers hosted the Indiana Pacers in game six of the championship finals. For three quarters, Indiana outplayed Los Angeles and led 84–79 at the start of the fourth. Finally, with the Pacers concentrating on the middle, Derek Fisher, Rick Fox, and Robert Horry opened up the Lakers offense by connecting for four three-pointers and igniting a 22–10 run. Shaq, who totaled 41 points and 12 rebounds for the game, contributed 10 points during the L.A. streak.

Indiana regrouped late in the fourth and pulled to within one at 110–109 with 1:27 remaining. But two costly fouls quashed the Pacers' comeback. Glen Rice sank two free throws at the 1:10 mark, and Kobe Bryant hit two more with 13 seconds left, putting Los Angeles in front 114–109. The Lakers held on for a 116–111 victory.

Sportswriters voted O'Neal the MVP, giving him his third major award of the season along with his All-Star game and regular season MVP honors.

EXTRA POINT < < < < < < < < < < < < < < < < < < < < < Shaquille O'Neal will someday be remembered as one of basketball's greatest big men. At 7-foot-1 and 315 pounds, Shaq towers over the court. But he moves well for someone who wears size 21EEE shoes. Not only does Shaquille possess a big body, he has big skills. He knows how to pass to his teammates and get others involved in the game.

Most of us will never be physically as big as No. 34, but we can grow a big heart for God. We can put others first. We can give our time to read to residents in a nursing home. We can share with a family that has less than we have. We can listen to a friend. And we can share the bigness of our God with the world.

GOAL! *Measure 7-feet-1-inch, Shaquille O'Neal's height. How many inches would you need to grow to be that tall? Perform an act of kindness to show that you're becoming a spiritual giant. Ask God always to make your actions big in his sight.*

NO GREATER GOLF CHALLENGE exists than winning the United States Open. Moving around the country to only the most beautiful and most difficult courses, the 2000 U.S. Open found itself on the Pacific coastline at Pebble Beach. And in the 100th Open, Tiger Woods conquered the course and the weather.

Some experts believed the 1997 Masters champion would never win the Open because he lacked patience. But Woods fought thick, gloomy June fog, storming to an opening round 65 and setting the course record.

Because of suspended play, almost 30 hours elapsed before Woods teed off for his second round. Darkness rapidly set in, allowing him only 12 holes. Arriving at 6:30 the following morning, Woods finished the remaining six holes, carding a 2-under 69.

Starting his third round immediately and battling a stiff wind, the golfer struggled early and shot a triple bogey on the third hole. But Woods rallied, registering an even-par 71 to put himself ten strokes in front.

The 24-year-old golfer provided spectators with a spectacular final round. After paring the front nine, Woods birdied four of the first five on the back nine. He concluded the final day with a 67 for a total of 272, besting the field by 15 shots.

Woods rewrote the record book. His margin of victory in a major tournament eclipsed the 13-stroke mark set in the 1862 British Open. He also broke the U.S. Open margin record of 11 shots held since 1899 by Willie Smith. In addition, Woods's 272 matched Jack Nicklaus and Lee Janzen for the lowest score in Open history.

EXTRA POINT < < < < < < < < < < < < < < < < < < < < < < When Tiger Woods broke onto the professional golf scene, he amazed everyone. But everybody wondered if he would last. Woods has lasted. He tames tough golf courses, battles bad weather, and continues to be one of the top golfers in the world.

But while Tiger Woods fights through tough weather, there is one man in history who *controls* the weather—Jesus Christ. If Jesus played golf, he could prevent a rain delay just by speaking a few words. Don't believe it? Just check out the story in Mark.

GOAL! *Read the story of Jesus calming the storm in Mark 4:35-41. Praise the Lord for his mighty power!*

> Then He arose and rebuked the wind, and said to the sea, "Peace, be still!" And the wind ceased and there was a great calm.
>
> MARK 4:39, NKJV

17 JUN

Jesus told
them, "If God
were your
Father, you
would love me,
because I have
come to you
from God. I am
not here on my
own, but he
sent me."

JOHN 8:42

FEW ATHLETES ENJOY the opportunity to perform in the same championship event as their father. In the 2002 College World Series, University of Texas pitcher Huston Street and his dad shared a Father's Day memory.

Huston's father, James Street, knew the journey to Omaha, Nebraska, well. Although more recognized for quarterbacking the Longhorns to a national collegiate football championship in 1969, he also pitched for Texas in two College World Series.

With eight teams vying for the collegiate baseball title, the competition proved stiff. In UT's first three games, the Longhorns held one-run leads in the late innings. Each time, Texas coach Augie Garrido called Huston from the bull pen to snuff out the opposition. And every time, the freshman saved the game. During each appearance, television cameras panned between the younger man on the mound and his father in the stands.

In the final game, UT led South Carolina 8–4 in the eighth. With two Gamecocks on base and one out, Garrido summoned Street for the fourth time. A fielder's choice produced an out and two runs. Then Huston struck out Yaron Peters to end the threat. Texas scored four insurance runs in the ninth, and Street closed the 12–6 win by getting a double-play ball and forcing a groundout.

The victory brought the Longhorns their fifth baseball national championship and Street the College World Series MVP award. Huston pitched 6.1 innings, allowed one run on two hits, struck out five, and notched four saves—the most ever in NCAA playoff history. His proud papa witnessed every pitch.

EXTRA POINT < < < < < < < < < < < < < < < < < < < < <
Reporters could hardly wait to interview the family. James expressed more excitement over his son's accomplishments than over his own. Huston's answers showed that he admired his father. When asked about following in his dad's footsteps, the son replied, "I don't know if I'll ever have bragging rights with my dad. Everything I am is because my dad taught it to me."

The Bible's New Testament tells the story of a father and a son. God the Father sent his Son, Jesus Christ, to earth. Jesus displayed the power and love of the heavenly Father. But Jesus also had an earthly father, Joseph, who loved and guided him too.

GOAL! *This Father's Day, write a thank-you note to your dad or a father figure in your life. Thank God for your earthly father, and then praise your heavenly Father.*

DISPUTES OFTEN ARISE in sporting events. But in 1999, the Stanley Cup finals ended with a questionable goal that upset many Buffalo fans.

Leading the Sabres three games to two, the Dallas Stars hoped to capture the Cup at Buffalo's Marine Midland Arena. The Stars opened a first-period lead, but Buffalo tied the contest in the second.

Knotted 1–1 at the end of three periods, the teams prepared for overtime. Two full extra periods elapsed. As the third overtime wound down, the Stars' Mike Modano took control of the puck at the half boards. He passed to Brett Hull, who took a shot that Dominik Hasek blocked. The puck left the crease for a second, but Hull's left skate didn't. The right wing then corralled the rebound and shoveled the puck past the prone goalie, setting off a celebration by the Stars.

Television replays, however, clearly showed Hull's skate in the crease. The Sabres refused to leave their dressing room for 20 minutes, claiming the goal should be disallowed. But NHL supervisor of officials Bryan Lewis clarified the rule, stating that an attacking player can stay in the crease as long as he maintains control of the puck. Although Buffalo remained dissatisfied, the goal counted and Dallas captured its first Stanley Cup.

EXTRA POINT < < < < < < < < < < < < < < < < < < < < < < The Sabres thought they got a raw deal. Professionals play hockey on a round-cornered rectangle 200 by 85 feet with a 4-by-6-foot goal cage. Any puck that completely clears the 2-inch-wide line in front of the goal counts. The crease in front of the goal is a semicircular area with a 6-foot radius marked by a red line. If the goalie is in the crease, no offensive player can enter unless the puck's there. If the goalie isn't in the crease, the opposing team can't enter.

Since the puck and the goalie weren't in the crease for that split second, the goal became questionable. But the officials' supervisor made the call. His decree ended the argument.

Making a judgment can be hard. Most of the time somebody's going to be upset by the call. But there is one perfect judge: God. Although everything might not go as we'd like, his decisions are always just.

GOAL! *Think about a time that a teacher, coach, or official made a judgment call that didn't go your way. Are you still mad about it? It's time to let go of that anger. Thank God for his perfect judgments and for his rules in the Bible.*

> For the Lord is our judge, our lawgiver, and our king. He will care for us and save us.
>
> ISAIAH 33:22

19 JUN

But when the Father sends the Counselor as my representative— and by the Counselor I mean the Holy Spirit—he will teach you everything and will remind you of everything I myself have told you.

JOHN 14:26

IN THE SPORTING WORLD, momentum sometimes switches

back and forth for no apparent reason. In the 1999 United States Open, Payne Stewart gained a slight advantage at the very last moment.

The former Southern Methodist University golfer led by one stroke over Phil Mickelson as the tournament entered its final day. Playing in the Open's last pairing, the duo battled neck and neck over the back nine. Mickelson pulled even on No. 10 on Stewart's bogey and went in front on No. 12 when his partner carded a second one.

Payne, clad in his signature knickers, regained a stroke with a birdie at 13 but lost it by bogeying 15. Mickelson seemed in command at the 16th, but he missed a 6-foot putt and took his only bogey of the day. Stewart, on the other hand, sank a 25-footer to save par and reclaimed the lead on 17 with a birdie.

On the final hole, Stewart drove into the rough. With no choice but to punch out, his second shot left him 77 yards from the green. Payne grabbed his wedge and lofted the ball high in the air, stopping it 15 feet short of the pin. After lining up his putt, he rolled the ball into the center of the hole just as church bells chimed in the distance. Stewart shot an even-par 70 for the day and finished at 279. Mickelson ended one stroke behind.

EXTRA POINT < < < < < < < < < < < < < < < < < < < < <

How fitting it was for Payne Stewart to win the U.S. Open on Father's Day. His own father influenced his love of the game, and Stewart loved his children, Chelsea and Aaron. The Lord's favor shone on the 42-year-old golfer, who was wearing a WWJD bracelet that day, demonstrating his dedication to ask, "What Would Jesus Do?"

Maybe you've wondered how you could live up to Jesus' high standards. It probably seems impossible. And it is . . . without God's help. The good news is that the heavenly Father sends the Holy Spirit to remind you of everything Jesus said.

GOAL! *Isn't it cool that God has a plan to help you act more like Jesus? Whenever you ask yourself, "What Would Jesus Do?" remember that the answer is already inside you. Then praise God for sending the Holy Spirit.*

A NEW LEAGUE BRINGS new excitement and hope for a sport. In 1997, women's basketball finally produced a professional league of its own.

The Los Angeles Forum hosted the first Women's National Basketball Association (WNBA) game between the Los Angeles Sparks and the New York Liberty. For months, fans anticipated the event featuring the matchup between Lisa Leslie of the Sparks and Rebecca Lobo of the Liberty. Over 14,000 witnessed the tip-off between the two post players.

Leslie won the opening tip and batted the ball to her teammate Jamila Wideman. Los Angeles forward Penny Toler sank the League's first basket with an 11-foot jumper less than a minute into the contest.

Both teams exhibited streaks of nervousness. They combined for 45 turnovers. But there were also glimpses of brilliance.

Midway through the first half, Leslie broke free to the Sparks' basket. The crowd urged the 6-foot-1 post to go for the dunk, but her legs couldn't quite propel her above the rim. Leslie finished the contest with 16 points and 14 rebounds, leading Los Angeles to a 67–57 victory. Lobo paced the New York scoring with 16 points.

> The good soil represents the hearts of those who truly accept God's message and produce a huge harvest—thirty, sixty, or even a hundred times as much as had been planted.
>
> MATTHEW 13:23

EXTRA POINT

‹ Generations ago, who would have thought that women would field a basketball league of their own? The All-American Girls' Professional Baseball League featured in the Hollywood movie *A League of Their Own* came into being only because major league baseball suffered with the men away during World War II. Even then, the women played only from 1943 until 1954. But women's basketball took off to produce a viable league with a fruitful crop of players and fans.

Jesus told a parable about producing another kind of crop. As a farmer scattered seed, some fell on a path, some on rocky land, some among the thorns, and some on good soil. Only the seeds that rooted in the fertile soil grew. And only when God's Word enters listening ears can it lead to understanding and a changed life.

GOAL! *Read the parable of the sower in Matthew 13:1-9; 18-23. Ask God to help your life be fertile soil for his Word so that you may help bring others to the Lord.*

21 JUN

HITTING A GOLF BALL into the branches of a tree usually results in two extra strokes. But in the 1998 United States Open, a timely gust of wind that shook the branches of a cypress pine prevented a costly bogey for Lee Janzen.

The 33-year-old golfer trailed tournament leader Payne Stewart by five strokes after the third round. Two bogeys on the first three holes on Sunday upped the margin to seven.

But Janzen turned things around on the 457-yard, par-4 fifth hole. His drive stuck the ball high in the branches of a tree lining the fairway. With Janzen already heading back to the box to hit a second drive, word came to him that a breeze had swayed the boughs, and the ball had dropped from the sky. The unusual event allowed Lee to chip for par instead of taking a double bogey.

Later on Stewart struggled. Bogeys on 12 and 13 knocked him from the lead, while Janzen forged ahead with birdies on 11, 13, 14, and 16. He closed with pars on 17 and 18, finishing the day with 68 and a total of 280.

Stewart trailed by one stroke on the final hole. He needed a 25-foot downhill putt for a birdie and a tie. But his ball broke low and rolled to the left. Janzen, watching the action on television from the clubhouse, breathed a sigh of relief and claimed the championship.

EXTRA POINT < < < < < < < < < < < < < < < < < < < < Nature, in the form of a tree, almost cost Lee Janzen the U.S. Open. And then nature, in the form of the wind, helped him save par and propelled him to the title. Golf courses utilize trees, sand, grass, water, and other natural objects to beautify the setting and challenge the players.

God's creation beautifies our lives, too. The book of Genesis describes how God created the world. He made plants and trees, and it's a good thing he did. We benefit in so many ways—whether building houses from wood or eating a piece of fruit—from God's creation.

GOAL! *The next time you eat a piece of fruit, thank God for his creation. Ask him to help you live a fruitful life for him.*

THE LAND WAS FILLED WITH SEED-BEARING PLANTS AND TREES, AND THEIR SEEDS

GENESIS 1:12

PRODUCED PLANTS AND TREES OF LIKE KIND. AND GOD SAW THAT IT WAS GOOD.

Honor your father and your mother, so that you may live long in the land the Lord your God is giving you.

EXODUS 20:12, NIV

AS MARTINA HINGIS MATURED and developed as a tennis player, her mother served as coach, adviser, and mentor. But when Martina and her mom parted in 1999, the superstar discovered the difficulty of facing competition alone.

In Wimbledon's first round, Hingis drew 16-year-old Jelena Dokic, who was ranked 129th in the world. These two players had met earlier in the year in the third round of the Australian Open with Hingis winning easily 6–1, 6–2.

But in this pairing, Dokic performed fearlessly from the baseline, answering Martina's desperate drop shots with drop shots of her own. Jelena served powerfully down the stretch. She controlled the match by keeping the ball deep and not allowing Hingis to push forward to the net or hit winning angles that traditionally accompanied her compact ground strokes.

The Yugoslavian-born player captured the match 6–2, 6–0 in only 54 minutes. On match point, when Hingis's backhand sailed long, Dokic wheeled around to face her father in the stands as she thrust both arms into the air. She became the lowest-ranked player to defeat a No. 1 seed in a Grand Slam event. Her victory also marked only the third time since 1968 that the top-ranked player had lost in a Grand Slam first round.

EXTRA POINT < < < < < < < < < < < < < < < < < < < < The 18-year-old Martina Hingis faced difficulty when she left her mom's guidance. And her actions cost her on the court. On the other hand, Dokic still enjoyed the loving support of her dad in the stands.

Many young people can't wait to go to college or move out on their own. And the time comes when this happens in every family. But when a daughter or son learns wisdom, independence, and maturity through years of loving instruction, everybody benefits from the move. If not, their decisions can prove disappointing, disgraceful, or disastrous.

God's plan is for parents to love and nurture their offspring to maturity. Then their sons and daughters leave the family nest for adult success.

GOAL! *What are some of the best things your parents have taught you?*

_____

_____

Praise God for moms and dads who help their daughters and sons mature through loving instruction.

THE SURF WAS UP at the 2003 X Games. For the first time in this adrenaline sports competition, teams from the East Coast and the West Coast squared off in Huntington Beach, California.

Two four-man squads from each team took turns riding the Pacific. While the waves crested at only about two to three feet (with an occasional four-footer), the athletes made the most of the conditions by busting big airs and carving out mean lines. The East Coast also showed its jawing abilities as captain Kelly Slater started the trash-talking early by asking his West Coast rivals during practice if they just "wanted to forfeit." The West Coasters laughed and the game was on.

The visitors surfed first with Shea Lopez, Aaron Cormican, Ben Bourgeois, and Damien Hobgood taking to the waves. Notching a combined score of 46.04, this fearsome foursome set the tone. The West Coast team didn't get any real waves and began with a low score.

The East Coast added to its lead when six-time world champs Slater, Cory Lopez, Taj Burrow, and Shane Dorian took to the ocean. The West countered with Rob Machado, Pat O'Connell, Tim Curran, and Kalani Robb. Curran led the group with a huge frontside 360 air. The first East Coast group went back in the water, and Cormican blasted a monster frontside 360 air and three additional technical moves to score a 9.0. The West's Dane Reynolds answered with a frontside grab five-foot air to score 9.07—the highest score of the day! But it was too little too late, and the East took home the first X Games gold medal for surfing.

> Don't use foul or abusive language. Let everything you say be good and helpful, so that your words will be an encouragement to those who hear them.
>
> EPHESIANS 4:29

EXTRA POINT
< < < < < < < < < < < < < < < < < < <

The East Coast beat the West on the waves, and they also battered them with their words. Throughout the competition, the East trash-talked the West. For some athletes, that's the way they psych out their opponents.

But as followers of Jesus, we should hold ourselves to a higher standard. The Bible tells us not to use abusive language. That applies to the sports field, the classroom, and our everyday life. Instead, our words should encourage others.

GOAL! *Next time you feel like trash-talking an opponent, think about what God says. Try to have your speech honor him at all times.*

24 JUN

If a widow has children or grandchildren, these should learn first of all to put their religion into practice by caring for their own family and so repaying their parents and grand-parents, for this is pleasing to God.

1 TIMOTHY 5:4, NIV

IN 2001, WHEN KARRIE WEBB accomplished one of the most amazing feats in golf, it came with a bittersweet ending. During the first day of the LPGA Championship, Webb's 71-year-old grandfather, Mick Collinson, suffered an unexpected stroke. After Saturday's third round, Karrie learned Collinson had taken a turn for the worse.

Webb considered skipping the LPGA Championship's final round and returning to Australia. But about seven hours before her tee time, she decided to compete. To reduce media hype, she and caddie Mike Patterson kept the news to themselves.

The 26-year-old golfer held a three-stroke lead as the tournament entered the last day. Playing with stoic determination, Webb birdied three of the first four holes, upping her spread to six. Laura Diaz closed with four birdies on the back nine, but Webb carded a 69 for a 270 total, claiming first place and her fifth Grand Slam by two strokes.

As soon as Webb tapped in her last putt, tears flowed. As much as she wanted to be with her family, she knew her grandfather wouldn't want her to miss a possible LPGA title. Her grandpa had taken her with him to play nine holes of golf every weekend since she was four years old. He owned a toy store and gave her plastic clubs, pulling her in a wagon when she got tired. He helped her struggle through 152 strokes on her first 18 holes at age eight, and for her 12th birthday he gave her a plane ticket to see Greg Norman play.

EXTRA POINT < < < < < < < < < < < < < < < < < < < < < < Mick Collinson died a few hours before his adoring grand-daughter reached Australia. He never knew she had become the youngest woman ever to complete a career Grand Slam and one of only five women ever to do it. But Karrie dedicated the tournament to her grandfather, repaying him the only way she knew how—by playing the sport he taught her to love.

God gives some of us very special grandparents. The apostle Paul wrote Timothy that repaying them pleases the heavenly Father.

GOAL! *If you can, plan a way to help repay your grandparents or other mentors in your life. It could be simple like a letter or something more elaborate. Thank God for grandparents.*

PLAYING IN THE FIRST GAME of a championship can make any team a little nervous. But in 1999, Mia Hamm calmed the U.S. National soccer team's fears as it entered World Cup competition.

With 78,972 fans at Giants Stadium—the largest crowd ever to view a women's sporting event—the Americans faced Denmark in the opening round. After 15 minutes of scoreless, chaotic play, the United States settled into a groove.

Brandi Chastain kicked a long pass to Hamm. Deftly dribbling the ball, the former North Carolina All-American cut back on Denmark's Katrine Pedersen just to the right of the goal. Using her left foot, she volleyed the ball into the top of the net.

Witnessing their star player score the first goal, her 110th in international matches, brought the United States team a sense of calm and control. Although the Americans missed several second-half chances to put away the game, the Danes eventually succumbed to the pressure of the relentless U.S. attack.

In the 73rd minute, Hamm sent a ball across the goal box to Julie Foudy. Julie controlled the ball and shot it into the net from ten yards away for America's second score. With a minute remaining, Kristine Lilly iced the contest with a goal from the top of the box to make the final score 3–0.

EXTRA POINT < < < < < < < < < < < < < < < < < < < Sometimes on the field, diamond, course, or court, athletes grow too excited and anxious to perform well. Nerves can cause the better team to lose. But the great ones in sports stay cool. Their heart may be thumping on the inside, but the exterior exudes calm.

The psalmist in the Bible knew the value of calmness. He wrote that we should take time to quiet ourselves and think of God's majesty. Often we're too busy or too nervous or have our mind going a million miles per hour, so we're unable to focus on God. But it's during those busy times that we need to be still.

GOAL! *Go outside to a calm, peaceful place or stay inside and turn off the TV, CD player, or anything making noise. Sit in the quiet as you let yourself slow down. Ask God to help you focus on his exalted glory.*

Be still, and know that I am God; I will be exalted among the nations, I will be exalted in the earth!

PSALM 46:10, NKJV

26 JUN

GIVING UP IS EASY. But coming back after failure shows character. Peter Fleck displayed his winning attitude by claiming back-to-back barefoot waterskiing jumping titles at the X Games.

Blessed is
the man who
trusts in the
Lord, whose
confidence is
in him.
JEREMIAH
17:7, NIV

Fleck's first two X Games didn't go well. In fact, they were horrible. He
made six jumps and landed zero. The results: no medals, no money, no glory,
and lots of embarrassment. But instead of giving up, Fleck returned to compete
in the 1997 X Games, where he won gold. Then Fleck came back again in 1998
to defend his title.

Heading into the two-day competition, Fleck oozed confidence—not because he was cocky but because he was prepared. After winning his first gold,
Fleck worked even harder to stay on top in his sport. He looked at hours of videotape, trying to find ways to get more distance from his jumps and discover
techniques to nail his landings. The extra effort paid off as Fleck landed his first
jump in every round and never trailed in the competition.

In the semifinals, Fleck jumped 87.5 feet to lead Ron Scarpa, Mamo
Colosio, and Lane Bowers into the finals. Fleck went 87.5 feet again in the finals
to edge out Scarpa by four feet. Colosio took third.

EXTRA POINT < < < < < < < < < < < < < < < < < < < <
Barefoot waterskiing is hard enough. Don't believe it? Just try it.
But being pulled by a boat at speeds of over 40 mph, zooming up a ramp, flying
through the air, and landing on the water on your feet seems impossible. And
soaring nearly 90 feet—that's like jumping nine cars—is amazing. Doing it once
would be an awesome feat. Landing it time after time is almost unthinkable. But
Peter Fleck developed the skills and confidence to do it and ended up winning
back-to-back gold medals.

Confidence makes a big difference in life and in athletics. As Christ's followers, we have a source for our confidence that's unbelievably powerful. The
prophet Jeremiah says we'll be blessed by putting our confidence in the Lord.

GOAL! *Can you think of something that you were awful at the first
time you tried? Praise God that he gave you the talent to practice and improve. Commit to putting your confidence in the Lord.*

THE UNITED STATES and Mexico rarely engage in athletic competition. But in the 2002 World Cup quarterfinals, the neighboring nations put on a spirited display on the soccer field.

The United States team, playing on two days' rest, surprised Mexico by coming out with an aggressive, high-energy style of play. The United States erupted for a goal in the game's eighth minute. U.S. captain Claudio Reyna made a long run up the right side after faking a defender. He passed to Josh Wolff standing near the goal. Wolff flicked the ball back to a wide-open Brian McBride, who drove it hard into the left side of the net.

But in typical fashion, the Mexicans controlled the ball for a majority of the game—keeping the attack in the U.S. end of the field nearly 70 percent of the time. But American goalie Brad Friedel refused to yield, blocking every shot, including two point-blank efforts in the 35th minute.

In the 65th minute, the United States broke Mexico's spirits with its second goal. Eddie Lewis sped upfield and fired a cross to Landon Donovan just inside the 6-yard box. Donovan headed the ball into the net for a 2–0 lead.

In the waning moments, tempers flared. Mexico's captain, Rafael Marquez, received an ejection for banging his head into Cobi Jones. Officials issued ten yellow cards, five for each team, for especially hard fouls in the 2–0 American victory.

EXTRA POINT < < < < < < < < < < < < < < < < < < < < < < < < The neighboring countries didn't end the game in very neighborly fashion. The Mexicans have long been a dominant soccer nation. For Americans, soccer's popularity lagged behind baseball, football, and basketball. Being beaten by anyone hurt Mexico, but losing to an upstart soccer nation brought threats of revenge and the beginnings of a grudge.

Sometimes neighbors have differences. Little irritations grow into big disagreements. Harsh words escalate into bad feelings. Grudges and revenge replace kindness and helpfulness. God's Word tells us to love our neighbors as ourselves. That may not be our way, but it's God's way . . . and it's the right way.

GOAL! *Think about your neighbors. If you have problems, will you work to make things right? Ask God to help you love your neighbors as yourself.*

Never seek revenge or bear a grudge against anyone, but love your neighbors as yourself. I am the Lord.
LEVITICUS 19:18

28 JUN

Similarly, encourage the young men to be self-controlled. In everything set them an example by doing what is good. In your teaching show integrity, seriousness and soundness of speech.

TITUS 2:6-8, NIV

LEARNING BY EXAMPLE

LEARNING BY EXAMPLE provides an excellent path to success, especially if the leader performs well. National League pitcher Fernando Valenzuela used Dave Stewart's example as a blueprint on the mound though the two played miles apart in 1990.

First, the Oakland A's flew over the border to face the Toronto Blue Jays. Stewart walked his first two batters but quickly settled into a groove, relying primarily on his crisp fastball. The right-hander retired 26 consecutive hitters before walking Junior Felix with two outs in the ninth. Tony Fernandez then flied to center, ending the game and giving Stewart his first no-hitter with a 5–0 victory.

More than 3,000 miles away, Valenzuela learned of Stewart's achievement 30 minutes prior to his start against the St. Louis Cardinals. The left-hander promised his Los Angeles Dodgers teammates they might witness a pitching gem as well. Valenzuela breezed through the game, throwing only 124 pitches. He struck out seven and allowed only four Cardinals on base with three walks and one error.

With one out in the ninth, Valenzuela walked Willie McGee. Former Dodger Pedro Guerrero then smashed a grounder that seemed destined for the outfield. But Valenzuela nicked the ball with his glove, ricocheting it to Juan Samuel, who stepped on second and threw to first for the double play. With the 6–0 win, Fernando collected his first no-hitter, and baseball recorded its first double no-hit day.

EXTRA POINT

< < < < < < < < < < < < < < < < < < < < < <

Fernando Valenzuela saw Dave Stewart's success and decided to follow his example. Their styles differed, but the outcomes didn't. Both notched one of baseball's greatest feats—a no-hitter.

Following a blueprint or watching an example makes any task easier. In the Bible, Paul wrote a letter urging Titus to set a positive example. Not only does God want us to follow positive patterns, he also wants us to live as a good example. We never know who's watching us or who might decide to follow us.

GOAL! *Who do you look to as an example? Write down one person and the quality of theirs you want to emulate.*

Person: *Quality:*

_____

Ask God to help you choose wise examples to follow and to be a good example to all who look to you.

OVERTIME GAMES can drain both players and fans. In a 1984 United States Football League playoff encounter, the Michigan Panthers and the Los Angeles Express played in the longest professional football game ever.

The two teams squared off in the opening round of the now defunct league. The Express trailed 21–13 with 8:57 remaining, but quarterback Steve Young directed Los Angeles to the Michigan 12-yard line with slightly over a minute left.

On third-and-goal, the former Brigham Young signal caller escaped a Panthers rush and ran to the 1. Facing fourth down, Young handed off to Kevin Nelson, who plunged in for the touchdown. Deciding to go for two points and the tie, Young rolled left and slipped into the end zone to knot the score.

In the first overtime, Michigan kicker Novo Bojovic pushed the ball wide left on a 37-yard field goal attempt, and neither team scored. Bojovic muffed another opportunity from 36 yards as the second overtime wound down, and the game moved to a third extra period.

Los Angeles took the kickoff and moved 75 yards. On first down from the Panther 24, Mel Gray took Young's handoff, darted into the line, cut outside, and headed for the corner. With defensive back Vito McKeever breathing down his neck, the exhausted running back thrust his body into the end zone. Los Angeles took a 27–21 win in the unbelievably long game.

EXTRA POINT < < < < < < < < < < < < < < < < < < < Players and fans alike thought the game would never end. Sometimes in life, we wish time would speed up. We can hardly wait for the big game, a birthday, Christmas, or another special occasion. Students feel that time crawls at the end of the school year.

At other moments, time flashes by at a whirling pace. We're not sure where the hours go, and we wish for more minutes in our days. We want the sun to stop in the middle of the sky and delay going down until we get caught up.

God gave all of us the gift of time—1,440 minutes in a day and 365 days in a year. And he knows exactly how long we will live. Treat each moment as a precious present from God . . . even if it feels like time is dragging.

GOAL! *Praise God for both his gift of time and his power over time. Commit to making the most of every day.*

> You have decided the length of our lives. You know how many months we will live, and we are not given a minute longer.
>
> JOB 14:5

30 JUN

JULY

HITTING TWO HOME RUNS in a road victory will help any baseball player make the headlines. But in 2000, Florida Marlins outfielder Mark Smith was not only a hero for his team on the field, but also on the drive home.

The reserve outfielder received a rare start in right field against the Montreal Expos, batting cleanup in place of Preston Wilson. After spending most of the season on the disabled list, the former Japanese League player belted a deep shot over the left-field fence in his first at bat. In his second plate appearance, Smith smashed a 415-foot homer to center. The two solo blasts provided all of Florida's offense in the 2–1 Marlins victory.

Elated after his successful day at Olympic Stadium, Smith and pitcher Brad Penny flew back to Florida and drove home together from the airport. Suddenly, the pair witnessed a car drift off the road, strike a concrete culvert, flip over the median, and catch fire. Smith quickly made a U-turn and called the police on his cell phone.

When the ballplayers arrived at the wrecked car, the driver had kicked out the rear window but couldn't squeeze out as fire raced from the engine. Smith grabbed the vehicle's occupant by the legs, pulled him through the window, and dragged him 20 yards before flames completely engulfed the automobile. The driver, 21-year-old Henry Oliva, was hospitalized but released the following day.

EXTRA POINT < < < < < < < < < < < < < < < < < < < < < < < Sports reporters sometimes talk about professional athletes having courage under fire. Was Mark Smith afraid when he saw that car on fire and a stranger's life in danger? Absolutely. But in that split second, Mark showed courage. He didn't allow fear to paralyze him. Instead, he exercised the kind of faith God gives.

It's okay to be afraid. But the Lord God offers the courage to conquer fear—whether of fire, failure, or something else. Numerous times during his life on earth, Jesus commanded, "Do not be afraid" and "Fear not."

Christ's words hold true today.

GOAL! *What makes you afraid?*

Someone said that fear and courage go together like macaroni and cheese. One's not much good without the other. Ask God for the courage to overcome your fears.

I am leaving you with a gift— peace of mind and heart. And the peace I give isn't like the peace the world gives. So don't be troubled or afraid.

JOHN 14:27

01 JUL

> All men are like grass, and all their glory is like the flowers of the field; the grass withers and the flowers fall, but the word of the Lord stands forever.
>
> 1 PETER 1:24-25, NIV

IN HIS PRIME, Pete Sampras owned Wimbledon. In the 1990s, he won six men's championships at the All England Lawn Tennis Club. And in 2001, Sampras was on a quest for his fifth straight title.

The 29-year-old American quickly advanced through the early rounds and came into the quarterfinals on a roll with 31 consecutive Wimbledon victories and 56 wins in his past 57 matches.

But in the quarters, Sampras squared off against 19-year-old Swiss upstart Roger Federer. Federer, the former Wimbledon Junior champion, refused to be awed. He established his presence, taking the first set 7–6. Sampras, the 13-time Grand Slam winner, evened the match with a 7–5 win in set two. The teenager bounced back to claim set three 6–4. And the battle between youth and age narrowed once again with a 7–6 Sampras victory in the fourth set to set up a decisive fifth.

Playing much like his former idol, Federer served confidently, returned consistently, and approached the net at every opportunity. His poise and ease forced his older opponent into a series of uncharacteristic errors.

With the score knotted 4–4, the seven-time Wimbledon champion held two break points, but Federer erased one with a volley and another with a sizzling forehand. Serving in the final game, Sampras misplayed two volleys. His young opponent finally cracked a return winner and fell to his knees after taking the match.

EXTRA POINT < < < < < < < < < < < < < < < < < < < <

Pete Sampras had an incredible run at Wimbledon. Few players achieve back-to-back Grand Slam titles. Still fewer three-peat. Four, five, or six in a row becomes rarer. Only Martina Navratilova (1982–1987) and W. C. Renshaw (1881–1886) won six Wimbledon singles titles in succession. Sampras tried for five, giving the match all he had.

It's impossible for an athlete to stay on top forever. Bodies age, injuries nag, and skills diminish. Younger players continually replace older ones. But there is something that lasts forever: God's Word. The Bible stands tall age after age, generation after generation.

GOAL! *Name some veteran athletes who retired or were replaced by younger ones. Thank God that his Word cannot be replaced. It's always fresh, always new . . . and always the best.*

ROCK CLIMBERS don't take chances. Safety comes first, as one false move could prove fatal on a gigantic rock face. But in speed climbing, risk is part of the sport. Because the competitors are top-roped to a wall as they go for the fastest time, slips and falls are expected. At the 1999 X Games Speed Climbing competition, Aaron Shamy used a risky strategy to fly up the wall for the gold.

Many speed climbers use a "ladder method," where arms and legs alternate in rapid succession so it looks like the athlete is running up the wall. Others simply pull themselves up the wall with their arms as their feet follow behind. But at X Games V in San Francisco, Shamy's unorthodox style of leaping up the wall took first and set a new record. By jumping at key points and skipping multiple holds, Shamy actually made the course shorter and his times lower . . . as long as he caught the next hold perfectly.

After overcoming some mistakes and barely defeating Andrii Vedenmieier in the semis, Shamy blew past Chris Bloch in the finals with a record-breaking time. He flew up the wall in just 12.61 seconds, shattering Vladimir Netsvetaev's previous mark of 15.38 by nearly three seconds. Netsvetaev settled for third in the 1999 Games after taking first the year before.

EXTRA POINT < < < < < < < < < < < < < < < < < < < < < Aaron Shamy may be famous for his superquick, unusual climbing style, but he's also known for his contagious smile and boundless energy. Win or lose, Shamy keeps a smile on his face and treats his competitors with respect. His happiness isn't tied to how he performs on the wall.

God wants his followers to have the same attitude. We should go through life smiling at the world—not scowling at our feet. Because of the awesome things Jesus has done and the hope we have in him, our outward appearance and actions should draw others to us. And nothing does more to attract friends than a smiling face and happy personality.

GOAL! *Sometimes it's not easy to smile. Difficult circumstances and bad moods often get in the way. But that's not God's desire for your life. He wants you to be happy and treat others well. Remember that your face will reflect your joy.*

They should be happy and do good while they live. I know there's nothing better for them to do than that.

ECCLESIASTES 3:12, NIrV

03 JUL

> So I will work
> hard to make
> these things
> clear to you.
> I want you
> to remember
> them long after
> I am gone.
>
> 2 PETER 1:15

FOR YEARS AMERICANS CELEBRATED the Fourth of July with baseball doubleheaders. In 1939, New Yorkers gathered to witness some great baseball, but more importantly, they came to Yankee Stadium to honor a hero and a friend.

The Yankees engaged the Washington Senators in the holiday twin bill. Following a 3–2 New York loss in the opener, more than 61,000 fans witnessed the legendary 1927 Bronx Bomber squad gather on the field facing home plate. After they were introduced, current players from both teams lined the base paths before Lou Gehrig, former Yankees first baseman, stepped from the dugout to receive gifts.

Following the presentation, Gehrig, who played in 2,130 consecutive games (a record that stood until 1995 when Cal Ripken Jr. broke it), choked up as he spoke. But former manager Joe McCarthy shouted words of encouragement, and the "Iron Horse" suppressed tears to deliver words of appreciation.

Forced into retirement with a deteriorating muscular disease, the ex-Yankee opened with, "For the past two weeks you have been reading about the bad break I got. Yet today, I consider myself the luckiest man on the face of this earth."

Gehrig continued by thanking his fans, teammates, organization, opponents, parents, and wife for their support and strength. He counted among his blessings an education, the chance to play baseball, and the love of those around him. The "Pride of the Yankees" closed his farewell address by stating, "I may have had a tough break, but I have an awful lot to live for."

EXTRA POINT < < < < < < < < < < < < < < < < < < < < Not only did Lou Gehrig fight back tears, fans at Yankee Stadium and those listening by radio swallowed weepy lumps in their throat too. They appreciated the brave ballplayer who was fighting amyotrophic lateral sclerosis (later renamed Lou Gehrig's Disease), which would ultimately take his life on June 2, 1941, when he was only 37.

But on that Independence Day, fans also remembered the brave patriots who had fought for a free nation. Fifty-six men risked their life to sign the Declaration of Independence. William Dawes, Paul Revere, and Samuel Prescott rode through dangerous territory to warn that the enemy approached. About 4,000 American soldiers died in the Revolution's battles.

In the Bible, the apostle Peter knew his days on earth would be short. He reminded us to remember the people and teachings of those who have gone before us to spread God's Good News.

GOAL! *Read a biography of Lou Gehrig or check out his farewell on the Internet. Ask God to help you appreciate those who lived their life well and left a legacy for others to follow.*

HAVING THE RIGHT EQUIPMENT can often help win championships. And when an athlete actually designs the gear, it gives him or her an even bigger edge. At the 1999 X Games in San Francisco, California, David Rogers took home street luge gold on his specially designed sled.

At first glance, street luge may look like a sport for athletes with a death wish. Traveling at speeds of more than 70 mph on a glorified skateboard, with their head inches from the pavement, street lugers certainly take some risks. But the fact is that many street lugers are in their 30s and hold down serious jobs. Rogers certainly fits that description. A mechanical engineer in his mid-30s, Rogers tinkered with his sled's design prior to the 1999 Games.

Starting with a group of competitors in the Super Mass competition down Seal Rock Run, Rogers wasn't expected to be among the winners. He had finished 21st in the previous X Games and claimed 32nd in the super mass in 1997. Plus, three-time X Games gold medalist Biker Sherlock was in the field.

Wearing a motorcycle helmet, a leather body suit, and thick gloves and shoes, the lugers rocketed down the course. With less than 100 feet remaining, it appeared as if Sherlock would claim his fourth gold. But Rogers accelerated through the Cliff House Turn and passed Sherlock 75 feet before the finish line. Sean Slate stuck his foot out at the line to edge out Bob Pereyra for third.

> I have filled [Bezalel] with the Spirit of God, giving him great wisdom, intelligence, and skill in all kinds of crafts.
>
> EXODUS 31:3

EXTRA POINT < < < < < < < < < < < < < < < < < < < < < < Top players in any sport demonstrate skill and craftsmanship. Natural ability coupled with practice creates excellence. David Rogers put his engineering know-how into his street luge and drove it to the gold.

Many people outside of athletics show knowledge in their craft as well. In Exodus, the second book of the Bible, God told Moses that he chose Bezalel to design the gold, silver, bronze, wood, and precious stone for the Tabernacle. Bezalel would help fashion a beautiful worship place.

Today, architects, sculptors, and stained-glass window artists create inviting settings for worship. They use their skills to build churches that glorify God.

GOAL! *Do you have a special skill? It's up to you to choose how to use your ability to praise the Lord. Thank God for the beauty that skilled craftspeople add to worship.*

05

"Should you

not fear me?"

declares the

Lord. "Should

you not

tremble in

my presence?

I made the

sand a

boundary for

the sea, an

everlasting

barrier it

cannot cross.

The waves

may roll, but

they cannot

prevail; they

may roar, but

they cannot

cross it."

JEREMIAH

5:22, NIV

SOME BARRIERS seem almost insurmountable in athletics, such as a 9,000-point score in the decathlon. But in 1999, Tomas Dvorak nearly exceeded that mark.

Through five events, the 27-year-old Czech stood 75 points behind Dan O'Brien's 1992 record pace of 8,891 points. Establishing personal bests in the 100 meters, long jump, and shot put gave Dvorak an opportunity for a strong closing.

The following day, the track star won the 110-meter hurdles and threw the discus 158-feet-6-inches. But Dvorak struggled in the pole vault, passing at 16-feet-2¾-inches due to injury. Still trailing O'Brien's mark by 76 points, the 1996 Olympic bronze medalist opted to save his strength.

The strategy proved successful. Dvorak heaved the javelin 237-3, moving 72 points ahead of O'Brien's pace. Needing 4:53.87 in the 1,500 meters to tie the world record and 4:36.34 to break 9,000, Dvorak appeared to be a lock early in the race. But then the decathlete erred. Slowing down to avoid burnout, Dvorak couldn't shave off enough time in his final lap and finished at 4:37.20, setting a new world mark of 8,944 points.

Although Tomas Dvorak missed the magical 9,000, his fellow countryman Roman Sebrle shattered the record only two years later with 9,026 points. And the decathlon barrier moved upward.

EXTRA POINT < < < < < < < < < < < < < < < < < < < < <

Competing in all ten decathlon events requires an exceptional diversity of skills. The 100 meters, triple jump, pole vault, discus, 400 meters, long jump, shot put, 110-meter hurdles, high jump, and 1,500-meter run could cause havoc for any athlete. Scoring in each event is based on a table that awards points for levels of proficiency. For example, a 10.0 in the 100 meters earns 1,037 points, while a 12.0 rates 605. Breaking 9,000 means earning an average of 900 points in each event.

In life, we too can overcome obstacles. We graduate from high school, and some of us go on to college. We may study to become a teacher or we may work hard to make the school track team.

The prophet Jeremiah says that God made some permanent barriers. But the heavenly Father himself knows no limits.

GOAL! *Think of barriers in your life. Write some down:*

_____

_____

Ask God to help you overcome them or live within them according to his plan.

WORDS ARE POWERFUL.

The right words can help someone accomplish big things. Don't believe it? Just look at what happened at the 2002 United States Women's Open.

Heading into the tournament's final day, Juli Inkster, a 42-year old mother of two, trailed Annika Sorenstam by two strokes for the lead. On Saturday night, Inkster had received an e-mail from her 12-year-old daughter. The encouraging message lifted the mother's attitude. Hayley's note read, "Good luck, Mom, you can do it."

After tweaking her swing on the driving range early in the morning, Inkster quickly shaved one stroke from the lead with a birdie on No. 3. Then she chipped in for a second birdie on 6 to tie. Another birdie at 7 followed as Inkster took the lead for good at the Prairie Dunes Country Club.

In the meantime, Sorenstam played cautiously, protecting her position. Although she birdied No. 5, the Swedish golfer took a bogey on 8 and didn't card another birdie until 14.

On the 15th hole, Inkster landed in the rough beside the green, pitched 15 feet past the hole, and sank a par-saving putt. A birdie on 16 propelled her to a three-stroke lead, and the California native finished the day with a 4-under-par 66. Her four-day total of 276 edged out Sorenstam for the title by two strokes.

EXTRA POINT

< < < < < < < < < < < < < < < < < < < < <

Juli Inkster gave high fives to the fans who praised her as she ran to the scoring tent after her victory. The support of her family and friends helped perfect her attitude, while the extra practice adjustments helped perfect her swing. And the encouraging words of her daughter made a difference too.

A woman in the Bible received similar accolades. And like Inkster, she worked hard to accomplish noble tasks. It's important to remember that our parents deserve and relish our praise and encouragement—no matter how old they are and no matter how old we are.

GOAL!

Read Proverbs 31:10-31. Write or e-mail encouraging words to older family members. Praise God for the noble things they do.

Her children stand and bless her. Her husband praises her: "There are many virtuous and capable women in the world, but you surpass them all!"

PROVERBS 31:28-29

---

07 JUL

TOP TRACK STARS set goals to break records. In 1999, Moroccan citizens nicknamed Hicham El Guerrouj "the Prince of the Desert" after he moved another step closer to achieving his ultimate ambition.

The 24-year-old distance runner competed in the mile at Rome's Golden Gala meet. On the same track a year earlier, El Guerrouj had set a world record in the 1,500 meters (3:26.00).

With warm weather conditions helping bring in fast times, the North African kept pace with the early leaders. At the bell lap, El Guerrouj raced to the front of the pack, but Kenya's Noah Ngeny stayed close. Pushed to his limits, the 1,500-meter world-record holder crossed the finish line two strides ahead of Ngeny in a time of 3:43.13—beating the old world record for the mile by 1.26 seconds.

El Guerrouj might have clocked a 3:42 or 3:41, but 300 meters from the end, he glanced at the large screen and caught a glimpse of Ngeny. The sight momentarily distracted the runner, adding at least a second to his time.

With two world records, El Guerrouj achieved another rung on his personal success ladder. The Moroccan hoped to eventually obtain world bests in every distance race between 1,500 and 5,000 meters, including the 2,000 meters, the 3,000 meters, and the steeple. Later in September he added the 2,000 meters to his resume.

EXTRA POINT < < < < < < < < < < < < < < < < < < < < Hicham El Guerrouj set high goals for himself. Achieving those goals and getting the most out of his talent required training hard and striving to win.

The apostle Paul knew a lot about goal setting. And he said we should have just one aim in life: pleasing God.

What are some things you'd like to accomplish for Christ? Do you want to lead somebody into a personal relationship with him? go on a mission trip? become a missionary in a foreign land? As Christians we too should set high goals. As great as your goals may be for God, he calls you to do one thing: Please him always. That's a tough goal.

GOAL! **Write down some of your goals.**

_____

_____

Ask God to help you please him with your thoughts, words, and actions, and you'll accomplish big things for him.

TIMING CAN MAKE the difference in any sport. In the 1998 World Cup, Lilian Thuram's feet spoke at a most opportune time.

Everyone enjoys a fitting reply; it is wonderful to say the right thing at the right time!

PROVERBS 15:23

The 26-year-old native of Guadeloupe in the French West Indies moved to Paris at age nine with his mother. Discovered at age 18 while playing for a local club, the defender signed with the French champion soccer team, AS Monaco, and represented his adopted country on the World Cup team.

The French squad advanced through the tournament's early rounds and faced Croatia in the semifinals. Confined primarily to a defensive role, Thuram had not tallied a single goal for the national team in 37 previous games.

But with Croatia leading 1–0 early in the second half, the player (who had once considered becoming a priest) stole the ball from Zvonimir Boban. Playing give-and-go with teammate Youri Djorkaeff, he blasted the ball past Croatian goalkeeper Drazen Ladic from close range to tie the score.

As the second half drew toward the midpoint, Thuram replied again in a timely manner. Moving forward from his defensive position, he robbed Robert Jarni of the ball, looked up, spotted an opening, and fired a shot into the lower left corner of the net from 20 yards away.

Despite losing captain Laurent Blanc because of a foul four minutes later, the ten-man French team held on for a 2–1 victory and the right to face Brazil in the finals. With 77,000 French fans screaming madly throughout the Stade de France, Thuram exited the arena on the shoulders of reserve goalie Bernard Lama as hundreds of photographers snapped the unexpected hero's picture.

EXTRA POINT < < < < < < < < < < < < < < < < < < < < < < < Lilian Thuram picked the perfect moment to come through for his team! Thuram discovered that timing meant everything as the French experienced the joy of moving into the World Cup finals.

In life, timing often means everything too. The writer of Proverbs understood the joy of offering an appropriate comment at the right moment. But he also knew the value of receiving a good word just when it's needed most. God wants us to help others with fitting replies and good words.

GOAL! *Sometime during the day, offer a positive word to a person who needs to hear a good message. Thank God for his good words in the Bible.*

WHEN A GAME HANGS in the balance, a coach must have faith that the players will execute the plan and come away with a victory. In the 1999 Women's World Cup, Brandi Chastain proved that her coach's faith was well-founded.

The American national soccer team drew China in the championship contest. More than 90,000 fans packed the Rose Bowl to cheer on the country's newest heroines.

But the Chinese provided formidable opposition. Through 90 minutes of regulation, the contest remained knotted in a scoreless tie. Then neither team could score in two 15-minute overtime periods as a United States defensive play prevented a China victory. With goalie Briana Scurry out of position, Kristine Lilly blocked a Fan Yunjie header off the goal line with her head in the 100th minute.

Moving to penalty kicks as the tiebreaker, U.S. coach Tony DiCicco selected team captain Carla Overbeck, Joy Fawcett, Lilly, Mia Hamm, and Chastain as his five kickers. Chastain replaced Michelle Akers, DiCicco's normal choice, after the veteran sustained a head injury in the game's late stages.

The United States caught a break on China's third attempt when Scurry deflected Liu Ying's shot wide of the net. The two teams were tied 4–4 with no Chinese players remaining as Chastain lined up against goalkeeper Gao Hong and blasted the ball past Hong for the winning goal. In a moment of jubilation, the California native fell to her knees, held her arms aloft, and shouted to the heavens.

EXTRA POINT < < < < < < < < < < < < < < < < < < < Coach DiCicco trusted Brandi Chastain with that final penalty kick. Fortunately she proved faithful as she won the game.

God is always faithful. Because he loves us, the Lord sent Jesus to earth to die for our wrongs. When we put our faith in Christ, he redeems us and offers us eternity with him. There is never any worrying about what the outcome will be. We don't have to fret on the sidelines like Coach DiCicco, wondering if we're going to win. We are *guaranteed* blessings when we put our faith in Jesus.

GOAL! *Write down some good definitions for faith and trust. Check a dictionary if you get stuck.*

_____

_____

Ask God to help you be faithful and put your faith in him.

AND SO IT IS:
ALL WHO PUT THEIR
FAITH IN
CHRIST
SHARE THE SAME BLESSING
ABRAHAM RECEIVED BECAUSE OF
HIS FAITH   GALATIANS 3:9

> I will give you
> a wise and
> understanding
> mind such as
> no one else has
> ever had or
> ever will have!
> And I will also
> give you what
> you did not ask
> for—riches
> and honor!
> 1 KINGS 3:12-13

BASEBALL HONORED CAL RIPKEN JR. at the 2001 All-Star game with the Commissioner's Historical Achievement Award, recognizing a lifetime of exploits. But the 21-year veteran also showed he had plenty of highlights left in his bat.

Although the Baltimore Oriole was voted the game's starting third baseman, shortstop Alex Rodriguez and American League manager Joe Torre pulled a switch in the first inning. Unknown to Ripken, Rodriguez, the starting shortstop, shifted over to third and allowed the future Hall of Famer to open at his original position.

In the third inning of a scoreless tie, the 18-time All-Star hammered Chan Ho Park's first-pitch fastball deep over the left-field wall. At age 40, Ripkin surpassed Stan Musial as the oldest player to homer in an All-Star contest. The 47,364 fans at Seattle's Safeco Field stood and showered their applause.

When Torre replaced Ripken with Angels third baseman Troy Glaus in the sixth inning, commissioner Bud Selig stopped play to award Ripken and Tony Gwynn lifetime achievement awards.

And following a 4–1 American League victory, Ripken captured his second All-Star MVP award—the only American League player ever to do so.

EXTRA POINT < < < < < < < < < < < < < < < < < < < < What would Cal Ripken have said if a reporter had asked him more than 20 years earlier what he hoped to accomplish in his baseball career? Perhaps his response might have been, "I want to earn a living playing the game I love."

But on July 2, 2001, when Cal Ripken Jr. announced his retirement effective at season's end, he had accomplished much more. He had appeared in 2,632 consecutive games, played in 18 All-Star games, and earned the record for most career hits by an Oriole.

At the beginning of Solomon's career as king of Israel and Judah, God asked him what he hoped to accomplish. When Solomon asked for wisdom, God granted the request and also added riches and honor.

Often when we seek to do our best, our Lord adds the extras we could only dream about.

GOAL! *Read more about Solomon in 1 Kings 3:5-14. If you could ask God for one thing, what would you choose? Praise God for all his gifts.*

WHEN SOMEBODY DOES something intelligent, people often say, "Now that's using your head." In the 1998 World Cup, Zinedine Zidane used his head in a smart way to bring France soccer's ultimate prize.

The French National Team hosted four-time champion Brazil at the Stade de France. More than 80,000 partisans, many with their faces painted the blue, white, and red of the French flag, filled the stadium to cheer for their native country.

Like most World Cup matches, the game began as a defensive struggle. In the 27th minute, Brazil's Roberto Carlos let the ball slip over the end line, setting up a French corner kick. Midfielder Emmanuel Petit left-footed the ball toward the Brazilian goal. Zidane, a 6-foot-1-inch midfielder better known for his passing than his jumping, outleaped Brazil's Leonardo and headed the ball past Taffarel, the Brazilian goalie, for the game's first score.

A similar situation occurred early in the second half. Youri Djorkaeff's corner kick attracted Zidane's head like a magnet, and the Algerian went airborne, powering the ball into the net. In the game's latter stages, Petit added another goal, and France shut out Brazil 3–0 to earn its first World Cup crown.

At the contest's conclusion, the crowd reverberated with shouts of Zidane's nickname, "Zizou! Zizou!" The following day, more than 600,000 French fans lined the Champs Élysées for the biggest celebration since France's liberation from the Nazis in 1944.

EXTRA POINT < < < < < < < < < < < < < < < < < < < < < < <
All of France took pride in the win and how Zinedine Zidane used his head. In the victory, he demonstrated two kinds of head power. Not only did Zizou use his skull to batter the ball into the net, he also used his brain to determine when and where to send it.

God wants us to use our head to make wise decisions in life. He created our brain so that we can learn, think, reason, and determine the right way to follow him.

GOAL! *Our brain may look like a three-pound mushroom, but it keeps us alive and holds all the information for who we are. You can learn more about your brain by looking in an encyclopedia or on the Internet. Ask God to help you use all of your brainpower and give you an understanding mind.*

So I turned my mind to understand, to investigate and to search out wisdom and the scheme of things and to understand the stupidity of wickedness and the madness of folly.

ECCLESIASTES 7:25, NIV

FOR ALMOST 70 YEARS, fans reveled as their favorite baseball players performed in the annual All-Star game. But in 2002, the commissioner's decision left everybody with an empty feeling.

The contest began with pageantry. An hour-long pregame ceremony featured Willie Mays, Hank Aaron, Cal Ripken Jr., and memorable moments in baseball history. Former Milwaukee Brave and Hall of Fame pitcher Warren Spahn threw out the first pitch to his ex-catcher turned announcer Bob Uecker.

Minnesota's Torii Hunter wowed the crowd early with a leaping catch in the first inning that robbed Barry Bonds of a home run. Bonds exacted revenge in his next at bat by blasting a 3-0 pitch into the second deck to put the National League in front 2–0.

Then both teams battled back and forth. Lance Berkman's two-run single in the seventh gave the NL a 7–6 margin, but Omar Vizquel tied it 7–7 with an RBI-triple in the eighth.

Heading into extra innings, managers Joe Torre and Bob Brenly eventually played everybody on their 30-man roster by the 11th inning. They had few pitching options left. After conferring with baseball commissioner Bud Selig, all parties agreed that no additional innings would be played.

Once Luis Castillo flied out to open the bottom of the 11th, the PA announcer informed the crowd of the decision. A couple of batters later, Freddy Garcia struck out Benito Santiago for the game's final out, and the players exited the field to a chorus of boos.

EXTRA POINT < < < < < < < < < < < < < < < < < < < Fans felt empty inside. Many had stayed up past midnight, only to see the second tie in the history of the game. (The other tie occurred in 1961 due to rain.) And on a night when the game's MVP award received Ted Williams's name, no one earned the honor.

The next day outraged fans flooded baseball's office with irate e-mails and calls. Too late, the commissioner vowed to never again let the game end in a tie except due to acts of God. But nothing removed the emptiness.

The apostle Paul used a lot of sports analogies in his writing. He encouraged Christians to press on to win the prize that God has called us to win. Achieving victory for Christ is important.

GOAL! *What are some occasions when ending in a tie would be okay? When it comes to a relationship with God, he doesn't want our second best. Ask God to help you win the prize that he's called you to achieve.*

A BOOST OF ENERGY can take a team to a higher level. In the WNBA's first All-Star game in 1999, an energized West surged past the East.

The best players in professional women's basketball gathered at New York's Madison Square Garden to showcase their sport. Whitney Houston turned up the electricity before the game with a rousing rendition of the "Star-Spangled Banner" that brought the sellout crowd of 18,649 to its feet.

A trio of Houston Comets—Sheryl Swoopes, Cynthia Cooper, and Tina Thompson—blitzed their Eastern opponents in the game's early stages. The three combined for 11 points in the opening minutes and paced the West to a quick 14–2 lead. Although the East closed to 31–29 with 4:39 remaining in the first half, Yolanda Griffith's turnaround jumper ignited a 12–0 run to close the half as the West held a 43–29 cushion.

Defense dominated the day for the West. Utah's Natalie Williams (14 points, 8 rebounds), Sacramento's Yolanda Griffith (10 points, 5 rebounds), and Los Angeles's Lisa Leslie (13 points, 5 rebounds) completely throttled the East offense and allowed the West to coast to a 79–61 victory. The East shot only 35 percent (26-of-74) for the game and pulled down 36 rebounds compared to 48 for the West. For her efforts, including a dunk in the pregame warm-ups, Lisa Leslie picked up the Most Valuable Player award.

EXTRA POINT < < < < < < < < < < < < < < < < < < < < < People watching WNBA basketball for the first time often seem amazed at the women's power. During games, the players sprint up and down the court, bang inside for rebounds, and play suffocating defense. They use all of their energy toward team victory.

The apostle Paul wrote about God's power. If God truly lives inside us, the Lord offers us power and stamina to do good for him.

GOAL! *Compare your physical energy and your spiritual energy. Are you lacking in any area? Exercise your body and your spirit by eating a nutritious diet of healthy food, working out, and taking part in sincere worship and Bible study. Ask God to give you the stamina needed to live for him.*

I pray that you will begin to understand the incredible greatness of his power for us who believe him.

EPHESIANS 1:19

14 JUL

Do to others what you would want them to do to you.

LUKE 6:31, NCV

AFTER THE 2000 X GAMES street luge competition, experts agreed it was the best track and deepest field of competitors ever. With street-luge pioneers and up-and-coming young competitors going head-to-head on specially designed luges (which look a lot like big skateboards), the competition and excitement soared—especially in the Super Mass finals.

Racing down Seal Rock Run in San Francisco, the final matched top-seeded Lee Dansie, No. 2 seed Bob "the Piranha" Pereyra, and four other top lugers that included Dennis Derammelaere, Sean Mallard, John Rogers, and Dave Auld. The speedy, hilly course provided the large crowd all the thrills it expected. Dansie bolted from the starting line and built a commanding lead. However, Pereyra kept things close and waited for an opportunity. His chance came at the Cliff House Turn when Dansie hit the brakes too late and skidded. The slight loss of speed was all Pereyra needed. With his head inches from the pavement and his body lying as flat as he could get it, Pereyra made a strong outside move and passed Dansie near the finish line. Dansie came in second, while John Rogers captured the bronze.

EXTRA POINT < < < < < < < < < < < < < < < < < < < <
Bob Pereyra and Lee Dansie helped create street luge more than 20 years before the 2000 X Games. Pereyra had even won the first X Games gold in street luge in 1995. Dansie had four medals, but no gold. So when Dansie held the lead right before the finish and saw Pereyra slipping up beside him, he admitted thinking about nudging his competitor into the hay bales that lined the course. But Dansie overcame those thoughts of turning to the "dark side" and let Pereyra safely pass. Dansie said his reputation of being a clean racer and his desire to have others treat him the same way in the future helped him make the decision.

God wants us to do the same thing as we choose how to treat people in our daily life and in our athletic endeavors. By treating others how we want to be treated, we're setting a good example.

GOAL! *Do you have a reputation on the athletic field? Strive to always be a fair competitor. Ask God for help.*

BIG CHALLENGES DEMAND big performances. At the 2003 X Games Skateboard Vert finals, the largest halfpipe in X Games history combined with an all-star field to leave the crowd breathless.

Once the fans caught their breath, they saw that Bucky Lasek had won the gold. The best-score-in-three-runs format allowed every boarder to go for broke with each trick. And Lasek's second run was near perfection. The Baltimore, Maryland, native strung together such a huge array of tricks that fans went into oxygen debt from screaming. His famous heelflip frontside gay twist (where he does a 360 at the lip while taking off backwards) came right after a massive frontside rodeo.

Lasek's score of 94.67 cemented him at the top, even though the ever consistent Andy Macdonald nailed five consecutive 540s on his final run to earn 92.67 points. The final piece of hardware went to Denmark's Rune Glifberg. Glifberg posted a 92.33 on his final attempt by landing a frontside heelflip, alley-oop 540 to a McTwist, and topped things off with a nosegrab switch kickflip.

> Even perfection has its limits, but your commands have no limit.
>
> PSALM 119:96

EXTRA POINT

< < < < < < < < < < < < < < < < < < < < <

Bucky Lasek brought fans to their feet with his amazing gold-medal performance. By stringing together trick after trick, Lasek rode his board to perfection and left no doubt who was the best in the world on that evening.

As believers in Jesus Christ, we're asked to pursue perfection. With Jesus as our example and the Bible as our guide, we try to live flawlessly. But the fact is we'll never score a perfect 100 in the ultimate Judge's eyes—just like Lasek's perfect run didn't garner 100 either. Instead we must realize that we can't be perfect. Our perfection has limits, but God—and his Word—are limitless. That's why we should look to God to forgive our shortcomings. God's grace makes us appear perfect in his eyes.

GOAL! *Try to live just one day following all of God's commands. Do you think you could do it? How about for a year . . . or a lifetime? It just can't be done. Praise God that his Word has no limits.*

16 JUL

I will lead the
blind by ways
they have not
known, along
unfamiliar
paths I will
guide them;
I will turn the
darkness into
light before
them and make
the rough
places smooth.
These are the
things I will
do; I will not
forsake them.

ISAIAH 42:16, NIV

EVER TRY RUNNING with your eyes closed? It's not a good idea . . . unless you enjoy head injuries. Running blind usually doesn't work out too well. But distance runner Marla Runyan runs nearly blind every time she takes the track.

A degenerative retina condition called Stargardt disease left the California native legally blind at age nine. Despite having 20/300 vision in one eye and 20/400 in the other, she competed as a high jumper at San Diego State. Later, she switched to the heptathlon and finished tenth in the 1996 Olympic trials. But eventually this courageous athlete concentrated only on the 1,500 meters.

One month before the 2000 Olympics trials, the 31-year-old suffered a training accident. While on a practice run, she injured her knee in a near collision with a child on a bicycle. With workouts limited to the swimming pool, the 1999 1,500-meter Pan American Games champion considered withdrawing.

After deciding she could block out the pain, Runyan set her sights on third and a berth to the 2000 Olympic Games in Sydney, Australia. Conceding the top positions to Regina Jacobs and Suzy Favor Hamilton, she focused on beating Shayne Culpepper.

Memorizing her uniform color and hairstyle, Marla found Culpepper as the pack entered the final lap. From her sixth-place position, she passed two runners and finished third in a time of 4:06.44.

EXTRA POINT ‹

Amazing! Not only did Marla Runyan compete with an injury, she did so without the sight most athletes enjoy. And in those 2000 Olympics, Runyan finished eighth with the best American time of 4:08.30, beating both Jacobs and Hamilton.

Many visually impaired people, like Runyan, learn to compensate in other ways. Their hearing becomes acute. They can sense the location of objects and people by movement, heat, and breathing. Runyan learned to distinguish fuzzy objects by shape and color.

In the Bible, God promises that he guides us when we can't find our way through life's changing and disappointing times. The Lord smoothes life's rough spots and shines his light in our darkness.

GOAL! *Ask God to guide the 16 million legally blind people worldwide. Praise him for helping you through dark days.*

NOTHING CRUSHES A GOLFER'S SPIRIT as much

as self-destructing at the end of a match. In the 1999 British Open, Jean Van de Velde became brokenhearted after turning an almost certain victory into an improbable loss.

The 33-year-old Frenchman held a three-shot lead over Paul Lawrie and Justin Leonard after 17 holes in Sunday's final round. Only a total collapse stood between him and the winner's check. But Van de Velde butchered No. 18.

His tee shot sailed 50 yards right of the fairway and landed on a small peninsula. Instead of playing safe and pitching out, he aimed for the pin with his 2 iron. But the ball hit a grandstand 40 yards short of the green and bounded into the rough. Van de Velde's third shot plopped into the water.

The Frenchman took off his shoes and socks and waded into the creek, hoping his ball would be playable. But before he could reach it, the ball sank into the water's depths, forcing him to take a penalty-shot drop. After sending his fifth shot into a greenside bunker, Van de Velde managed to pitch out and sink a six-foot putt for a triple-bogey seven.

Van de Velde tied with Paul Lawrie and Justin Leonard at 6-under at the end of four rounds, and the trio entered a four-hole playoff. All three golfers struggled on 15 and 16. But Lawrie birdied the final two holes for the title, forcing Van de Velde to accept a disappointing loss.

He heals the brokenhearted and binds up their wounds.

PSALM 147:3, NKJV

EXTRA POINT

< < < < < < < < < < < < < < < < < < <

Nothing hurts athletes more than having victory in the palm of their hand and letting it slip away. And the same holds true in life. Losing an honor, a good grade, a scholarship, a job opportunity, or a good relationship creates deep wounds.

And when the hurt stays in the pit of the stomach and the what-ifs replay over and over in the mind, Jesus understands. The psalmist says that God can heal our broken heart and bandage our wounds. Then the Father lovingly offers time to repair the damage and fade the scars.

GOAL! Remember a time a sure thing slipped away from you. How did you feel? Praise God for his ability to heal hearts and hurts.

18 JUL

Remember the
days of long
ago; think
about the
generations
past. Ask your
father and he
will inform you.
Inquire of your
elders, and
they will
tell you.
DEUTERONOMY
32:7

SOME PEOPLE SAY lightning never strikes the same place twice. But others know that's not the case. In 1999, the Yankees of yesteryear watched David Cone electrify the crowd with another record-making performance.

A Sunday afternoon crowd of 41,930 gathered at Yankee Stadium for "Yogi Berra Day." As part of the festivities, former pitcher Don Larsen threw out the ceremonial first pitch to Berra, recreating their historic role in Larsen's perfect game in the 1956 World Series.

Then Cone took the mound for the Bronx Bombers, and his teammates staked the 36-year-old right-hander to an early 5–0 lead. In the second, Ricky Ledee and Derek Jeter blasted two-run home runs sandwiched around Joe Girardi's RBI-double.

Despite the 95-degree heat, the 13-year veteran grew stronger as the game went on. Through seven innings, Cone retired 21 straight hitters. However, with one out in the eighth, Jose Vidro rapped a ground ball up the middle that appeared headed for the outfield. But second baseman Chuck Knoblauch ranged to his right, speared the ball with a backhand, traveled four steps, and fired a perfect throw for the 23rd out.

Chris Widger opened the ninth by striking out on three pitches, and Ledee made an awkward running catch of Ryan McGuire's fly ball for out number two. With the fans screaming, Cone faced Orlando Cabrera for the final out. On a 1-1 pitch, Cabrera popped up into foul territory. Third baseman Scott Brosius gloved the ball, giving Cone a 6–0 victory over Montreal and the 14th perfect game in baseball's modern era.

EXTRA POINT < < < < < < < < < < < < < < < < < < < <
Those fortunate enough to see or listen to the 1956 perfect game surely told the story to their children and grandchildren. But who would have thought David Cone would duplicate the feat on the day honoring Berra and Larsen? However, the unbelievable happened, and all those watching or listening earned the right to pass down their stories.

The writer of Deuteronomy explained the value of passing down stories—God's stories. Remembering and learning from the past adds richness to the present . . . and the future.

GOAL! *Ask an older person to tell you stories about sports, family, or one of their favorite subjects. Praise God for the gift of generations past and their stories.*

IN LESS THAN FIVE YEARS, Eldrick Woods ascended to the pinnacle of professional golf and demonstrated the validity of his nickname—Tiger.

The 24-year-old Californian entered the 2000 British Open's last round six strokes ahead of David Duval at 16-under-par. Through Sunday's front nine, Duval sliced the margin in half with a sizzling 32. But in typical Woods fashion, he overcame a slow start with a fantastic finish.

On No. 10, Woods, the previous month's United States Open winner, carded his second birdie of the day with a 12-foot putt. Two holes later, he regained his six-stroke lead by tapping in a three-footer for birdie, while Duval three-putted for bogey.

With six holes remaining, Duval faded with another bogey on 15 and a quadruple bogey at 17. Woods closed out with a 69, the first time he had recorded four rounds of a Grand Slam tournament in the 60s. The former Stanford golfer captured the British Open with a 269, which was 19-under-par and broke Nick Faldo's record of 18-under-par set in 1990. Ernie Els and Thomas Bjorn tied for second at 11-under-par.

With the British Open title, Woods added his name to the list of Jack Nicklaus, Gary Player, Gene Sarazen, and Ben Hogan as winners of all of golf's Grand Slam events: Masters, U.S. Open, British Open, and PGA Championship. Nicklaus completed the cycle at age 26, Player at 29, Sarazen at 33, and Hogan at 40. Meanwhile Woods swept the quartet at age 24.

EXTRA POINT < < < < < < < < < < < < < < < < < < < < < Like the source of his nickname, the golfer exhibited a tenacious attitude and fighting spirit. Lt. Col. Earl Woods gave young Eldrick the nickname "Tiger" after Vietnamese soldier Vuong Dang Phong. Earl hoped his son would be as courageous as his friend. And Tiger lived up to his dad's hopes.

In the Bible, God gave Jacob a new name. The twin experienced both an extraordinary struggle and an extraordinary encounter with God. The life-changing experience began a new era. God left his mark on Jacob, and Jacob became Israel, a man at peace with himself and surrendered to God.

GOAL! *Think about your nickname. What does it mean? Do you like it? Ask God to help you earn a nickname that reflects him. Read more about Jacob, also known as Israel, in Genesis 27 and 32.*

Then the man said, "Your name will no longer be Jacob, but Israel, because you have struggled with God and with men and have overcome."
GENESIS 32:28, NIV

BUT AS FOR ME, MY FEET HAD ALMOST STUMBLED; MY STEPS HAD NEARLY SLIPPED. FOR I WAS ENVIOUS OF THE BOASTFUL, WHEN I SAW THE PROSPERITY OF THE WICKED.

PSALM 73:2-3, NKJV

ERIC KOSTON PROVED it's better to show up late than never at the 2003 X Games. The star skateboarder attended a friend's wedding the morning of the street skateboard competition and arrived at the Staples Center in Los Angeles ten minutes after the event was supposed to start.

No problem. Organizers delayed the start time so Koston could compete— and that's exactly what he did. With no practice time at all, Koston wowed the crowd with his fearless tricks and ended up taking home the gold.

The Staples Center (home of the L.A. Lakers) is normally off-limits to skateboarders, with 24-hour guards enforcing the rules. However, it welcomed the X Games fans and competitors by setting up a two-level course separated by two nine-stair handrails in the middle and cement ledges on either side. Plus, handicap ramps, picnic tables, short boxes, and various obstacles allowed the athletes to show off their skills. The competition allowed each of the ten skaters to make three 75-second runs.

Koston trailed after the first run, but on his second attempt he pulled a switch tailslide to fakie down the rail and threw in a kickflip across the picnic bench for good measure. His second-run score proved high enough for top honors. Rodil Jr. nailed a flawless first run that showcased a backside lipslide and a noseblunt slide on the rail, which was good enough for second. Paul Rodriguez used his technical artistry to claim third.

EXTRA POINT < < < < < < < < < < < < < < < < < < < < <
Professional skateboarders show exceptional balance as they slide across tables and down railings. The risks of slipping are great. One wrong move could end in a gnarly wipeout and a serious road rash.

But slipping on a skateboard isn't the worst thing that could happen to us. The psalmist warned against sliding away from God. Sometimes we find ourselves in danger of slipping into bad groups, bad language, or bad choices. When we begin to slide, the heavenly Father offers to help us find solid footing in his Word.

GOAL! *Slide across a wood or vinyl floor in your socks. Be careful; it's easy to slip. Praise God for helping you find a foothold when you slip in life.*

21 JUL

> I will be with you, and I will protect you wherever you go. I will someday bring you safely back to this land. I will be with you constantly until I have finished giving you everything I have promised.
>
> GENESIS 28:15

BRITISH GOLF COURSES typically contain high roughs, rolling fairways, and deep weeds, which present a challenge to foreigners not used to the conditions. In the 2001 British Open, David Duval navigated the rugged turf of Royal Lytham & St. Annes to capture his first major title.

The Jacksonville, Florida, native shared the lead with Ian Woosnam, Bernhard Langer, and Alex Cejka heading into the final day. Because the competition boasted the greatest number of coleaders in any Grand Slam in 23 years, most observers expected a shoot-out for the title or possibly even a playoff.

But Duval, noted for his wraparound sunglasses and stoic expression, took charge. A birdie on 3 and back-to-back birdies on 6 and 7 gave the American a two-stroke lead.

A tee shot into the rough resulted in a bogey for Duval on 12, but instead of collapsing in the backstretch as he had done the previous year, the golfer rallied with a birdie. Despite hitting two drives into the knee-high grass on 14 and 15, he recovered for par on both and approached the final three holes with a three-stroke margin.

Duval parred the rest of the round, finishing the day with a 4-under 67. His four-day total of 274, 10-under-par, bettered Sweden's Niclas Fasth by three shots. Duval became the sixth American in seven years to claim the British Open crown.

EXTRA POINT < < < < < < < < < < < < < < < < < < < < < < < Athletes usually find competing at home easier than on the road. Events held in foreign countries present even greater challenges. Jet lag, time changes, unfamiliar foods, and sometimes even different languages contribute to the difficulty. But David Duval found a comfort zone in the British Open.

As Christians we can feel at home no matter where we are. God created the entire world and is Lord of all. In the Old Testament, God told Jacob that he would always be with him—no matter where he went. The same thing is true today: God is with you no matter where you go.

GOAL! *God could take you to a multitude of places during your lifetime. Perhaps you'll travel to a different nation. Maybe you'll live in the inner city or out in the country. But it doesn't matter where you are because God's there too. Praise him for that fact.*

MISTAKES ON THE GOLF COURSE

pull players off their path of trying to win a major title. In the 2002 British Open, Ernie Els overcame a huge blunder and returned to the pack.

The 32-year-old South African led by two strokes as the tournament wound down on the final day. Through 12 holes on Sunday, Els increased the margin to three and appeared to have clinched his third Grand Slam title. But a tee shot into the bunker on 14 led to a bogey. Then a bad drive and a poor chip resulted in a double bogey on 16, leaving the two-time United States Open champion a stroke behind the leader.

However, on the par-5 No. 17, Els reached the green in two and two-putted for birdie. He finished with a par on 18, and for the first time in British Open history, four golfers—Els, Thomas Levet, Stuart Appleby, and Steve Elkington—tied at the top with 278s at the end of regulation.

In the four-hole playoff, Els and Levet posted pars and eliminated Appleby and Elkington, who both went 1-over. Forced into sudden death, the remaining pair returned to the 18th. Levet's tee shot found a bunker as did Els's second shot. But the South African blasted from the sand and placed his ball five feet from the hole. While Levet two-putted for bogey, Els sank the 5-footer for par and the victory.

EXTRA POINT

< < < < < < < < < < < < < < < < < <

Ernie Els had the British Open in his grasp. Then things started to fall apart. His shots went astray. Fortunately, the champion managed to turn his game around in time to tie for a playoff spot and then earn the trophy.

Sometimes in life, we stray from God's prepared path. Like stubborn sheep, we follow whoever or whatever appeals to us most. Eventually, we move so far that we're lost. But Jesus, the Good Shepherd, always leaves the flock to find the one wandering lamb. He returns us to the safety of his care. Praise God!

GOAL! *Practice hitting a golf ball. Does it always go where you want? Ask God to help you go where he wants, and when you don't, to bring you back into his fold.*

Once you were wandering like lost sheep. But now you have turned to your Shepherd, the Guardian of your souls.

1 PETER 2:25

AN APPEALS BOARD rarely overturns a judge in a swim meet. In 2001, the Australian and United States 800-meter relay teams learned that fact.

At the World Championships in Fukuoka, Japan, the Australian quartet, comprised of Elka Graham, Linda Mackenzie, Petria Thomas, and Giaan Rooney, edged out their American counterparts for first place. Encouraged by photographers and fans behind the Australian bench, the young women jumped in the pool to celebrate.

But the four failed to notice the final swimmer for the last place team hadn't completed the race. Since Federation Internationale de Natation Amateur (FINA) rule SW 10.11 prohibits participants from reentering the pool until all competitors have finished, judge Andriy Vlaskov disqualified the Australians. His ruling appeared to hand the gold to the Americans.

But the United States squad also suffered a disqualification. Based on touch-pad recordings, officials ruled that Julie Hardt started before teammate Cristina Teuscher touched the wall. However, the Americans claimed the equipment malfunctioned, and other teams had been allowed more leeway to compensate.

Both teams appealed, but a FINA jury upheld the decisions the following day. As a result, Great Britain's team of Nicola Jackson, Janine Belton, Karen Legg, and Karen Pickering captured the gold medal. Germany and Japan claimed the silver and the bronze.

EXTRA POINT < < < < < < < < < < < < < < < < < < < < < < What a strange race! Did the Australian swimmers know the rule about celebrating in the pool before the race concluded? Probably. But in the magical moment, the women listened to the crowd and their emotions. Did the touch pad malfunction? Probably. But in the excitement, Hardt left a hair too soon. Did Great Britain earn the gold? Some argued that their medals should have been bronze.

Sometimes, but not often, officials hear appeals from athletes' ambassadors and change their ruling. In the Bible, the roles are reversed. God, the official judge of the universe, sends his ambassadors. He wants us, as his representatives, to encourage individuals to be reconciled to him. The Lord offers relief from indifference, resentment, selfishness, and guilt. We can help people make good judgments for God.

GOAL! *Think of what it means to represent Christ—to be his ambassador in a world that's sometimes hostile to his teachings. Ask God to help you stay close to him as you speak to others for his sake.*

MANY CLAIM that winning the 23-day, 2,287-mile Tour de France requires miraculous endurance. And in 1999, Lance Armstrong experienced three miracles en route to his victory.

Armstrong's push-it-to-the-limit style brought him to American bicycle racing's forefront. Coach Chris Carmichael selected the 20-year-old for the 1992 Barcelona Olympic team. But Armstrong faltered, finishing 14th, and turned professional after the disappointment.

Success on the European tour proved elusive. In his first race, the American placed dead last. However, Armstrong slowly improved. Then in October 1996, doctors delivered tragic news. Tests confirmed cancer. Physicians rated his chances at 50-50. Surgery and four rounds of chemotherapy followed before Armstrong resumed training—only five months after the diagnosis.

The near-death experience altered the Texan's attitude. He developed quiet determination and relentless resolve. Armstrong steadily accumulated four victories in 1998.

In 1999, during the Tour de France's second stage, the American seized a six-minute lead over rival Alex Zuelle when a rider crashed, knocking ten racers off their bike. After stage eight, Armstrong donned the leader's *maillot jaune* (yellow jersey) and never relinquished it.

With victory virtually assured, the cancer survivor completed the final stage by leisurely pedaling up the Champs Élysées. Armstrong bested Zuelle by 7 minutes and 37 seconds, becoming only the second American to capture the prestigious bicycle race.

You are the God who performs miracles; you display your power among the peoples.

PSALM 77:14, NIV

EXTRA POINT

< < < < < < < < < < < < < < < < < < < < < < <

By all counts, there's no way Lance Armstrong should have won the Tour de France—not to mention his amazing victory over cancer. Imagine racing more than 2,000 miles up and down mountains with 100 riders crowding hairpin curves. Consider spending three weeks biking almost every daylight moment. Muscles would ache and the body would almost give out. But Armstrong's cancer-free body excelled.

How did he do it? Personal fitness, a positive attitude, and perseverance played a significant role. But God performed miracle after miracle in Armstrong's life.

God continually does miracles, many of which go unnoticed. Many people take the credit for God's miracles when he deserves all the honor. We should always be on the lookout for God's hand in our life and praise the Lord for his greatness.

GOAL! *Consider the miracles in Lance Armstrong's life. Praise God for miracles he performs today.*

25 JUL

> The Lord does whatever pleases him throughout all heaven and earth, and on the seas and in their depths.
>
> PSALM 135:6

SOMETIMES THE ACTIONS of a few people can ruin everybody's fun. That was the case in 1976 when the College All-Stars faced the Pittsburgh Steelers at Chicago's Soldier Field.

In 1934, *Chicago Tribune* sports editor Arch Ward first came up with the idea of an exhibition game that would match a squad of former college senior stars against the defending National Football League champions. For more than 40 years, the contest raised money for charity and served as the kickoff to football season.

But in 1976, a few rowdy fans and bad weather destroyed Ward's vision. Although the collegians generated little offense, a strong defensive effort held the Steelers to three Roy Gerela field goals in the first half. But after the intermission, the Steelers dominated. A safety and two Pittsburgh touchdowns left the All-Stars down 24–0 as the third quarter drew to a close.

Suddenly, a thunderstorm unleashed its fury on Soldier Field. With lightning flashing in all directions, officials stopped play and sent the teams to the safety of the locker rooms. But the crowd of 52,895 lost control of their senses. Fans spilled onto the playing surface, using the wet field as a gigantic slip-and-slide. The unruly crowd tore down both goalposts. As numerous fistfights erupted throughout the stadium, NFL Commissioner Pete Rozelle announced that the game would not continue.

EXTRA POINT < < < < < < < < < < < < < < < < < < < < < < The officials lost control of the game *and* the fans after the storm hit. The teams never finished. Really, the collegians didn't stand much of a chance. After all, the pros had won every contest since 1963. The lightning, thunder, and rain only ended the game sooner.

Then because of waning interest and opposition from owners and players, the game was canceled for good. A great tradition came to a sad conclusion because of some fans.

The fact is, we can't do whatever we want. Society says to do what feels good or right. But as followers of Jesus Christ, we know we have to obey God's rules.

God, on the other hand, can do whatever he wants. He controls the heavens and earth. All of his ways are perfect and just.

GOAL! *Make up a short psalm or poem praising God for his mighty power. Offer your words as a prayer to the Lord.*

LANCE ARMSTRONG OVERCAME CANCER to win the 1999 Tour de France. But the following year, the question remained whether he could endure the pain and repeat as the champion of the world's most famous bicycle race.

The Texan began training for that year's 23-day, 2,256-mile endurance contest seven months prior to its beginning. Shunning all fattening foods, including his favorite—peanut butter, Armstrong committed to a weight-loss program and trained by cycling over every mountain in the physically demanding French course.

During the 87th annual Tour de France's early stages, Armstrong stayed in the pack to conserve his strength. By day nine, he had fallen to 16th place. But the defending champion shot into first place by 4:14 as the bikers entered the Pyrenees Mountains.

Adorned with the leader's yellow jersey, the 28-year-old cyclist extended his lead by almost five minutes with a run up Mont Ventoux. Moving into the French Alps, Armstrong increased the margin to over seven minutes with only six stages remaining.

Despite losing two minutes the following day, Armstrong refused to yield. On day 19, he won his only stage and upped the lead to 6:02. On the day's final run, which began at the Eiffel Tower and ended at the Champs Élysées, American students painted their faces with stars and stripes and cheered for their countryman. Lance Armstrong had won the 2000 Tour de France.

Then [Jesus] said to them all: "If anyone would come after me, he must deny himself and take up his cross daily and follow me. For whoever wants to save his life will lose it, but whoever loses his life for me will save it."

LUKE 9:23-24, NIV

EXTRA POINT < < < < < < < < < < < < < < < < < < < < < < Lance's discipline paid off. His willingness to forego simple pleasures like his favorite food helped bring victory. Armstrong's biking over every single mountain on the 2,000-plus mile course gave him unprecedented experience and endurance.

Few individuals in life choose to exercise the self-discipline needed for incredible success. Most choose moderate discipline and moderate success. But in the Bible, Jesus told his followers to deny themselves and follow him.

GOAL! *Make a list of your favorite foods.*

_____

_____

Could you deny yourself the taste as part of a disciplined training program? Ask God to help you discipline yourself for him.

27 JUL

Oh, clap your hands, all you peoples! Shout to God with the voice of triumph!

PSALM 47:1, NKJV

SPORTS FANS OFTEN CLAP in rhythm to encourage favorite athletes or teams to perform well. In the 1989 Caribbean Zone Track and Field Championships, the sound propelled high jumper Javier Sotomayor to unprecedented heights.

After Sotomayor missed his first attempt at 8 feet, the stadium scoreboard flashed the quiet sign. With every event except the high jump completed, the crowd focused on the 21-year-old Cuban.

The arena grew still as everybody watched Sotomayor perform his prejump ritual of slapping his thighs, arms, and face. Suddenly, the sound of a single person clapping punctuated the silence. One of his Cuban teammates pounded his hands together to inspire the jumper.

A few more joined in. Within moments the entire venue reverberated with fervent clamor. Pumped with adrenaline, Sotomayor bounded from the right side of the crossbar, planted his foot, and soared. The 6-foot-3-inch, 180-pound athlete grazed the bar slightly, making it shiver for a few tense seconds. After the crosspiece had firmly settled in place, applause boomed. The track star leaped from the pit, performed a backflip, and collapsed beneath a mob of teammates.

Officials measured his jump at 2.44 meters, or 8 feet-1/8 inch. Sotomayor became the first high jumper to clear the 8-foot barrier. His historic leap occurred 33 years after Charles Dumas became the first to break the 7-foot mark.

EXTRA POINT < < < < < < < < < < < < < < < < < < < < < < Could Javier Sotomayor have broken the elusive 8-foot barrier without the clapping crowd? Absolutely. After all, as a youngster he had practiced high jumping with dried sugarcane sticks stretched across a rusty oil drum. He definitely possessed internal strength and determination.

But *would* Sotomayor have cleared the record height without the reverberating claps? Possibly not. He needed the rush, the push, the knowledge that everybody was supporting him echoing in his head.

Like the teammate who began the rhythmic applause, the psalmist urged people to clap their hands in praise to God. He asked for shouts of joy to the Lord. Does God need our praise to be our God? Absolutely not. But we need to praise him to express our awe and adoration.

GOAL! *Attend a sporting event or watch one on TV. Note the crowd's involvement, particularly their clapping. Praise God with clapping and shouts of joy.*

CYCLISTS CONCENTRATE on where they're headed and not where they've been. In the 1984 Olympics, Connie Carpenter-Phinney managed to move ahead at the last moment using a technique known to every young biker.

The Los Angeles Games hosted women's cycling for the first time. Despite the 92-degree temperature, over 200,000 spectators lined the 9.85-mile course winding around the suburb of Mission Viejo. As the race unfolded, six competitors, including Americans Carpenter-Phinney and Rebecca Twigg, emerged from the 45-member contingent to battle for the lead.

They raced neck and neck until the final 500 meters, when Italy's Maria Canins broke for the finish. Almost like a choreographed routine, Carpenter-Phinney, Twigg, Norway's Unni Larsen, and West Germany's Sandra Schumacher formed a line behind her rear wheel. Schumacher moved in front with 200 meters remaining, flanked on either side by the two Americans.

Twigg gained a slight advantage 100 meters from the finish, but Carpenter-Phinney, a former Olympic speed skater, caught up with three meters to go. Remembering her husband's advice, she lifted her body from the saddle, throwing the handlebars toward the finish line like a kid jumping a curb. The trick propelled the bike forward about eight inches, her margin of victory over Twigg.

Both riders received official times of 2:11.14, but Carpenter-Phinney's extra push forward claimed the gold. Twigg took the silver, and Schumacher received the bronze.

EXTRA POINT < < < < < < < < < < < < < < < < < < < < < < < < < Connie Carpenter-Phinney's little trick gave her an exciting victory in an incredible race. Her eyes misted atop the medal stand watching the Stars and Stripes ascend as the "Star-Spangled Banner" played. As she'd pressed for the prize, eight inches had meant that gold now hung around her neck.

The apostle Paul must have been an athlete. Or at least he may have been a fan of sports. He wrote to the Philippians, comparing his life with Jesus to a race. He urged Christians to live as athletes, pressing on toward the future.

GOAL! *Ride a bike, walk in a park, or jog through your neighborhood. Concentrate on pressing forward instead of remaining behind. Praise God that when you ask him, he forgets your past as well.*

I am still not all I should be, but I am focusing all my energies on this one thing: Forgetting the past and looking forward to what lies ahead, I strain to reach the end of the race and receive the prize.
PHILIPPIANS
3:13–14

29 JUL

> Don't let evil get the best of you, but conquer evil by doing good.
>
> ROMANS 12:21

WHEN FORMER COLLEGIATE baseball players signed with the independent Salt Lake City Trappers in 1987, most were just glad to be able to continue playing the game they loved. But the team of castoffs accomplished a feat to remember.

The franchise, with no major-league affiliation, stocked its roster with undrafted free agents. Salt Lake City opened the season with three victories and two defeats. A 6–5 loss to the Pocatello Giants on June 24 lowered the Trappers' record to .500. But suddenly the independent team started winning, and the string didn't stop.

Game by game, the Trappers approached the all-time consecutive win streak of 27 games held jointly by the 1902 Corsicana (Texas) Tigers and the 1921 Baltimore Orioles. Salt Lake City broke the record at home on July 25 with victory number 28 in a 13–3 decision over Pocatello. The Trappers added another win for good measure, edging the Giants 8–6 the following day.

Going on the road in quest of No. 30, Salt Lake City faced the Billings Mustangs. The Trappers took a 2–0 lead in the first, but Billings countered with six runs in the bottom of the inning, capped by Eddie Taubensee's three-run homer. Mike Malinak closed the gap to 7–5 with a solo shot in the sixth, but reliever Quinn Marsh escaped jams in the eighth and ninth to preserve the Mustang win.

EXTRA POINT < < < < < < < < < < < < < < < < < < < < < The streak ended at 29 wins in a row, but the Salt Lake City Trappers had made history. Signing with the independent team kept the young athletes in the game. The players could have been upset by not being drafted by a big-league team. They could have given up because of their "bad luck." But instead they made the most of their situation. They overcame their unfortunate circumstances with a good attitude.

The Bible tells Christians to do the same thing. As believers, we shouldn't let evil surroundings or circumstances get us down. Instead, we should overcome our circumstances by doing good.

GOAL! *If you look around, you'll probably notice a lot of evil in the world. And that makes sense, because Satan rules the earth. But when you know Jesus, you have power in you that's greater than anything in this world. And God's power will help you overcome evil.*

PAIRING THE WORLD'S BEST male and female golfers in a mixed team, alternate shot, match-play format sounds like a great idea. But in 2001, Tiger Woods, Annika Sorenstam, David Duval, and Karrie Webb may have wished they hadn't agreed to compete, as wild weather forced them to put into practice everything they'd learned about golf.

ABC television hosted the event at Palm Desert's Bighorn Golf Club. When the foursome teed off at 5 p.m., the temperature registered 103 degrees. The rules called for men to tee off on odd holes and women on even ones. The unique format coupled with high crosswinds and dusty conditions created problems in this made-for-television event. Shots headed into bunkers, banged against trees, landed in the rough, and got caught up in bushes.

The Woods-Sorenstam team built a two-hole lead through seven, but double bogeys on 10 and 11 allowed Duval and Webb to move in front. Woods and Sorenstam fell two holes behind with three remaining, but a late rally and 12-foot birdie putt by Sorenstam on the final hole tied things up.

Moving back to the 18th tee for a playoff, Woods connected a three-foot putt for par, giving his team the win after a 4-hour and 29-minute match. Afterward, Sorenstam and Webb rushed to catch a flight to London to compete in the British Women's Open.

> Keep putting into practice all you learned from me and heard from me and saw me doing, and the God of peace will be with you.
>
> PHILIPPIANS 4:9

EXTRA POINT < < < < < < < < < < < < < < < < < < < < < < In such weather conditions, most amateurs would pack in their clubs and head for home. Sorenstam and Webb probably wanted to zip up their bags and board their flight. But the golfers had signed contracts. On that difficult evening when bogeys were like pars, they put into practice all they'd ever learned about golf.

In life, some days hand us dusty, gusty winds of change. Others bring dark clouds of disappointment or storms of grief. A few dawn with the cooling rain of refreshment or the bright sunshine of spiritual renewal. But whatever life holds, God asks that we put into practice all we have learned from him. Then his peace will go with us.

GOAL! *Spend some time practicing a skill you have learned. Ask God to help you put into practice what you've learned from him.*

31 JUL

AUGUST

PATIENCE IS A VIRTUE—in life and in the batter's box. In 1978 as Pete Rose pursued Joe DiMaggio's 56-game hitting streak, a little impatience might have cost Rose an amazing opportunity.

After the Cincinnati Reds first baseman extended his string to 44 games, he admitted to reporters that threats of thundershowers increased his desire to collect an early hit. Although fair skies prevailed the following evening, frustration clouded Rose's efforts.

Rookie left-hander Stan Williams of the Atlanta Braves walked the 37-year-old player in the first inning and speared a vicious line drive near his shoe top in the third, robbing Rose of a sure hit. Facing baseball's all-time hit leader once more in the fifth, Williams made the first baseman ground out.

Gene Garber took the mound for Atlanta in the seventh. Rose crushed an early offering, but the ball headed straight for third baseman Bob Horner's glove. He snared it without moving.

Trailing 16–4, the Reds' captain batted with two outs in the ninth. After bunting the first pitch foul, Rose took two balls and then foul-tipped a changeup. For the 2-2 pitch, Garber threw another changeup. The first baseman's swing barely nicked the ball as it settled into catcher Joe Nolan's glove for strike three, ending Rose's quest for baseball's longest hitting streak.

EXTRA POINT

< < < < < < < < < < < < < < < < < < < < < <

Although Pete Rose didn't break DiMaggio's record, Rose's 44-game hitting streak tied with Willie Keeler for the longest in the National League and second longest all-time. (Keeler earned his record in 1897 with the Baltimore Orioles.)

But Pete Rose badly wanted to hit safely in game 45 to keep the streak alive. After great defensive plays twice robbed him of hits, the star put all his hopes on one last try. He appeared anxious, replacing his normal relaxed style with a tension everyone in the stadium felt. Rose tried too hard.

That's an easy trap for us in life, too. We want something so much that tension takes its toll. We commit an error on a routine catch. We forget our lines. We press too hard and hit a bad note. We freeze.

But God knows our thoughts and our anxieties. He whispers to our heart that we can relax because he loves us no matter what.

GOAL! *Put yourself in Pete Rose's place. Would you have felt anxious? How does your body react to tension? You can relax knowing that God loves you no matter what.*

Search me, O God, and know my heart; test me and know my anxious thoughts.

PSALM 139:23, NIV

01 AUG

Yet I reserve
seven thousand
in Israel—all
whose knees
have not bowed
down to Baal
and all whose
mouths have
not kissed him.

1 KINGS
19:18, NIV

A 7,000-POINT SCORE in the heptathlon represents the pinnacle of the sport. In the 1992 Barcelona Olympics, Jackie Joyner-Kersee targeted that mark as her goal.

The East St. Louis native captured the 1988 heptathlon gold with a world record 7,291 points. But Spain's heat and humidity limited her chances for another record-breaking performance. Then Joyner-Kersee's disappointing throw in the shot put made a new record impossible.

Just prior to the 200 meters, her final event of the first day, Jackie watched fellow American Gail Devers claim the 100-meter gold medal. Inspired by her friend's efforts, Joyner-Kersee vowed to raise her performance to the next level. A first-place finish in the 200 with a time of 23.12 seconds gave her 4,136 points through four events and a lead of 127 over Germany's Sabine Braun.

Day two opened with the long jump, the 30-year-old's strongest event. A leap of 23-3.5 extended her lead to 239 points, and a javelin throw of 147-feet-7-inches put her in front by 298. In the final event, the 800 meters, Joyner-Kersee needed a time under 2:15 to reach 7,000 points. She clocked a 2:11.78, finishing with 7,044 points and back-to-back gold medals. Irina Belova of the Unified team took silver, and Braun claimed the bronze.

EXTRA POINT < < < < < < < < < < < < < < < < < < < <
Jackie Joyner-Kersee stood atop the medal stand not with a record but with another 7,000-point milestone. Only seven times had an athlete reached that magical number in the high jump, long jump, shot put, javelin, 800-meter run, 400-meter hurdles, and 200-meter sprint. And of the seven 7,000-point performances, Joyner-Kersee reached it six times while Russia's Larisa Nikitina scored 7,004 in 1989.

The number 7,000 not only has significance in the heptathlon, but also in the Old Testament. Wicked King Ahab and Queen Jezebel worshipped Baal rather than God. They killed God's prophets and required the people to bow to their false god. Elijah felt alone. But God told his prophet that 7,000 others in Israel resisted the evil rulers too.

When we feel alone in our faith, God remains faithful and ready to lead us to others who also follow him.

GOAL! *Read more about Elijah, Ahab, and Jezebel in 1 Kings 19 and 2 Kings 9. Praise God for all who stand firm in faith. And next time you feel alone as a Christian, remember that there are millions of others who feel the same way about Jesus as you do.*

JESSE OWENS CAPTIVATED crowds with his performance in the 100 meters in the 1936 Berlin Olympics. But even though Owens earned a gold medal and set an Olympic record, German leader Adolph Hitler refused to acknowledge his accomplishments.

Owens, an Alabama sharecropper's son, had already established himself as a track star for Ohio State at the 1935 Big Ten championships. In 45 minutes, he broke five world records and tied a sixth in the sprints, hurdles, and long jump. Yet Owens faced strong Olympic competition from his teammate Ralph Metcalfe.

The former Buckeyes sprinter peaked at an opportune time. In his three preliminary heats, Owens turned in times of 10.3, 10.2, and 10.4 seconds. With the field narrowed to six competitors, Owens broke out in front and pulled ahead by two meters at the halfway point. Metcalfe pulled closer but still trailed by a meter at the tape. Owens captured the gold with a clocking of 10.3, while Metcalfe claimed the silver at 10.4. Holland's Martinus Osendarp won the bronze at 10.5.

EXTRA POINT < < < < < < < < < < < < < < < < < < < < < < Prior to Owens's triumph, Nazi propaganda portrayed African-Americans as inferior and taunted the United States for relying on "black auxiliaries" to fill their Olympic roster. However, the message appeared not to affect German fans. The crowd of 110,000 at Reich Sports Field Stadium thundered their approval of Jesse Owens's victory. Although Adolph Hitler ignored every African-American gold medalist, hundreds of fans clamored for Owens's autograph at every public sighting.

Jesse Owens proved to be one of the greatest athletes of all time. But the track star also exhibited strong character. Although the Nazi leader and German newspapers put him down, Owens showed love to German fans and athletes. In fact, Owens and German jumper Luz Long developed a friendship that continued with Long's family even after he lost his life in 1943 at the battle of San Pietro.

And God wants us to do the same thing by demonstrating his love to our enemies.

GOAL! *It's easy to hate your enemies. But God wants more from you. Ask God to help you show love and pray for people who put you down.*

You have heard that the law of Moses says, "Love your neighbor" and hate your enemy. But I say, love your enemies! Pray for those who persecute you!
MATTHEW 5:43-44

03 AUG

BEFORE THE INVENTION of television, millions of fans followed baseball over the airwaves. In 1921, an enterprising engineer discovered radio's power to bring sports into the life and home of fans.

Less than a year before, KDKA in Pittsburgh, Pennsylvania, became America's first working radio station. The initial broadcast opened with Harold Arlin, a 26-year-old Westinghouse engineer, reading the results of the 1920 presidential election.

The following summer, Arlin decided to test the possibility of remote broadcasting from Pittsburgh's Forbes Field. Setting up a field-level box behind home plate, the engineer constructed a miniature transmitter and described every hit, run, and error into a converted telephone.

The game itself meant little. The first-place Pirates dispatched the last-place Philadelphia Phillies 8–5 by scoring three runs in the bottom of the eighth. The highlights reported by Arlin included a two-run home run by Philadelphia's Cy Williams in the third and an injury to Pittsburgh first baseman Charlie Grimm's shoulder after being hit with a pitch in the sixth.

Sometimes the arrangement worked well, but occasionally the equipment failed. Crowd noise created problems. But despite the difficulties, people listened and demanded more. As a result, sales of radios boomed and radio stations popped up all over the country.

EXTRA POINT < < < < < < < < < < < < < < < < < < < < < < Radio helped expand sports, and sports helped expand radio. Today, both sports and media extend to the ends of the earth. More than 80 years after its first broadcast, KDKA still airs Pirates baseball.

Radio and television not only enable fans to keep up with favorite teams, but satellites beam up-to-date news and programs around the globe. The airwaves also send God's Good News into countries where missionaries cannot visit. Christ's message reaches television sets and radios in homes that have never heard the name of Jesus. Jesus' story touches the heart of people who have never seen a Bible or can't read.

Like Harold Arlin, who discovered radio's power to bring sports into the homes of fans, Christians discovered the media's ability to bring the Lord into the life of those who need Jesus' saving grace.

GOAL! *Look at your newspaper's TV guide. What kind of Christian programming do you find? Praise God for dedicated broadcasters who use this medium to share Christ.*

IN 1999, GEENA DAVIS PROVED she wasn't just another pretty Hollywood actress. She took the concentration, stamina, and dedication she had built up on movie sets and focused those characteristics on archery.

Davis, the 1988 Academy Award winner for best supporting actress, had always been an athlete. The former high school hurdler and high jumper fell in love with archery while watching the 1996 Olympics. Enthralled by American gold medalist Justin Huish, she contacted the Simi Valley, California, native, who taught her the basics.

Huish also recommended hiring Don Rabska as a coach. Although skeptical at first, the Van Nuys, California, instructor soon realized that his new pupil was serious about the sport. Starting with a once-a-week lesson, Davis soon progressed to a six-days-a-week, five-hours-a-day training program.

Her two years of practice reaped dividends when the 43-year-old finished 29th out of the 300 women archers in the national target championships at Oxford, Ohio. The top-32 placing earned the movie star a spot in the Olympic trials semifinals held in Bloomfield, New Jersey.

Although hopeful of a berth on the 2000 U.S. Olympic team, Davis faltered. Hampered by rain, intense media coverage, and motion-picture fans, she finished 24th out of 28 competitors. Despite her disappointing showing, archery fans and enthusiasts welcomed the actress's entry into the sport, bringing it newfound exposure.

Finally, brothers, good-by. Aim for perfection, listen to my appeal, be of one mind, live in peace. And the God of love and peace will be with you.

2 CORINTHIANS 13:11, NIV

EXTRA POINT < < < < < < < < < < < < < < < < < < < Geena Davis's steady hand and discerning eye made her a successful archer. The actress often scored ten points by hitting the tiny gold circle in the target's center.

The Bible occasionally mentions archery and taking good aim. In 2 Corinthians, Paul ends his letter by encouraging fellow believers to aim for perfection.

The Lord wants us to concentrate steadily on him. Then we can listen to good advice from friends and live at peace with ourselves and with the people around us.

GOAL! *Remember these archery tips and apply them to your life as you ask God to help you concentrate on him.*
- *Keep your eye on the target.*
- *Don't let the crowd distract you.*
- *Steady your hand and don't waver.*

> If one falls down, the other can help him up. But it is bad for the person who is alone and falls, because no one is there to help.
>
> ECCLESIASTES 4:10, NCV

WITH ATHLETES RUNNING full speed and colliding without pads, injuries are bound to occur in soccer. But the best teams in the world always have solid players to step in when a star suffers an injury. The U.S. Women's National Soccer team proved that to be true at the 2003 Women's World Cup.

Defender Brandi Chastain broke her foot in the Americans' opening game, and 20-year-old Cat Reddick replaced her on the field. Reddick, the youngest player and the only collegian on the team, excelled for Team USA in her first World Cup. In fact, when the United States played North Korea in the final game of the first round, Reddick earned player of the game honors in a 3–0 win.

With the United States already ahead 1–0 at the break, Reddick tallied two goals in the second half to cement the victory. Her first came early in the second off a corner kick by Aly Wagner. Julie Foudy got her head on the ball and flicked it toward the Korean goal. As the ball appeared to be going past the far post, Reddick flew in and hipped it into the net. Reddick's second goal came 18 minutes later on a perfect cross from Shannon MacMillan that Reddick hammered into the net with her head.

EXTRA POINT < < < < < < < < < < < < < < < < < < < Defenders don't usually score a lot of goals. But Cat Reddick's tallies helped the U.S. team push past North Korea. While Reddick claimed her first two World Cup goals against the Koreans, she was no stranger to finding the back of the net. She scored 78 goals at Briarwood Christian High School in Birmingham, Alabama. And her knack for scoring also came in handy at the University of North Carolina. Reddick continued to play well as the United States finished third at the 2003 World Cup, even though Brandi Chastain missed the rest of the tournament.

Teams need solid subs who can step up to a challenge. The same thing is true in our Christian walk. Sometimes we may feel beaten and injured. That's when we need a friend to come in and help us continue in the most important game of all—the game of life.

GOAL! *Who are some of your Christian "teammates"? Make sure you have a buddy or two who can help you through difficult times.*

SHANE HAMMAN IS ONE of the most dominant weight lifters in U.S. history. He proved that at the 2003 National Championships by winning the super heavyweight division for the seventh straight time.

When it comes to pumping iron, nobody can match this 5-foot-8-inch, 350-pound athlete with a 62-inch chest, 35-inch thighs, and 22-inch biceps. And he's been proving his power in weight-lifting competitions since 1990.

First, as a power lifter competing in bench press, dead lift, and squat, Hamman broke 14 world records. His record-setting squat of 1,008 pounds is almost unbelievable. And his personal bests of 738 in the dead lift and 551 in the bench aren't too bad either.

Then in 1996, Shane decided to switch to Olympic weight lifting—where athletes compete in the snatch and in the clean and jerk—to pursue his dream of becoming an Olympian.

"These lifts are way more technical than the power lifts," Hamman says.

In the snatch, the weight goes from the ground to above the head in one motion. Then the lifter stands up. The clean and jerk requires the athlete to first clean the bar from the ground to his chest and then jerk it over his head.

Hamman quickly picked up the techniques, setting numerous American records. At the 2003 U.S. championships in Chattanooga, Tennessee, Shane outmuscled the competition by lifting 407 pounds in the snatch and added 484 in the clean and jerk to win the Best Male Lifter award.

EXTRA POINT < < < < < < < < < < < < < < < < < < < < < < Shane Hamman is obviously one powerful dude. And if you asked him why he's so strong, he'd have just one answer—and it's not because he has big muscles.

"I realized early on my strength was a gift from God," Hamman says. "I totally dedicated my weight lifting to him to be used for his glory. And he's really blessed me for putting him first in my life."

God wants all his children to put him first in their lives—whether they're 98-pound weaklings or 350-pound Olympic weight lifters. By putting God first, everything else falls into place.

GOAL! *Commit to beginning a weight-lifting regimen. Make a chart of where you begin and see how fast you progress. Find a weight-lifting partner and get some good advice from a trainer or a gym teacher. And as you get stronger, don't forget where your strength truly comes from.*

The Lord is
my strength
and my song;
he has become
my victory.
He is my God,
and I will
praise him;
he is my
father's God,
and I will
exalt him!
EXODUS 15:2

07 AUG

AND YOU SHOULD **FOLLOW MY EXAMPLE,** JUST AS I **FOLLOW CHRIST'S.**
1 CORINTHIANS 11:1

A STARTING BASEBALL PITCHER must lead from the mound. His confidence and determination should inspire teammates. In 2000, Darren Dreifort not only provided direction with his pitches, but he also led at the plate.

The Los Angeles Dodgers played host to the Chicago Cubs. Dreifort's second-inning single spurred the Dodgers to a 1–0 lead, but the right-hander surrendered three runs in the third with shortstop Kevin Elster's error plating two.

Elster cut the margin to a single run with a fourth-inning homer. Three pitches later, Dreifort, a three-time All-American pitcher and designated hitter at Wichita State, tied the score with his fourth career round-tripper. The power surge continued for Los Angeles as Gary Sheffield and Shawn Green both connected on long balls, putting the Dodgers in front 6–3.

Dreifort continued his hot hitting the following inning, blasting a shot off Todd Van Poppel 462 feet over the center-field fence. No Dodgers pitcher had hit two home runs in a game since Don Drysdale in 1958.

In the seventh, Dreifort gave up two singles and a run before leaving the contest, with the Dodgers leading 7–4 with two outs. Mike Fetters and Jeff Shaw relieved and allowed only one more Cubs run as the game ended 7–5. And Dreifort earned the pitching win thanks to his own two RBIs.

EXTRA POINT < < < < < < < < < < < < < < < < < < < < < < Darren Dreifort exhibited leadership both on the mound and in the batter's box. He showed poise under pressure, particularly when his teammate's error put him two runs behind. Dreifort led the way, and his actions set an example that others followed.

Leadership is also important in your relationship with Christ. Surrounding yourself with solid Christian friends and following a strong Christian leader will help you grow. People who set a good example for you will encourage you to act as God wants you to. And, of course, Jesus is your ultimate example. If you always strive to act like him, you'll develop your leadership potential.

GOAL! *Write down qualities of leadership, both in sports and in other aspects of life.*

_____

_____

Praise God for good leaders. Ask the Lord to help you follow their example.

08 AUG

MOST HURDLERS NEED 13 strides between hurdles to achieve optimum speed in the 400-meter hurdles. But Kevin Young discovered he could run faster by taking 12.

The former UCLA athlete followed in the steps of Edwin Moses, a four-time world-record setter in the event. Moses, who compiled a 122-race winning streak in the 400-meter hurdles during the 1970s and '80s, perfected the art of taking 13 strides between each hurdle. But Young's 6-foot-4-inch frame and his ability to lead with both feet allowed him to run only 12 steps before leaping hurdles four through eight of the ten-hurdle event.

Prior to the 1992 Barcelona Olympics, Young predicted he would break the 47-second mark. He reinforced the prediction by covering the walls of his Olympic Village room with papers marked 46.89.

In the 400-meter Olympic finals, Young's years of practice paid off. He took control of the race after the fifth hurdle, opening a huge lead. Without a single close challenger, the American held his index finger aloft ten meters away from the finish line. Young broke the tape in a world-record time of 46.78 seconds, shaving almost a quarter second from Moses's previous mark and becoming the only man ever to run the hurdles in under 47 seconds.

EXTRA POINT < < < < < < < < < < < < < < < < < < < < < Twelve steps became the key for Kevin Young's amazing victory. Instead of competing in the event in the same manner as everybody else, Young came up with a new way. His unique style brought him the Olympic gold and a world record.

The book of Romans encourages us to live in a new way. People in the Old Testament who believed in God had to obey a lot of laws. But once Jesus came, we were allowed to live in a new way and experience total freedom in Christ. Praise God!

GOAL! *Think about all the sacrifices and rules that people in the Old Testament had to follow to show their devotion to God. You can read about them in the book of Leviticus. Then you can check out Romans to learn how freeing your life with God is because of Jesus' sacrifice. Thank Jesus for allowing you to serve God in a new way.*

> But now we have been released from the law, for we died with Christ, and we are no longer captive to its power. Now we can really serve God, not in the old way by obeying the letter of the law, but in the new way, by the Spirit.
>
> ROMANS 7:6

RETURNING TO A SPORT after a catastrophic injury is never easy. But Dennis "D-Rom" Derammelaere came back to the 1999 X Games Street Luge competition and won one of the closest races of all time.

D-Rom had missed the previous year's event after an accident during practice shattered his lower leg and ankle. Competing with six screws in his ankle and a titanium plate in his leg, Derammelaere reached the dual competition finals against street luge legend Lee Dansie. With nearly 10,000 fans lining San Francisco's Seal Rock Run, D-Rom and Dansie put on a show.

Neither athlete gained an edge out of the gate as the two competitors traveled side by side almost the entire course. Coming to the historic Cliff House Turn, Dansie went for the pass. But with little room between Derammelaere and the hay bales, the two sleds collided and locked together. With an accident imminent, Dansie pushed the sleds apart. The finalists screamed through the final turns and went toe-to-toe past the finish line.

The photo finish showed Dansie had edged out D-Rom by a fraction. However, the judges ruled that Dansie caused unnecessary contact, and they gave the victory to hometown favorite Derammelaere.

EXTRA POINT < < < < < < < < < < < < < < < < < < < < < < < Dennis Derammelaere endured surgery, hours of rehabilitation, and days of physical therapy to return to street luge. And after his hard-fought victory, D-Rom said it was the best moment of his life.

During the course of our existence, we're bound to suffer through our share of injuries. All of them won't be as bad as Derammelaere's crushed ankle, but chances are we'll go through our share of physical pain. God's prophet Jeremiah went through a lot for his Lord, but he stayed confident of God's healing and saving power. And since Jesus Christ has come to earth, now he can save you forever and ever.

GOAL! *Check your family's medicine cabinet for bandages and other medical supplies. Those are great to have, but they can't compare to the heavenly Father's healing power. When Jesus saves you from your sins, you're saved forever. The Lord's ability to heal physical and emotional injuries is unmatched.*

Lord, heal me, and I will truly be healed. Save me, and I will truly be saved. You are the one I praise.
JEREMIAH 17:14, NCV

10 AUG

> If the Lord
> delights in a
> man's way,
> he makes his
> steps firm;
> though he
> stumble, he
> will not fall,
> for the Lord
> upholds him
> with his hand.
>
> PSALM
> 37:23-24, NIV

WITH TIGHTLY PACKED RUNNERS jockeying for position, distance races run around a track sometimes look like an accident waiting to happen. And in the 1984 Olympics, a tragic stumble cost Mary Decker a gold medal.

The 26-year-old California native missed the 1976 Games due to injury and the 1980 Games because of an American boycott. Running in the 3,000 meters in the 1984 Los Angeles Olympics, Decker led the pack from the outset.

A little over halfway through the event, South African Zola Budd and Romanian Maricica Puica challenged the former world-record holder in the 5,000 and 10,000 meters. Budd, an 18-year-old who had immigrated to England to sidestep the Olympic boycott, attempted to pass Decker coming out of a turn.

The tightly bunched pack allowed Decker no maneuvering room. She shortened her stride for a couple of steps, but her right thigh grazed Budd's left foot. Knocked off balance, the barefoot South African runner swayed slightly to the left, causing Decker's right foot to strike Budd's left calf.

The American fell to the track and rolled to the infield. Hoping to rejoin the race, Decker jumped to her feet but quickly fell back to the ground due to a pulled hip-stabilizer muscle. Shaken by the incident involving Decker, Budd lost her lead. She finished seventh. Track officials originally disqualified the South African for illegal contact, but a videotape review prompted an appeal jury to unanimously reinstate her placement.

EXTRA POINT < < < < < < < < < < < < < < < < < < <
Both Zola Budd and Mary Decker stumbled during that important Olympic race. Although Budd still had a chance, she didn't hold up under pressure. Budd had grown up admiring Decker. The American's exit from the race after training for eight years rattled the South African. Neither runner was blessed with a good race.

The psalmist sang about God's blessings and about our tendency to stumble. If we live in a way that delights the Lord, we may stumble, but we won't fall. God will hold us up and help us back to our feet. With God's help, you can finish life's race as a winner.

GOAL! *Watch a long race on TV and see how easy it would be to fall. Now think how simple it is to make a mistake and stumble in everyday life. God will keep you firmly on his path if you keep following him.*

NEAR MISSES, synchronized stunts, and off-the-charts creativity have made the skateboard vert doubles one of the most popular events at the X Games. So it didn't surprise anybody when fans filled the Staples Center to watch the finals at the 2003 competition.

With practice kicking off at 2 p.m., riders got together to hone their skills and work out the perfect run. For some competitors, this marked their first opportunity to skate together. Neil Hendrix and Buster Halterman—newcomers to vert doubles—made the most of this time to tweak their performance. The extra work paid off in a third-place finish.

But the night belonged to veteran vert skaters Bucky Lasek, Bob Burnquist, Rune Glifberg, and Mike Crum. The "CrumBerg" duo came superclose to each other on several over-under moves including Crum's huge heelflip frontside air over Glifberg's kickflip backflip. The team displayed great amplitude and used the entire halfpipe in finishing second. And second was as close as Team CrumBerg was going to get to the top, because the Killer Bs were on their game.

Bucky and Bob stunned the crowd by pulling out the hardest tricks after barely using any of the practice time. Truth be told, Lasek and Burnquist had been secretly practicing on Burnquist's backyard ramp. The pair executed several tough board exchanges, such as when Lasek held a board on the ramp and Burnquist rode across the halfpipe, jumped on Lasek's board, and pulled a tailslide revert.

EXTRA POINT < < < < < < < < < < < < < < < < < < < < < < Bucky Lasek and Bob Burnquist surprised everybody with their gold-medal-winning performance. But the Killer Bs earned their medal by practicing hard. Their secret runs in Burnquist's backyard paved the way for victory.

The Bible says God sees everything—even things done in secret. And he rewards our good behavior even when nobody else notices. The Killer Bs were rewarded for their secret practices by taking home the gold and a lot of prize money. God rewards us in a lot of ways . . . some of which we won't see until we get to heaven.

GOAL! *Doesn't it feel good when others recognize your good actions? Commit to God to do the right thing, even if nobody notices—because he always does.*

> Your Father can see what is done in secret, and he will reward you.
> MATTHEW 6:4, NCV

12 AUG

NO ABSOLUTES EXIST in the sports world. As Gail Devers learned in the 1992 Barcelona Olympics, a sure thing can turn unexpectedly bad.

Devers, who had battled Graves disease four years earlier, captured a surprise gold medal in the 100 meters at the Games in Spain. With one gold in hand, the former UCLA sprinter aimed for a second gold in her best event—the 100-meter hurdles. The sprint/hurdles first-place combination would match Fanny Blankers-Koen's accomplishment in the 1948 London Games.

In the finale, Gail took command after the fourth hurdle and appeared to have a cinch victory with only one hurdle remaining. But as she approached the final barrier, her lead foot glanced the hurdle and sent her sprawling onto the track.

Quickly rolling to her hands and knees, Devers crawled the final eight meters and finished in fifth place.

After barely qualifying with a third-place finish in her semifinal heat, Greece's Paraskevi Patoulidou emerged as the unexpected victor with a time of 12.64 seconds. The 27-year-old athlete claimed the first Olympic gold medal for Greece since 1912 when Konstantin Tsiklitiris won the standing broad jump.

EXTRA POINT < < < < < < < < < < < < < < < < < < < < < < Gail Devers caught her foot on the last hurdle and fell to the track, out of medal contention. The obstacle prevented the athlete from an anticipated win.

The Bible says that people who give you advice contrary to God's Word are putting obstacles in your way. And just like Devers learned, any obstacle can cause problems.

While we can't avoid all ungodly ideas and advice, we can be prepared. Walking daily with God in prayer and grounding ourselves in Scripture help us recognize people who might lead us astray. Then we can avoid them.

GOAL! *Do your friends give you advice and encourage you to do things that honor God or dishonor him? Ask God to keep you grounded and help you stay away from people who are an obstacle to your walk with Jesus.*

> I urge you, brothers, to watch out for those who cause divisions and put obstacles in your way that are contrary to the teaching you have learned. Keep away from them.
>
> ROMANS 16:17, NIV

RUSHING IN THE MIDST of competition can lead to disappointing results. In the 1992 Barcelona Olympics, a quick clock forced Sergei Bubka into a poor pole vault performance.

The 28-year-old Ukrainian opted to forego his initial attempt until the crossbar registered 18-feet-8.25-inches. American Tim Bright insisted officials equally enforce the Olympic rule permitting only two minutes of prep time once a vaulter is cleared to jump. Bubka, accustomed to more time, appeared agitated as he readied for his attempt.

Sensing his time expiring, the four-time world champion sailed under the bar. The 30-time world-record setter cleared the bar safely in his second attempt, but Bubka's leg dislodged the crossbar on the way down.

Only one attempt away from elimination, Sergei passed to gain more time and waited to vault until the bar stood at 18-10.25. With crosswinds swirling, Bubka decided on a softer pole. However, the strong winds subsided. Awkward in his final attempt, the 1988 Olympic gold medalist struck the bar with his shins.

Without Bubka as a factor, his Russian teammates Maxim Tarassov and Igor Trandenkow tied for the best vault at 19-0.25. Tarassov claimed the gold with fewer misses. Local favorite Javier Garcia Chico captured the bronze at 18-10.25.

EXTRA POINT

< < < < < < < < < < < < < < < < < < < < < < < < Whether the track-and-field officials rushed him or whether Sergei Bubka hurried himself, the world-record holder lost. Rushing forced the defending Olympic champion and pre-event favorite out of contention.

Sometimes we rush into poor decisions. Satan makes wrong choices look very attractive, and we move too quickly. But God urges us to take time to think and pray before we act. We must move first with our brain and then with our feet. That way we avoid wrong choices and follow Christ's way.

GOAL! *How much time does a person need to choose between right and wrong? It takes time to weigh the options, pray, and follow God's will. Ask God to keep you from rushing into poor choices.*

There are six things the Lord hates, seven that are detestable to him: haughty eyes, a lying tongue, hands that shed innocent blood, a heart that devises wicked schemes, feet that are quick to rush into evil, a false witness who pours out lies and a man who stirs up dissension among brothers.
PROVERBS 6:16-19, NIV

14 AUG

> Lord, give
> to me your
> unfailing love,
> the salvation
> that you
> promised me.
> Then I will
> have an answer
> for those who
> taunt me,
> for I trust in
> your word.
>
> PSALM 119:41–42

TAMPA BAY BUCCANEERS defensive tackle Warren Sapp is known for his big mouth almost as much as his big plays on defense. Sapp enjoys verbally sparring with opponents to get an edge during the game. Plus, his offbeat quotes often show up in newspapers or get broadcast on television. But in 2003, the NFL felt Sapp went too far when his taunting began even before the kickoff.

During a Monday night game against Indianapolis, Sapp skipped through the Colts' area as they stretched before the game. And at 6-feet-2-inches tall and 303 pounds, he wasn't trying to sell anybody Girl Scout cookies.

Following complaints by the Colts, the NFL reacted with a fine and a penalty warning. The 2003 season marked the first time that officials took the field 50 minutes prior to kickoff to keep a check on pregame taunts.

With the possibility of costing his team 15 yards and precious field position during the game, Sapp stopped his pregame shenanigans and refocused from trash talking to the playing field.

EXTRA POINT

< < < < < < < < < < < < < < < < < < < <

No one likes to be taunted or ridiculed. But in some sports it all seems like part of the game—like when a baseball catcher chatters to a batter or when a receiver shoves the football in the face of a defensive back after making a big catch. Some players even jump around and celebrate after making a tackle.

But taunting doesn't have a place in the Christian life. That's not Christ's way, so it shouldn't be our way. And if we're ever taunted, all we have to do is think about how God would respond. By focusing on his unfailing love, we can deal with other people's taunts. He'll show us how to answer put-downs in a way that pleases him.

GOAL!

Think about a time when someone ridiculed you or your team. Then remember an experience when you or your team taunted an opponent. Ask God to help your words and actions be like his.

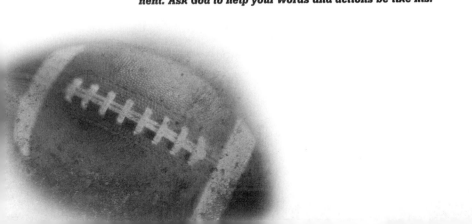

YOU WANT DOMINATION? All you have to do is think about Ken Climo. As much as Michael Jordan and the Chicago Bulls dominated basketball or the Dallas Cowboys ruled the NFL in the early 1990s, Climo reigned over the professional disc golf world even more.

The Clearwater, Florida, pro won nine consecutive Professional Disc Golf Association (PDGA) World Championships from 1990–98. And in 1999 Climo won 14 events and finished second at Worlds.

Never heard of disc golf? Just imagine playing regular ball golf with specially designed Frisbees. Instead of putting a ball into a hole, competitors throw discs into metal baskets lined with chains that "catch" the disc. And unlike traditional golfers who earn millions of dollars and appear on network television every week, professional disc golfers travel the world in virtual anonymity and don't earn huge sums of money. In 1999, Climo's best year, he brought home only $22,839 in prize money.

But "the Champ," as Climo is simply called, doesn't play disc golf for the money. He throws massive drives, lofts in pretty approach shots, and nails 50-foot putts because he loves the sport.

EXTRA POINT < < < < < < < < < < < < < < < < < < < Ken Climo's fierce competitive nature is legendary. Every year the world's best disc golfers tried to knock Climo from the pinnacle of the sport. But Climo continually worked on his game, made himself mentally tough, and came through with the world title. Climo showed he loved disc golf by practicing every day. He helped disc companies create new discs that improved the sport. And he treated competitors and tournament directors with respect.

As Christians, we all want to show God that we love him. But how can we do that? Reading the Bible every day, treating others as we want to be treated, and sharing our faith in creative ways are all good ideas. And the Bible gives us another: following God's commands.

GOAL! *God shows us that he loves us in so many ways. List some of them.*

_____

_____

Now think how you can show God that you love him. The answer doesn't have to involve something difficult.

Rise in the
presence of
the aged,
show respect
for the elderly
and revere
your God. I
am the Lord.

LEVITICUS
19:32, NIV

SOME ATHLETES NEVER seem to age. Jesse Orosco, who pitched for more than ten major league teams during his career, is one such player. In 1999, Orosco rose to the pinnacle of major league pitching appearances with the Baltimore Orioles.

The 42-year-old California native debuted with the New York Mets in 1979. Over more than 25 seasons, the left-hander started only four games, pitching the remainder in relief. After serving as a closer early in his career, Orosco moved to a setup role and often hurled less than one inning per game.

With the Baltimore Orioles hosting the Minnesota Twins, Orioles manager Ray Miller summoned the reliever from the bull pen with two outs in the top of the seventh and his club leading 4–3. The JumboTron scoreboard flashed "1,072" to indicate the pitcher's record-breaking number of appearances that pushed him past Dennis Eckersly.

When the reliever reached the mound, his infielders gathered to congratulate him, and the crowd of 40,805 at Camden Yards roared its approval. His first adrenaline-filled pitch to Twins second baseman Todd Walker sailed high and tight. Walker drilled Orosco's next offering, but center fielder Brady Anderson scarcely moved and gloved the hard-hit fly ball for the inning's final out.

Removed after his two-pitch outing, Orosco walked to the dugout and hugged his 12-year-old son, Jesse, the team's batboy. Moving to the stands, he kissed his wife, Leticia, and daughters, Natalie and Alyssa.

EXTRA POINT < < < < < < < < < < < < < < < < < < < What a wonderful moment for the Orosco family and the Baltimore Orioles. All showed appropriate honor and respect for the aging pitcher. Family members hugged and kissed him. Players shook his hand. Fans stood and cheered. Orosco continued to add to his record and had tallied more than 1,250 appearances through 2003.

We regularly honor older athletes for their achievements. But the Bible urges us to show respect for all those who are older. We should listen to their advice and speak to them with respect.

But more than respecting the elderly, we should revere and honor God by our words and through our actions.

GOAL! *What are some ways you can show respect to older people? How about God? It's even more important to spend time praising the Lord with honor and respect.*

THE 100-METER DASH stands out as the marquee event at track meets. Sprinters race at speeds of more than 20 mph, trying to reach the finish line first. The 100 meters at the 1988 Olympics in Seoul proved to be one of the most memorable races ever . . . but not for a positive reason.

The world's fastest athletes gathered at the starting line in South Korea, poised to make Olympic history. At the gun, Canada's Ben Johnson bolted from the line and blistered down the track in a world- and Olympic-record time of 9.79. Muscles bulging and veins popping, Johnson beat second-place finisher Carl Lewis by a surprising .13 seconds, which is an eternity in a sprint. Lewis' time of 9.92 also bettered the previous Olympic record.

But the surprises weren't over. Just 62 hours after the completion of the race, Olympic officials entered Johnson's room and walked out with his gold medal. Johnson had tested positive for steroids—a performance-enhancing drug banned by the Olympics and many professional sports. As it turned out, Johnson had been using the drugs for six years before he was caught breaking the rules.

With Johnson disqualified, Lewis took home the gold. Great Britain's Linford Christie claimed silver, and USA's Calvin Smith earned bronze.

> We know that we belong to God, but the Evil One controls the whole world.
>
> 1 JOHN 5:19, NCV

EXTRA POINT

< < < < < < < < < < < < < < < < < < < < < <

Ben Johnson was willing to do whatever it took to win—even if it meant breaking the rules and risking his health. He tried to control his own destiny and win Olympic gold. But instead he lost his prize medal and was shown all over the world to be a cheater.

If we take an honest look at our life, we spend a lot of time trying to control situations. We try to control getting good grades by sneaking a peak at our neighbor's paper. We control our relationships by not showing our true selves to others. But whenever we think we've gained an edge, we discover we've made a terrible mistake.

Although we're children of God, the devil controls the world. Sometimes he gives us a false sense of control so we make bad decisions. Here's the truth: When it comes to control, it's best to leave it up to God.

GOAL! *Write down something you control.*

_____

_____

Now give over control of it to God. His power is always greater than Satan's.

18 AUG

If you love
sleep, you will
end in poverty.
Keep your eyes
open, and there
will be plenty
to eat!

PROVERBS 20:13

OUTFIELDERS MUST REMAIN ALERT even though a

lack of action may cause some to become bored. In 2000, Ron Gant's physical
and mental drowsiness allowed the New York Yankees to tie an unusual major
league record.

The Anaheim Angels faced the two-time defending world champions at
Yankee Stadium. In the bottom of the third with runners on second and third
and no outs, Jorge Posado sliced a wicked line drive to Anaheim left fielder Ron
Gant. Gant managed to get his glove on the ball, but then dropped it for an error
as Posado raced to second. Since a run would have scored even if Gant caught
the ball, the Yankee catcher earned a sacrifice fly.

Scott Brosius followed with a second fly ball that scored Tino Martinez
from third. The next batter, Clay Bellinger, lofted yet another high fly to left,
sending Gant all the way to the warning track for the catch. But instead of firing
the ball back to the infield, the Angel outfielder casually tossed it to his cutoff
man.

Posado, who had tagged at second on the catch, alertly noted the mental
mistake. Never slowing down, he motored all the way home for the inning's
third run. Staked to the early lead, the Yankees cruised to a 9–1 win.

But interestingly enough, the three sacrifice flies in the third inning tied a
major league record first set July 1, 1962, by the White Sox against the Indians
and matched by the Yankees the previous June in a shutout over the Tigers.

EXTRA < < < < < < < < < < < < < < < < < <
POINT Ron Gant's usual alertness took the day off. The athlete might

have been standing in the outfield, but he mentally slumbered.

God gave the gift of sleep to rest our body and restore our mind. But the
writer of Proverbs says if we sleep too much, then we'll be lacking in life. Too
much rest can lead to laziness—and that's a bad thing. By keeping your eyes
wide open and staying mentally alert and ready to work, you'll be able to succeed.

GOAL! *Do you ever feel lazy? As your body grows, it's natural to feel
sluggish. But don't get in the habit of dozing through days. Stay alert and
be ready for opportunities that God gives you.*

INSPIRATION CAN CARRY an athlete a long way in a competition. In the 2000 PGA Championship, it took Tiger Woods and Bob May into a playoff.

The 31-year-old California native trailed Woods by a single stroke after three rounds. May shot a 72 in the opener, and then successive scores of 66 placed him at 204, 12-under-par. In Sunday's final round, Woods struggled. Hampered by a bogey six on hole 2, he fell behind May by a stroke. But Woods' back-to-back birdies on 7 and 8 knotted the golfers at 13-under-par as they entered the back nine.

Triple birdies on 10, 11, and 12 put the 43rd-ranked May back in front by one until Woods launched a massive 350-foot drive on 17. With his wedge, Woods pitched four feet from the pin and sank the birdie putt. May recorded a par. As the tension mounted, both golfers carded incredible birdies on the final hole, finishing at 18-under-par and forcing a three-hole playoff to begin at 16.

Woods sank a 20-foot birdie putt on the first playoff hole to go one up. After the duo parred 17, fatigue and pressure forced ugly shots on 18. But both golfers salvaged pars, and Woods claimed his third major tournament victory in 2000. With the win, Woods matched Ben Hogan as the only golfer to capture three Grand Slam tournaments in a single year.

EXTRA POINT < < < < < < < < < < < < < < < < < < < < < < Bob May held his own against the No. 1 golfer in the world. Faith in his ability, love of the game, and hope of victory allowed the underdog to force a playoff. While Woods rewrote the record book, May worked, labored, and endured. Golf fans remember his inspired effort, even though Woods overcame in the end.

The apostle Paul remembered the efforts of the Christians at Thessalonica. Their faith in Jesus produced good work. Their love prompted labor for God. Their hope inspired endurance for other Christ followers.

We can follow their example in faith, hope, and love.

GOAL! *Think about what faith, hope, and love mean for your favorite athlete and for you in life. Ask God for faith that produces work, love that prompts labor, and hope that inspires endurance.*

> We continually remember before our God and Father your work produced by faith, your labor prompted by love, and your endurance inspired by hope in our Lord Jesus Christ.
>
> 1 THESSALONIANS 1:3, NIV

Then the word
of the Lord
came to
Jeremiah: "I
am the Lord,
the God of all
mankind. Is
anything too
hard for me?"

JEREMIAH
32:26-27, NIV

DEFEATING A PROVEN CHAMPION is never easy. Not only must you mentally convince yourself that you can win, but you must also perform flawlessly physically. In the 2001 World Track and Field Championships, the Ukraine's Zhanna Pintusevich-Block did all of those things in the 100 meters.

The field of sprinters included American Marion Jones, who had accumulated a string of 42 consecutive victories. The world's top 100-meter runner had not lost since her final race in 1997 when Jamaica's Merlene Otley bolted past her in Japan.

In the 1997 World Championships, the Ukrainian runner battled the former University of North Carolina track star to the wire. Pintusevich-Block and Jones finished neck and neck in the 100 meters, and the native of the small village of Nezhin celebrated at the conclusion thinking she had won. But moments later, the scoreboard posted times, and Jones edged her opponent by .02 seconds.

Pintusevich-Block again proved to be Jones' best competition in the 2001 World Championship. In the semifinal heat, she nipped Jones at the tape by .01 seconds. Then she made it two victories in a row over the 2000 Olympic gold medalist. In the championship race, the 29-year-old Ukrainian never let Jones pull ahead. Running side-by-side, Zhanna lunged forward at the tape and recorded a 10.82, .03 seconds better than her previous personal best.

Marion, who collected the silver medal with a 10.85 timing, exhibited great respect following her defeat, hugging her rival and saluting her determination. Greece's Ekaterini Thanou finished third at 10.91.

EXTRA POINT < < < < < < < < < < < < < < < < < < < Many sprinters would have conceded the gold to Marion Jones and strived for silver, but not Zhanna Pintusevich-Block. Her mother raised her alone and in poverty. Nothing seemed too hard for her after her childhood. She wanted to rule the 100 meters, and she did.

Many of us shy away from difficult challenges, fearing they're too hard. We choose sports that we already play well. We take easy classes in school. We try for cushy jobs.

But that's not God's way. He's the Lord of all. Nothing proves too hard for our heavenly Father. And we should work to follow his lead.

GOAL! *Think of things you haven't tackled because you think they're too hard.*

Now try one of them. Keep crossing items off your list. Praise God for helping you accomplish challenging tasks.

BASEBALL CATCHERS PLAY a defined position. But in 2000, Brent Mayne helped his team by taking on a different role.

Mayne, the Colorado Rockies starting catcher, had missed six games before the Rockies hosted the Atlanta Braves. The game was tied 6–6 with two outs in the 11th inning when Colorado manager Buddy Bell brought in John Wasdin, his only remaining reliever. But Wasdin hit Andres Galarraga with a pitch; a scuffle ensued and the umpires ejected both players.

With his team out of fresh pitchers, Brian Bohanon—the previous night's starter—entered the game and retired Javy Lopez to end the inning. In the 12th, Bell sent Mayne to the mound, the first position player to ever pitch for the Rockies. The catcher picked up two quick outs before surrendering a single and a walk. With the ever-dangerous Chipper Jones in the box, Mayne induced a groundout to end the inning.

In the bottom of the 12th, the Rockies loaded the bases. Colorado sent in third-string catcher Adam Melhuse to pinch hit. Melhuse greeted Braves reliever Stan Belinda with his first major league hit, and Neifi Perez scored in the winning run in the 7–6 victory. Mayne collected the win, the first position player to earn the honor since outfielder Rocky Colavito pitched for the Yankees on August 25, 1968.

EXTRA POINT < < < < < < < < < < < < < < < < < < < < < Manager Buddy Bell encouraged Brent Mayne to show his versatility. Going from catcher to pitcher wasn't easy, but Mayne did it to help his team. And the Colorado Rockies earned the victory.

In the Bible, the apostle Paul gives us the example of his versatility. He adapted to his surroundings and reached people where they were to help expand God's team. Paul was willing to change his "position" in life to introduce others to Jesus Christ.

GOAL! *What "position" do you have in school? Are you a jock, brain, or computer guru? Be willing to follow Paul's example by breaking out of your clique to share Christ with others. Ask God for the courage and opportunity to be all things to all people.*

When I am with those who are oppressed, I share their oppression so that I might bring them to Christ. Yes, I try to find common ground with everyone so that I might bring them to Christ.

1 CORINTHIANS 9:22

22

AUG

I ask you to
pray for us.
Pray first that
the Lord's
message will
spread rapidly
and be honored
wherever it
goes, just as
when it came
to you.

2 THESSALONIANS
3:1

FEW PITCHERS START their first major league game with greater performance than Bob Feller. In 1936, his astounding number of strike-outs led sportswriters to nickname him "Rapid Robert."

After drawing statewide attention as a high school pitcher, the Van Meter, Iowa, native signed with the Cleveland Indians at age 16. When word leaked of the illegal arrangement, baseball commissioner Kenesaw Landis fined Cleveland $7,500 and declared Feller a free agent. Although the Detroit Tigers made a strong bid for his services, the Iowa farm boy decided to go to the Indians.

Although Feller still lacked a year of high school and any minor league experience, Cleveland pitched him in a July exhibition game against the St. Louis Cardinals. The 17-year-old hurler quickly notched eight strikeouts in three innings.

After several relief appearances by Feller, manager Steve O'Neill granted the ballplayer a start against the St. Louis Browns. Working his fastball perfectly, the youthful pitcher fanned 15 batters in a complete game 4–1 victory. He allowed only six hits and walked four. And his 15 strikeouts were just one short of the American League record at the time and two shy of the major league mark.

EXTRA POINT < < < < < < < < < < < < < < < < < < < < < Just imagine being 17 years old and pitching in the majors. Then picture yourself winning by striking out more than half the batters that you face. Your photograph appears on the front page of the sports section. Your story headlines radio and movie theater newsreels. Word of your accomplishment spreads. Everyone knows about you.

More than 2,000 years ago, word of a gifted man spread even though there weren't any newspapers, radios, or TV stations. Word of Jesus Christ crossed the world. Everyone soon knew about his gift of salvation. The apostle Paul took the gospel into new cities. Sometimes the Good News spread rapidly with many people becoming Christians. Paul asked the Thessalonians to pray that would continue.

And we should pray for the same thing today.

GOAL! *Listen and watch for sports news that spreads quickly. Pray that the Good News of Jesus Christ will spread rapidly, too.*

EVERY YOUNG ATHLETE DREAMS of his first day in the big leagues. But few experience the amazing debut that Jason Jennings had in 2001.

The rookie pitcher for the Colorado Rockies drew his first major league assignment against the New York Mets at Shea Stadium. A 62-minute rain delay postponed Jennings' first pitch, and the Texan attempted a *New York Times* crossword puzzle to calm his nerves and pass the time.

When the skies cleared, Colorado staked the 23-year-old right-hander to a 3–0 lead. Jennings survived two shaky innings, getting an assist from right fielder Larry Walker for the game's first out and starting a 1-6-3 double play on Rey Ordonez's grounder to end the second. The Rockies padded the lead to 5–0 with two runs in the fifth. For the game, Jennings, the 1999 Collegiate Player of the Year, allowed only five hits and struck out eight.

Jennings added to his terrific pitching outing with a 3-for-5 performance at the plate. In his second at bat, he singled to left. With runners on first and second in the seventh, the pitcher lined an RBI-single to right. The rookie capped the night by shooting Donne Wall's first pitch in the ninth over the right-field wall for the game's final run in a 10–0 triumph.

Jennings' performance marked the first time since 1900 that a hurler threw a shutout and hit a home run in his first major league game.

> Therefore do not worry about tomorrow, for tomorrow will worry about itself. Each day has enough trouble of its own.
>
> MATTHEW 6:34, NIV

EXTRA POINT < < < < < < < < < < < < < < < < < < <

The former Baylor University player accomplished a feat no one had matched in a century! Although he must have been afraid and nervous all at the same time, Jennings didn't show stress after the second inning. He relaxed enough to get three hits, including the homer, and a shutout victory on the mound.

In the Bible, Jesus tells us not to worry about the future. Instead we should concentrate on each moment. By living in the present, we'll be able to deal better with the troubles that come our way.

GOAL! *Practice some of these stress-reducing methods as you praise God for his calming presence.*

- *Breathe slowly and consciously.*
- *Tense and then relax each muscle, beginning at your neck.*
- *Wash your face or take a warm bath or shower.*
- *Recall a pleasant memory.*

24 AUG

> For the Lord
> your God is
> going with you!
> He will fight
> for you against
> your enemies,
> and he will give
> you victory!
> DEUTERONOMY
> 20:4

SOME PLAYERS JUST SEEM to be winners. Chris Drury is one of those players. Championships are drawn to him like a magnet.

In 1989, he claimed his first while playing Little League baseball. His Trumbull, Connecticut, squad advanced to the Little League World Series in Williamsport, Pennsylvania, after winning the United States East Region. Few expected the American 12-year-olds to provide strong competition, since foreign teams had captured 18 of the previous 22 titles.

But following victories over Davenport, Iowa, and San Pedro, California, the New Englanders faced Kaohsiung, Taiwan, in the championship. The Taiwanese used their ace left-hander, Hsu Ming-Lan, in a 13–0 semifinal win over Maracaibo, Venezuela, and were forced to throw Lee Chien-Chih in the final. The United States team countered with Drury, a pitcher adept at throwing fastballs and off-speed junk.

Taiwan opened the scoring with a run in the first when left fielder Dan McGrath misjudged a deep fly ball. But after seeing Chien-Chih's unorthodox pitching style once, Trumbull rocked the Taiwanese hurler for two runs in the third, two in the fourth, and a home run by Ken Martin in the fifth.

In the meantime, Drury handled the pitching duties masterfully by using slow-breaking pitches to keep the Taiwanese off balance. The 5-foot-1-inch, 126-pound hurler limited Kaohsiung to five hits while striking out two and walking four. In the final inning, the youngster walked the lead-off hitter but retired the next three. McGrath gloved a fly ball on the warning track for the game's last out in Trumbull's 5–2 triumph for the Little League World Championship.

But Williamsport wasn't Chris Drury's only championship. His Boston University hockey team won the NCAAs, his Colorado Avalanche won the Stanley Cup, and his USA hockey team won silver in the 2002 Olympics. Incredibly, Drury met 41st President George Bush with his Little League team and 43rd President George W. Bush with the Avalanche.

EXTRA POINT < < < < < < < < < < < < < < < < < < < Victory seems to follow Chris Drury. And victory followed the Israelites in the Old Testament. God issued instructions for his people and joined their battle. He expected them to prepare, to take care of unfinished business before reporting for duty, and to treat their enemies according to his rules. When they obeyed God, they won.

GOAL! *Read God's instructions in Deuteronomy 20 about victory in war. Praise God for his presence in the victories in your life.*

GOLFERS OFTEN REQUIRE only a single hole to settle tie-breakers. But in the 2001 NEC Invitational, Tiger Woods and Jim Furyk battled through seven playoff holes to determine a winner.

Furyk led the field by two strokes heading into the tournament's final day at Akron's Firestone Country Club. Woods, however, tied his playing partner with an 8-foot birdie putt on hole 16. The pair finished knotted at 13-under-par.

Moving back to the 18th tee box for sudden death, Woods appeared in command when Furyk's second shot landed in the right bunker and his third shot remained lodged in the sand. However, the former University of Arizona golfer blasted his fourth shot into the hole to save par and stay tied.

On the following three holes, Furyk missed great victory opportunities when a series of 12-foot birdie putts failed to fall. The duo struggled through six extra holes, but neither golfer could break par.

Back on 18 for the seventh playoff hole, both Woods and Furyk drove into the rough, but Furyk's ball nestled beneath a tree, while Woods's lay just to the right of the fairway. Woods used his wedge to pitch within two feet of the hole and sank the birdie putt. Furyk punched out of the rough and settled for bogey, giving Woods his 29th career victory. The 25-year-old's triumph tied Jack Nicklaus for most PGA Tour wins before turning age 30.

Seven times a day I praise You, because of Your righteous judgments.
PSALM 119:164, NKJV

EXTRA POINT < < < < < < < < < < < < < < < < < < < < Seven times Jim Furyk had a chance to win and couldn't. But on the seventh try, Tiger Woods finally claimed the victory.

In the Bible, the number seven held great significance to the Israelites because it symbolized completion. It's mentioned 261 times in the Old Testament and 66 times in the New.

God created the world in seven days. Seven people lived on the ark with Noah. Joseph's dream showed seven years of plenty and seven of famine. Leviticus lists seven feasts. The battle of Jericho featured seven priests with seven trumpets surrounding the city's walls for seven days. God cured army commander Naaman after he washed seven times in the Jordan River. Job's friends sat with him seven days.

GOAL! *Explore Scripture for other uses of the number seven. Praise God for his completeness.*

26 AUG

WINNING A PROFESSIONAL sports league's first championship happens only once. But for Cynthia Cooper, coming home meant more than capturing the WNBA's first title in 1997.

Boasting the best record in the Women's National Basketball Association, the Houston Comets tangled with the New York Liberty on their home court in front of 16,285 fans. Despite Houston's stellar mark, the Liberty had beaten the Comets in all three regular season encounters.

With New York's Rebecca Lobo scoring 16 points in the Liberty's 59–41 semifinal win over Phoenix, Houston coach Van Chancellor handed rookie Tina Thompson the assignment of guarding the all-star center. The first player taken in the WNBA draft responded like a veteran by holding Lobo to nine points.

Tough defense from both teams dominated the contest as Houston pulled in front 28–24 at the half. Early in the second half, the Comets erupted for a 10–0 run, but the Liberty closed to 50–43 with a little over three minutes remaining. Down the stretch, Cooper took command. The 32-year-old guard sank eight successive free throws to clinch the 65–51 victory, giving the Comets the first WNBA crown.

Playing the entire 40 minutes, the former USC All-American scored 25 points, grabbed four rebounds, dished out four assists, made two steals, and blocked a shot to claim the league's first championship series Most Valuable Player award.

EXTRA POINT < < < < < < < < < < < < < < < < < < < < Cooper not only came home to Houston and a victory, she came home to play in front of her mother Mary Cobbs, who battled breast cancer. Cynthia Cooper cherished home and family. And we should do the same. Our parents may come down on us every once in a while and our siblings may occasionally annoy us—nothing on earth is perfect. But deep down we have to admit that we love our family.

God created homes to provide loving, safe places for kids to grow and thrive. The heavenly Father made mothers and fathers to teach their offspring right from wrong and to show them his way. Then the Lord planned for the children to grow up to establish their own homes and teach their children and their children's children until the end of time.

GOAL! *Trace the branches of your family tree on a free Internet site. Thank God for family members who cherish you.*

CHILDREN'S CHILDREN ARE A CROWN TO THE AGED, AND PARENTS ARE THE PRIDE OF THEIR CHILDREN.

PROVERBS 17:6, NIV

Now all of you together are Christ's body, and each one of you is a separate and necessary part of it.

1 CORINTHIANS 12:27

CARL LEWIS REIGNED over the track world for nearly two decades. In 1997, he crowned his career with an encore performance at the end of the European summer track season.

The 36-year-old athlete, who captured nine gold medals in four Olympics, ran his final race at Berlin's Olympic Stadium. At the same site where Jesse Owens made Olympic history, Lewis anchored the 400-meter relay team.

Prior to the event, the former University of Houston sprinter entered the stadium in regal style. A chauffeur-driven Mercedes squired Lewis and fellow retiree Linford Christie around the track to a standing ovation of 60,000 fans. A group of the runner's supporters held up a sign reading, "Thank you for all the great moments, Carl."

Few doubted the race's outcome. Donovan Bailey, who set a world record in the 100 meters at the 1996 Olympics, opened and handed off to Leroy Burrell. Burrell then passed off to Frankie Fredericks, who gave Lewis the baton and a slight push in the back to send him on the anchor leg. Carl crossed the finish line in a time of 38.24 seconds, far ahead of the rest of the field.

EXTRA POINT < < < < < < < < < < < < < < < < < < < < Carl Lewis sat on track's throne for almost 20 years. He set 11 world records, 16 American records, and 4 world and American indoor records. The 6-foot-3-inch, 195-pound runner experienced career bests running 60 yards in 6.02 seconds, 100 meters in 9.86 seconds, 200 meters in 19.75 seconds, and jumping 8.87 meters or 29 feet-1-inch. God endowed Lewis with the incredible physical and mental ability to rule his sport.

God gives everybody different talents. Some can shoot a basketball. Others play beautiful music or create useful things with tools. Every gift and talent comes from God and fits together beautifully in the body of Christ.

GOAL! *Make a list of abilities you think God has given you. They can be related to sports, school, or regular life.*

_____

_____

_____

Read about the body of Christ in 1 Corinthians 12:12–31. Pray that God will help you use your gifts for his glory as part of his body.

KICKING AN EXTRA POINT rarely excites the crowd. But in 2001, Jacksonville State's backup kicker drew a standing ovation.

Second-year football coach Jack Crowe sought a reserve kicker and some extra attention for his Jacksonville, Alabama, team that moved from Division II to Division I-AA. After hearing from one of his assistant coaches about Ashley Martin, a midfielder on the women's soccer team, he invited her to spring practice. She earned her position on the football squad by connecting on 20 of 22 extra point attempts against a full-scale rush.

Martin learned the basics of football before coming to Jacksonville State. She kicked for Georgia's East Coweta High, where she was also voted homecoming queen.

In the Gamecocks' first game against Cumberland University, Crowe sent in the 20-year-old psychology major following Jacksonville State's second touchdown. With her ponytail hanging out of her red helmet, Ashley swung her right leg and sent the ball through the uprights. The crowd of 11,312 cheered, and her mother, Stacy, received high fives from more than 30 family members and friends.

Ashley booted two more extra points in the 72–10 victory, and Crowe awarded his kicker the game ball. The following morning the first female football player to score in a Division I-AA game flew to New York and appeared on *Good Morning America*.

EXTRA POINT < < < < < < < < < < < < < < < < < < < < < The Gamecocks won, but Ashley got the glory because she achieved something no other woman had accomplished. She scored in an NCAA Division I-AA football game. She proved that her gender could contribute to a gridiron victory.

In the Bible, another woman proved herself. God chose Deborah to lead Israel. King Jabin of Canaan cruelly ruled God's people for 20 years. The Lord told Deborah to prepare Barak to lead the Israelites against Jabin's General Sisera. When Barak hesitated and would go only if Deborah went too, she warned him that he wouldn't receive the glory. A woman would. Nevertheless, he insisted, and God did as he said.

GOAL! *Come up with some first-time accomplishments by women. You may want to check out the Internet or go to the library. Praise God that he uses both males and females in his work.*

Barak told her, "I will go, but only if you go with me!" "Very well," she replied, "I will go with you. But since you have made this choice, you will receive no honor. For the Lord's victory over Sisera will be at the hands of a woman."
JUDGES 4:8-9

I don't mean to say that I have already achieved these things or that I have already reached perfection! But I keep working toward that day when I will finally be all that Christ Jesus saved me for and wants me to be.

PHILIPPIANS 3:12

DURING HIS CAREER, Michael Johnson pursued Olympic gold and world records. The sprinter achieved an unparalleled feat capturing both the 200- and 400-meter gold medals in the 1996 Olympics in Atlanta. He set a world record in the 200-meter finals. But his quest for the 400-meter top mark eluded him. In the 1999 World Track and Field Championships in Spain, he obtained his final goal.

After Johnson clocked a 43.95 in the semifinals, most people predicted he would set a 400-meter world record in the finals. USA Track and Field officials prepared a press release announcing his feat, leaving out only the new time.

When the starting gun sounded, the Texan bolted from the blocks. With a 10.9 in the first 100 meters, Johnson reached the race's midpoint at 21.0. Coming around the final curve, the 32-year-old runner calmly continued his blistering pace despite leading the field by ten meters. He crossed the finish line in 43.18 seconds, topping Butch Reynolds' old world record by .11 seconds.

Spying an American flag, Johnson rushed over and slapped hands with the fans in the front row of Seville's Olympic Stadium. In his victory lap, the runner walked slowly, savoring his lifelong goal.

EXTRA POINT < < < < < < < < < < < < < < < < < < < < Michael Johnson didn't begin as a star. His education-oriented parents demanded that schoolwork precede athletics. At Dallas' Skyline High School, he ran an average track career. He didn't attract much college attention, but Baylor University's coach saw potential. Johnson chose "Quarter Miler U."

Under Clyde Hart's tutoring and with a freshman-year growth spurt, Michael became a five-time NCAA champion and world-class runner while earning a business degree. But most agree that Michael Johnson's success came because of his dedication and attitude—an attitude that led him to quit high school football in spite of peer pressure.

Michael Johnson became his own person who pressed on to win educational and athletic prizes and accomplish his goals. And that's what the apostle Paul says we should do.

GOAL! *Think about your educational, athletic, and life goals. Ask God for the dedication and attitude to accomplish them.*

ONLY SEVEN AMERICAN professional sports teams have captured four consecutive championships. The Houston Comets did it in stunning fashion by winning the first four WNBA titles. But their quest for trophy number four in 2000 required some last-second heroics.

The Comets hosted the New York Liberty in game two of the best-of-three WNBA championship series. After defeating New York 59–52 on the road, Coach Van Chancellor's team sought to join men's basketball's Boston Celtics, baseball's New York Yankees, and hockey's Montreal Canadiens and New York Islanders as four-in-a-row title holders.

Despite being the underdogs, the Liberty battled gamely and overcame a 12–2 first-half deficit and a 44–35 second-half margin to lead 64–61 with 31 seconds remaining. Unfazed, Cynthia Cooper, the three-time WNBA championship MVP, fired a shot from beyond the men's three-point line. The ball touched nothing but net, tying the score and sending the contest into overtime.

Three-pointers by Crystal Robinson and Sue Wicks gave the Liberty a 70–69 edge with a little over two minutes to play, but Sheryl Swoopes put the Comets back in front with two free throws. Cooper hit a running jump shot with just under a minute left, making the score 72–70. Two free throws each by Tina Thompson and Coquese Washington iced the 79–73 victory. For her 25-point effort in her final professional game, Cooper received her fourth MVP award.

EXTRA POINT < < < < < < < < < < < < < < < < < < < < Cynthia Cooper rescued the Houston Comets from defeat. Her strength and rock-solid play saved the victory and gave Houston a four-peat.

Cooper's job was to play basketball. But other people earn their pay as rescuers in much more stressful arenas. Firefighters, police, and emergency medical personnel save people from injury or death—often putting themselves at risk.

From 1993 to 2002, 1,655 law enforcement officers died in the line of duty, an average of one death every 53 hours.

God wants us to remember the brave people who put their lives on the line for us. And he wants us to know that he's our ultimate rescuer.

GOAL! *Would you risk your life as a police officer, firefighter, or emergency medical rescuer? Praise Jesus for his willing sacrifice to rescue us from sin.*

The Lord will rescue me from every evil attack and will bring me safely to his heavenly kingdom. To him be glory for ever and ever. Amen.

2 TIMOTHY 4:18, NIV

31 AUG

THOUSANDS OF ATHLETES have participated in the Olympic Games. Hundreds have won gold medals. But only a single athlete has captured a gold in both the Winter and Summer Games.

Eddie Eagan grew up in a poor family in Denver, Colorado. As a youth, he idolized Frank Merriwell, an athlete featured in dime fiction novels. Eagan followed his hero's footsteps, attending Yale, Harvard Law School, and Oxford. Eventually, the Colorado native became a successful attorney.

Like Merriwell, the young man from Denver excelled in sports. In 1920, Eagan won the light heavyweight division at the Games in Antwerp, Belgium. Later, he won the United States Amateur Heavyweight title and the Amateur Championship of Great Britain.

Twelve years later, the boxer competed on the U.S. four-man bobsled team in Lake Placid, New York. Eagan, Billy Fiske, Jay O'Brien, and Clifford Gray claimed the gold for the USA over Germany and Switzerland.

So far nine Americans have competed in summer and winter Olympic events. Eagan, however, holds the honor as the only Olympian to capture gold in both.

EXTRA POINT < < < < < < < < < < < < < < < < < < < < < Eddie Eagan found success in both hot weather and cold—in both Lake Placid and Antwerp. People honored Eagan for the gold medals he won. But his achievement went beyond the boundaries of countries and of seasons. His accomplishments transcended sports. He made a name for himself in life. God says an honorable name is more valuable than money. We should treasure it more than gold.

How do we make a good name for ourselves? We must be honest, truthful, kind, considerate, true to our promises, and willing to admit when we're wrong.

But we can't do all those things alone. We must depend on our heavenly Father for help. The Bible provides principles for living. Prayer gives us strength.

GOAL! *When your name surfaces in conversation, what do you think people say? If you honestly don't know, ask a friend you can trust to tell you the truth. Commit to God to working hard to earn a good name.*

01 SEP

MOST FOOTBALL TEAMS begin their seasons with high expectations. But in the 2000 opener, the Dallas Cowboys failed to play as well as many fans thought they should.

The Texas Stadium thermometer registered 109 degrees for the noon kickoff against the Philadelphia Eagles. The heat didn't faze Philadelphia, however, as coach Andy Reid called for an onside kick to start the game. Eagles kicker David Akers popped the ball short, and Philadelphia's Dameane Douglas caught the pigskin. Phillies quarterback Donovan McNabb needed only eight plays to score, and the contest quickly turned into a rout.

The Philadelphia defense smothered Cowboys quarterback Troy Aikman, sacking him three times on his first four pass attempts. The Eagles scored again in the first quarter on an eight-play, 61-yard drive. Early in the second quarter, Jeremiah Trotter intercepted an Aikman pass and returned it 27 yards for a touchdown, putting the Eagles up 21–0. The Dallas quarterback left for the hospital a few plays later following his fourth sack, which resulted in a concussion.

Ahead 24–6 at the midpoint, the Eagles scored 17 second-half points before Dallas tallied a late touchdown on a 4-yard pass from Randall Cunningham to Joey Galloway. However, Galloway suffered a season-ending knee injury later in the fourth quarter.

Philadelphia's 41–14 victory not only spoiled Dave Campo's coaching debut, it also represented the worst drubbing for Dallas since a 28–0 loss in 1989.

EXTRA POINT < < < < < < < < < < < < < < < < < < < <

Dallas fans left the stadium deflated. A new coach, a new season, and a few superstars had inflated their expectations. But a couple of quarters into the first game, Cowboys faithfuls knew 2000 would be a season to forget.

On the other hand, the cool-weather-based Eagles prepared for the heat. Team members ingested extra fluids the week before and drank pickle juice during the game to ward off dehydration. Whether the odd drink worked or not, Philadelphia exceeded expectations in the 100-plus degree weather.

In life, we hope to exceed expectations. The Corinthian Christians did. They first committed themselves to the Lord and then gave of themselves to doing God's will.

GOAL! *What expectations do you have for your favorite football team this fall? What expectations do you have in your Christian life?*
Ask God to help you meet his expectations.

DAVE WOTTLE always wore an old golf cap when he ran. But in the 1972 Olympics, his failure to remove his hat led to a tearful and apologetic moment.

The 22-year-old Ohio native shocked track followers when he equaled the 800-meter world record at the Olympic tryouts. In the Munich, Germany, Games observers rated Russia's Yevhen Arzhanor the favorite due to Wottle's tendinitis and lack of experience.

Kenyans Michael Boit and Robert Ouko set a blistering pace. Wottle, following his typical strategy of lingering toward the back and saving his strength for a strong finish, trudged along in sixth place at the halfway point. In the second lap, the Kenyans faded and Arzhanor took control. Wottle shifted into overdrive, but winning appeared hopeless with 50 meters remaining.

Still gaining ground, the American realized Arzhanor had exhausted his reserves. Drawing on one last ounce of strength, Wottle leaned forward and nipped the Russian at the tape. He finished the course in 1:45.86—.03 seconds faster than Arzhanor.

The victory shocked both fans and Wottle. Still reeling from his surprise win, Dave failed to remove his cap during the "Star-Spangled Banner" at the medal ceremony. Unaware of his action until a reporter asked if he was making a protest, the Bowling Green Air Force ROTC member issued a formal apology.

> Nothing in all creation can hide from him. Everything is naked and exposed before his eyes. This is the God to whom we must explain all that we have done.
> HEBREWS 4:13

EXTRA POINT < < < < < < < < < < < < < < < < < < < < Hat etiquette calls for removal of caps during the passing of the flag and the playing of the national anthem. Dave Wottle obviously learned the rules in his college military course. He simply got caught up in the moment and the cap felt like such a part of him that he forgot. When the reporter pointed out the mistake, Dave Wottle sincerely apologized.

We often make unintentional mistakes. We accidentally break something. We forgot to complete a chore. We space out on a commitment. But we can't hide any of our mistakes from God. He sees and knows everything. Like Dave Wottle did, the right thing to do is to apologize sincerely.

GOAL! *Isn't it cool that when we mess up we can immediately ask God for forgiveness—and he gives it to us! Praise God for his understanding when we unintentionally do wrong.*

03 SEP

One day Jesus
told his
disciples a
story to
illustrate their
need for
constant prayer
and to show
them that they
must never
give up.
LUKE 18:1

WHEN A TEAM FACES playoff elimination, it plays with determination. In 1999, Teresa Weatherspoon's never-give-up attitude helped extend the New York Liberty's season.

The Liberty met the Houston Comets in game two of the best-of-three WNBA finals. After the Liberty lost 73–60 on its home court, another loss would result in a sad return trip to New York and a jubilant celebration for the Comets' third straight crown.

In the contest's early stages, Houston appeared headed for the two-game sweep. Leading by as many as 18 points in the first half, the Comets held a 37–23 advantage at the intermission. That's when Liberty coach Richie Adubato instructed Crystal Robinson to take command in the second half. The former Southeast Oklahoma State guard found her shooting eye and tallied 16 points in a 19–2 New York run to open the second half.

Houston regrouped, however, and the two teams fought back and forth. With 2.4 seconds remaining, Tina Thompson banked a shot off the glass, putting the Comets in front 67–65 and apparently cementing the Houston three-peat.

After calling a time-out, the Liberty inbounded the ball to Teresa Weatherspoon in the backcourt. Taking two dribbles, the 33-year-old veteran launched the ball from behind the midcourt line. From 53 feet, the ball arced through the air, bounced off the backboard, and ripped through the net at the buzzer. The improbable shot brought New York a 68–67 victory and knotted the series at a game each.

EXTRA POINT < < < < < < < < < < < < < < < < < < < Teresa Weatherspoon didn't give up. Although chances for victory appeared bleak, Weatherspoon gave her best effort and was rewarded with victory.

One day Jesus Christ told his followers a story about never giving up. In the story a widow bugs a judge so much that he finally gives her justice. The point is: The Lord rewards persistence; he wants us to keep trying.

You never know when your final efforts will result in a victory for God . . . or a 53-foot three-pointer.

GOAL! *Read the story of the persistent widow in Luke 18:1–8. What can you learn from this parable? Pray that God gives you a never-give-up attitude when it comes to following his will.*

PHYSICIANS HELP ATHLETES overcome injuries and prolong their career. But at the 1972 Olympics, oversights by American doctors cost swimmer Rick DeMont a gold medal.

The 16-year-old California native suffered from asthma and allergies to wheat and fur. By using the prescription drug Marax, he was able to alleviate his symptoms. After qualifying for the Munich Games, he completed a form listing his medications. However, doctors for the U.S. Olympic team failed to check the drug's components for substances banned under International Olympic Committee rules.

After edging out Australia's Bradford Cooper by .01 seconds for the gold medal in the 400-meter freestyle, DeMont submitted to a drug test. Two days later, while the swimmer waited to compete in the 1,500 meters, officials informed him that he'd tested positive for ephedrine—a compound contained in Marax—and could not swim.

Over the next few days, confusion and endless legal proceedings occupied the American's time. At the conclusion, the IOC stripped DeMont of his gold medal and issued a stern reprimand to U.S. officials.

In 1996, DeMont filed suit against the United States Olympic Committee, claiming mishandling of his medical disclosure. As part of the settlement, the USOC issued a press release stating the swimmer properly informed officials of his prescriptions. The committee updated the visitor's kiosk at its Colorado Springs headquarters to reflect DeMont's accomplishment in the 1972 Games.

> On this day, atonement will be made for you, and you will be cleansed from all your sins in the Lord's presence.
>
> LEVITICUS 16:30

EXTRA POINT

< < < < < < < < < < < < < < < < < < < < <

Rick DeMont did everything right. He openly discussed his asthma and allergies. He completely disclosed his prescription drugs. But the doctors failed to check the chemicals in Marax. A mistake cost DeMont an Olympic medal, a leg on the relay team, and his reputation as a clean, drug-free athlete.

In life, we also should strive to be clean. The great thing is that Jesus can make us that way. In the Old Testament Moses wrote about a day when the Lord will cleanse us from our sins. That's exactly what happens when we pray to ask Jesus into our life.

GOAL! *If you haven't prayed to invite Jesus into your life, you can do it now. Simply tell God you've made a lot of mistakes and believe that Jesus can cleanse your sins. Ask God to help you live for him and to give you a spotless reputation.*

05 SEP

UTILITY PLAYERS SECURE their spot on baseball rosters by being able to play multiple positions. In 1999, Scott Sheldon proved to be one of the most useful players of all time.

The 30-year-old rookie played every position except pitcher for the Texas Rangers during a spring training game, which locked in a spot for him on the team. Then late in the regular season, Rangers manager Johnny Oates decided to give Sheldon a chance to make history.

Mired in last place and trailing the Chicago White Sox 10–1 in the second inning, Oates informed Chicago manager Jerry Manuel of his idea and put Sheldon in the game as catcher in the fourth inning. After moving to first base for the fifth, Sheldon played second and short in the sixth, and right and center field in the seventh.

In the eighth inning, the versatile player opened at left field and with one out shifted to the mound. Facing pinch hitter Jeff Liefer, Sheldon struck him out swinging on five pitches. Without hesitation, he tossed the ball to Oates and moved to third base for the Rangers' final defensive out in the 13–1 loss.

By playing all nine positions in a single game, Sheldon joined Bert Campaneris and Cesar Tovar as the only players in major league history to accomplish this unique feat.

EXTRA POINT < < < < < < < < < < < < < < < < < < < < < < Anyone who can play every position and strike out a batter helps a team. Even though the Rangers lost, Johnny Oates's experiment proved Scott Sheldon's versatility.

The Bible tells about another useful person in a 25-verse book. Philemon, tucked between Titus and Hebrews in the New Testament, describes Onesimus's story. He was a slave who had run away to Rome. There he met Paul and became a Christian.

Paul pled with Philemon to forgive Onesimus because of his usefulness to Paul while the apostle was in prison. He urged Philemon to treat Onesimus as a Christian brother rather than punishing him as a runaway slave.

GOAL! *Read the book of Philemon. If Onesimus had been your runaway slave, how would you have treated him after hearing Paul's pleas? How can you be useful to God?*

PICKING THE TIME and place to retire is a special treat for an athlete. In 2001, Michael Johnson elected to conclude his career at the Goodwill Games in Australia.

The world-record holder in the 200- and 400-meter run began sprinting professionally at the 1990 Goodwill Games in Seattle. He also competed in two other Goodwill contests: St. Petersburg, Russia, in 1994 and in the 1998 Games at Uniondale, New York.

After capturing his second 400-meter Olympic gold medal at the 2000 Sydney Games, the former Baylor University star ran only relay races in his final professional year. Then at his final Goodwill Games appearance at Brisbane's ANZ Stadium, he participated, along with Derrick Brew, Leonard Byrd, and Antonio Pettigrew in the competition's final event, the 1,600-meter relay.

Running the anchor lap, the 33-year-old runner took the baton just ahead of Jamaica's Michael Blackwood. The Caribbean runner matched Johnson's pace for 300 meters, but the nine-time world champion blistered down the stretch and won by eight meters.

The American relay team took first place in a time of 3:00.52, and Johnson walked a victory lap with his three teammates. More than 30,000 fans cheered as the five-time Olympic gold medalist stood listening to the "Star-Spangled Banner" for the final time atop the winners' stand.

> Now all has been heard; here is the conclusion of the matter: Fear God and keep his commandments, for this is the whole duty of man.
> ECCLESIASTES 12:13, NIV

EXTRA POINT < < < < < < < < < < < < < < < < < < < < < < < < Michael Johnson accomplished all his goals on the track—world records, Olympic medals, and meet titles. The star hadn't lost many steps, but training and recovery grew more difficult. His wife, Kerry, his son, Sebastian, and business opportunities helped Johnson make the decision to conclude his running career.

The author of Ecclesiastes made a final conclusion. He told everybody to fear God and obey his commands. That's the duty of every person. And if we do those things, God will applaud when we meet him in heaven.

GOAL! *Think about the things God commands you to do. If you need a refresher, read the Bible to learn how God wants you to live. At the conclusion of your life, God will judge your actions and whether or not you did your best to achieve his will for you on earth.*

07 SEP

You will enjoy
the fruit of your
labor. How
happy you will
be! How rich
your life!

PSALM 128:2

NOTHING THRILLS FANS like a towering home run. In 1998, Mark McGwire's massive blasts generated enthusiasm and etched his name in baseball's record book.

The St. Louis Cardinals first baseman commenced the 1998 campaign by belting 11 round-trippers in April and 16 in May. The 6-foot-5-inch, 250-pound slugger reached the 50-homer plateau on August 20. Not only did the single-season record of 61 set by Roger Maris in 1961 appear to be in jeopardy, but enthusiasts relished the neck and neck competition supplied by Chicago Cubs outfielder Sammy Sosa, who was also hitting home runs at an incredible pace.

On September 5, Big Mac smashed his 60th. The nation waited anxiously for Maris's mark to fall. Two days later, millions watched televised coverage of the Cardinals and the Cubs. In McGwire's first at bat, he lined Mike Morgan's 1-1 pitch just inside the left-field foul pole to tie the record.

The following evening, McGwire ripped a slider to left that barely cleared the eight-foot wall for the record-breaking number 62. The hometown crowd of 49,987 erupted. First-base coach Dave McKay almost caused the slugger to miss the bag with his embrace. Receiving high fives from every Cub, McGwire slowly rounded the bases before being mobbed by teammates and his ten-year-old son, Matthew.

After stepping into the stands to hug Maris's three sons and daughter, the record holder thanked the fans and his rival, Sammy Sosa.

EXTRA POINT < < < < < < < < < < < < < < < < < < < < What a night for baseball fans! The game between the Cardinals and the Cubs wasn't an ordinary contest. Instead, it proved to be a drama of past heroes versus current stars and two men respectfully battling each other.

McGwire and Sosa worked hard. They spent hours in the batting cage. They lifted weights. When that 62nd home run cleared the fence, McGwire earned the fruits of his labor. The crowd roared, reporters lined up for interviews, and his name was written in the record books.

Most of us will never know that kind of athletic success. But we can enjoy the fruits of our labor. The psalmist promises that if we work hard, we'll enjoy the Father's blessings.

GOAL! *Take a trip to some batting cages. Note the effort required to successfully hit a baseball. Think about the effort required to be a successful Christian. God will help you work hard for him if you ask him to.*

MAUREEN CONNOLLY'S PASSION for tennis translated into success on the court. And despite injury and an illness that cut both her career and her life short, her legacy endures.

In 1951, the San Diego, California, native burst on the tennis scene, claiming the United States Open at age 16. Two years later, she captured the Australian Open, French Open, and Wimbledon titles before advancing to the U.S. Open finals for the third straight year.

After going through the preliminary rounds undefeated, Connolly drew longtime adversary Doris Hart in the finals. The pair had recently met in the Wimbledon finals.

Using her speed and strong ground strokes, the blond teenager broke Hart's serve twice in the first set and coasted to a 6–2 win. Connolly dispatched her opponent with almost the same ease in set two, winning 6–4. The entire match lasted only 43 minutes. Together with her triumphs in Australia, France, and Great Britain, Connolly became the first woman to claim all four Grand Slam titles in the same year.

EXTRA POINT
< < < < < < < < < < < < < < < < < < < <

The press nicknamed Maureen Connolly "Little Mo," comparing her power to the big guns of the Battleship Missouri, known as "Big Mo."

From 1951 to 1954, Little Mo won nine Grand Slams. But two weeks after her 1954 Wimbledon win, tragedy struck. While she was horseback riding, a cement truck knocked her from her mount. The star's fall injured her leg so severely that she could no longer compete.

Married to 1952 Olympic equestrian Norman Brinker, the two settled in Dallas where Maureen dedicated herself to developing young tennis talent. In 1968, she established a foundation to promote junior tennis but six months later died of cancer at age 34.

When tragedies strike and death takes a person at a young age, we ask why. But God doesn't promise answers, fairness, freedom from pain, or long life. He simply promises his comforting presence. And he wants us to show that same comfort to others who are going through tough times.

GOAL! *Is there a family you know that has experienced tragedy? If so, there are certainly ways to offer loving support. Ask God to help those people feel his presence and comfort even in the midst of the sadness.*

Praise be to the God and Father of our Lord Jesus Christ, the Father of compassion and the God of all comfort, who comforts us in all our troubles, so that we can comfort those in any trouble with the comfort we ourselves have received from God.

2 CORINTHIANS 1:3-4, NIV

09 SEP

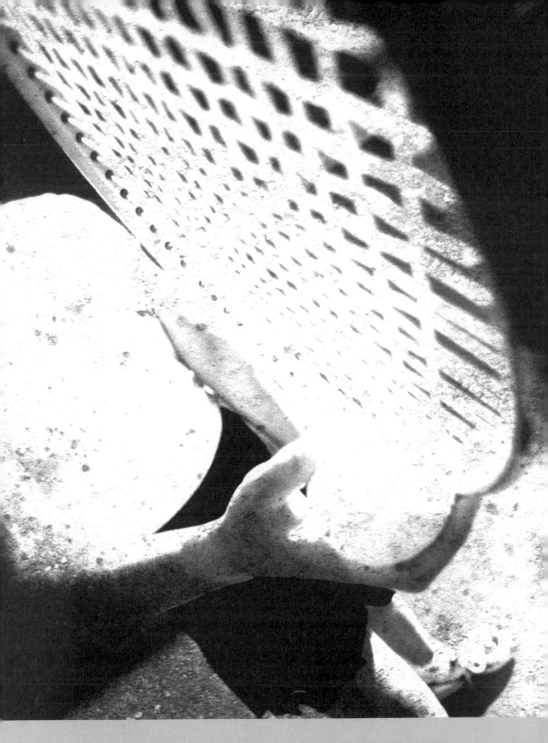

WISDOM BELONGS TO THE AGED, AND UNDERSTANDING TO THOSE WHO HAVE LIVED MANY YEARS.

JOB 12:12

SATCHEL PAIGE DOMINATED Negro League baseball for more than two decades. But in 1948, the legendary pitcher showcased his talent in the majors.

The Cleveland Indians signed Paige on July 7 in a move that many considered a publicity stunt by owner Bill Veeck. Although the Alabama native's age was officially listed as 42, estimates of his actual age added between two and six years.

After several relief appearances, Veeck and manager Lou Boudreau inserted the aging hurler as a starter. Lasting seven innings, Paige won his first start against the Washington Senators. Ten days later, he drew the assignment to face the Chicago White Sox in Comiskey Park.

Over 50,000 packed the stadium, and 15,000 more were turned away. After four scoreless innings, the Indians tallied a run with Lary Doby's triple and Jim Hegan's sacrifice fly. In the eighth, Cleveland added another run on Ken Keltner's single, Hegan's sacrifice, and Dale Mitchell's RBI-single. The Indians iced the 5–0 victory with three runs in the ninth fueled by singles from Boudreau and Doby and two White Sox errors.

On the mound, Paige performed superbly, walking none and allowing only five singles. The White Sox threatened to spoil the shutout in the ninth, putting runners on first and third with one out. But the veteran pitcher retired Aaron Robinson and Ralph Hodgin for his fourth win and first complete game victory in the major leagues.

EXTRA POINT

‹ ‹ ‹ ‹ ‹ ‹ ‹ ‹ ‹ ‹ ‹ ‹ ‹ ‹ ‹ ‹ ‹ ‹ ‹ ‹

The Indians gratefully added gray-haired Satchel Paige to their roster. Later in the season, the pitcher who was as old as some of his teammates' fathers aided Cleveland's pennant drive with a 6–1 record. Even while in his 40s, Satchel Paige made the most of his opportunity to finally play in the major leagues.

Baseball had already discriminated against Paige and the others in the Negro League because of the color of their skin. How wonderful that Bill Veeck and Lou Boudreau decided not to discriminate against Paige because of his age. And the older player helped Cleveland into the postseason.

Older people can add a lot to our life too. Because they've lived longer, they can give us wisdom that they've learned from experience. That's what the Bible says.

GOAL! *This is the month we celebrate Grandparents Day. Think about what you've learned from your grandparents or other older adults. Thank God for their wisdom and support.*

10 SEP

Greater love
has no one than
this, than to lay
down one's life
for his friends.

JOHN 15:13, NKJV

THE TRAGIC EVENTS of September 11, 2001, brought the sports world to a standstill. Although professional and collegiate teams postponed games, many high school squads elected to play.

One football contest pitted Bloomington, Minnesota's, Jefferson High against Eastview. Although Jefferson emerged victorious 20–10, the pregame activities overshadowed the action on the field. Jefferson's helmets bore two decals—an American flag and a No. 10 honoring former quarterback Tom Burnett Jr.

Before the game, the high school recognized the player who had led Jefferson to a state championship in 1981. The 38-year-old father of three girls had been a passenger on United Flight 93.

After hijackers took over the airplane, Burnett called his wife, Deena, on his cell phone. In two later calls, she told him about the destruction of New York's World Trade Center and the attack on the Pentagon. Burnett telephoned a final time, telling his wife that he and several other passengers would attempt to retake the airplane. They wanted to prevent the hijackers from completing their destructive mission of crashing the plane into a Washington, D.C. building.

Family members of those on board confidentially listened to tapes of the flight's last moments. Recordings indicated that the pilots had already been killed when the group bravely managed to take control of the jet. Although their specific actions remain unknown, the flight never reached the nation's capitol. Instead, it crashed in western Pennsylvania, killing all aboard.

EXTRA POINT < < < < < < < < < < < < < < < < < < < < In addition to Tom Burnett, who played football at St. John's University in New York, three others credited with heroic actions on Flight 93 were college athletes. Todd Beamer played basketball and baseball at Wheaton College in Illinois, Mark Bingham competed in rugby at UC–Berkeley, and Jeremy Glick won a national judo championship.

Burnett and the others knew they probably would die, but they understood the devastation that would have been caused by crashing into the White House or the Capitol Building. The heroes treasured their nation and her people. With bravery and love, they sacrificed their life for their country.

Jesus Christ also laid down his life for his friends, including you and me.

GOAL! *Who would you be willing to die for? If you'd been on Flight 93, would you have joined Tom Burnett Jr. in the attempt to retake the plane? Ask God to bless the families of all who died on September 11, 2001. Thank Jesus for dying for you.*

LINDSAY DAVENPORT'S PARENTS always believed in their daughter's abilities. Her mom spent endless hours taking Lindsay to tennis lessons. In the 1998 United States Open, Lindsay rewarded their faith.

After moving through six preliminary rounds without losing a set, the 22-year-old Californian faced defending champion Martina Hingis in the finals. Many considered Davenport to be too slow to win a Grand Slam event, but a strength and conditioning program resulted in 30 fewer pounds and renewed self-confidence.

The 6-foot-2-inch player took a 2–1 lead over Hingis with a service break in the first set and then received a favorable call in game seven. With the game at deuce, the wind blew off Lindsay's baseball cap on a return she hit into the net. Umpire Dessie Samuels ruled a let and ordered the point replayed. Davenport won the replay and took another service break to move in front 5–2. She eventually won the set 6–3.

After the American went up 4–2 in set two, Hingis rallied. But Davenport regained her control with a series of sharp volleys and passing shots, winning 12 of the final 15 points en route to a 7–5 victory. Davenport's triumph marked the first win for an American-born female player in the U.S. Open since Chris Evert in 1982. As an added bonus, the new champion claimed the title on her mother's birthday.

Listen, my child, to what your father teaches you. Don't neglect your mother's teaching. What you learn from them will crown you with grace and clothe you with honor.

PROVERBS 1:8-9

EXTRA POINT < < < < < < < < < < < < < < < < < < < < < < Lindsay Davenport's parents played an important role in her success. The tennis star listened to her mother's advice and responded to the caring she showed. Davenport remembered the teachings of the instructors her parents had hired. She followed in her father Wink's footsteps as an Olympian, winning tennis gold at the 1996 Atlanta Games. He played on the fifth-place USA men's volleyball team in the Mexico City Olympics in 1968.

The writer of Proverbs explained the importance of listening to parents. He compared the value of their teachings to garlands and necklaces awarded for achievement.

GOAL! *Thin of some advice your mother or father has given you.*

Read God's advice in Proverbs 1:8-19. Ask the heavenly Father to help you put your parents' advice and instructions into action.

12 SEP

You shall have
no other gods
before me. You
shall not make
for yourself an
idol in the form
of anything in
heaven above
or on the earth
beneath or in
the waters
below.
EXODUS
20:3-4, NIV

SOMETIMES AN ATHLETE is so on his game that the audience—as well as his competitors—stand up and cheer. That was the case at the bike dirt competition at the 2003 Gravity Games.

From the moment Ryan Nyquist stepped on his bike, he was pure gold. Nyquist was the only rider to tally more than 90 points on every run, and his average of 96 points had him solidly in first even before his last ride.

But although this 24-year-old North Carolinian could have coasted through his final ride, he put on a show for the fans. He flew down the 55-degree, 35-foot ramp and stuck his first trick, a 720, perfectly. For his second stunt, Nyquist calmly landed a double bar spin. He followed that with a no-hander raise the roof. And finally, Nyquist brought everybody to their feet with a double bar spin backflip.

With the perfect round complete, Nyquist slipped off his seat and let his bike fly—nearly taking out a cameraman. As Nyquist raised his hands in victory, fellow bike dirt riders tossed their bikes off the platform and began bowing down to the champion.

EXTRA POINT

< < < < < < < < < < < < < < < < < < < < <

Ryan Nyquist could do no wrong at the 2003 Gravity Games. Every one of his rides scored huge points. Nobody could hang with him. Even though he already had the gold, Nyquist ended with a bang. And once Nyquist nailed his final stunt, the crowd stood and his competitors dropped to their knees.

Although bike dirt riders were joking a bit when they bowed before Nyquist, the Bible is clear: God doesn't want you to worship idols. Anything that takes your focus off Jesus can be an idol, whether it's money, perfect grades, the opposite sex, or a sports star. As you go through life, make sure you have God in his deserving place: first.

GOAL! *We don't hear too much about people bowing to a golden calf today, yet thousands of people—young and old—worship various idols. Commit to follow the one true God and bow only to him.*

QUICK STARTS often can lead to great games. And in a 2003 football contest between Baltimore and Cleveland, Ravens running back Jamal Lewis used some fast footwork to break the NFL single-game rushing record.

Lewis knew early in the week that he might have a record-breaking day. He even told a teammate that if he got the ball enough, he thought he'd have a career game. And Lewis was right.

After just two carries, Lewis had amassed 100 yards—thanks to an 82-yard touchdown jaunt. By halftime he had 180 yards, and all the Ravens started talking about breaking the single-game record of 278 yards, which was held by Cincinnati's Corey Dillon.

In the second half, Lewis continued to gain yards in bunches. His 63-yard touchdown run in the fourth quarter gave Baltimore a 23–13 lead. And by game's end, he had carried the ball 30 times for 295 yards in the Ravens' 33–13 victory. That's an average of 9.8 yards every time he wrapped his hands around the ball! Plus, Lewis would have been the first player to break 300 yards in a game, but a 60-yard touchdown run in the first half was called back because of a holding penalty.

EXTRA POINT

< < < < < < < < < < < < < < < < < < < < < < <

Cleveland had a tough time stopping Jamal Lewis. With his teammates' help and support, Lewis set a new NFL record and played an amazing game.

In Bible times, the Jewish authorities also had a hard time trying to stop some people. They couldn't hinder the disciples from spreading the gospel. They arrested the apostles and questioned them in the temple court. But Peter and the others said they had to obey God and do their job. The furious council plotted to kill the disciples.

But Gamaliel, a Pharisee, offered his council members some sound advice. He said if the disciples' words came from themselves, their efforts would fail. But if their purpose came from God, no one could stop them. And no one did.

GOAL! *Imagine breaking an NFL rushing record. You'd feel unstoppable! Praise God that nobody can stop the gospel. Will you ask him to use you in his awesome plan?*

So my advice is, leave these men alone. If they are teaching and doing these things merely on their own, it will soon be overthrown. But if it is of God, you will not be able to stop them. You may even find yourselves fighting against God.
ACTS 5:38-39

14 SEP

As iron
sharpens iron,
so one man
sharpens
another.

PROVERBS
27:17, NIV

MARCO DE SANTI MADE HISTORY at the aggressive

inline vert finals of the 2003 Gravity Games when he hit a double flat spin and a double backflip in the same run. But this Brazilian star wasn't finished. He tossed in a couple of 900s and tore off his shirt as he took over the leaderboard with an 89.25.

And although de Santi had a history-making run, he knew his lead wasn't safe as Eito Yasutoko took to the ramp. Yasutoko has been called "the most feared competitor in the world of inline vert" for good reason. He goes higher, does bigger moves, and pulls tricks that nobody in the world can match.

Yasutoko quickly electrified the crowd with his insane amplitude and speed. After cranking up some momentum soaring 20 feet above the ramp, he threw every trick in the book with style. His double backflip 180 was magnificent. His double flat backflip looked impeccable. And his 1080 California roll left the judges and audience with their jaw on the ground.

At the end of his run, the judges awarded him a 91.75, making him the only competitor to break 90 at the Games.

EXTRA POINT < < < < < < < < < < < < < < < < < < < < < <

What makes Eito Yasutoko such an awesome competitor? Hours of practice? Sure. A no-fear attitude? Yup. But if you asked Yasutoko why he's so good, he'd give a lot of credit to his brother, Takeshi. Takeshi is also one of the world's best inline vert skaters. And although he hasn't risen as high in the rankings as his brother, Takeshi pushes Eito in practice. The brothers love each other, but they also challenge each other to try new things and get better and better. Then at competitions they hang out together and cheer each other on.

The Bible talks about this concept of brothers encouraging each other to improve. The book of Proverbs compares a godly, healthy relationship to two pieces of iron sharpening each other. Get the point?

GOAL! Do you have a brother or sister who can help push you to greatness? If not, maybe a best friend or other family member can keep you accountable. Thank God for people in your life who encourage you to improve.

A KICKOFF RETURN for touchdown to start the half gives a team a tremendous boost. In 1989, Notre Dame's Raghib "Rocket" Ismail's speedy efforts helped upset No. 1 Michigan.

The Fighting Irish faced 105,912 Wolverines fans and a tough Michigan team at Ann Arbor. Following a first-half defensive battle that left Notre Dame leading 7–6, Michigan kicked off to begin the third quarter.

Ismail, a 5-foot-10-inch flanker with 4.28 speed over 40 yards, fielded the ball on his 12-yard line. Following a terrific block by Rodney Culver, the speedy sophomore wide receiver bolted up the middle for an 88-yard touchdown. Rocket's score represented the first kickoff returned for a touchdown against Michigan since Minnesota's Ron Engel performed the feat on October 26, 1957.

With sophomore Elvis Grbac subbing for an injured Michael Taylor, Michigan closed to 17–12 on a 5-yard touchdown pass to Derrick Walker early in the fourth quarter. On the ensuing kickoff, however, Ismail collected the ball on the 8. Again following Culver, Rocket blasted straight down the field for a 92-yard score. No other runner had ever blistered Michigan for two kickoff return touchdowns in a single game.

Grbac led the Wolverines to another touchdown, hitting split end Greg McMurtry on a 4-yard pass with just over four minutes remaining. But the Irish held on for a 24–19 win, extending their winning streak to 14 games.

EXTRA POINT < < < < < < < < < < < < < < < < < < < < < Rocket Ismail made the difference in the ball game. His quickness gave Notre Dame two touchdowns and a terrific mental advantage. Like it did in the Notre Dame–Michigan contest, speed frequently wins competitions.

After Jesus' death and burial, some women went early in the morning to his tomb. But when they got there, they were in for a big surprise. Instead of finding a dead friend and teacher, they discovered an empty tomb and an angel with a message: Go quickly and tell the disciples that Jesus has risen from the dead!

Sometimes in life, we too must move quickly and without hesitation as we follow God's plan.

GOAL! *Think of times when moving quickly made a difference. Ask God to help you move with speed when you should.*

Then go quickly and tell his disciples: "He has risen from the dead and is going ahead of you into Galilee. There you will see him." Now I have told you.
MATTHEW 28:7, NIV

God is not a man, that he should lie. He is not a human, that he should change his mind. Has he ever spoken and failed to act? Has he ever promised and not carried it through?

NUMBERS 23:19

MISTY HYMAN ALMOST QUIT swimming due to a rule change and health problems. But after changing her mind, she returned to garner a 2000 Olympic gold medal.

The 21-year-old swimmer perfected a unique underwater fish kick that brought her times to an elite level. However, FINA, the sport's international governing body, banned the maneuver in 1999, which forced Hyman to alter her style. The ruling, combined with her continual sinus and asthma difficulties, almost caused the Phoenix, Arizona, native to walk away from the sport just months prior to the Games in Sydney, Australia.

Few considered the first-time Olympian a serious threat in the 200-meter butterfly. Australia's Susie O'Neill, who had broken the event's 19-year-old record the previous May, was rated as the favorite.

Prior to the start, the crowd of 17,500 filled the venue with shouts for O'Neill, their hometown hero, affectionately known as "Madame Butterfly." But a small contingent of Americans shouted, "U-S-A, U-S-A" to encourage Hyman.

The American surged to an early lead and held a body-length margin over the Australian at the 150-meter mark. O'Neill pushed valiantly but never caught Hyman as she swam a personal best and pulled the biggest early upset of the Games. She captured the gold in an Olympic record time of 2:05.88, only .07 off O'Neill's world-record pace. O'Neill claimed the silver at 2:06.58, and fellow Australian Petria Thomas took the bronze at 2:07.12.

EXTRA POINT < < < < < < < < < < < < < < < < < < < <
Some people joke that it's a woman's prerogative to change her mind. Actually, people can change their mind anytime—and often they should. Misty Hyman rightly reversed her decision to compete and captured Olympic gold as a result.

But sometimes people who change their mind cause difficulties. We can't depend on them. They promise and don't come through. They talk big, but they don't follow their words with action.

However, we can depend on God. He always does what he says. He always keeps his promises.

GOAL! *Think of a time you've changed your mind and things turned out well. Remember another time when the opposite happened. Thank God that you can depend on him to never change. Praise him for always keeping his promises.*

ONCE AN ATHLETE STEPS AWAY from competitive sports it's hard for him to regain his form. But in 1999, Jim Morris discovered he still had what it took.

When injuries forced the pitcher to retire at age 25, he entered Angelo State University in San Angelo, Texas. He walked on to the Division II football team and led the nation in punting. But pro football scouts weren't interested, so Morris earned his degree and began coaching and teaching at a West Texas high school. Morris limited his baseball activity to throwing batting practice for his team.

But after seeing and feeling his coach's stinging fastball, catcher Joel DeLaGarza presented a challenge to Morris and his teammates. If the Owls captured the district title, their coach would have to attend a major league tryout.

Morris agreed, thinking a little motivation wouldn't hurt but never believing his team could do it. But the Owls won, fulfilling their end of the bargain. So the ex-minor leaguer attended a Tampa Bay Devil Rays camp. When the 35-year-old took the mound, his first pitch registered 94 mph. The rest followed at 96 to 98. Scout Doug Gassaway shook his head in wonder.

After Morris's second tryout, the Devil Rays inked him to a minor league contract and shipped him to their AA club. A few weeks later, Tampa Bay promoted him to AAA. And in September, Morris suited up for the big show.

He joined the Devil Rays in Arlington to face the Texas Rangers. With most of his players and nearly the entire town of Big Lake watching, the former coach entered the game with two out in the eighth. Relying on his blazing fastball, he struck out Royce Clayton on four pitches—all strikes.

EXTRA POINT < < < < < < < < < < < < < < < < < < < At age 35, Morris became the second oldest rookie pitcher in the majors. He credited his success to the long rest plus a smooth motion that allowed him to pitch every day. But his achievement really came because he followed his dream and was thankful for every opportunity he received.

God gives us dreams, but sometimes they don't come true right away. But we need to be thankful no matter what.

GOAL! *Watch the movie* **The Rookie** *about Jim Morris's life. Think about your dreams. God can help you wait for his timing for your dreams to come true.*

No matter what happens, always be thankful, for this is God's will for you who belong to Christ Jesus.
1 THESSALONIANS 5:18

18 SEP

THE BEST MOUNTAIN BIKERS in the world must possess powerful legs, huge lung capacities, and fearless nerves. And nowhere are those characteristics more needed than in the relatively new sport of four-cross. At the 2003 Mountain Bike World Championships, the 4X event thrilled spectators with its high speeds, tight turns, and big jumps under the lights in Lugano, Switzerland.

Four cross pits four riders against each other on a relatively short, technical track. Competitors go all out as they jockey to be the first to cross the finish line. In the men's final, three Americans—Eric Carter, Brian Lopes, and Brian Schmith—faced off against the Czech Republic's Michal Prokop, the No. 1 ranked rider in the world. Prokop proved his champion status again that night, exploding from the starting gate. Carter and Lopes tried to challenge, but Prokop held them off to earn the gold medal. Carter took home the silver with Lopes claiming the bronze.

On the women's side, two Americans (Jill Kintner and Melissa Buhl) matched against the French duo of Anne-Caroline Chausson and Sabrina Jonnier. Kintner had the best jump out of the gate, but Chausson and Jonnier caught her by the first turn. Chausson, possibly the best female mountain biker of all time, added another gold to her collection of medals, while Jonnier ended up second, and Kintner picked up the bronze.

EXTRA POINT < < < < < < < < < < < < < < < < < < < < < The Americans challenged at the World Mountain Biking Championships, but in the end the top-ranked riders stayed alert and walked away with the gold that crisp Swiss evening. Night contests under the lights can add a lot of excitement to sporting events. The fans in Switzerland certainly enjoyed the action of the 4X.

The Bible says Christians belong to the light. We aren't part of the darkness. God's light brings things to life and makes everything more vibrant and exciting, just like lights at a sporting event. Life without Christ is dull and pointless . . . like competing in the dark.

GOAL! *Have you noticed that just a little light brings life to the darkness? Commit to God to be his light. Pray that he'll give you the power to live an exciting life for him.*

IN THE PAST YOU WERE FULL OF DARKNESS,

BUT NOW YOU ARE FULL OF LIGHT IN THE LORD.

SO LIVE LIKE CHILDREN WHO BELONG TO THE LIGHT.

EPHESIANS 5:8, NCV

TRAVIS COLLINS LOVED SPORTS, but instead of playing professional ball, he became a preacher and eventually served God as a missionary overseas. Once Collins returned to the United States, he wanted to remain close to football and dreamed of becoming an official. He worked hard learning all the rules for each level in his state. He practiced all the signals until he knew them without thinking. He went through game situations in his head. And he passed the test to earn the right to step onto the gridiron.

Reverend/referee Collins received his official assignment. He arrived early for the Oldham versus Christian School of Louisville, Kentucky, middle-school game. Clad in his new uniform with a whistle around his neck, he couldn't wait for action.

Working with an experienced crew, Travis made a few early calls, expressing them clearly and assertively. He refused to let the game grow out of control. Finally, the preacher watched intently as one of the teams neared the end zone.

At last the ball crossed the goal line . . . or so he thought. Collins's hands moved from his side. He blew his whistle as his arms reached over his head. *Touchdown!*

The action stopped. The players looked around. The head of the officiating crew walked over to Collins to confer: "You called a touchdown on the 5-yard line."

EXTRA POINT < < < < < < < < < < < < < < < < < < < < Travis Collins was so excited about calling his first touchdown that he had watched the wrong line on the field. His face reddened with embarrassment as he corrected the situation.

A friend later teased him that officials who are afraid to call a touchdown they think they see on the 5-yard line will never call a touchdown at all. Collins was a strong and courageous referee in the first of many games he would officiate.

God wants his people to be strong and courageous. Without the courage to make dreams a reality, we might as well not dream. Without the strength to follow through, we'd get nothing accomplished.

GOAL! *With your family or friends, share stories of embarrassing but well-intended mistakes. Ask God for the strength and courage to dream big dreams, even if it means making a few mistakes.*

SCREAMING AROUND CORNERS and flying down steep straightaways at 45 mph sounds like a good event for a car—or perhaps a bicycle. But racing that fast standing on a skateboard sounds insane. At the 2001 Gravity Games, Dane van Bommel proved otherwise as his carefully crafted runs led to two gold medals in the two-man and four-man downhill skateboarding events.

In the two-man event, van Bommel used his quick starts and perfect lines to cruise to an uneventful victory. Gary Hardwick—who holds the standing skateboarding speed world record at 62.55 mph—settled for second.

The four-man event—where riders attacked College Hill four at a time— featured more thrills and spills. Almost every heat saw riders eat pavement (fortunately they all wore a full-length protective bodysuit and a helmet). The second heat was especially wild as Eli Smouse went down and sent John "Dread" Gwiazdowski catapulting into the hay bales and Dave Bryant sliding face-first down the road. When the carnage finally cleared, van Bommel won the finals in a tight race over Alex Wenk. Lee Dansie finished third.

EXTRA POINT < < < < < < < < < < < < < < < < < < < < < When Dane van Bommel won two Gravity golds in 2000, many felt it was a fluke. He returned in 2001 and received everything he could have hoped for as he won two more golds . . . and brought home $20,000.

As followers of Jesus Christ, we can also receive everything we hope for. God isn't a candy dispenser who gives us whatever we want, but the Bible says that when we ask for things that line up with his will, we can be confident he hears us and will give us what we ask for. That might not make us a four-time gold medal winner in the Gravity Games, but it can give us the assurance that God hears our prayer requests and does what's best for us.

GOAL! *What is God's will for your life? If you're not sure, pray, read the Bible, and ask God to reveal his plan to you. Thank God that he hears and answers your prayers.*

And this is the boldness we have in God's presence: that if we ask God for anything that agrees with what he wants, he hears us. If we know he hears us every time we ask him, we know we have what we ask from him.

1 JOHN 5:14-15, NCV

21 SEP

THE UNITED STATES OLYMPIC softball team won 110 consecutive games before journeying to Sydney, Australia, for the 2000 Olympics. The favored Americans sparkled in game one as Lori Harrigan threw the first no-hitter in Olympic history in a 6–0 defeat of Canada. The following day, Danielle Henderson and Christa Williams combined for a 3–0 blanking of Cuba.

But the tide shifted in the next game. Captain Dot Richardson committed two 11th-inning errors, allowing Japan to take a 2–1 decision. Two extra-inning losses to China and Australia followed.

Still in uniform, the team gathered in a large shower at the athletic village. Standing under the pouring water, they vowed to wash away their misfortunes.

And the strategy worked. Shutouts over New Zealand and Italy vaulted the United States into the medal round. In the first game, Stacy Nuveman blasted a three-run homer in the bottom of the tenth to defeat China 3–0. That same day, Richardson plated the winning run to edge out Australia 1–0. With the victory, the red-white-and-blue earned a place in the gold-medal game.

In the championship game, Japan's Reika Utsugi crushed a changeup for a solo home run in the fourth. One inning later, Nuveman tied the game with an RBI-single. Knotted 1–1, the contest went to extra innings.

As a light rain fell, Nuveman walked and Jennifer McFalls substituted as a pinch runner in the bottom of the eighth. With one out, Richardson walked, and Laura Berg launched a deep line drive. Shiori Koseki snagged the ball in her outstretched glove. But Koseki slipped, and the ball popped free as McFalls raced home. Gold for USA!

> I will bless them and the places surrounding my hill. I will send down showers in season; there will be showers of blessing.
>
> EZEKIEL 34:26, NIV

EXTRA POINT < < < < < < < < < < < < < < < < < < < Showers of runs and errors marked the team's first five games at the 2000 Olympics. Dedicated to a fresh start, they symbolically washed the slate clean. And ironically, they won the gold medal during a rain shower.

The prophet Ezekiel talked about showers. We must first be willing to stand under the water of God's love to wash away our sin. Then the Lord sends down showers of blessings.

GOAL! *Imagine the smell of light rain and the sound of drops splashing. Think about the way the world looks after a shower. Praise God for the showers of blessings he brings into our life.*

STEALING 50 BASES and hitting 50 doubles requires a rare combination of speed and power. In baseball's history, only two players have achieved the feat.

In 1998, the Houston Astros engaged the St. Louis Cardinals at Busch Stadium. Having clinched the National League Central title, the Astros played to maintain their competitive edge and accomplish team and individual goals.

The crowd of 38,997 hoped to witness Cardinals first baseman Mark McGwire add to his record-setting season home run total. But Astros pitcher Randy Johnson shackled the St. Louis hitters.

Houston erupted for three runs in the first and one in the second, coasting to a 7–1 victory—the club's 100th of the season and the highest total in team history. But in the sixth, Craig Biggio accomplished an amazing individual honor.

With two out, Biggio singled. Two pitches later, the second baseman stole second, his 50th successful steal. Coupled with his 51 doubles for the season, the 32-year-old infielder joined Tris Speaker as the only two players in baseball's 50-50 club. In 1912, Speaker clubbed 53 doubles and stole 52 bases. Biggio celebrated the occasion by ripping the base from the ground and carrying it back to his Houston home as a souvenir.

EXTRA POINT < < < < < < < < < < < < < < < < < < < Hitting 50 doubles and stealing 50 bases isn't Biggio's only record. He's also the only player ever to be named to the All-Stars both at catcher and second base. But the 50-50 is pretty impressive. Speaker, the only other player to do it, entered baseball's Hall of Fame in 1937 as the seventh player selected. That's good company.

The Bible encourages us to keep good company. Friends who inspire us and lift us up help our Christian walk. But buddies who drag us down can ruin what we've worked for. Strive to find friends who help you reach your full potential.

GOAL! *Evaluate the company you keep. Do they encourage you or drag you down? Ask the Lord to surround you with godly people.*

> Don't be fooled by those who say such things, for "bad company corrupts good character."
> 1 CORINTHIANS 15:33

23 SEP

A cheerful heart is good medicine, but a broken spirit saps a person's strength.

PROVERBS 17:22

MOST DIVERS STAND on the 33-foot platform locked in total concentration and showing no emotion. But before every dive in the 2000 Sydney Olympics, Laura Wilkinson flashed her brightest smile.

A broken foot almost denied the Texas native a spot on the U.S. team. The 22-year-old former University of Texas diver spent weeks in a cast. She delayed surgery and healed in time to qualify for the Games.

In the preliminaries and semifinals, Laura did okay and ended up fifth. But in the final round of five dives, she enjoyed herself and earned drastically better results. At the same time, the favored Chinese faltered. Sang Xue splashed on her third and fourth dives. Her inward 3½ somersault tuck devastated her gold medal hopes. Li Na fared no better. On her third dive, a forward 3½ somersault pike, she earned only 5.5s and 6.0s.

Laura shot up the scoreboard. Beaming, she nailed a reverse 2½ somersault, barely disturbing the water's surface. The American nervously approached her fourth and weakest dive, an inward 2½ somersault in the pike position. Before she scaled the platform, Coach Ken Armstrong whispered a word of encouragement to his gutsy competitor.

The 1998 Goodwill Games champion climbed the tower and removed the protective kayak boot. With her smile gleaming, Laura produced a solid effort, increasing her lead.

The Texan clinched gold on her final attempt, edging out Li 543.75 to 542.01. Canada's Anne Montminy claimed the bronze. Wilkinson's first-place finish broke a string of four consecutive 10-meter Chinese gold medals.

EXTRA POINT < < < < < < < < < < < < < < < < < < < < Experts speculated that Laura had little chance of reaching the medal stand, much less the top step. How did an injured Texan win gold over four-time champions and prohibitive favorites?

The secret lay inside. Laura Wilkinson's wise smile reflected her heart and captured the crowd. Her confidence came from the encouragement of a coach and family she knew applauded her no matter what.

In the Bible, King Solomon knew that power of being positive and staying happy. He wrote about it in the book of Proverbs.

GOAL! *Think about Christians you know. Picture their faces. Do their expressions reflect their heart? The Lord wants to help your face show the brightness of God's love, if you let him.*

THE GOAL OF SPORTS centers on winning. In 1998, the New York Yankees won more regular-season games than almost any team in baseball history.

He holds victory in store for the upright, he is a shield to those whose walk is blameless.
PROVERBS 2:7, NIV

In their final series of the season, the Yankees entertained the Tampa Bay Devil Rays. With three games remaining, New York's record stood at 111–48, one victory short of the American League record.

Joe Torre's club took a 1–0 lead in the first on a double by Derek Jeter and a Bernie Williams's RBI-single. After the Devil Rays tied the game in the third, the Yankees broke open the contest with five runs. Scott Brosius delivered the crowning blow—a two-run single to right center that scored Darryl Strawberry and Jorge Posada.

Orlando Hernandez threw five innings and collected the historic 112th victory in a 6–1 decision. Andy Pettitte even came in on a rare relief appearance to pitch three scoreless innings.

With the win, the Yankees bettered the American League mark of 111 victories set by the 1954 Cleveland Indians and their own team record, held by the 1927 Yankees team that included Lou Gehrig and Babe Ruth, and finished 110–44.

Although the Yankees didn't break the 1906 Chicago Cubs' National League mark of 116–36, New York won their two remaining games and finished 114–48. The Yanks also joined the 1954 Indians as the only AL teams with winning percentages over .700.

EXTRA POINT ‹ Surely everyone called the New York Yankees winners. But what must we do to be called winners in life? Do we have to be the best at sports or graduate at the top of the class? Is popularity important? What about money, power, and honors?

The writer of Proverbs tells us that God holds the victory for those who love him. He protects those who try to live according to his laws. God makes us winners.

GOAL! *Watch the news or read a newspaper and make a list of winners. You may find athletes, politicians, celebrities, business executives, and others.*

God wants to guide you in your walk to make you a winner. Pray that he'll give you chances to tell others what makes a real winner.

Then God told
Noah and
his sons . . .
"I solemnly
promise never
to send another
flood to kill all
living creatures
and destroy
the earth."

GENESIS 9:8, 11

SINCE 1992, WHEN BASEBALL was officially included in the Summer Olympics, Cuba has dominated the sport. The Caribbean nation remained undefeated en route to two gold medals. But in the 2000 Sydney Games, Tommy Lasorda's band of minor leaguers made the most of an opportunity.

Lasorda, a former Los Angeles Dodgers manager, opted for a squad of athletes with AA and AAA experience rather than the usual collegians. But the Cubans humiliated the young players 6–1 in a preliminary round.

After advancing to the gold-medal game with a 3–2 victory over Korea, the United States drew a return encounter with Cuba in the championships. On offense, Team USA took charge early. With two out in the first, Mike Neill slammed a solo home run off Pedro Luis Lazo. The Americans iced the contest in the fifth, scoring three runs on Pat Borders's double and a two-run single by Ernie Young.

On the mound, Ben Sheets pitched masterfully. The 22-year-old allowed only three hits and no runs through eight innings. Leading 4–0 in the ninth, he struck out the first two Cubans. Yassar Gomez then sliced a wicked fly, but Neill snagged the ball with a sliding catch for the final out.

EXTRA POINT < < < < < < < < < < < < < < < < < < < < < Getting a second chance to redeem yourself can provide special moments in sports and in life. And God is a God of second chances. He gives us a chance at new life by believing in Jesus Christ. Then every time we mess up, he gives us the chance to pray and ask for forgiveness. That's just who God is, and he's always been that way.

At one point in the Old Testament, all the people—except for one family—had turned away from God. Their actions were incredibly evil. But instead of wiping out the earth, God gave humans a second chance by telling Noah to build a boat to save the animals and his family. After the Flood, God promised to never destroy the world with water again.

GOAL! *Can you think of a time when you needed a second chance? Isn't it great that God gives you that opportunity? Thank God for being who he is.*

EVERYONE THOUGHT Alexander Karelin of Russia would crush his competition in Greco-Roman wrestling at the 2000 Olympic Games. But American Rulon Gardner discovered a way to dethrone the champion.

The Russian wrestler hadn't lost a match in 13 years, capturing three Olympic gold medals in the super heavyweight class during that time. No wrestler had even managed to score a point against Karelin for ten years.

But Gardner, a former University of Nebraska wrestler, devised an unusual strategy. Rather than allowing Karelin to use his strength and throwing skills, the 29-year-old stayed chest-to-chest and shoulder-to-shoulder with him so that his opponent couldn't gain leverage.

Following a scoreless three-minute period, the wrestlers switched to a clinch. In this position, the pair must remain locked until one executes a scoring move or releases his lock. As the two powered to the edge of the mat, Gardner maintained his grip, but Karelin broke his hands slightly. Judges needed 90 seconds of replay for confirmation, but the video clearly showed the break, and the American went up 1–0.

Neither wrestler scored another point. As the nine-minute match neared its conclusion, the 33-year-old Karelin looked visibly tired because he had already wrestled twice that day. Gardner had only competed once. With eight seconds remaining, the defending Olympic champion conceded the match and walked away, giving Gardner the gold.

EXTRA POINT < < < < < < < < < < < < < < < < < < < <
Rulon Gardner traveled a long way from his childhood state of Wyoming to the top of the medal stand in Australia. Physically, he had changed too. Gardner walked on to the University of Nebraska football team but quit to concentrate on his favorite sport, wrestling. Before the Olympics, he had managed only a fifth in world competition.

But Gardner's greatest change came in respect. As a child, he had been cruelly called "Fatso" by many of his classmates. But Gardner didn't have to wrestle with the unflattering comments and taunts anymore. He wore a gold medal.

Words do hurt. Enemies damage as much through words as by actions. Jesus' half brother wrote about the dangers of the tongue in the New Testament.

GOAL! *Think about words that have hurt you. Consider words you've used to hurt others. God wants your speech to honor him.*

No one can tame the tongue. It is an uncontrollable evil, full of deadly poison.
JAMES 3:8

27 SEP

I tell you the
truth, if you
have faith
as small as
a mustard
seed, you can
say to this
mountain,
"Move from
here to there"
and it will
move.
Nothing will
be impossible
for you.

MATTHEW
17:20, NIV

RYDER CUP CAPTAIN Ben Crenshaw believed in his 1999 American team. On the final day of competition, they rewarded his faith.

The United States trailed their European counterparts 10–6 after the four-ball and foursome rounds. With 12 singles matches remaining, the Americans needed 8½ points to reclaim the gold chalice. In an emotional Saturday meeting, every team member spoke passionately.

On Sunday, Tom Lehman, Davis Love III, Phil Mickelson, Hal Sutton, David Duval, Tiger Woods, Steve Pate, and Jim Furyk all edged out their opponents to earn a point. But 14 points weren't enough; Justin Leonard needed at least a tie to give the United States the victory.

The situation appeared hopeless, however. Spain's Jose Olazabal led by four holes with seven remaining. But the Texan won the next four, nailing a 35-foot putt on 15. Two holes later, Leonard connected on another incredible shot. Facing a 45-foot uphill putt, he stroked perfectly and watched the ball bang the back of the cup for a birdie. Olazabal sank an 18-footer for a birdie on 18 to tie, but Leonard's ½ point gave the Americans a 14½ to 13½ edge. The victory brought the Ryder Cup back to U.S. soil for the first time since 1993.

EXTRA POINT < < < < < < < < < < < < < < < < < < < < <
Despite being played every other year, many call the Ryder Cup golf's fifth major tournament. Samuel Ryder, an English nurseryman, had helped found and fund the inaugural event in 1927 and commissioned the trophy to encourage American and British golfers to compete officially as teams.

Ryder's seed money literally came from seeds. The son of a corn merchant, Ryder dreamed of selling penny seed packets to English citizens. When his father questioned the idea, Ryder began the business himself. The seed packets sold, but in his 50s the wealthy man became ill from overwork. Doctors encouraged him to start exercising outdoors, so he took up golf. In the 25 years he enjoyed the sport, Ryder sowed seeds promoting the game.

Jesus knew the value of tiny seeds. He compared faith to the smallest of all seeds, the mustard seed. Faith that small, he said, can move mountains.

GOAL! *Examine a seed. Imagine what it can grow into. God can use your faith to change the world.*

CATHY FREEMAN RACED for more than medals in the 2000 Olympics. Representing both her country and its native people, the Australian Aborigine carried a huge burden.

Australia honored its popular track star by having Freeman light the flaming cauldron atop Olympic Stadium in the opening ceremonies. Ten days later, she faced the race of a lifetime in the 400 meters. Despite her three-year undefeated streak, the 27-year-old sprinter felt the pressure of performing well before her native fans in addition to the 386,000 members of her mostly impoverished, minority race.

With 112,524 chanting her name, Freeman bolted from the blocks. Jamaica's Lorraine Graham and Great Britain's Katharine Merry led through the final turn, but Freeman pulled ahead with about 20 meters remaining. The first Aborigine gold medalist recorded a 49.11 with Graham clocking a 49.58 and Merry a 49.72.

After catching her breath, Freeman sat and pulled off her shoes, which reflected the Aboriginal colors. Clad in a gold, green, and gray bodysuit, she took her victory lap barefoot. To celebrate her win, Cathy carried two flags around the stadium. One bore Australia's Union Jack and Southern Cross. The other waved the red, yellow, and black of the Aborigine people.

EXTRA POINT < < < < < < < < < < < < < < < < < < < < < < Freeman descended from a culture dating back thousands of years. But beginning from the British settlement of Sydney in 1788, the natives became disadvantaged. Government policy dictated thousands of their children be removed from their mother's care. Aborigines live an average of 20 years less than other Australians. Many face unemployment and violence.

Cathy Freeman wanted to be a beacon of light for her people. Sure, she wanted to claim the gold, but she ran with a deeper purpose in each stride—to give her people hope.

God wants us to do the same thing. He wants us to run straight to our goal and not waver or miss.

GOAL! *Imagine having all the hopes and dreams of your people resting on your shoulders. Cathy Freeman did, and she reached her goal. With God's help, run strong and straight to your goal.*

So I run straight to the goal with purpose in every step. I am not like a boxer who misses his punches.

1 CORINTHIANS 9:26

There is no
longer Jew or
Gentile, slave
or free, male
or female. For
you are all
Christians—you
are one in
Christ Jesus.

GALATIANS 3:28

ALTHOUGH THE GREEKS founded the Olympics, the country's success has been limited in recent years. But in the 2000 Sydney Games, Konstantinos Kenteris pulled off a stunning upset.

Hamstring pulls forced Michael Johnson and Maurice Greene to skip the 200 meters and left the event wide open. Kenteris, a 27-year-old former 400-meter runner, also battled injuries caused by one leg being shorter than the other.

Few considered the Greek a serious medal threat. Following the preliminary heats, experts rated John Capel of the United States as the favorite based on his 19.85 clocking. But in the finals, Capel anticipated the start and rocked forward. Off on his timing, he settled back as the gun sounded.

The poor start pushed Capel to the rear. Coming off the turn, Atop Boldon, Darren Campbell, and Obadele Thompson fought for the lead. But in the final 20 meters, Konstantinos eased past the group and onto the medal stand.

Kenteris clocked a personal best of 20.09 for the gold medal. Great Britain's Campbell took the silver at 20.14, and Trinidad's Boldon claimed the bronze with a 20.20. The triumph stunned the gold medalist. Konstantinos clasped his hands to his face in surprise, grabbed his country's flag from a spectator, and dashed around the track in a victory lap.

EXTRA POINT < < < < < < < < < < < < < < < < < < < < < The Olympic Games began at least 3,500 years ago. By 600 BC, four Greek cities, including Olympia, hosted important sporting festivals. The contests grew from values and beliefs that idealized physical and mental fitness. History records Olympic champions from 776 BC to AD 217, but Roman emperor Theodosius I abolished the every-four-year games in 393.

Near the turn of the last century, 24-year-old Frenchman Pierre de Coubertin worked seven years reviving the Olympic Games before an international congress adopted his plan in 1894. Athens hosted the first modern Games in 1896 with 13 nations and 300 athletes participating. But nationality and status didn't matter in the competition. Athletes were simply athletes, competing to do their best.

In Christ, nationality, status, and gender don't matter either. We're all one in him.

GOAL! *Search the Internet for information about Olympic competition. Note that medalists hail from many countries. Praise God that we're all one in him.*

OCTOBER

They will reject
the truth and
follow strange
myths.

2 TIMOTHY 4:4

OVER TIME, some sports accomplishments reach legendary proportions. Babe Ruth's "called shot" in the 1932 World Series may contain more myth than reality.

The New York Yankees faced the Chicago Cubs in game three at Wrigley Field. With New York victorious in the first two contests, emotions ran high as the Cubs attempted to regroup.

The Yankees felt particular anger toward Chicago over the club's treatment of former New York player Mark Koenig. Barbs flew continually from both dugouts with Ruth serving as the Yankees' ringleader.

In the top of the first, Ruth's homer contributed to a 3–0 Yankees lead. But the Cubs matched New York and tied the game 4–4 in the fourth. With 49,986 fans screaming on every pitch, the Sultan of Swat worked the count to 2-2 in the fifth. Suddenly, the Yankee slugger stepped from the box and made a sweeping gesture toward center field.

He then powered Charlie Root's pitch deep into the center-field stands. Lou Gehrig, the following batter, also homered. The Yankees held on for a 7–5 win and went up 3–0 in the best-of-seven series.

EXTRA POINT < < < < < < < < < < < < < < < < < < < < About 100 or so reporters covered the game that day. Only one, Joe Williams of the *New York World*, mentioned Ruth's gesture. Williams concluded that the star pointed to the place he planned to homer.

Other columnists picked up the hype a few days later. Although Babe Ruth originally denied the story, he later embraced the legend. For years no one knew the truth. But 16mm film shot by Harold Warp, made public in 2000, indicates that Ruth actually pointed toward the Cubs' dugout, perhaps continuing the taunting.

Over time, legends seem to become reality. The apostle Paul wrote to young Timothy about the danger of myths among Christ's people. When Christians listen to legend, they turn away from truth and can follow strange ideas.

GOAL! *Can you think of any historic myths, such as George Washington's chopping down the cherry tree, or stories about gods from other countries? Remember that myths usually originate to explain something. Ask God to help you know the difference between fact and fable.*

BEST TRICK COMPETITIONS force riders to pull stunts they'd never try under normal circumstances. An athlete only has to complete a stunt once to win the top prize. At the 2003 Gravity Games, Richie Velasquez tried until he nailed an amazing stunt to win.

When it comes to these titles, technical mastery matters little. The judges and crowd are looking for two things: danger and amplitude. Sixteen prequalified skaters broke into four heats. The four skaters in each heat were given ten minutes to pull their best stunt. Only the top skater in each heat continued in the competition. After the opening rounds, only four skaters remained: Velasquez and Brian Aragon from the United States and France's Stephane Alfano and Wilfried Rossignol. Velasquez won his heat with a flatspin 540 over the gap-of-death channel.

In the finals, everybody took it up a notch. Velasquez went for a mind-blowing transfer from a 6-foot quarterpipe, over a rail to a larger quarterpipe ten feet away. Needless to say, Velasquez had to go big to make it. And after eight attempts, the New Yorker nailed his stunt to bring the crowd to its feet.

Alfano claimed second with a large gap transfer to disaster soul grind. And Aragon earned third with a huge 540 acid drop.

> But God is faithful and fair. If we admit that we have sinned, he will forgive us our sins. He will forgive every wrong thing we have done. He will make us pure.
>
> 1 JOHN 1:9, NIrV

EXTRA POINT
< < < < < < < < < < < < < < < < < < < < < <

Richie Velasquez tried seven times to complete his stunt in the finals. And seven times he failed. But on his eighth attempt, Velasquez pulled his dangerous trick to win the gold. The judges didn't count his seven misses against him; they awarded Velasquez points based on his perfect attempt.

Just like in the best trick competition, God doesn't care how many times we mess up. He judges us if we do the right thing once—and the right thing is admitting we're sinners and asking his forgiveness. If we do the correct thing by turning to God, he forgets our past mistakes and awards us with the gold medal of purity.

GOAL! *Have you ever messed up? You'd better say yes! Praise God that he doesn't hold your mistakes against you when you ask for his forgiveness. Thank him for his faithfulness.*

Show me,
O Lord, my
life's end and
the number
of my days;
let me know
how fleeting
is my life.

PSALM 39:4, NIV

MOST PROFESSIONAL ATHLETES retire in their 30s. A few survive into their 40s, but virtually none compete past 50. In 1997, however, Gordie Howe strapped on his skates as his 70th birthday approached.

Beginning in 1947, the five-time National Hockey League MVP played 25 years for the Detroit Red Wings. After a brief retirement, he signed with the Houston Aeros of the new World Hockey Association, joining sons Mark and Marty as teammates. Howe finished his hockey career in 1980.

Since the 21-time All-Star had suited up professionally from the '40s to the '80s, the Detroit Vipers of the International Hockey League offered him the opportunity to add the '90s to his resume. At age 69, Howe relished the chance to skate once more in his adopted city.

Wearing his familiar No. 9, the Hall-of-Famer entered the arena to a standing ovation of 20,182 fans. Howe remained on the ice for only 47 seconds and never touched the puck. However, Brad Shaw's shot did deflect off his leg toward the Kansas City Blades' net before being stopped by goalie Jon Casey.

The former Red Wing skated off to a final rousing ovation and took a seat on the bench. After the second period, he left the game for a quick press conference.

EXTRA POINT < < < < < < < < < < < < < < < < < < < < < Gordie Howe accomplished many feats in his long career. He scored 801 goals, made 1,049 assists, played in 1,767 regular-season games, and won four Stanley Cups. And it was a real bonus for him to put on his skates and play just before turning 70.

The Bible says our days are numbered and our life is fleeting. Like Gordie Howe, we should make the most of all the years we have. There's no time like now to begin.

GOAL! *Think about your goals for the next few decades of your life.*

Goals for my teens: _____

_____

Goals for my 20s: _____

_____

Goals for my 30s: _____

_____

Goals for my 40s: _____

_____

Does this list include spiritual accomplishments? The real measure of your success is whether you make each year count for the Lord.

ROGER MARIS'S MAJOR LEAGUE RECORD of 61

home runs in a season stood for 37 *years* before Mark McGwire broke it with 70 in 1998. However, McGwire's mark lasted only 37 *months* when Barry Bonds slugged 73 in 2001.

With three games remaining in the season, the San Francisco Giants outfielder tied McGwire on the road with a blast in Houston. Facing the Dodgers' Chan Ho Park less than 24 hours later, Bonds drove a 1-0 fastball out of the deepest part of Pacific Bell Park in the first inning to the delight of his hometown fans.

His next time up, Bonds connected again, hammering the pitch 405 feet to center field. The two massive home runs gave Bonds 72 with two games to go.

On the season's final day, the 37-year-old outfielder squared off against knuckleballer Dennis Springer. The crowd of 41,257 expected Bonds to walk or fly out since slow pitches rarely generate homers. But in the first, Springer served up a 3-2 knuckler that wobbled to Bonds like a slow-pitch softball. He crushed the offering into Pacific Bell's arcade for his 73rd round-tripper.

Besides the record-breaking home run mark, Bonds finished the 2001 campaign with a .515 on-base percentage—the highest in the National League since John McGraw's .547 in 1899. He set a major league record by belting a home run every 6.52 at bats. Bonds's slugging percentage of .863 obliterated Babe Ruth's mark of .847 set in 1920.

EXTRA POINT
< < < < < < < < < < < < < < < < < < < < <

Barry Bonds broke several seemingly unbreakable marks. And speaking of *Bonds* and *breaking*, it seems like many people today enjoy breaking bonds. New ideas catch on. New friends replace old ones. Change becomes certain.

But there's one bond we should never break. The Bible says when we draw near to God he draws near to us. A relationship with him isn't something that can be replaced.

GOAL! *Think about things in your life that are unbreakable. Maybe it's your commitment to God or your love for your family. Are there other bonds you should break? Ask God to help you always stay close to him.*

> Draw near to God and He will draw near to you. Cleanse your hands, you sinners; and purify your hearts, you double-minded.
>
> JAMES 4:8, NKJV

Perseverance
must finish its
work so that
you may be
mature and
complete,
not lacking
anything.

JAMES 1:4, NIV

SKATEBOARDING TYPICALLY isn't a sport that displays the common etiquette of "ladies first." Men dominate the highlight films and headlines. But at the 2003 Gravity Games in Cleveland, Ohio, the women had a time to shine on the 12-foot halfpipe.

Although the event was a demonstration, spectators packed the bleachers and stood near the action to get a glimpse of five fearless riders. San Diego's Mimi Knoop nailed numerous backside 5-0s and a handful of handplants. Vert skate veteran Cara-Beth Burnside also displayed how far women's vert has come. Other riders, such as Jen O'Brien, showed a graceful style up and down the halfpipe, throwing in fluid backside ollies and frontside airs for good measure. Holly Lyons caught some nice air, but perhaps 13-year-old Lyn-Z Adams Hawkins captured the crowd's fancy more than anyone else. The fearless and energetic teen squared off in an unspoken battle with Burnside to see who would be the first to land a kickflip indy before the end of the competition.

With every attempt, the crowd cheered, hoping one of the women would land the stunt. But at the end of the 45-minute competition, neither had ripped the elusive trick and time had run out . . . or had it?

While the women cleared out and the men warmed up for their competition, Hawkins refused to walk away. She kept working at it and finally stuck a clean kickflip indy.

EXTRA POINT < < < < < < < < < < < < < < < < < < < < The 2003 women's vert demonstration surprised everybody. Despite having the men's skate street finals going on at the same time, the women's competition drew a large crowd and awed those in attendance. Plus, it gave all eyes a glimpse of what's ahead in women's vert—and it's going to be big.

Then a teen showed her championship drive by trying time after time—risking injury with every attempt—to nail a tough trick. And Lyn-Z's perseverance was rewarded. She hit the kickflip indy.

God wants his followers to show that same kind of perseverance. He wants us to keep pursuing him as he makes us more like him.

GOAL! *Is there anything you want to do or any character trait you want to develop for God . . . but you just can't seem to do it? Commit to keep trying and not give up until you've succeeded.*

PROFESSIONAL BEACH VOLLEYBALL

PROFESSIONAL BEACH VOLLEYBALL requires supreme teamwork and athletic ability. During the 2003 season, nobody showed more of those traits than Kerri Walsh and Misty May.

In the American pro beach circuit, May's quickness and Walsh's power ruled the sand. The duo went undefeated in all eight American events. With the 6-foot-2-inch Walsh dominating the net with 104 blocks in the season and the speedy May making 254 digs, this team had the perfect combination. And the pair ended the 2003 season with a bang by winning the Beach Volleyball World Championships in Rio de Janeiro, Brazil. It marked their fifth victory on the world tour.

May and Walsh narrowly defeated the Australian team of Natalie Cook and Nicole Sanderson in the semifinals—in a match where May and Walsh had to fight off two match points. Then in the finals, the Americans beat the Brazilian team of Adriana Brandao Behar and Shelda Kelly Bruno. Not only were Behar and Bruno the defending world champions, but May and Walsh looked up to this pair and tried to learn from them. Again the going was difficult for the U.S. team, but it pulled out the key points to claim a 21–19, 21–19 victory.

EXTRA POINT < < < < < < < < < < < < < < < < < < < <
Kerri Walsh and Misty May experienced a dream year in 2003. Of the 16 biggest beach volleyball events (eight on the American tour and eight more on the world tour), the pair took first 13 times and claimed one silver, one bronze, and one fourth-place finish. Time after time, Walsh and May were able to win the big point. With perfectly complementing styles, the duo proved nearly impossible to beat.

God wants his followers to be part of an unbeatable team as well. Wise King Solomon wrote that two people are better than one because they can help each other. Of course, it's even better to have three on our team—especially if the third player is God.

GOAL! *Do you like competing in individual or team sports better? Why?*

Thank God that he's the perfect teammate to make your team strong.

> An enemy might defeat one person, but two people together can defend themselves; a rope that is woven of three strings is hard to break.
>
> ECCLESIASTES 4:12, NCV

06 OCT

Husbands, take good care of your wives. They are weaker than you. So treat them with respect. Honor them as those who will share with you the gracious gift of life. Then nothing will stand in the way of your prayers.

1 PETER 3:7, NIrV

FEMALES HAVE OFTEN BEEN CALLED the "fairer sex." That point may be up for debate, but there's no way to argue that Manon Rheaume was a pretty fair hockey goalie. No, make that a great hockey goalie.

In 1992 the Canadian-born Rheaume became the first woman to play in a National League Hockey game. At 5-feet-7-inches and 130 pounds, Rheaume wasn't an imposing figure in the net. But her lightning-fast reflexes, quickness around the net, and knowledge of the game earned her a spot on the team. Rheaume made history in late September when she took to the ice for the Tampa Bay Lightning in a preseason contest against the St. Louis Blues.

Of course, making history was nothing new to Rheaume. At age five, she was already playing hockey and fending off her brothers' shots in the net. By 11, Rheaume became the first girl to play in the International Pee Wee Hockey Tournament. Then at 19 she was the first woman player for the Trois-Rivieres Draveurs, a major men's junior hockey team from Quebec. She also led the Canadian Women's National Team to World Championships in 1992 and 1994.

Although Rheaume's NHL tenure proved short, she continued to play professional hockey for the Atlanta Knights, the Las Vegas Thunder, the Charlotte Checkers, and other teams.

EXTRA POINT

< < < < < < < < < < < < < < < < < < < < < <

When most people think of hockey, they picture toothless guys smashing into each other on the ice. It doesn't seem like a girl-friendly sport. Manon Rheaume proved women could play on the highest level of hockey with the men. Her skills between the pipes earned her the right to play in the NHL.

Sometimes in life women don't seem to gain the same opportunities as men. But the truth is God created men *and* women in his image. Both genders reflect the Creator, although we're not the same. God wants us to treat each other equally—as brothers and sisters in Christ.

GOAL! Write down some differences between males and females.

Men	Women
_____	_____
_____	_____
_____	_____
_____	_____

While there are certain differences, God sees us equally as his children. Ask him to help you treat the opposite sex with proper respect.

ARGUMENTS WITH UMPIRES have occurred in baseball almost since the game began in the 1800s. But in 1998, New York Yankees second baseman Chuck Knoblauch allowed a quarrel to distract his play.

Leading 1–0 in the American League Championship Series, the Yankees hosted the Cleveland Indians for the second game. The contest turned into a pitchers' duel with the score tied 1–1 heading into the 12th inning.

Cleveland first baseman Jim Thome opened the 12th with a single, and manager Mike Hargrove inserted Enrique Wilson as a pinch runner. Playing for the lead, Travis Fryman dropped a perfect bunt down the first-base line. New York first baseman Tino Martinez charged the ball, wheeled around, and threw to Knoblauch, who had covered first.

But Martinez's throw hit Fryman in the back and rolled about 20 feet behind the bag. Knoblauch, believing the runner should have been called out for interference, fumed and launched into a tirade with home plate umpire Ted Hendry.

Meanwhile, play continued. Wilson raced to third and was waved home. Ignoring his teammates' screams, Knoblauch remained locked in the argument before finally retrieving the ball. But his hurried throw arrived too late as Wilson dove into the plate for a 2–1 advantage. The Indians added two more runs in the 12th, and Mike Jackson clinched the save as Cleveland took a 4–1 victory.

EXTRA POINT < < < < < < < < < < < < < < < < < < < < < < Chuck Knoblauch's dispute cost the Yankees the ball game and could have made the difference in the series. Fortunately for Knoblauch, the Yankees came through to win the pennant four games to two after dropping the second and third playoff contests. The apologetic second baseman credited his teammates with giving him support when his emotions got the better of him.

Sometimes arguing gets the better of us, too. During those times, it's hard for others to see Christ in us. The writer of Proverbs said that disputes should be stopped before they cause too much damage.

GOAL! *Are there arguments in your family or among your friends that have led people to stop talking to each other? If so, do what you can to mend the relationships. Ask God to keep you from arguing.*

> Starting a quarrel is like breaching a dam; so drop the matter before a dispute breaks out.
> PROVERBS 17:14, NIV

08 OCT

NUMEROUS SONS have followed their fathers into professional sports. In 2000, Brett Hull of the Dallas Stars not only proved his ability to follow his Hall of Fame father, Bobby, in the National Hockey League, he also achieved success in his own way.

Dallas traveled to Canada to engage the Toronto Maple Leafs. Early in the first period, Toronto scored and held a 1–0 lead until late in the third.

That's when Hull, using stealth and cunning, worked free ten feet from the Toronto goal. Taking a pass from teammate Brendan Morrow, he fired the puck past Maple Leafs goalie Curtis Joseph, tying the game.

Hull's goal, the 611th of his NHL career, raised him past his father to the ninth spot on the all-time scoring list. It also left him only two behind former Pittsburgh Penguins star Mario Lemieux as the NHL's eighth–most prolific scorer.

Less than two minutes later, Hull passed to Derian Hatcher, who sent a shot to Morrow that deflected off the boards. The left wing fired the rebound past Joseph to put the Stars in front 2–1. Joe Nieuwendyk's goal with a little over six minutes remaining clinched the 3–1 victory for Dallas.

EXTRA POINT < < < < < < < < < < < < < < < < < < <
Often family members make comparisons such as "Like father, like son." In some ways Brett Hull plays hockey like his father. Both skate with intensity and have the drive to win. But Brett and his dad offer divergent styles. Fans love Bobby for his skating ability and speed. They admire Brett for his smarts, his moves, and his finesse.

We may never break huge records like Brett did by moving up the list of hockey's all-time greatest scorers. But we can make our parents proud in other ways. The fact is, our parents gave us life and want the best for us. Following God and acting wisely are two ways you can bring joy to your family. Plus, you won't have to lose any teeth at the hockey rink!

GOAL! *Think of ways you can make your parents proud. Maybe it's by taking out the trash or doing the dishes without being asked. Commit to God to always try to be wise.*

THE FATHER OF GODLY CHILDREN
HAS CAUSE FOR JOY. PROVERBS 23:24
WHAT A PLEASURE IT IS
TO HAVE WISE CHILDREN.

Above
everything
else, guard
your heart.
It is where
your life
comes from.
PROVERBS
4:23, NIrV

THE SPORT OF FENCING originated nearly 2,000 years before Jesus Christ's birth as a way for soldiers to prepare for battle. And when the modern Olympics began in 1896, fencing was part of the competition. In every Summer Olympics, fencing allows the world's top swordsmen to battle for supremacy. At the 2000 Games in Australia, Romania's Mihai Claudiu Covaliu surprised the field to win gold in the men's sabre.

A sabre blade is about 35 inches long and weighs less than a pound. Athletes score points by touching their opponent with the tip of the blade anywhere between the top of the head and the hips. A point can also be scored with a slashing motion in the same area. The first player to 15 points wins.

Covaliu, who entered the Games ranked tenth in the world, beat the No. 2 seeded Damien Touya in the quarterfinals. He advanced to the finals to face France's Mathieu Gourdain—who had upset No. 1 ranked Stanislav Pozdniakov of Russia in an earlier round. With an unlikely pairing in the gold-medal match, Covaliu wasted little time earning the title. He quickly slashed his way to an 11–7 lead and claimed the gold 15–12 before the first of three 3-minute periods had elapsed.

EXTRA POINT < < < < < < < < < < < < < < < < < < < < Steel clashing and slicing through the air highlighted the men's sabre finals at the 2000 Summer Olympics. Both competitors wore metallic masks and chest protectors for safety. But as Romania's Mihai Claudiu Covaliu attacked, France's Mathieu Gourdain couldn't guard himself, and Covaliu quickly won the gold.

The Bible says to guard our heart—and that doesn't mean wearing a steel vest. Instead, God wants us to be careful about what we see and hear. Letting impure images or crude song lyrics into our life pollutes our heart. If our heart is left unguarded, that pollution affects all areas of our life.

GOAL! *Tell God you want to protect your heart . . . it's one of the most important things you can do. Ask him for discernment about what to let into your life.*

WHEN ANSON DORRANCE began coaching college soccer, his attention was pulled in many directions. But the University of North Carolina coach refused to give his women's team less than his best, and eventually he helped guide the ladies to an amazing 500 victories.

Born in Bombay, India, Dorrance grew up playing soccer all over the world. Three years as an All-Conference soccer player at UNC cemented his love for the game. While attending law school, Dorrance held a part-time job as a UNC men's soccer coach. In 1979, the University offered him a full-time position for $12,500 if he would take over the women's program too.

The law student accepted the challenge. Eventually, he realized something had to give, and Dorrance bade farewell to the legal profession.

For ten years, the soccer coach led both programs, posting a 172–65–21 mark—even winning six NCAA titles with the women's team. In 1989, Dorrance began devoting his energies solely to the UNC women's team and helped them capture 11 national collegiate crowns.

Ranked No. 1 in the nation during 2001, the Tar Heels faced 14th-ranked Clemson for the Atlantic Coast Conference lead. Anne Morrell of the Tar Heels scored a goal in the game's first three minutes, and Anne Remy added two in the second half as North Carolina coasted to a 3–0 triumph. Dorrance became the first NCAA women's soccer coach to record 500 victories, moving his career mark to 500–22–11.

> We must pay more careful attention, therefore, to what we have heard, so that we do not drift away.
> HEBREWS 2:1, NIV

EXTRA POINT

< < < < < < < < < < < < < < < < < < < <

People wondered when Anson Dorrance slept. Dividing his time between law school, men's soccer, and the women's team left little time. Finally, Dorrance realized he should give more careful attention to the UNC women. And his devotion paid off with success.

The writer of Hebrews urged the people to pay attention to what they had learned about God. That way, they wouldn't drift away from their faith.

In life, we need to realize the same thing. Busyness and inattention can cause problems. It's easy for our mind to wander in church or when we read the Bible and pray. Our heavenly Father wants us to pay close attention to what's important.

GOAL! *Make a list of things that are important to you.*

_____

_____

Ask God to help you give careful attention to what is important to him.

11 OCT

So then, let us
not be like
others, who are
asleep, but let
us be alert and
self-controlled.

1 THESSALONIANS
5:6, NIV

BASEBALL PLAYERS ENDLESSLY WORK on being in the proper position during spring training, ensuring that someone backs up every throw. In 2001, Derek Jeter's alert maneuver kept the New York Yankees in the playoffs.

After dropping the first two games of the best-of-five series to the Oakland A's, the Yankees faced elimination at Network Associates Coliseum. With New York's Mike Mussina dueling Oakland's Barry Zito, the Yankees grabbed a 1–0 lead in the fifth on Jorge Posada's solo home run.

In the seventh, A's designated hitter Jeremy Giambi singled with two out. Terrence Long followed with a double into the right-field corner that Shane Spencer fielded cleanly. Meanwhile, third-base coach Ron Washington waved the lumbering Giambi home. Spencer unleashed a long throw that sailed over the outstretched gloves of both second baseman Alfonso Soriano and first baseman Tino Martinez.

But shortstop Derek Jeter alertly drifted over to the first-base line and fielded the throw on one hop. Without turning around, he flipped the ball backhanded to Posada at the plate. Since Giambi failed to slide, the catcher managed to tag the runner on his calf just before he touched the plate for the inning's final out. Then Mariano Rivera hurled two shutout innings to preserve the 1–0 New York victory.

EXTRA POINT < < < < < < < < < < < < < < < < < < < < Not only did the game depend on Derek Jeter's alert defensive play, the entire series turned around for the Yankees after that out. New York took game three and never looked back by winning game four 9–2 and game five 5–3.

In baseball, every player isn't involved in every play. But by being aware of what is happening, a player can make the difference. That's exactly what Jeter did.

Being alert also yields success in the Christian life. Hanging out in questionable places or surrounding ourselves with sinful activities with our mind turned off harms our good influence. And we may be tempted to do wrong. On the other hand, keeping our mind alert and staying self-controlled positions us to influence others for God while avoiding temptation.

GOAL! *Next time you watch baseball either in person or on television, pay particular attention to defensive positions. See how the players move for every play and keep their mind in the game. Ask God to help you stay alert for him.*

VENUS WILLIAMS'S POWERFUL SERVE has taken her to the top of the world tennis rankings. But in 1998, her serve wasn't enough to defeat Lindsay Davenport in the European Championships.

In the quarterfinals, Williams drew France's Mary Pierce. Williams, already the world's fastest female server at 125 mph, fired three consecutive aces in the set's final game. On her last serve, Williams hit the ball perfectly, registering 127 mph on the speed gun and breaking her old world record. The California native totaled 13 aces against Pierce and took the match 6–4, 6–1.

After defeating Nathalie Tauziat in the semifinals, Williams faced Davenport in the championship. With the first set tied 5–5, Venus served, leading 40–30. But she lost the next seven points, giving Davenport the service break and a 7–5 win.

In the second set, Davenport broke her opponent's service at 2–2 and held serve for a 4–2 lead. Trailing 5–3, Williams handed Davenport the set and the match when she smashed a forehand into the net. The victory brought Davenport her sixth title of the year and solidified her status as the No. 1 player on the world tour.

EXTRA POINT

< < < < < < < < < < < < < < < < < < < < < < < Powerful serves help win tournaments. Aces and service winners make for quick matches and easy points. Good players practice for hours on their serve. They learn how to put spin on the ball, hit a power serve, and place it wherever they want. Professional players expect to win all their service games.

God wants us to serve him, too. But he doesn't want us to work softly and timidly for him. He desires that we serve him with strength and power, not doing anything halfheartedly or halfway. Then the heavenly Father receives the glory and praise.

GOAL! *Practice serving—whether it's tennis, table tennis, or racquetball. Work on power, speed, and accuracy. Now think of ways you can serve God.*

———————————————————————————

———————————————————————————

Plan to do at least one act of service this week. Praise God for the strength he provides.

If anyone speaks, he should do it as one speaking the very words of God. If anyone serves, he should do it with the strength God provides, so that in all things God may be praised through Jesus Christ. To him be the glory and the power for ever and ever. Amen.

1 PETER 4:11, NIV

The Lord will
sustain him on
his sickbed and
restore him
from his bed
of illness.

PSALM 41:3, NIV

NO ATHLETE WANTS to be on the injured list when the team is competing for a championship. In 1997, Kevin Brown arose from his sickbed to pitch the Florida Marlins to the National League pennant.

The Marlins led the Atlanta Braves three games to two in the seven-game series. Brown had been scheduled to pitch in game four and later in five, but a viral infection sidelined the right-hander. Fighting off the illness, the 32-year-old pitcher summoned his strength to take the mound for game six.

His teammates provided tremendous support, erupting for four runs in the top of the first on Bobby Bonilla's two-run single, Charles Johnson's bases-loaded walk, and Craig Counsell's RBI groundout.

Although Brown's sickness left him unsettled, he survived a shaky first two innings and nursed a 4–3 lead into the sixth. The Marlins scored another three runs on Braves starter Tom Glavine to force him to the showers. Bonilla's infield single plated a run for his third RBI of the game.

Brown's pitch count went over 140 in the ninth as he allowed one run. The Braves put runners on first and second, but Brown induced Atlanta's third baseman to hit into a game-ending fielder's choice. Florida had won its first National League title with a 7–4 triumph!

EXTRA POINT < < < < < < < < < < < < < < < < < < < < < Many athletes play through injuries. Medication, determination, and tolerance to pain enable them to compete. However, most never get on the field when serious illness strikes. Fever, chills, and other symptoms make competition difficult if not impossible. And of course, contagious viruses can spread to the team, coaches, umpires, and all who come in contact with the sick athlete. But Kevin Brown managed to defeat his illness and the Atlanta Braves.

God desires that we stay healthy. The Lord wants us to take care of our body to prevent sickness. But the psalmist wrote that the heavenly Father cares for us when we're sick in bed.

GOAL! *Do all you can to keep from catching a cold, the flu, or another illness. If you know someone who is ill, pray that God will help him or her get well.*

CONSISTENCY, ENDURANCE, and hard work characterize professional football's great runners. In 1984, Walter Payton of the Chicago Bears rose to the top with those traits.

The Bears were entertaining the New Orleans Saints at Soldier Field. Coming into the season's sixth game, Payton had rushed for 12,245 career yards, leaving him 67 shy of Jim Brown's all-time National Football League mark.

On the second play of the third quarter, with the Bears leading 13–7, quarterback Jim McMahon called Toss-28-Weak, a sweep to the left with Payton carrying the ball. Payton took the toss, skittered along in the backfield, found an opening, and burst through for a 6-yard gain, giving him 12,317 career rushing yards—five more than the legendary Jim Brown, who retired in 1965.

With the record, play stopped. Photographers scrambled. Payton dashed to the Saints sideline and shook hands with opposing coach Bum Phillips. Circling back to the Bears bench, he handed the historic ball to coach Johnny Roland for safekeeping until it went to the NFL Hall of Fame.

EXTRA POINT < < < < < < < < < < < < < < < < < < < The new all-time rushing leader finished the game with 154 yards on 32 carries in a 20–7 Chicago victory. Walter Payton would go on to play three more seasons, upping his record to 16,726 yards in 13 years. The powerful running back, nicknamed "Sweetness" for both his kindness to people and his grace on the field, missed one game as a rookie before playing in 186 consecutive contests.

Just as he rushed again and again on the field, Walter Payton rushed to help others. He established a foundation to give neglected and abused children self-esteem and hope. Sadly, Payton died of a liver disease in 1999 at age 45. Today his family celebrates his July birthday with an event called "Sleigh Bells in July" to collect Christmas toys for children.

Payton's hard work left a legacy on the gridiron and in his community.

GOAL! *Why not begin now to collect toys for underprivileged children for Christmas? With hard work and God's help, you can become a leader at school, in your church, and around your neighborhood.*

> Work hard and become a leader; be lazy and become a slave.
>
> PROVERBS 12:24

My dear children, I write this to you so that you will not sin. But if anybody does sin, we have one who speaks to the Father in our defense— Jesus Christ, the Righteous One.

1 JOHN 2:1, NIV

GOALIES ALMOST NEVER SCORE; therefore, fans and

sportswriters rate their effectiveness based on keeping the puck out of the net. In 2000, Colorado Avalanche goalie Patrick Roy earned distinction as the National Hockey League's greatest all-time defender.

The Avalanche traveled cross-country to engage the Washington Capitals. In the early stages of the NHL campaign, Colorado remained undefeated through the first five games while the Capitals sought their first victory.

Despite falling behind 2–0, Washington tied the game on two goals by Peter Bondra and went up 3–2 on Ulf Dahlen's score. But Colorado's Joe Sakic nailed his first goal of the season and tied the contest early in the third period.

As the game ticked down, Jan Bulis almost pulled a last-second Capitals victory. His shot zipped toward the net but struck Roy's pads and bounded away.

Less than two minutes into overtime, officials penalized Washington's Richard Zednik for cross-checking. With a 4-on-3 advantage, Colorado mounted a savage attack on Capitals goalie Olaf Kolzig. Ray Bourque attempted a slap shot that went awry, but Peter Forsberg hammered the deflection into the net for a 4–3 Avalanche victory.

EXTRA POINT < < < < < < < < < < < < < < < < < < <

Roy, who stopped 27 of Washington's 30 shots, leaped in jubilation and was mobbed by his teammates. Highlights of his 16-year career flashed on the video screens as he cut away the historic net. In the postgame press conference, he took a telephone call from Canadian Prime Minister Jean Chrentien.

With the win, Roy collected his 448th career victory, breaking the record held by legendary goalie Terry Sawchuk. A goalie stands in the crease, defending the boundaries of the goal, daring opponents to get the puck past him. Roy finished his career as hockey's best defender between the pipes by amassing 551 regular-season wins and another 151 playoff victories.

As Christians, we also have a strong Defender—Jesus Christ. The Lord defends us against Satan's attacks. He speaks on our behalf to God when we sin. And he always keeps our scoreboard clean.

GOAL! *Think of ways that God defends you. Thank Jesus for taking up your defense.*

AMAZING UPSETS ALWAYS seem to happen in the Olympics. At the 2000 Summer Games in Sydney, Australia, the women's individual épée saw a virtual unknown from Hungary defeat the reigning champion and claim a fencing gold medal.

Hungary's Timea Nagy entered the épée competition ranked third on her team and in the double digits globally. She'd never won a major individual championship and had finished 12th at the world championships. So when she met defending Olympic gold medalist and current world champion Laura Flessel-Colovic in the semifinals, most thought the French favorite would slice through.

If you've never heard of épée, it's a 35-inch sword that weighs about 27 ounces. Rules state that a player earns a point by touching the tip of the blade on any part of her opponent. Sensors in the blade signal a score. The first athlete to score 15 points during three 3 minute rounds wins the match.

Flessel-Colovic used her quickness and stinging attacks at her opponent's feet to push the semifinal match to the end. But Nagy refused to blink against the higher ranked opponent. Tied 14–14, both women knew they'd advance with the next point. And when Nagy scored, she continued to the finals against Gianna Habluetzel-Buerki of Switzerland. Nagy trailed early in the gold-medal match 6–3, but she rebounded to win 15–11.

EXTRA POINT < < < < < < < < < < < < < < < < < < < < Timea Nagy showed she had the sword skill to go toe-to-toe with the world's best. Her speed made things uncomfortable for her opponents as she thrust her way to the top.

While Nagy's piercing strokes won the gold, her blade doesn't compare with God's Word. The writer of Hebrews says that God's Word is sharper than any sword as it cuts into our life. Sometimes we become uncomfortable as we read the Bible because its truth convicts us when we stray from God's plan. But that's exactly why we should read it: so we can stay close to God.

GOAL! *Commit to reading God's Word for five minutes every day. Start in the Gospels and find out about Jesus' life. By tapping into the Bible, you can strengthen your relationship with God.*

God's word is alive and working and is sharper than a double-edged sword. It cuts all the way into us, where the soul and the spirit are joined, to the center of our joints and bones. And it judges the thoughts and feelings in our hearts.
HEBREWS 4:12, NCV

17 OCT

NOW ABOUT
TITUS—HE IS MY
PARTNER WHO IS
WORKING WITH ME
TO HELP YOU. AND
ABOUT THE OTHER
BROTHERS—THEY
ARE SENT FROM
THE CHURCHES,
AND THEY BRING
GLORY TO CHRIST.

2 CORINTHIANS 8:23, NCV

WHEN TWO ACCOMPLISHED ATHLETES combine

their forces, the results can be impressive. During the 2003 beach volleyball season, Brazil's Ricardo Alex Costa Santos joined with Emanuel Rego to create an incredible duo. The pair started the season slowly but then won five of the last seven Federation of International Volleyball (FIVB) tournaments, including the Beach Volleyball World Championships in Rio de Janeiro, Brazil.

Santos and Rego played two matches together during the 2002 season and decided to compete together full-time in 2003. After cruising through their earlier matches at the world championships, the Brazilian pair met Americans Dax Holdren and Stein Metzger in the finals. Holdren and Metzger had only played in one tournament before the world championships. Their hustling, aggressive style had surprised a lot of teams . . . but not the experienced Brazilians.

In the finals, Santos and Rego defeated the U.S. pair 21–18, 21–15 to claim the title. The Americans had played a nearly flawless semifinal to qualify for the last match, but they couldn't repeat their performance as the Brazilians proved too powerful and skilled in front of their home-country fans.

The 44-minute victory marked Rego's 41st gold on the FIVB circuit, while Santos earned his 20th.

EXTRA POINT < < < < < < < < < < < < < < < < < < <

Ricardo Alex Costa Santos and Emanuel Rego made a powerful pair. They dominated the beach volleyball circuit in 2003 and brought home the world championship. Their teamwork proved unbeatable.

In the New Testament, a lot of God's followers showed amazing teamwork. Many times in the book of Acts a pair of Christians would go off to spread God's Good News. The apostle Paul had a lot of partners who helped him on his missionary trips. He always had somebody with him to assist in preaching the gospel. One of Paul's helpers was Titus—and the two of them made a dream team for Christ.

GOAL! *Standing alone for Jesus Christ can be hard. Sometimes you have to do it, but it's nice to have a partner to help you. Thank God for friends who can help you bring glory to God.*

18

SWITCHING FROM CANADIAN football to the American game usually causes difficulties. But in 1998, Doug Flutie's quick thinking brought the Buffalo Bills a comeback victory.

Bruised ribs sidelined starting quarterback Rob Johnson, and Flutie drew the assignment against the undefeated Jacksonville Jaguars. The backup signal caller signed with the Bills after eight seasons with the Calgary Stampeders. He hadn't started in a National Football League game since 1989 and ironically took the game's first snap on Canada's Thanksgiving Day. A soloist sang "O Canada," and many of the CFL's Toronto Argonauts watched from the stands.

The contest turned into a defensive struggle as Jacksonville led 16–10 with a little under two minutes remaining. Following a Jaguar punt, the Bills took over at their own 30-yard line. With 39 seconds left, Buffalo faced second-and-6 at the Jacksonville 39. The 35-year-old quarterback found wide receiver Eric Moulds running free down the left sideline. Hauling in the pass at the 7, the receiver made a diving stab for the end zone. One official signaled touchdown, but another marked the ball short, and the clock continued to run.

Buffalo hurried to the line of scrimmage, and Flutie spiked the ball to stop the clock. After throwing two incompletions, the quarterback called a toss sweep to the left with 13 seconds on the scoreboard. But running back Thurman Thomas ran right. With no one there to take the ball, Flutie tucked it under his arm and rambled into the end zone. His quick action gave the Bills a surprising 17–16 triumph.

EXTRA POINT < < < < < < < < < < < < < < < < < < < < < < Everyone makes mistakes in sports. Thurman Thomas made one that day. He possibly didn't hear the quarterback's call over intense crowd noise. But Doug Flutie didn't get flustered. He didn't ponder what he should do. He thought quickly and acted decisively to bring victory.

Sometimes we take too long to make a decision. We go back and forth, and then we act too late to make a difference. Sometimes we also wait too long to call on God. We try to take care of situations ourselves when we should seek his help. God always wants us to go to him first.

GOAL! *Think of decisions you've waited too long to make. Ask God to remind you to go to him first.*

Seek first the kingdom of God and His righteousness, and all these things shall be added to you.

MATTHEW 6:33, NKJV

TENSIONS BETWEEN PITCHERS and hitters run high, especially in championship play. In the 2000 World Series, Roger Clemens allowed his emotions to rule his actions.

The American League's New York Yankees and the National League's New York Mets tangled in the first all–Big Apple series since 1956. After the Yankees took game one, the two teams met again at Yankee Stadium, with Mike Hampton hoping to even the score for his National League squad against Roger Clemens.

Earlier that year, the New York press reported a brewing feud between Clemens and Mets catcher Mike Piazza. The controversy stemmed from an incident when Clemens beaned Piazza's batting helmet and sent him to the hospital with a concussion.

After striking out the first two Mets batters, Clemens went ahead 1-2 in the count to Piazza and threw a fastball inside at the hands. Piazza fouled off the pitch, but his bat shattered. The barrel skidded along the ground toward the mound.

Clemens fielded the lumber as it bounced toward him. The pitcher then spun toward the plate and fired the broken bat at Piazza's feet as he ran toward first. Piazza calmly walked toward the Yankee pitcher before home-plate umpire Charlie Reliford intercepted him. Both benches emptied, but no punches flew, and order resumed after a few minutes. Finally, the catcher ended the inning with a groundout.

Calm prevailed through the remainder of the game. Clemens handcuffed the Mets, allowing two hits and striking out nine in eight shutout innings. Relievers Jeff Nelson and Mariano Rivera survived home runs by Piazza and Jay Payton to preserve a 6–5 Yankees victory.

EXTRA POINT < < < < < < < < < < < < < < < < < < < < What was Roger Clemens thinking? No one can plan to break a bat and aim the splintered barrel at a player. The pitcher's emotions got the best of him as he did something stupid. No injuries occurred, and fortunately for Clemens, the umpire didn't eject him from the game.

God wants us to learn self-control. In Galatians, the apostle Paul describes what a Christian's life should look like when the Holy Spirit is in control. Will you strive to have those characteristics in your life?

GOAL! *How should Rogers Clemens have reacted to the broken bat? Ask God to help you show self-control in difficult situations.*

> When the **Holy Spirit** controls our lives, he will produce this kind of fruit in us: love, joy, peace, patience, kindness, goodness, faithfulness, gentleness, and self-control.
> **GALATIANS 5:22-23**

20 OCT

OCT 21

HOW MANY PUSH-UPS can you do in a minute? Jump down and time yourself for 60 seconds. But before you do, here are the rules. For a push-up to count, your body has to stay totally straight throughout the entire exercise. You must lower yourself toward the ground until your elbows achieve at least a 90-degree angle. Finally, you need to push yourself up until your arms are straight. All right. Go! Write down how many you pounded out: _____

Now how many push-ups do you think you could do in an hour? a day? a year?

Great Britain's Paddy Doyle has set more than 120 national, European, and world records. In 1993, he did 1,750 push-ups in an hour, which was a world record at the time. But one of his most amazing feats is completing 1,500,230 documented push-ups in a year—and he wasn't even in gym class! From October 21, 1988, to October 21, 1989, he averaged more than 4,000 a day. In May of that same year, he also set a 24-hour push-up world record with 37,350. Do your arms ache just thinking about that?

EXTRA POINT < < < < < < < < < < < < < < < < < < < < < < Paddy Doyle lives for physical fitness. He constantly trains, eats healthy foods, and keeps his body in top shape. By doing thousands of push-ups a day, he set a gigantic world record and earned a spot in *Guinness World Records*. He built a rock-hard body with consistent hard work.

While many of us will never have Paddy Doyle's physique or determination, we can learn to treat our body with respect. The Bible says our body is a temple of the Holy Spirit. Because God's Spirit lives in Christians, we need to honor our body. That definitely means staying away from drugs, alcohol, and premarital sex. But it also means we should try to exercise and eat right to stay healthy.

You should know that your body is a temple for the Holy Spirit who is in you. You have received the Holy Spirit from God. So you do not belong to yourselves, because you were bought by God for a price. So honor God with your bodies.

1 CORINTHIANS 6:19-20, NCV

GOAL! *Write down some things you can do to stay in shape.*

_____

_____

_____

Thank God for perfectly designing your body exactly the way it is.

THE IDEA FOR THE X GAMES Global Championship in 2003 was a good one. Held simultaneously in Whistler, British Columbia, and San Antonio, Texas, the Games gave the world's best extreme athletes the chance to compete for their country. Just one problem: Some sports—such as freestyle motocross—are totally ruled by the United States.

So when Team USA, Team Europe, and Team Asia got together for the Moto X freestyle competition, there was really no doubt that Americans Kenny Bartram and Nate Adams would take the top two spots. The only surprise was how hard these athletes battled each other. Neither wanted silver, and both pulled every trick in their arsenal.

Bartram nailed his first run to claim the initial lead. But Adams's second run nearly made him the winner in everybody's eyes, including Bartram's. Adams nailed a backflip and threw in a lazyboy (where the rider comes out of the seat with only his feet hooked under the handlebars while sailing 40 feet in the air) and a look-back Hart attack for good measure. His score put him on top. Bartram didn't think he could do better than he did in his first run—but he was wrong. By stringing together a McMetz-to-no-handed landing, a no-handed whip, no-footed nac-nac, and backflip, there was no doubt Bartram earned first.

EXTRA POINT < < < < < < < < < < < < < < < < < < < Kenny Bartram and Nate Adams will go down in history as two of the biggest names in freestyle motocross. Many of their opponents at the X Games Global Championships were competing for the first time. After the victory, Bartram did television interviews for three countries as the world got to see the latest freestyle stunts—including the backflip. Nate and Kenny gave people in many nations a glimpse of what FMX is all about.

God wants us to follow Adams's and Bartram's example with our faith. We need to think globally. We tend to get caught up in our own little world and miss God's big picture. His Word is spreading. More than two billion people call themselves Christians, but there's still plenty of work to be done.

GOAL! *You're a light for God in a dark world. Don't hide your faith. Think of ways you can share Jesus Christ. And don't forget to pray for Christians around the world.*

> This is what the Lord told us to do, saying: "I have made you a light for the nations; you will show people all over the world the way to be saved."
> ACTS 13:47, NCV

His anger lasts
for a moment,
but his favor
lasts a lifetime!
Weeping may
go on all night,
but joy comes
with the
morning.

PSALM 30:5

CIRCUMSTANCES DICTATE a coach's decisions during a football game. Winning always comes ahead of individual accomplishments. But in 2000, kicker Gary Anderson broke a long-time record at the exact moment he desired.

The Minnesota Vikings took on the Buffalo Bills at the Metrodome. Heading into the game, Anderson trailed George Blanda, the National Football League's all time leading scorer, by nine points. The South Africa native hoped for a high-scoring day to break the record in front of his mother and two sons, who were at the game.

Early in the fourth quarter, the kicker's chances to pass the former Oakland Raider appeared remote. Although Anderson booted field goals of 38 and 20 yards in the first half, the Vikings trailed Buffalo 24–13, and the 41-year-old assumed Minnesota would need every second to score two touchdowns.

Dante Culpepper closed the gap with an 11-yard touchdown pass to Cris Carter, and the Vikings converted the two-point attempt on a throw to Moe Williams, making the score 24–21. After falling behind 27–21, Minnesota forced Buffalo to punt, and Troy Walters returned the kick 28 yards to the Buffalo 34. Two plays later, Culpepper connected with Randy Moss for a 39-yard scoring pass, and Anderson's extra point put the Vikings in front 28–27.

Still needing one point for the record, Minnesota mounted a final drive and moved inside the Bills 10. With a minute left, Anderson booted a 21-yard field goal, giving him the all-time scoring record with 2,004 career points in 19 NFL seasons.

EXTRA POINT < < < < < < < < < < < < < < < < < < < < Everyone knew that, barring injury, Gary Anderson would break the record. The question was when. The kicker so wanted the moment to be while his mother and sons watched. For three quarters, Anderson didn't think that would happen, but it did. He reached the milestone.

Occasionally things don't go well in life. We desire something so badly we can taste it. Then the chance slowly slips away. But sometimes it seems that God's favor rests on us. We grasp the achievement at God's perfect time and experience his grace. The fact is, as his children, God's favor always rests on us.

GOAL! *In a sports encyclopedia or on the Internet, review all-time NFL scoring leaders. Note how many are kickers. Think about the victories they achieved. Thank God for his favor.*

BALANCING THE DEMANDS OF FAMILY and team

always poses a challenge for professional athletes. In 1997, an injury to Wayne Gretzky's wife during a game forced him to choose between being by her side and remaining in the game.

The New York Rangers were hosting the Chicago Blackhawks at Madison Square Garden. Chicago claimed a 1–0 lead in the second period on Eric Daze's chip shot that floated over New York goalie Mike Richter. Then neither team could crack the opponent's defense.

Midway through the third period, New York's Ulf Samuelson and Chicago's Sergei Krivokrasov collided at the wall near the Rangers' penalty box. The shock wave caused a protective Plexiglas panel to break and fall into the stadium seats. A large fragment grazed Gretzky's wife, former actress Janet Jones, cutting her lower lip and rendering her semiconscious. Play halted for more than ten minutes as medical personnel placed Jones on a stretcher and took the mother of the four Gretzky children to a local hospital.

Rangers' trainer Jim Ramsay assured Gretzky that his wife's condition was fine, and teammate Kevin Stevens's wife accompanied Janet in the ambulance. Gretzky continued to play, but the Rangers lost 1–0. The following day, he expressed second thoughts about his decision, even though his wife was released after receiving several stitches and spending the night in the hospital for observation.

And you husbands must love your wives with the same love Christ showed the church. He gave up his life for her.

EPHESIANS 5:25

EXTRA POINT < < < < < < < < < < < < < < < < < < < < < <

What should Wayne Gretzky have done? Should he have stayed by his wife's side? Should he have put the team first since he got paid millions to play hockey and win games? How could "the Great One" balance his two roles?

Only Janet and Wayne can answer those questions for themselves and their marriage. But the Bible offers some guidance. A husband should love his wife as he loves himself. The apostle Paul compares the love of a husband to the love of Christ for the church. Christ gave his life for his followers. And God expects a husband to love his wife that much.

GOAL! What should a wife expect from her husband during family emergencies? What should a husband expect from his wife under the same circumstances? Ask God to help you learn—and recognize—unselfish love as you look for a future mate.

24 OCT

Trust in the
Lord with all
your heart and
lean not on
your own
understanding;
in all your ways
acknowledge
him, and he
will make your
paths straight.

PROVERBS
3:5-6, NIV

EVERY DEFENSIVE PLAYER DREAMS of rumbling into the end zone for six points. But in 1964, when Minnesota Vikings defensive end Jim Marshall thought he tallied a touchdown, he actually put two points on the board . . . for the other team.

The Vikings were visiting the San Francisco 49ers. The Niners held a 17–13 lead early in the fourth quarter, but a pair of San Francisco turnovers produced two quick Minnesota touchdowns.

Roy Winston intercepted a George Mira pass on the 49ers 11-yard line, and three plays later quarterback Fran Tarkenton rolled around the end for an 8-yard score. On San Francisco's subsequent possession, defensive tackle Carl Eller scooped up a Mira fumble and galloped 45 yards for a touchdown to put Minnesota in front 27–17.

Marshall, hoping to make the highlight film with another big defensive play, found the opportunity on San Francisco's next drive. Mira completed a short pass to tailback Billy Kilmer, who took a few steps before fumbling. Trailing the play, the Vikings defensive end grabbed the ball in midair and bolted toward the goal line. Unfortunately for Vikings fans, Marshall had been trailing the play, so when he grabbed the ball he was running toward the San Francisco goal line.

Marshall ran untouched all the way through the end zone and hurled the football into the stands. Puffed with excitement, his elation soon turned to dejection when officials signaled a San Francisco safety. The defensive end's wrong-way jaunt scored two points for the 49ers. *Oops.* Despite Marshall's mistake, Minnesota managed to edge out San Francisco 27–22.

EXTRA POINT < < < < < < < < < < < < < < < < < < < < Imagine the rush of recovering a fumble and scoring a touchdown for your team. Then consider the embarrassment of knowing you hadn't helped your team at all. You'd actually given your opponent two points because you took the wrong path. That's what Jim Marshall did.

The writer of Proverbs warns against leaning on ourselves and following our own paths. Only by trusting God completely, acknowledging him, and not following our own plans will the Lord make our paths straight.

GOAL! *Ask God to keep the paths of your life moving straight to him. You might just avoid some embarrassing moments, and you definitely will live a more rewarding life.*

FOOTBALL COACHES SELDOM RISK

FOOTBALL COACHES SELDOM RISK kicking a field goal longer than 50 yards, because missed attempts give the opposing team the ball at the spot of the kick. But in 1998, Denver Broncos kicker Jason Elam made the most of his long-range opportunity.

Denver battled Jacksonville in Mile High Stadium. Leading 24–10, the Broncos faced fourth-and-3 at Jacksonville's 48-yard line with no time-outs left and time expiring in the first half. Coach Mike Shanahan originally called for a punt but changed his mind at the last second. The delay, however, resulted in a five-yard penalty and forced the kick to be attempted from 63 yards away.

The snap fired back, the ball was placed down, and Elam swung his leg hard. The pigskin exploded off his foot toward the goalposts. The ball sailed through the uprights and cleared the crossbar with room to spare. When it cleared the uprights and tied the NFL record for longest field goal, Elam sprinted toward the pigskin, retrieved it, and beamed all the way to the locker room.

Elam's field goal knotted him with Tom Dempsey of the New Orleans Saints. Dempsey hit his 63-yarder against the Detroit Lions on November 8, 1970. Ironically, Dempsey was watching Elam on television. He cheered when the ball sailed through the goalposts.

EXTRA POINT

< < < < < < < < < < < < < < < < < < < < < < <

Coach Mike Shanahan took a big risk. Even though the clock showed little time, a miss would have given the Jaguars a first down on the 47-yard line of Denver and the chance for a quick score. Seven points could have put Jacksonville back in the game.

But the risk paid dividends. The Broncos ran to the dressing room three scores ahead. And Elam tied the NFL record.

In the Bible, Priscilla and Aquila took risks. They fled from Emperor Claudius in Rome. They accompanied Paul to Syria. They witnessed to and discipled Apollos in Ephesus. And they established a church in their home. Their risks paid dividends as many came to know Christ.

GOAL! *Are you a risk taker? If not, think of something you need to do despite your fear. Then take the wise risk. Ask God to help you.*

Greet Priscilla and Aquila. They have been co-workers in my ministry for Christ Jesus. In fact, they risked their lives for me. I am not the only one who is thankful to them; so are all the Gentile churches.

ROMANS 16:3-4

26 OCT

IN 2001, PENN STATE'S Joe Paterno proved to be one of the best college football coaches ever.

Nearly 110,000 fans packed Beaver Stadium to watch Penn State and Ohio State, hoping to witness a historic scene. Paterno, Penn State's 74-year-old coach, needed one more victory to bypass the late Paul "Bear" Bryant as the NCAA's winningest major college football coach.

Early in the third quarter, Paterno's prospects appeared bleak. Ohio State's Derek Ross intercepted a pass and returned it 45 yards for a touchdown, putting the Buckeyes in front 27–9. However, freshman quarterback Zack Mills quickly righted Penn State with a 69-yard touchdown romp. Later in the third quarter, he connected with Tony Johnson for 26 yards to narrow the margin to 27–22. As the contest entered the final quarter, Mills found running back Eric McCoo for a 14-yard touchdown, and the Nittany Lions surged in front 29–27.

A missed Penn State field goal gave Ohio State a final scoring opportunity. The Buckeyes moved from their own 31-yard line to the Penn State 21. But Paterno's defense held and forced an Ohio State field goal. At the snap, 330-pound Jimmy Kennedy leaped in the air and batted Mike Nugent's attempt away with his left hand. The Nittany Lions ran out the clock and gave Paterno his 324th career victory with the 29–27 win.

EXTRA POINT < < < < < < < < < < < < < < < < < < < < Joe Paterno wrote his name in the record book. But he also wrote his name elsewhere on campus at the new Paterno library wing. He and his wife, Sue, donated $250,000 to the facility and cochaired the fund-raising campaign for the library dedicated in their honor on September 8, 2000. The Paternos supported the library because it's the heart of a great university.

But as many books as the 490,000-square-foot Penn State library holds, it isn't large enough to contain all that could be written describing what Jesus Christ did on earth. No library ever built is big enough. No library ever will be.

GOAL! *Visit a local library. Check out and read a book on a subject that interests you. Praise God that there aren't enough words or books to describe Christ's glory.*

ATHLETES SOMETIMES PERFORM better when they don't know what the competition is doing. In 2000, Karrie Webb won the AFLAC Champions golf tournament by focusing on her own game—not her opponents'.

After three rounds, the 25-year-old Australian trailed coleaders Sherri Steinhauer and Nancy Scranton by two strokes. Despite needing only a top-ten finish to capture the LPGA Player of the Year award, she refused to check the standings. She also instructed her caddie to keep silent.

On the back nine, Webb opened with five straight pars and then hit three consecutive birdies on 15, 16, and 17 to tie Dottie Pepper for the lead. Both finished the final round with a 15-under-par 273. This score proved to be the best of the day, and the two women entered a playoff.

Pepper teed off first, hitting her drive into the rough. Webb originally planned to use her driver but switched to a 3 wood after observing the bad shot. The winner of six 2000 LPGA titles kept her drive in the fairway. Her approach shot landed on the green, 20 feet behind the pin.

Dottie's approach advanced only about 50 yards, settling well short of the green behind some small trees. A great chip and a 30-foot putt almost salvaged par. In the meantime, Webb two-putted for par to claim the victory and Player of the Year honors.

EXTRA POINT < < < < < < < < < < < < < < < < < < < < < < Sometimes athletes choose not to learn competitors' scores. The lack of knowledge keeps them focused on their own game and avoids the distraction of opponents' excellent or poor play. Karrie Webb obviously made the right choice to mind her own business and pay attention to her own game.

Sometimes in life we become wrapped up looking at other people's lives. We focus on them and don't pay attention to what we're doing. Jesus talked about that at the Sermon on the Mount. He said we should look at the big issues in our own life before we go looking for other people's minor mess-ups. That way we won't lose sight of what's really important.

GOAL! *Do you ever look at the bad things other people do to make yourself feel better? God wants to keep you focused on your own life.*

Why worry about a speck in your friend's eye when you have a log in your own?
MATTHEW 7:3

28 OCT

PRACTICE MAKES PERFECT. It's an old saying, and a true one. But as New York Yankee Tino Martinez learned in game four of the 2001 World Series, watching television can also be helpful.

The Yankees trailed the Arizona Diamondbacks two games to one and hosted the fourth contest in the best-of-seven series at Yankee Stadium. A New York defeat would almost certainly clinch the world title for Arizona.

The Diamondbacks appeared to be on the brink of their third victory, taking a 3–1 lead into the eighth inning. Manager Bob Brenly brought in Byung-Hyun Kim, a submarine-style closer, to shut down the Yankees.

New York had never faced Kim, and Martinez elected to watch his motion on the clubhouse television. Tino saw the Diamondbacks' reliever strike out Shane Spencer, Scott Brosius, and Alfonso Soriano.

Then in the ninth, Derek Jeter bunted into a groundout, Paul O'Neill singled, and Bernie Williams struck out. Martinez stepped to the plate as the Yankees' last hope. Seeing a fastball he could handle, Martinez ripped it over the wall in short right field to tie the game.

In the tenth, Kim coaxed Brosius and Soriano into fly outs, and Jeter came to bat with the score tied. After working the count full and fouling off a pitch, the shortstop belted a fastball over the right-field fence, giving New York a 4–3 win and tying the series at two games each.

EXTRA POINT < < < < < < < < < < < < < < < < < < < < Tino Martinez could have sat in the dugout anticipating a pitcher he had never seen. But he had a better idea. He hurried into the clubhouse to watch the televised game. Martinez scouted the opposition, looking for pitch patterns and speed. Watching and learning paid off with the two-run homer that kept the Yankees alive.

Watching and learning are important in our life too. Moses reminded God's people to watch, learn, and remember. Then he urged them to teach the Lord's lessons to their children and their children's children.

GOAL! *Watch a broadcast of your favorite sport, paying particular attention to learning something new. Ask God to help you remember all you've learned about him.*

Only be careful, and watch yourselves closely so that you do not forget the things your eyes have seen or let them slip from your heart as long as you live. Teach them to your children and to their children after them.

DEUTERONOMY 4:9, NIV

WHEN MICHAEL JORDAN returned to professional basketball with the Washington Wizards after a 40-month absence, no one knew exactly what to expect. But in Jordan's first game, the New York Knicks discovered times had changed.

The Wizards opened the 2001–02 season against the Knicks at Madison Square Garden before a sellout crowd of 19,763. Although Jordan still wore number 23, he could no longer dominate contests like he used to.

Washington played well in the first half and led 43–41 at the break. But the Knicks regrouped. Latrell Sprewell's three-pointer put New York in front 84–83 with a little under four minutes to play. The Knicks upped the lead to 89–86 with 1:43 to go.

Two free throws by New York's Othella Harrington made the score 91–88 with 34 seconds on the clock. On Washington's next possession, Jordan tried a lob pass that Kurt Thomas intercepted. But Thomas lost the ball on the dribble, and the Wizards passed to Jordan for a wide-open 3-point shot on the wing. His attempt clanged off the rim, and Thomas rebounded. Drawing a foul, Thomas made two free throws to clinch a 93–91 Knicks victory.

EXTRA POINT < < < < < < < < < < < < < < < < < < < < < Ask people to name the top ten NBA players of all time, and most include Michael Jordan on their list. Narrow the selections to five, and Michael Jordan's name usually still appears. Some would even place him at No. 1. But time changes things. After three years away from his sport, he no longer connected on every key shot.

Things change; it's a fact. Kings, presidents, and other rulers lose power. Some people gain wisdom and discernment. But only God has the power to make times and seasons change. Only God brings rulers in and out of power. Only God offers wisdom and discernment. The prophet Daniel learned that and praised the Lord.

Then Daniel praised the God of heaven and said:

"Praise be to the name of God for ever and ever; wisdom and power are his. He changes times and seasons; he sets up kings and deposes them. He gives wisdom to the wise and knowledge to the discerning."

DANIEL 2:19-21, NIV

GOAL! *Read about Daniel's learning experience in Daniel 2:1-23. Praise God using Daniel's words in verses 20-21.*

30 OCT

WE USUALLY THINK of ghosts in terms of movies and the imagination. But when Harold "Red" Grange ran wild against Michigan in 1924, sportswriter Grantland Rice could describe Grange's performance in no other terms.

The Wheaton, Illinois, native earned the nickname "the Wheaton Iceman" from his summer job working on an ice truck. After scoring 75 touchdowns in high school, he enrolled at the University of Illinois. Although the 5-foot-11-inch, 175-pounder enjoyed a solid sophomore season rushing for 723 yards and scoring 12 touchdowns, national acclaim didn't follow until the Fighting Illini hosted the University of Michigan the following year.

The Wolverines had allowed only 32 points in their past 20 games, but Grange returned the opening kickoff 95 yards for a touchdown. On the next three Illinois possessions, he scored on runs of 67, 56, and 44 yards. After taking a breather, the running back returned and scored on an 11-yard run and threw a 20-yard touchdown pass in a 39–14 victory. In total, Grange tallied 212 rushing yards, 64 passing yards, and 126 return yards as Illinois snapped a 20-game Michigan winning streak.

Rice, covering the game for the *New York Herald-Tribune*, described Grange as "a streak of fire, a breath of flame eluding all who reach and clutch; a gray ghost thrown into the game that rival hands may never touch."

EXTRA POINT < < < < < < < < < < < < < < < < < < < <

Red Grange made the Wolverine defense appear like it was chasing a ghost. When Michigan players neared the running back, he eluded and eventually brought fear to his opponents every time he touched the ball.

The Bible often mentions the three persons of God: Father, Son, and Holy Spirit. Some Christians refer to the Holy Spirit as the Holy Ghost. But the Holy Spirit isn't elusive or scary. He offers guidance and comfort.

GOAL! *Today is a day when many people celebrate and dress like evil spirits. As Christians, we need to be set apart. Focus on the Holy Spirit. And thank the Father for giving us his Spirit to help us.*

And this expectation will not disappoint us. For we know how dearly God loves us, because he has given us the Holy Spirit to fill our hearts with his love.

ROMANS 5:5

NO-
VEM-
BER

By the seventh day God had finished the work he had been doing; so on the seventh day he rested from all his work.

GENESIS 2:2, NIV

OVERTIME COLLEGE FOOTBALL GAMES don't give the teams much time to rest. In 2001, the Arkansas Razorbacks and the University of Mississippi Rebels needed seven extra periods to decide a winner.

After 60 minutes of strong defensive play, the visiting Razorbacks and host Rebels remained knotted at 17–17. In the first overtime period, Arkansas took the ball first, and Cedric Cobbs bolted 16 yards for a touchdown. Facing fourth-and-goal on their next possession, Mississippi managed to tie the game with a 12-yard scoring pass from Eli Manning to Jason Armistead.

Neither team scored in the second overtime with the Razorbacks missing a game-winning field goal. Beginning with the third OT, squads were forced to run or pass for two-point conversions rather than kicking a point after touchdown.

Staggering and reeling like exhausted heavyweight boxers, the Razorbacks and Rebels tallied touchdowns and missed two-point conversions for another four periods. In the seventh OT, Arkansas went on offense first, and Mark Pierce took the ball into the end zone from two yards away. With the successful two-point conversion, the Razorbacks led 58–50.

Knowing his team needed eight points to stay alive, Manning threw a two-yard touchdown pass. On the extra point attempt, he connected with tight end Doug Ziegler at the three, but linebacker Jermaine Petty tackled the receiver short of the goal line. And Arkansas survived with a 58–56 win.

EXTRA POINT < < < < < < < < < < < < < < < < < <   Not only did the contest break the record for the longest overtime game played in NCAA history, the Razorbacks and Rebels set the mark at 198 for the most plays in a game. And the 47,464 fans enjoyed the highest scoring Southeastern Conference contest ever.

But Arkansas players, coaches, and fans alike ended the game quietly, too tired to celebrate winning the four-and-a-half-hour event. And both teams needed a good rest after the game to get themselves rejuvenated for the next contest.

Rest can be a good thing. Even God rested on the seventh day of creation. And he commanded the Israelites to do the same. The heavenly Father knows the value of slowing down, and so should we.

GOAL! *Do you rest regularly? If not, plan to slow down to rejuvenate and refocus your life. Thank the Lord for times of rest.*

BETHANY HAMILTON EXPERIENCED as memorable a 2003 as any professional athlete in the world. The 13-year-old surfer won the women's division at the Local Motion-Ezekiel Surf Into Summer contest in Oahu, Hawaii, defeating much older and more experienced competitors. Then Hamilton took first in the women's division of the National Scholastic Surfing Association's Open and Explorer Event on her home island of Kauai.

But Hamilton gained worldwide notoriety early in November when news spread after a 14-foot tiger shark bit off her left arm. She was surfing early in the morning with some family and friends off Kauai's north shore. As she dangled her left arm in the water, waiting for a decent wave, the shark came out of nowhere and bit her arm off at the shoulder—and it also took a huge chunk out of her surfboard. A supreme athlete, Hamilton didn't panic; she calmly paddled with one arm over to her friends. Once everybody realized what happened, they quickly returned to shore and rushed her to the hospital.

Soon everybody wanted to know more about this amazing teenager. Friends, doctors, and family members—including her older brothers, Noah and Tim—were interviewed by the national news media. And when asked how Bethany made it through this ordeal, Noah had just a two-word response: "Jesus Christ."

EXTRA POINT < < < < < < < < < < < < < < < < < < < < < < Bethany Hamilton was regarded as the top up-and-coming women's surfer in the world. She had five sponsors and a bright future. After the shark took her arm, her spirits didn't dampen. In fact, she told one of her friends that she was glad this happened to her because then she could tell the whole world about God.

Even without her arm, Hamilton knows her future is bright—whether it's in surfing, photography, or whatever she wants to do. With God as her Savior, Bethany's not worried. She even competed again ten weeks after the accident. As followers of Jesus Christ, we shouldn't fret about what's going to happen to us, either. No matter what happens—good or bad—God can use it for our benefit.

GOAL! *Next time something bad happens to you, think about Bethany Hamilton. Ask God to help you totally trust him with your life.*

"For I know the plans I have for you," says the Lord. "They are plans for good and not for disaster, to give you a future and a hope."

JEREMIAH 29:11

UNTIED SHOELACES can frustrate runners. In the 1997 New York City Marathon, John Kagwe's shoelaces kept him from a record-breaking performance.

Although the race kicked off in 60-degree temperatures, entrants struggled with steady rain and a stiff breeze throughout the course. Despite stops at miles 3 and 10 to retie a problem shoelace, Kagwe, a native of Kenya, led his closest competitors by seven seconds as the race reached the 22 mile mark and wound into Central Park.

Still bothered by the pesky, unraveling lace, Kagwe decided to let it dangle rather than lose more time retying it. Previous experience running with an untied lace gave Kagwe the confidence to believe he could continue without stumbling. A 5:02 time in mile 23 gave the African runner a 25-meter lead. He upped the margin to 50 meters with consecutive 4:56s in miles 25 and 26.

With his shoelace still flapping at the finish, Kagwe, who had finished fourth the previous year, claimed first place in a time of 2:08.12—only 11 seconds off the course record of 2:08.01 set by Tanzania's Juma Ikangaa in 1989. Fellow Kenyan Joseph Chebet's 2:09.27 time earned him second place, and Italy's Stefano Baldini took third at 2:09.31.

> The worries of this life, the deceitfulness of wealth and the desires for other things come in and choke the word, making it unfruitful.
>
> MARK 4:19, NIV

EXTRA POINT < < < < < < < < < < < < < < < < < < < <
What a pain—a flopping, untied shoestring! That lace kept John Kagwe from a record, but it didn't stop the runner from winning the race. The Kenyan decided not to sweat the small stuff, and his decision paid off.

Too often in life we let pesky, little things interfere with what's important. We spend time worrying about having the right sports equipment when we should focus on enjoying the sport and learning the proper skills. We search for the perfect present when we should be focusing on the person.

God cares about the small stuff in our life, but he doesn't want us to get caught up in it and miss out on the power of his Good News. The heavenly Father really wants us to look at the big picture of his kingdom—not the little things of this earth.

GOAL! *Try walking around with an untied shoelace. How much did the string bother you? Ask God to help you focus on his Word and not worry about the small problems in life.*

A CHAMPIONSHIP DECIDED in the last moments thrills one team and crushes the other. In the 2001 World Series, the New York Yankees saw their hopes dashed in the final at bat.

With the series tied at three games each, Arizona Diamondbacks pitcher Curt Schilling muzzled the defending world champions, taking a 1–0 lead into the seventh inning. But the Yankees tied on singles by Derek Jeter, Paul O'Neill, and Tino Martinez. Then the pinstripers went ahead 2–1 in the eighth on Alfonso Soriano's home run.

Going with their best, New York brought in closer Mariano Rivera, who had converted 23 consecutive postseason saves over four years. The reliever shut down Arizona in the eighth.

But in the ninth, the Diamondbacks refused to lose. Mark Grace opened with a single, and Arizona put runners at first and second when Rivera threw wide of second base on Damian Miller's sacrifice. Jay Bell reached on a fielder's choice when pinch runner David Delluci was forced out at third.

With two on and one out, Tony Womack pulled an RBI-double down the right-field line, tying the game. Rivera hit Craig Counsell to load the bases. Then Luis Gonzalez blooped a single, scoring Bell for the 3–2 victory. Randy Johnson, the game six starter who closed out game seven for Arizona, earned his third win in a Series to become the first pitcher to achieve the feat since Mickey Lolich in 1968.

EXTRA POINT < < < < < < < < < < < < < < < < < < < < <
Coming back to take a lead in the eighth inning took the Yankees to the heights of expectation. Losing in the ninth plunged them to the depths of despair.

In life, our greatest disappointments often follow our highest expectations. We lose the game we're favored to win. We receive the practical present instead of the gift we really wanted. Our best friend moves far away.

But no matter how we feel or where we find ourselves in life, the Bible is clear: Nothing can separate us from God's love. We may feel outcast, low, and alone, but God is there.

GOAL! *Think about a time you felt on top of the world. Now remember when you were in the dregs. Don't forget that God is always with you. His love follows you wherever you go.*

> Neither height nor depth, nor anything else in all creation, will be able to separate us from the love of God that is in Christ Jesus our Lord.
> ROMANS 8:39, NIV

04 NOV

FOR WHEN THE SON OF MAN RETURNS, YOU WILL KNOW IT BEYOND ALL DOUBT.
IT WILL BE AS EVIDENT AS THE LIGHTNING THAT FLASHES ACROSS THE SKY.

LUKE 17:24

LIGHTNING NEVER STRIKES the same place twice. Have you heard that before? It's a popular saying, but it's not true. In 2001, Mike Brown of the Chicago Bears proved that with back-to-back electrifying overtime interceptions.

In week six of the season, the Bears and the San Francisco 49ers played to a 31–31 tie. Just 16 seconds into overtime, the Bears safety returned an interception 33 yards for a touchdown and a Chicago victory.

The following week, the Bears met the Cleveland Browns. In the third quarter, Cleveland led 21–7 on a Tim Couch–to–Kevin Johnson 55-yard touchdown completion. Still trailing by 14 points with 28 seconds remaining, Chicago needed a miracle. Bears signal caller Shane Matthews cut the margin in half with a nine-yard scoring pass to Marty Booker. After the extra point, Paul Edinger booted an onside kick, and Bobbie Howard recovered for Chicago on the Cleveland 47-yard line.

On the game's final play, Matthews lofted a desperation pass deep into the end zone. David Terrell leaped, batting the ball toward the goal. James Allen, trailing the play, grabbed the pigskin out of midair and dove into the end zone for the tying touchdown.

The Bears won the overtime toss and took the ball, but Cleveland forced a punt. Brad Maynard pinned the Browns on their own 12. Three plays later, defensive end Bryan Robinson slapped Couch's pass into the air. Mike Brown caught the ball in stride, bolting 16 yards for the game-winning score in the 27–21 Chicago win.

EXTRA POINT

< < < < < < < < < < < < < < < < < < < <

Two weeks in a row, lightning—in the form of safety Mike Brown—struck the National Football League. His flashes of brilliance brought important victories to the Chicago Bears.

But one person in history totally electrified the world. Jesus Christ is the most significant person ever to walk the earth. His book—the Bible—has sold more copies than any other book. And his second return to this planet is going to be like a huge lightning storm. Jesus struck the earth once already, but lightning will strike again when he returns.

GOAL! *When you view majestic lightning flashing across an inky sky, remember how Jesus powers up your life. Praise God for the glory of his Son and the fact that he will return.*

> He lifted me out of the slimy pit, out of the mud and mire; he set my feet on a rock and gave me a firm place to stand.
>
> PSALM 40:2, NIV

A MUDDY FOOTBALL FIELD

A MUDDY FOOTBALL FIELD often puts teams on an even playing field, even if one is supposed to be a lot better. In 1925, the muck and mire at Chicago's Soldier Field sank Michigan's national championship.

Five days of torrential rain soaked the field before the Wolverines' encounter with Northwestern. Although 40,000 people bought tickets, only half braved the elements to watch Michigan, a team that had outscored five opponents 180–0, play the Wildcats. Heavy rainfall continued at kickoff, causing every player to sink ankle deep in mud.

Northwestern capitalized on an early Wolverines turnover. Michigan quarterback Benny Friedman fielded a punt inside his own 5-yard line but fumbled. The Wildcats pounced on the ball, and Northwestern's Tiny Lewis kicked an 18-yard field goal to lead 3–0.

Late in the third quarter, Michigan pushed the Wildcats back toward their own goal. Lewis lined up in punt formation, eight yards deep in the end zone. But rather than kicking, he dropped to a knee and awarded the Wolverines an intentional 2-point safety. Under the rules at that time, Northwestern kept possession and received the ball on its own 40-yard line.

The Wildcats defense continued to thwart Michigan, and Northwestern held on for the 3–2 victory. For the game, the Wildcats limited Michigan to 35 offensive yards and no first downs.

EXTRA POINT

EXTRA POINT < < < < < < < < < < < < < < < < < < < < Muck makes any ball slimy and slippery. Running—let alone scoring—becomes difficult. The weather conditions bogged down the game. Michigan's offense got stuck in the mud.

In the Bible, David wrote about the Lord rescuing him from the mud. David, just like us, made some poor decisions and wandered from God's plan for his life and into some sticky situations. But God was faithful—he rescued David and put him back on solid ground. God does the same thing for us when we reach out and ask him.

GOAL! *Have you ever played football or soccer in the mud? It can be slippery and frustrating, yet fun. But being stuck in the mud in life is never fun. Praise God that he rescues you.*

FROM HIS BOYHOOD DAYS, Daniel "Rudy" Ruettiger envisioned playing football for Notre Dame. Although slow and undersized, his dream finally came true in 1975 as the Fighting Irish faced off against Georgia Tech.

After graduating with great difficulty from Joliet Catholic High School in Illinois, Rudy served in the U.S. Navy and returned home to work in a power plant. Only his best friend, Pete, believed in the dream. When Pete died in an accident, Rudy quit his job and at age 23 applied for admission to Notre Dame. However, the university rejected his application due to mediocre grades and low test scores.

Ruettiger enrolled instead at a neighboring junior college, where counselors discovered Rudy suffered from dyslexia, a learning disability characterized by reversing letters and numbers. After three semesters of hard work and help from friends at the junior college, Rudy got into Notre Dame, fulfilling part one of his dream.

Pursing part two of his goal, Ruettiger played on the Fighting Irish scout team, winning the respect of his teammates and coaches. His football friends pressured head coach Dan Devine into allowing Rudy to suit up for the Fighting Irish's final home game against Georgia Tech.

Devine inserted the walk-on in the contest's final moments. The former scout team defensive end responded with a sack of the Yellow Jackets quarterback. At the game's end, several teammates hoisted Rudy on their shoulders and carried him off the field.

EXTRA POINT < < < < < < < < < < < < < < < < < < < < < <

Rudy Ruettiger dreamed big dreams. No one—not even his family—could imagine him achieving those goals. After all, his too-slow, too-small body couldn't play college football for any school, much less a powerhouse like Notre Dame. And his learning disability would keep him from attending a school with such a strong academic reputation. But with faith and the help of his friends, Rudy lived his impossible dream.

In the Bible, Joseph dreamed dreams. He also had to overcome a lot of obstacles—including disbelief from his family—but God helped him live his dream too. Some people may try to squelch your dream, but God can use those setbacks for your good.

GOAL! *Read about Joseph in Genesis 37, 39–41. Thank the Lord for helping you overcome obstacles to achieve your dreams. Also ask him to help you do what you can to make other people's dreams come true.*

You intended to harm me, but God intended it for good to accomplish what is now being done, the saving of many lives.
GENESIS 50:20, NIV

Moses was there with the Lord forty days and forty nights without eating bread or drinking water. And he wrote on the tablets the words of the covenant— the Ten Commandments.

EXODUS 34:28, NIV

IN FOOTBALL, ILLEGAL PLAYS should result in penalties.

But in the 1997 Missouri–Nebraska football game, a questionable play gave the Cornhuskers a key victory.

Before a crowd of 66,846, the Tigers stunned the top-ranked and undefeated Nebraska Cornhuskers by scoring on four of their first six possessions and taking a 24–21 halftime lead. Missouri continued to keep pace with the Cornhuskers in the second stanza, going ahead 38–31 on a 15-yard touchdown pass from Corby Jones to Eddie Brooks.

However, Nebraska drove to the Missouri 12 with seven seconds remaining. On the third down, quarterback Scott Frost threw to Shevin Wiggins in the end zone. A Tigers defender batted the ball, and Harold Piersey appeared ready to make the interception. But before the Tiger could clutch the pigskin, Wiggins fell to his back and booted the ball. Cornhuskers receiver Matt Davison dove and caught the flying football for the tying touchdown just before it hit the turf.

Missouri fans stared in disbelief. Forced into overtime, Nebraska scored first on a Frost 12-yard option. The Tigers failed to score on their offensive series, and the Cornhuskers escaped with a 45–38 victory.

EXTRA POINT

< < < < < < < < < < < < < < < < < < < <

Missouri fans discussed the game for days. Football experts wondered if Nebraska had scored illegally. Rules provide a penalty for deliberately kicking a football to keep it in bounds. If Wiggins deliberately kicked the pigskin, Nebraska's penalty would be 15 yards plus the loss of down.

However, according to the technical adviser for Big 12 officials, an accidental kick isn't a penalty. If officials are in doubt, they shouldn't make a call. The referees did the right thing . . . although later Wiggins admitted that he deliberately kicked the ball.

Rules play an important role in athletics. Enforcing the standards makes contests fair and the playing field level. Some directives also help prevent injuries. Ignoring the regulations ruins the integrity of the sport.

In the same way, ignoring God's laws costs us our integrity and separates us from him. Fortunately, his rules are outlined for us in the Bible.

GOAL! *Do you know the rules of your favorite sport? Take time to read God's laws in Exodus 20:1-17. Ask the Lord to help you keep his rules.*

OVERTIME BASKETBALL GAMES add a few minutes to the clock so the contest can be decided. But in 1989, the Seattle Supersonics wished they could've wrangled another couple of seconds in the longest NBA contest played under the 24-second shot clock rule.

Hosting Seattle, the Milwaukee Bucks led 102–97 as the season's fourth game wound to a close. But the Supersonics ran off six straight points and went ahead 103–102 with 36 seconds remaining. Milwaukee's Fred Roberts drew a late foul but connected on only one of two free throws, so the contest went to overtime tied at 103–103.

At the end of the first extra period, the scoreboard read 110–110. Another five-minute span elapsed, and the score stood knotted at 120–120. With five seconds left in the third overtime, the Bucks took a 127–125 lead, but Seattle forward Dale Ellis, who led all scorers with 53 points, nailed a shot to tie the game for a fourth time.

The contest remained locked at 138–138 after four overtimes. In the fifth, Milwaukee took command with a 9–0 run and moved in front 155–146 with 31 seconds left to play. But the Supersonics countered with Dana Barros's three-pointer, Nate McMillan's free throw, and Sedale Threatt's rebound basket. Xavier McDaniel missed a desperation shot for Seattle as the clock ticked down, but he was fouled. Unfortunately for the Sonics, the infraction occurred inside the three-point arc. Although two points weren't enough to claim the victory, McDaniel hit both free throws, and Milwaukee survived with a 155–154 five-overtime win.

EXTRA POINT < < < < < < < < < < < < < < < < < < < < The Supersonics and the Bucks managed to add 25 minutes to the normal 48-minute NBA game. They played more than an extra half, although Seattle may have wished for a little more time.

In life, many people may wish they had a few more hours, days, or years to live. But God gives us just one chance. Only he knows the length of our life. And he wants us to make the most of our time.

The book of Psalms records a prayer of Moses. This early leader asked God to teach him to get the most out of every moment. It was a wise thing to ask for in his day, and it's a wise thing to ask for today.

GOAL! *Memorize Psalm 90:12. Ask God to help you make the most of every second you have on earth.*

> Teach us to make the most of our time, so that we may grow in wisdom.
>
> PSALM 90:12

09 NOV

A word fitly
spoken is like
apples of gold
in settings
of silver.

PROVERBS
25:11, NKJV

FOOTBALL COACHES REGULARLY USE halftime pep talks to inspire their team. In 1928, Notre Dame's Knute Rockne delivered perhaps the most famous words in the history of sports.

A 4–2 Fighting Irish squad faced the unbeaten Army Cadets at New York's Yankee Stadium. After a scoreless first half, Rockne elected to share an anecdote about former Notre Dame running back George Gipp.

The Michigan native arrived in South Bend in 1916 to play baseball, but Rockne convinced him to try football. In four years, he rushed for 2,341 yards—a school record that stood for 50 years.

Toward the end of Gipp's senior season, he contracted a streptococcus infection that led to pneumonia. His condition worsened, and Rockne stayed by the player's bedside as Gipp's life drained away. Gipp voiced a last request the day before he died. He asked Rockne to tell his Notre Dame players to "win just one for the Gipper," at a time when things were going wrong. Rockne inspired his players as he told them this was the time.

The fired-up Irish rushed to the field for the second half. Army took a 6–0 lead, but Notre Dame tied the contest on Jack Chevigny's one-yard plunge. As the fourth quarter drew to a close, halfback Butch Niemiec hit reserve receiver Johnny O'Brien for a 32-yard touchdown pass, putting the Fighting Irish in front 12–6. On its final possession, Army drove to Notre Dame's 1-yard line, but time expired before the Cadets could run a final play. Rockne's squad had pulled off the stunning upset.

EXTRA POINT < < < < < < < < < < < < < < < < < < < < <

The coach had filed away George Gipp's story to use at the appropriate time. Playing an undefeated team and needing a win seemed right. Would Notre Dame have beaten Army without Knute Rockne's speech? We'll never know. But the truth is, words possess power. Inspiring words change outcomes. Good coaches like Rockne know that.

The writer of Proverbs knew that too. The right comment at the correct moment can prove as precious as gold. And each time we open our mouth, our speech can inspire with results as valuable as silver.

GOAL! *Name three people whose words inspire you:*

_____

_____

_____

Why do they motivate you to do good things? Ask God to help you use your speech as an inspiration to others.

WHEN DOES FINISHING FOURTH feel like taking first?

Not often. Fourth usually feels one place worse than third. But at the 2003 Pop Secret 400, Matt Kenseth's fourth-place finish helped him wrap up first place in the Winston Cup points standings.

The Pop Secret went like a lot of races had gone for Kenseth. He started near the back, steadily moved past other drivers, stayed out of trouble, and finished near the top. Bill Elliot won the race with Jimmie Johnson taking second and Jeremy Mayfield earning third. Kenseth's fourth kept him 226 points ahead of Johnson with Dale Earnhardt Jr. sitting in the next spot. But with those points, Kenseth couldn't be knocked out of first in the Winston Cup, as only one race remained.

Kenseth ended up claiming the overall racing title by 90 points over Johnson, despite winning just one race all season. The Wisconsin driver began the year with a mediocre 20th-place finish at Daytona. He followed that with a third at Rockingham, and then he won the UAW-Daimler Chrysler 400 at Las Vegas. His fourth place in Atlanta moved him into the Winston Cup points lead—a lead he didn't give up for eight months. Kenseth tallied 25 top ten finishes in 36 races to win nearly $9.5 million.

EXTRA POINT < < < < < < < < < < < < < < < < < < < < < <

Matt Kenseth isn't the biggest name in NASCAR. He didn't make a lot of headlines in 2003 with his amazing victories. Instead, he performed well every week and quietly moved his way to the top. And once Kenseth stood at the pinnacle of the Winston Cup standings, nobody could knock him off.

That's the kind of life God wants us to lead. Our heavenly Father doesn't want us to rise to the top quickly only to fade back into the pack. He desires that we consistently live for him day after day and stay first with him.

GOAL! *How dependable are you in your Christian life? God already knows the answer. Do you read your Bible every month? every week? every day? Do you pray often? God wants to help you to live consistently for him.*

> But be careful to obey the teachings and laws Moses, the Lord's servant, gave you: to love the Lord your God and obey his commands, to continue to follow him and serve him the very best you can.
>
> JOSHUA 22:5, NCV

THE IRONMAN TRIATHLON is a grueling test of endurance. Athletes must swim for more than two-and-a-quarter miles, bike over 111 miles, and run a full marathon in excess of 26 miles. For many people that would be a week's . . . or maybe a month's worth of activity. But at the Ironman Triathlon World Championships in Kona, Hawaii, competitors complete the course in about a third of a day.

At the 2003 Hawaii Ironman, Canada's Peter Reid outworked the competition to win his third championship. Reid had been experiencing a disappointing season heading into the World Championships. His training had gone well, but he couldn't put anything together in a race. On the advice of a past champion, Reid went to Hawaii early and started training by himself. He pushed himself on solitary seven-hour bike rides and long runs to sharpen himself physically and mentally. And on race day, his efforts paid off.

Reid completed the ocean swim in 50 minutes, 36 seconds. Next he jumped on the bike and pedaled out a time of 4 hours, 40 minutes, and 4 seconds. Transitioning into the run, Reid found himself neck and neck with Belgium's Rutger Beke. Reid beat Beke by nearly seven minutes in the marathon to earn the title.

> There are a great many people to harvest, but there are only a few workers. So pray to God, who owns the harvest, that he will send more workers to help gather his harvest.
>
> LUKE 10:2, NCV

EXTRA POINT < < < < < < < < < < < < < < < < < < < < The Hawaii Ironman is the toughest and most competitive triathlon in the world. Winning it once is an amazing feat. Only three athletes have claimed two victories. Two men, Dave Scott and Mark Allen, earned six wins apiece. And with his 2003 championship, Peter Reid tallied his third title. Many athletes try to rise to the top, but few claim multiple victories.

The same thing can be true in the Christian church. Many people have good intentions of spreading God's Word, but few step forward and do it. Jesus told his followers that many people wanted to hear his truth, but the workers were few.

The world hasn't changed that much. There still aren't enough Christians to tell all the people on the earth about Jesus.

GOAL! *Pray that God will send out more workers. Will you be available to rise to the top and work in the heavenly Father's harvest?*

WINNING STREAKS don't last forever. Eventually every team loses. But in 1998, the University of Tennessee Lady Volunteers saw an opportunity for renewal after their lengthy unbeaten streak snapped.

Riding the crest of 46 straight victories and three consecutive NCAA basketball championships, the Lady Vols faced Purdue in the Women's Tip-Off Classic. The Boilermakers presented a strong challenge, returning all five starters from the previous year's squad that made it to the Elite Eight.

As expected, the game remained close early. Tennessee led 11–10 at the 15:58 mark, but Purdue forged ahead. The Boilermakers built a 46–33 halftime margin.

The Lady Vols battled back, using a 14–6 spurt to narrow the gap with 4:10 left to play. But Ukari Figgs hit a jumper, and Stephanie White-McCarty made a layup for Purdue. Then four Purdue free throws down the stretch clinched a 78–68 Boilermakers victory. Purdue would go on to emerge as the 1999 NCAA national champion.

EXTRA POINT < < < < < < < < < < < < < < < < < < < < The loss marked the first Tennessee defeat since a 61–59 decision to Auburn in the championship game of the Southeastern Conference tournament on March 2, 1997. But after the frustration over the loss subsided, the renewed Lady Vols returned to their winning ways. The women posted a 31–3 record during the 1998–99 season, winning the Southeastern Conference championship. Plus, Tennessee drew a record 413,580 fans.

Only one team in any sport can win the championship. And even then, few teams run the table and end up undefeated. Athletics and life become a cycle of restoration and renewal from losses to wins, from valleys to peaks.

The disciple Peter may have experienced more highs and lows than any other of Christ's early followers. From the thrill of walking on water to the devastating failure of denying Jesus, he felt the feelings of loss and renewal. And he knew God's grace was enough to restore him and make him strong.

GOAL! *Search the Internet to see how many college basketball teams—both men's and women's—have won a national championship with a perfect record. Do you need to ask God to restore your relationship with him?*

In his kindness God called you to his eternal glory by means of Jesus Christ. After you have suffered a little while, he will restore, support, and strengthen you, and he will place you on a firm foundation.

1 PETER 5:10

RESULTS SPEAK LOUDER than insults.

In the 1998 Kansas State–Nebraska encounter, K-State quarterback Michael Bishop discovered that silence served his team better than his mouth.

The 70-degree weather and sunshine made KSU Stadium the perfect venue for college football. At 9–0 and ranked No. 2 in the nation, the Wildcats looked to end 29 years of Nebraska Cornhuskers domination.

But the Cornhuskers struck first on an 80-yard drive with Eric Crouch throwing an 8-yard touchdown pass to Sheldon Jackson. Kansas State tied, but Bishop's fumble led to another Nebraska touchdown. Bishop's second dropped ball resulted in a Cornhuskers field goal and a 17–7 Big Red lead.

On KSU's next possession, the Wildcats moved to the 3-yard line, where Bishop coughed up the ball a third time. Ranting and raving, Kansas State coach Bill Snyder ordered the quarterback to the bench with strict instructions to remain silent.

Regaining his composure, Bishop directed KSU on a 76-yard touchdown march in less than a minute, narrowing the halftime gap to 17–14. In the third period, the Wildcats defense decimated the Cornhuskers, allowing only nine yards on 17 plays. KSU took leads of 21–17 and 27–24 before Bishop tossed an 11-yard scoring pass to Darnell McDonald with five minutes remaining. Jeff Kelly iced the 40–30 victory for the Wildcats with a 23-yard fumble return for a touchdown in the final three seconds.

EXTRA POINT

Fans wondered what Coach Snyder said to his quarterback after the third fumble. What could he have laid on the young man that made such a tremendous difference? The simple request, "Silence," made a profound impact on Michael Bishop and the game. The quiet enabled the player to focus on his task and to concentrate on his responsibility.

In our own life too, silence can make a difference. Spending quiet time alone with God every day helps us focus on our Creator and Savior and the task he has for us. We communicate with the Lord, express our love to him, and listen to his still voice leading us in the right way.

GOAL! *Begin or continue to spend quiet time alone with God every day. If you're just starting, try for about three to five minutes. Pray, read your Bible, and listen to him. Praise the heavenly Father for silence.*

But when you pray, go away by yourself, shut the door behind you, and pray to your Father secretly. Then your Father, who knows all secrets, will reward you.

MATTHEW 6:6

GYMNASTICS MIGHT NOT HAVE achieved its popularity with American sports fans without the accomplishments of Cathy Rigby. But despite her success, the gymnast harbored a longtime secret.

At age 15, the Los Alamitos, California, native garnered a berth on the 1968 Olympic squad and placed 16th overall in Mexico City. However, at the 1970 World Championships in Ljubljana, Yugoslavia, Rigby made history for the United States.

No American, male or female, had ever medaled in international gymnastics competition. But performing on the balance beam, the 4-foot-11-inch, 95-pound athlete posted scores of 9.70 and 9.35 for a 19.05 total. Her rating earned a silver medal on the beam. Rigby finished 15th overall with a 74.45 that led the United States to seventh place in the team standings at 360.20.

Although hopeful at the 1972 Munich Games, Ribgy failed to medal but improved to tenth and brought new excitement and interest to the sport. She retired from competition following the 1972 Olympics to become a sports commentator as well as a television and theater actress.

EXTRA POINT < < < < < < < < < < < < < < < < < < < < < After gymnastics Rigby appeared to be a happily married mother enjoying a successful career, but her life teetered. Like many gymnasts who maintain a slight body needed for competing, she suffered from an eating disorder. But in the early 1980s, Cathy recognized her problem, got the help she needed, and overcame the potentially fatal condition.

Even though many people didn't know Cathy Rigby's secret, God did. He knows all our secrets. He's available to listen to our heart and has prepared Christian friends, family members, pastors, and professionals to help.

GOAL! *Do you or somebody you know suffer from an eating disorder? Maybe you're hiding other secrets from your parents or friends. Praise God for knowing all about you and caring about all the details of your life. Then ask him to give you the courage to share your troubles with people who love you and can help you.*

God would surely have known it, for he knows the secrets of every heart.
PSALM 44:21

15 NOV

Therefore, prepare your minds for action; be self-controlled; set your hope fully on the grace to be given you when Jesus Christ is revealed.

1 PETER 1:13, NIV

BUD WILKINSON EMPHASIZED preparation during his 17-year tenure as head football coach at the University of Oklahoma. And his hard work resulted in huge success for the Sooners, including a 47-game winning streak—the longest in NCAA Division I history. But in 1957, Notre Dame caught the Sooners slightly unprepared.

Hoping to snap Oklahoma's historic unbeaten streak, the Notre Dame squad visited Owen Field with two losses. After being shut out 40–0 by the Sooners the previous season, the Fighting Irish entered the contest as 19-point underdogs with revenge on their mind.

Despite its high-octane offense, Oklahoma failed to move the ball consistently. But the stout Sooner defense stopped Notre Dame three times inside the 10-yard line. With the game tied 0–0, the Fighting Irish took possession on their own 20 with less than 13 minutes remaining. Working the ball up the middle, Notre Dame drove to the Sooners 3-yard line in 19 plays.

Facing fourth-and-goal with four minutes to play, Oklahoma bunched its defense, expecting Notre Dame fullback Nick Pietrosante to bull up the middle. But quarterback Bob Williams pitched to Dick Lynch, who swept the right side for a touchdown and a Notre Dame lead.

The Sooners answered by moving to the Irish 24, but on first down, Williams intercepted an Oklahoma pass in the end zone. When the final gun sounded, the Sooners crowd sat in stunned silence, then rose and gave both teams a standing ovation. In the locker room following the game, Wilkinson shouldered the entire blame himself, citing lack of preparation for the loss.

EXTRA POINT < < < < < < < < < < < < < < < < < < < < < < < Players play the game, but coaches prepare players to succeed. Sometimes a team loses because of a lack of talent. Often a squad tastes defeat because it didn't prepare as well as its opposition.

The heavenly Father wants us to prepare for the Christian life. He gives us what we need, but we must prepare to receive his gifts. Bible study, prayer, worship, Christian fellowship, and sharing our testimony prepare us for his presents . . . and his presence.

GOAL! *Think about how an athlete prepares for a game. Consider how you prepare to lead a Christian life. None of us can do it without God's help.*

EVEN FOOTBALL OFFICIALS make mistakes—no surprise there, right? But in the 1940 Dartmouth–Cornell game, the crew managed to turn around its error.

The Dartmouth Indians hosted the undefeated, No. 2-ranked Cornell Big Red. Playing in bitter cold, Dartmouth took a 3–0 lead on Bob Krieger's 27-yard field goal in the fourth quarter. With 45 seconds remaining, Cornell mounted a drive and faced first-and-goal at the Indian 6-yard line.

Three straight runs left the Big Red a foot short. With nine seconds left, Cornell called a time-out, but referee Red Friesell penalized Cornell five yards for illegal substitution, bringing up fourth-and-goal from the 6. Quarterback Walt Scholl threw for the end zone, but Ray Hall broke up the pass, apparently returning the ball to Dartmouth.

The home crowd roared with excitement over the upset. With three seconds still on the clock, Friesell handed the ball to the Indians, but lineman Joe McKenny stopped him. Cornell retained possession. On the "fifth down" play, Scholl connected with Bill Murphy for a touchdown. The extra point gave the Big Red a 7–3 win.

After the game, a scout from a rival Ivy League team approached Friesell and informed him of the mistake. Viewing game films confirmed the error. The ball should have gone to Dartmouth. The official filed a report with the Eastern Intercollegiate Football Association admitting his crew's mistake. Cornell president Ezra Day telegraphed the findings to Dartmouth athletic director William T. McCarter, and the Big Red relinquished the victory.

EXTRA POINT < < < < < < < < < < < < < < < < < < < Sometimes, but not very often, officials reverse their call after instant replay review. But in 1940 instant replay didn't exist, and even in the 21st century officials don't use it in college ball. But the football association admitted the mistake, and Cornell agreed to give up the win.

Rarely in the Bible does God reverse his decisions. But one time he did was when he sent Jonah to preach judgment to Nineveh. The people saw their errors and showed genuine sorrow, so God spared them, turning their defeat into victory.

GOAL! *Read Jonah 1–4. Was God right to reverse his judgment? Should Jonah have been upset? Praise God for turning defeat to victory.*

When God saw what they did and how they turned from their evil ways, he had compassion and did not bring upon them the destruction he had threatened.
JONAH 3:10, NIV

17 NOV

YOUNG TENNIS PLAYERS FACE tremendous pressure in championship matches. But in the 2001 Tennis Masters Cup, Lleyton Hewitt rose to the world's top ranking.

In the invitational round-robin affair, players draw outstanding opponents in each match. The fast-paced contests over a relatively short period of time appeal to fans who want to watch competition between international tennis superstars.

Hewitt defeated Sebastien Grosjean in his opener and marched through matches with Andre Agassi, Pat Rafter, and Juan Carlos Ferrero before surprisingly meeting Grosjean again in the finals.

Battling a groin injury, the 20-year-old Australian pummeled the Frenchman's backhand. Hewitt, the 2001 United States Open champion, bolted to a 4–1 lead in set one with two service breaks. But Grosjean rallied with a break of his own and narrowed the score to 4–3. However, Hewitt, playing in front of 10,000 countrymen at Sydney's SuperDome, held on to take the set 6–3.

In set two, the Adelaide, Australia, native broke Grosjean's service and claimed another 6–3 victory. He repeated with a service break in the final set and took the match in three straight sets with a 6–4 win. Although his opponent clouted 21 winners compared to only 12 for Hewitt, the Frenchman committed 47 unforced errors, while Hewitt limited his mistakes to just 19.

EXTRA POINT < < < < < < < < < < < < < < < < < < < < < < < For his efforts, Lleyton Hewitt claimed a purse worth $1.5 million and gained 150 points in the world rankings to vault over Brazil's Gustavo Kuerten to the No. 1 spot. The strong young athlete battled through world-class players to the top of the invitational field.

In the Bible, God exalted a strong young man to the top. He anointed David to wear the crown. The shepherd-turned-warrior loved God and served him with all his heart and strength.

God may not expect us to be great warriors. He may not exalt us to an earthly throne or anoint us with royal oil. But he does ask us to love and serve him with all our heart and strength.

GOAL! *Have you given God your heart and strength? If not, ask the Lord to use you as he did David.*

PSALM 89:19-21, NIV

I HAVE EXALTED A YOUNG MAN
FROM AMONG THE PEOPLE.

I HAVE FOUND DAVID MY SERVANT;
WITH MY SACRED OIL
I HAVE ANOINTED HIM.

MY HAND WILL SUSTAIN HIM;
SURELY MY ARM WILL
STRENGTHEN HIM.

The Lord is
good to those
who hope in
him, to those
who seek him.
It is good to
wait quietly
for the Lord
to save.

LAMENTATIONS
3:25-26, NCV

MANY ATHLETES HAVE SAID IT BEFORE, and millions more will say it in the future: It's not over till it's over. Whether it's baseball, football, auto racing, or tiddlywinks, fighting hard to the finish can garner some surprising victories. That certainly was the case at the 2003 Ford 400 at Homestead-Miami Speedway.

Bill Elliott led for nearly two-thirds of the race and appeared to be driving towards his second-straight Winston Cup victory. Elliott had held off Bobby Labonte on a restart nine laps from the finish and built a comfortable lead. But when Elliott came out of turn two on the final lap, his right rear tire flew apart and started a fire in the wheel well. Forced to throttle back, Elliott settled for eighth. In the meantime, Labonte took advantage of the situation by blowing past Elliott and taking the checkered flag. Labonte led for only one lap in the 267-lap race, but it was the most important one.

EXTRA POINT < < < < < < < < < < < < < < < < < < < < < <

For many athletes, waiting for the right opportunity seems harder than any other aspect of their sport. Players don't tend to be patient. They like to force the action and make things happen. Sometimes that works; other times it ends in disaster. In auto racing, being impatient can lead to an accident and big-time injuries . . . even death. Bobby Labonte accepts the risks he takes on the racetrack. And he knows his fellow racers do the same. They trust each other to be patient and make the right moves, but it's hard to wait.

Most people don't like to wait. Children eagerly anticipate Christmas and birthdays. Moms and dads anxiously await the birth of a baby. Every Monday, we start looking forward to the weekend. But waiting is key to a successful relationship with God. So many times we want things to happen according to our time schedule. But that's not always God's plan. Sometimes he wants us to wait for his perfect timing. At those instances, we need to trust that he knows best.

GOAL! *Count the number of days until Christmas, the end of the school year, or your next birthday. Can you wait? Ask the Lord to help you wait for him.*

WORLD-CLASS TRIATHLONS tend to lack surprise endings. Barring an injury or mechanical problem, the top athletes usually finish where everybody expects them to. Leading into the 25th Ironman Triathlon World Championships in Kona, Hawaii, many expected Germany's Nina Kraft and Switzerland's Natascha Badmann to battle for the 2003 title. But somebody forgot to tell that to Canada's Lori Bowden.

Bowden, the 1999 champ, entered the race after stringing together a number of second- and third-place finishes in big-time events. Instead of putting pressure on herself to win, Bowden went into the race planning to smile and have fun the whole time. While it's hard to smile during more than nine hours of torturous swimming, biking, and running, Bowden's positive attitude took her to the top.

She completed the 2.4-mile swim through Kailua Bay in 56 minutes and 51 seconds, which kept her minutes from the lead. She biked the grueling 111-mile course in five hours and nine minutes. As Bowden started the 26-plus mile marathon, she knew she was within striking distance of four time champion Badmann. Bowden kept her legs pumping and made up ground with every stride. She ended up beating Badmann by more than ten minutes in the run to claim the championship by 5 minutes and 13 seconds. Badmann finished second with Kraft taking third.

> Training the body has some value. But being godly has value in every way. It promises help for the life you are now living and the life to come.
>
> 1 TIMOTHY 4:8, NIrV

EXTRA POINT

‹ ‹ ‹ ‹ ‹ ‹ ‹ ‹ ‹ ‹ ‹ ‹ ‹ ‹ ‹ ‹ ‹ ‹ ‹

Heading into the 2003 Ironman Triathlon World Championships, Lori Bowden focused her training on the race. She competed in the course many times and knew what it would take to win: a lot of hard work. And all of Bowden's training showed as she blistered the competition in the marathon to claim the victory.

The Bible talks a lot about physical training. As a creation in God's image, we need to treat our body well and try to stay in shape. But the apostle Paul tells us that there's something more important than physical exercise—spiritual exercise. When we read the Bible, pray, and treat others as Jesus would, we become more godly. And godliness reaps rewards on earth and in heaven.

GOAL! *Is your body getting enough exercise? How's your spiritual training going? As you work to keep your physical body strong, don't forget to focus on spiritual exercise as well.*

20 NOV

Our God is
a God who
strengthens
you and cheers
you up. May
he help you
agree with
each other
as you follow
Christ Jesus.

ROMANS
15:5, NIrV

THE BAJA 1000 is the oldest off-road race in the world, not to mention one of the toughest. Beginning in Tijuana, Mexico, and ending in La Paz, it covers nearly the entire Baja peninsula south of California. And in the 2003 competition, the Mark Miller racing team of Mark Miller and Ryan Arciero ran away from the competition in the Trophy Truck division, despite fighting steering problems.

Even without mechanical difficulties, the Baja 1000 tests a driver's endurance. The steering wheel vibrates like a jackhammer. The world flies past in a blur of browns and greens as the truck whips through the desert, over hills, and through rivers.

Miller started the race for his team and drove 180 of the first 205 miles with almost no power-assist steering. Once his team fixed a loose power-steering hose at a pit stop, Miller blazed through the pack. He took the lead at mile 325 and built a nine-minute edge by the time he handed over the truck to Arciero after 442 miles. Once Arciero got behind the wheel, he continued to add to the lead. He was ahead by 24 minutes by the time he passed mile 580—and he continued to push the truck's Bilstein shocks and General Motors Vortec 6-liter V-8 engine to the limit. He charged through the finish line to win by 48 minutes over second-place finishers Tim Herbst and Ed Herbst from Las Vegas. The Miller team won the grueling race with a time of 16 hours, 28 minutes, and 45 seconds.

EXTRA POINT < < < < < < < < < < < < < < < < < < < < The Baja 1000 tests a driver's endurance and driving skills. Only a high-functioning team can win. When Mark Miller fought with steering problems, his copilot, Wade Weaver, encouraged him and helped him stay hydrated. Then team mechanics diagnosed and fixed the problem.

God wants his team of believers to encourage each other and have one purpose too. By working together as we follow Jesus, we can be a more effective team.

GOAL! *Where do you turn when temporary difficulties hit your life? God is a great source of strength and encouragement. Thank him for also putting people in your life to help.*

TEAMS OFTEN SCORE 100 points in a basketball game. But in 1968, coach Bill Yeoman and his University of Houston Cougars reached that mark in *football*.

During the 1964 season, Yeoman experimented with his quarterback taking the snap, faking to the fullback, and continuing down the line of scrimmage—an offense called the veer option attack. The signal caller had the option to pitch the ball to a trailing halfback or keep the pigskin himself. Houston practiced the play the following season but never utilized it in a game.

With five straight losses to open the 1965 campaign, however, the Cougars added the veer option attack and didn't lose again. Over the next three years, Houston rolled up incredible offensive numbers.

In the final game of the 1968 season, the Tulsa Golden Hurricanes visited the Astrodome. The Cougars dominated, leading 24–0 at halftime. Tulsa opened the third period with a touchdown, but then Houston's veer shifted into overdrive.

The Cougars added 27 third quarter points and 49 in the fourth quarter, scoring 14 touchdowns, 13 extra points, and a field goal to reach triple digits. Twelve different UH players scored in the 100–6 victory as Houston totaled 762 offensive yards, including 555 rushing.

Still other seed fell on fertile soil and produced a crop that was thirty, sixty, and even a hundred times as much as had been planted.

MARK 4:8

EXTRA POINT < < < < < < < < < < < < < < < < < < Coach Bill Yeoman developed one of the most productive offenses of all time. Because of its success, hundreds of high school and college teams—including Air Force and Rice—continue to run the largely unchanged veer attack.

Jesus told his followers how to be productive in sharing the gospel. But instead of talking about scoring points, he told a story about planting seeds. Birds ate some seeds. Other plants couldn't grow because of shallow soil. Thorny weeds choked out some young sprouts. But some seeds fell on good soil, multiplying 30, 60, or 100 times. When we share the gospel with others, some never hear. Others become excited at first, but fall away. Satan chokes out the Word for some. But a few hear about Christ, accept him, and tell others the Good News. They reproduce themselves 30, 60, or 100 times. Now that's success!

GOAL! *Read Jesus' parable in Mark 4:3-20. God can reproduce your faith when you witness to others.*

22 NOV

> It is a good thing to receive wealth from God and the good health to enjoy it. To enjoy your work and accept your lot in life—that is indeed a gift from God.
>
> ECCLESIASTES
> 5:19

UNTIL RECENTLY, goalies never scored in a National Hockey League game. In 1979, however, the first goalie goal occurred more by gift than by ability.

The New York Islanders faced off against the Colorado Rockies on the road. The Rockies, who would later relocate to New Jersey and change their name to the Devils, had never beaten the New Yorkers, losing 13 games and tying two in their previous matchups.

After two periods, the Rockies held a 4–3 advantage. But early in the third period, New York tied on a freak goal. The Islanders skated shorthanded due to a delayed penalty during which Colorado pulled its goalie, Bill McKenzie, and inserted a sixth attacker. Rockie defenseman Rob Ramage gained control of the puck on the Islanders' end. He fired a pass toward the point but missed his target.

The puck skidded backward straight into the Colorado net, tying the score. Under NHL rules, the last Islander to touch the puck received credit for the goal. In this instance, New York goalie Billy Smith had blocked the deflected shot and thus scored a goal without actually taking the shot. Although the Rockies eventually won 7–4, Smith garnered many of the headlines with the first goalie goal.

EXTRA POINT < < < < < < < < < < < < < < < < < < < < < < Hockey goalies remain buried by the net and disguised by equipment. While they receive credit for saves, those occur frequently and with little glory. Billy Smith's goal provided a rare spark of happiness in a rather disappointing game for him.

Believe it or not, God wants us to be happy in our work, regardless of what we do. That may mean school, a job, or doing things around the house. The heavenly Father desires that we enjoy the wealth and possessions that our work brings. Enjoying work and accepting our position in life are gifts from God.

GOAL! *What are some jobs or responsibilities that would make you happy? Thank God for happiness in work.*

AS A GENERAL RULE, any loose football should be pounced on as soon as possible. However, in 1993, Leon Lett's mental lapse during a blocked kick cost the Dallas Cowboys a victory.

The Cowboys entertained the Miami Dolphins on Thanksgiving Day at Texas Stadium. A freak, early-winter storm dropped the temperature to 32 degrees with wind chills in the single digits. Plus, the turf turned into an icy, slippery rink.

Dallas took a 14–7 halftime lead with two Kevin Williams touchdowns, but the Dolphins closed to 14–13 on second-half field goals of 20 and 31 yards. With 2:16 remaining, Miami took over on its own 20-yard line. Quarterback Steve DeBerg connected on 8 of 11 passes and directed the Dolphins to the Cowboy 24. The drive stalled, and Pete Stoyanovich lined up to try a 41-yard field goal.

But Dallas defensive lineman Jimmie Jones got a hand on the ball, and it rolled toward the Dallas goal line. Under NFL rules, the pigskin belonged to the Cowboys unless one of their players touched it and created a live ball. Lett, who instinctively thought he needed to recover the football, mistakenly jumped on it at the 7-yard line. But on the icy surface, the ball squirted free.

A mad scramble ensued, and Miami center Jeff Dellenbach recovered the pigskin at the 1. Given second life, Stoyanovich booted a 19-yard field goal as time expired, bringing the Dolphins an unexpected 16–14 victory.

EXTRA POINT < < < < < < < < < < < < < < < < < < < < All the Cowboys needed to seal the victory was not to touch the football. Perhaps Dallas coach Jimmy Johnson should have called a time-out to remind the players, "Do not touch the ball if you block the field goal." But he didn't, and Lett touched it.

When Jesus rose from the dead and appeared to his disciples, he asked them to touch him so they would know he had truly risen from the dead. They believed and celebrated the Lord's victory over death.

> Look at my hands and my feet. It is I myself! Touch me and see; a ghost does not have flesh and bones, as you see I have.
>
> LUKE 24:39, NIV

GOAL! *Name some things you shouldn't handle.*

_____

_____

_____

Ask God to help you stay away from the things you shouldn't touch and focus on the things that matter to him.

God blesses those who mourn, for they will be comforted.

MATTHEW 5:4

TRADITIONS ABOUND at Thanksgiving. But in the 1999 Texas A&M versus Texas game, players paid homage to fellow students who died preparing for an honored Aggie tradition.

Every year before this annual game, Texas A&M students build a massive bonfire for a pep rally the night before the game. In the early morning hours eight days prior to the contest, the 55-foot stack of tiered logs collapsed. Hundreds of huge pieces of wood tumbled down, killing 12 volunteers.

A pall hung over the crowd of 86,128 gathered at A&M's Kyle Field. Under his jersey, each Aggie player wore a T-shirt listing the victims' names.

Texas led 16–6 at halftime, but the Aggies closed to 16–13 on fullback Ja'Mar Toombs's 9-yard run. As the clock ticked down, A&M quarterback Randy McCown capped a 48-yard drive with a 14-yard touchdown pass to Matt Bumgardner, giving the Aggies a 20–16 lead. Texas failed to record a first down on its next possession but forced an A&M punt and took over at its own 11-yard line with two minutes remaining.

Major Applewhite directed the Longhorns to the Aggie 45, but Jay Brooks sacked the Texas quarterback on first down, creating a fumble that was recovered by A&M linebacker Brian Gamble with 23 seconds left. After the play, Gamble dropped to his knees, clutched his helmet, then raised both hands and pointed to the sky with teary eyes.

EXTRA < < < < < < < < < < < < < < < < < < < < <
POINT That day and many following, the Texas A&M family needed compassion. Each walk past the bonfire ruins brought sadness. Yet the students were thankful they had known those who died. They mourned the loss of their friends, but they celebrated their memory.

Tragedies often occur in life. Many times we can't explain why. We have to trust God and his will for the world. And we can know that God comforts those who lose loved ones. He cares for everybody in the world. His grace and strength help people through difficult times.

GOAL! *Consider talking with a mature Christian about why bad things happen. Thank the Lord for his comfort when calamity comes.*

A COIN TOSS BEGINS every football game and any overtime period. In 1998, a referee's mistake during a coin toss may have cost the Pittsburgh Steelers a victory.

"You have eyes—can't you see? You have ears—can't you hear?" Don't you remember anything at all?

MARK 8:18

The Detroit Lions hosted the Steelers in their traditional Thanksgiving Day game at the Silverdome. Pittsburgh's Norm Johnson, who kicked field goals of 30 and 38 yards in the second quarter, booted a 25-yarder with one second remaining in regulation to tie the game 16–16. With the contest headed into overtime, the teams met at midfield to determine possession.

Pittsburgh Steelers captain Jerome Bettis called "tails." But referee Phil Luckett claimed to hear "Heads-tails." The official credited the Steelers captain with his first word. The coin turned over in the air, hit the turf, and flipped over to reveal tails. The referee awarded first choice to the Lions, who elected to receive. Unfortunately for Luckett, the stadium microphones, which were piped into the national television feeds, clearly picked up the Steeler running back saying "tails."

No NFL rule allowed Pittsburgh to protest, so the team kicked off to Detroit. Following a 21-yard return by Terry Fair, the Lions moved 41 yards in seven plays. On third down from the 25, Jason Hanson lined up for a 42-yard field goal. His kick sailed true, and the Lions escaped with a 19–16 victory less than three minutes into overtime.

EXTRA POINT

< < < < < < < < < < < < < < < < < < < <

Referees make mistakes, but usually their errors result from judgment calls or quick decisions. Phil Luckett's lapse involved neither. Relaxed coin-toss meetings involve little stress and no time constraints. Why the official erred, no one knows. Perhaps he simply misunderstood, but millions of people from coast to coast listened to him make the wrong call.

The truth is, we all have eyes and ears, but sometimes we misunderstand as well. After Jesus fed the 5,000, he became a bit frustrated by the disciples. Although they had witnessed the amazing event, they didn't comprehend God's power. They were still worried about little things.

GOAL!

Read through the Gospels or just think about all the amazing things Jesus did. List some of them.

_____

_____

_____

Ask God to open your eyes, ears, and mind to understand his greatness.

For even I, the
Son of Man,
came here not
to be served but
to serve others,
and to give my
life as a ransom
for many.

MATTHEW 20:28

UNSELFISH PLAYERS REWARD their teams and teammates by putting others first. In 1999, Detroit Red Wings center Steve Yzerman achieved a personal goal while attempting to unselfishly assist another.

The Red Wings entertained the Edmonton Oilers at the Joe Louis Arena. On a power play opportunity midway through a scoreless first period, Yzerman won a face-off to the right of Oilers goalie Tommy Salo. He circled and took several purposeful strides behind the goal line. The Red Wings captain then headed toward the net, searching for a teammate with a better shooting angle.

The 34-year-old center spotted Slava Kozlov cutting toward the crease and flipped the puck toward him. But instead of hitting Kozlov's stick, it struck Salo's glove, bounced off the goalie's left skate, and scooted into the net, putting the Red Wings in front 1–0.

Stunned by the unusual goal, the 19,983 fans sat silent for a moment before standing in thunderous applause. Teammates rushed to Yzerman's side. After fist-bumping his friends, Yzerman stood in the bench area, punched his right arm into the air, and raised his stick to those in attendance. With his goal, Yzerman became the 11th player in National Hockey League history to record 600 goals and only the fifth to total both 600 goals and 900 assists.

EXTRA POINT < < < < < < < < < < < < < < < < < < < How ironic that a player with more assists than goals found the back of the net his 600th time while attempting to make a pass. Yzerman's unselfish play not only benefited the Detroit Red Wings, but gave him personal gain as well.

Everyone enjoys playing on a team with selfless teammates. Games become easier for everyone, and often the squad's record shows the generous attitude. But not everyone enjoys being a team player. Some athletes think only of themselves and try to be the star.

But that's not what Jesus wants us to do in athletics or in life. We should follow his example. Christ came to earth with all the power in the universe, yet he served others—even giving his life for us.

GOAL! *Watch a game in person or on television. Look especially for unselfish players. Notice the selfish ones too. Which athletes help the team most? Ask God to help you serve your teammates.*

NORMALLY A CLOUD of smoke on a motorsports track is a sign of something bad. A blown engine, a car spinning out of control, a fire—smoke and racing just don't mix. But the 2003 Ford 400 ended in a white cloud, and Matt Kenseth couldn't have been happier.

Although Kenseth finished dead last in the Ford 400 after his engine blew 28 laps into the race, his loss couldn't wipe the smile off his face. Normally if a racer is eliminated from a NASCAR event that early, he jumps into a helicopter, flies to the airport, and jets home. But Kenseth wasn't going anywhere—he still had to celebrate his season-long Winston Cup championship. Even his last-place finish in NASCAR's final race of the year didn't knock him out of the top spot in the points standings. So once Bobby Labonte took the checkered flag, it was time for Kenseth to get back on the track.

He stepped into his backup car, eased its nose against the wall, and gunned the engine. The madly spinning tires created an enormous cloud of smoke and a memorable way to cap off a Winston Cup championship. Nobody had ever seen a stunt like that before, and it proved to be a great way to celebrate.

EXTRA ‹
POINT Matt Kenseth may have lost the battle at the Ford 400, but he won the war by taking first in the Winston Cup standings. His season-ending setback at the Homestead-Miami Speedway didn't dampen his spirits because he knew he was the champion no matter what happened. So when the race ended, Kenseth celebrated in grand style.

In our Christian life, we'll often suffer setbacks. We won't win every race. All of our papers won't be As. Everything won't go perfectly. But we have reason to celebrate every day because of what Jesus Christ has done in our life. We may lose a lot of battles, but Jesus won the war. You're already a champion if the Lord is in your life.

GOAL! *Suffering loss isn't easy. But it is a part of life. Instead of dwelling on your loss, try to focus on Christ and the ultimate victory he gives you. He's already won the war . . . so celebrate!*

> They will celebrate your great goodness. They will sing with joy about your holy acts.
>
> PSALM 145:7, NIrV

28 NOV

No discipline seems pleasant at the time, but painful. Later on, however, it produces a harvest of righteousness and peace for those who have been trained by it.

HEBREWS 12:11, NIV

SOMETIMES BEING DISCIPLINED for improper actions can help a person get back on track in life. In 2001, Richard Morales overcame two arrests for fighting to lead Uruguay's soccer team into the World Cup.

Uruguay matched up against Australia before almost 70,000 fans at Montevideo's Estadio Centenario to determine the final 2002 World Cup spot. The South American host team threatened to take the lead in the game's 13th minute when Alvaro Recoba sent a corner kick crashing off the goalpost.

However, a minute later, Uruguay lit up the scoreboard. A long pass from Gianni Guigou caught the Australians napping. Dario Silva collected the ball outside the box, held off a challenge from Shaun Murphy, advanced toward the goal, and fired a shot past goalie Mark Schwarzer.

The 1–0 lead held through the intermission. Midway through the second half, Morales substituted into the contest for Federico Magallanes. A year earlier, the striker had been arrested following a fight between his Nacional team and the opposing Penarol. After eight days in jail, all players were released. Shortly afterward, Morales again faced charges following an altercation, but they were later dropped as well.

In the 71st minute, Recoba won a free kick on the left side and floated the ball across to Morales. Morales headed the ball into the net, putting his team up 2–0. During the added time at the end of the game, he iced the victory by scoring a breakaway goal after receiving a pass from Recoba. The 3–0 victory earned Uruguay its first World Cup berth since 1990.

EXTRA POINT < < < < < < < < < < < < < < < < < < < Richard Morales's violent actions deserved punishment. The first imprisonment didn't make the kind of impression it should have, but the second problem did. The soccer star returned to competition ready to focus on the game—not on his temper or on difficulties with opposing players or officials.

Sometimes in life, we deserve punishment. Although it may be painful, punishment has a purpose. God wants us to learn from discipline so we don't make the same mistakes again.

GOAL! *Can you think of any punishments you didn't like? Good! Thank God for loving discipline and commit to him to learn from it.*

FEW ATHLETES can play two professional sports with equal ability. But in 1987, Auburn's Bo Jackson proved he wasn't an ordinary athlete.

Jackson, the first pick in the 1986 NFL draft, shunned football and opted to play baseball for the Kansas City Royals. After half a season in the minors, Jackson joined the majors, but football continued to beckon. The Los Angeles Raiders drafted Jackson again in the seventh round. Jackson and Raiders owner Al Davis agreed on a contract allowing Jackson to play both sports.

The outfielder/running back joined the Raiders the week following the 1987 NFL players' strike. Jackson saw limited action in the next five games before facing the Seattle Seahawks on *Monday Night Football.*

Seattle jumped in front 7–0, but Los Angeles tied the game on a 46-yard touchdown pass to James Lofton. In the second quarter, Jackson stunned the Kingdome fans and the national television audience. First, Jackson put the Raiders in front with a 14-yard touchdown catch. Then when Los Angeles faced third-and-six on its own 9-yard line, the 230-pound running back bolted around the left end and blazed past a baffled Seattle defense for a 91-yard touchdown.

The Raiders added two field goals before halftime, and on their first possession in the third quarter, Jackson broke for a 42-yard run to set up a 2-yard touchdown blast straight over linebacker Brian Bosworth. Jackson finished the night with 221 yards on 18 carries, setting a new Raiders rushing record in the 37–14 win.

EXTRA POINT 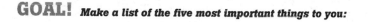 In baseball, Bo Jackson hit, fielded, and ran bases well. In football, the college superstar ran wild. But few athletes manage to play two sports beyond high school or college. Usually players excel more at one than the other or enjoy one more. They have to choose and put one first.

The same is true in life. Something must hold first place in our heart. Jesus said that for most people, the choice comes down to God and money. Which do you serve: God or material things?

GOAL! *Make a list of the five most important things to you:*

_____

_____

_____

_____

_____

Rank them. What's on top? Ask God to help you put him first.

No one can serve two masters. For you will hate one and love the other, or be devoted to one and despise the other. You cannot serve both God and money.
MATTHEW 6:24

DE–
CEM–
BER

LONG ROAD TRIPS wear down professional athletes. At the start of the 1993 National Basketball Association season, weariness finally ended the Houston Rockets' winning streak.

The Rockets triumphed at the beginning of the season with 15 consecutive wins, the 15th victory coming against the New York Knicks at Madison Square Garden. The following day, however, found the Rockets in Atlanta for an encounter with the Hawks at the Omni.

Atlanta also entered the contest on a roll, reeling off nine straight wins. Before 16,368 hometown fans, Mookie Blaylock continued the Hawks' torrid pace, scoring 16 first-quarter points to fuel a 38–27 edge. In the second quarter, former Rocket Craig Ehlo came off the bench and grabbed three key steals to intensify the pressure on Houston. Mario Elie's broken hand allowed Ehlo to ignore the Rockets forward's shooting and to play the ball. Turnovers resulted in Atlanta's 30–19 scoring advantage, boosting the Hawks' halftime lead to 68–46.

Strong defense thwarted Houston's leading scorer and rebounder, Hakeem Olajuwon, who totaled only 17 points and 7 rebounds. Vernon Maxwell keyed the Rocket offense with 26, but Atlanta matched the Rockets over the second half and coasted to a 133–111 victory. With the loss in game 16, Houston's 15-game winning streak tied the NBA's best opening record, set by the Washington Capitols in 1948.

EXTRA POINT

< < < < < < < < < < < < < < < < < < < < < < <

The basketball season lasts a long, long time. Teams begin playing in November and move through 82 regular season games. Four playoff rounds await the top teams. The NBA champions continue the sport into June. Depending on playoff wins, a team could compete in 97 to 108 games.

The Houston Rockets' 15-in-a-row wins to start the year represented quite an accomplishment. But they grew weary and eventually lost. Great teams pace themselves for the long term.

We also must pace ourselves in life. The apostle Paul reminded the Galatians that we sometimes burn out doing too many positive things. But if we pace ourselves and make wise choices, our good works will pay off.

GOAL!

Examine your calendar and your activities during the upcoming holidays. Be careful not to schedule so many things—even if they're all good—that you grow weary. Ask God to help you pace yourself.

Let us not become weary in doing good, for at the proper time we will reap a harvest if we do not give up.

GALATIANS 6:9, NIV

01 DEC

The path of life is level for those who are right with God; Lord, you make the way of life smooth for those people.

ISAIAH 26:7, NCV

DOWNHILL SKIING and cross-country skiing are such different sports that they almost shouldn't share the word *ski*. Sure, both activities require athletes to strap skis on their feet. But downhill allows competitors to ride up the mountain on comfortable lifts or gondolas, while cross-country athletes must power and glide their way up hills and across flat meadows for great distances. Downhill skiers gracefully glide down the slopes. Cross-country skiers grind their way over obstacles.

Cross-country skiing, also called Nordic skiing, is arguably one of the most aerobically challenging sports on the planet. Using both upper and lower body strength, Nordic skiers have to work for every inch of ground they cover—and they can traverse some pretty serious territory.

In 1988, Seppo-Juhani Savolainen covered more than 258 miles on cross-country skis in 24 hours. The Finnish skier took to the country near Sarriselk, Finland, and ended up somewhere in Hawaii (just kidding!) after his record-breaking effort.

EXTRA POINT < < < < < < < < < < < < < < < < < < < <

Seppo-Juhani Savolainen worked tirelessly to set his world record in Nordic skiing. By consistently planting his poles and pushing with his skis, Savolainen skied farther than the distance between New York and Baltimore. He stayed on a level path and endured to the end.

In life, we may know people for whom every activity is a downhill ski race. They float to the top of a mountain only to come crashing down. Everything turns to tragedy or triumph. Their life is filled with peaks and valleys. They rarely walk on level ground. But God doesn't want our life to be that way. He desires that we glide through life on a level path. There will still be some ups and downs and we'll still have to work hard to succeed—like in Nordic skiing—but he'll make our paths smooth.

In the Old Testament, the prophet Isaiah praises people who follow God's path. They live a consistent, level life just as God planned.

GOAL! *Study successful sports stars. Note that their wins usually flow from consistency. Pray for God to give you consistency in your Christian life.*

TY TRYON'S FATHER started giving his son golf instruction at age three. In 2001, the years of practice and hard work reaped dividends as Ty earned a Professional Golfers' Association playing card.

The junior at Dr. Phillips High School in Orlando, Florida, competed in the PGA's annual qualifying school at Bear Lakes Country Club in West Palm Beach. The top 35 finishers received memberships, granting them entry into PGA-sponsored tournaments for the following year.

After five rounds of the six-round event, Tryon stood three shots away from 35th place. But on the final day, he carded a 66 and vaulted 27 spots into a tie for 23rd, just nine strokes in back of top finisher Pat Perez. The 17-year-old golfer, who began studying under the tutelage of golf guru David Leadbetter at age seven, posted an 18-under-par 414 in his six rounds.

Unfortunately, the previous September the PGA Tour had adopted a new policy requiring players to be 18 for full membership. Tryon, who turned 18 on June 2, was permitted to play in 12 tournaments prior to his birthday before gaining full playing privileges.

EXTRA POINT < < < < < < < < < < < < < < < < < < < < < Ty Tryon most likely would never have qualified for the PGA Tour at age 17 if he hadn't begun playing golf as a toddler. Consistent lessons and constant practice paid great rewards. His game became second nature and part of his everyday life.

That's what God wants us to do with the Bible. He desires that we consistently learn and constantly search through his Word. The Lord asks that we keep verses near us, teach them to children, talk about them wherever we are, and think of them every waking moment.

Then his Word will be hidden in our heart and mind.

Fix these words of mine in your hearts and minds; tie them as symbols on your hands and bind them on your foreheads. Teach them to your children, talking about them when you sit at home and when you walk along the road, when you lie down and when you get up.

DEUTERONOMY 11:18-19, NIV

GOAL! *Write down a special verse on a separate piece of paper. Fold the paper several times and keep it in your pocket as a reminder. Recite the verse each time you touch the paper until you memorize the words. Then begin with another passage. Praise God for fixing his Word in your heart and mind.*

03 DEC

Have no fear of
sudden disaster
or of the ruin
that overtakes
the wicked, for
the Lord will be
your confidence
and will keep
your foot from
being snared.

PROVERBS
3:25-26, NIV

FEW AMERICANS HAVE EXCELLED at alpine skiing.

But in 2001, Bode Miller's risky style brought the United States two long-over-due World Cup victories.

The 24-year-old Franconia, New Hampshire, native grew up admiring European skiers such as Michael von Gruenigen and Hermann Maier. Miller adapted their styles, taking chances and using speed to overcome mistakes.

At the event in Val d'Isère, France, Miller stood third in the giant slalom with a time of 1:14.40. Going for broke on his second run, Miller lost control for an instant and went down on his hip as he attacked the icy course. Somehow he managed to prevent a disastrous spill and regrouped to charge down the mountain in a time of 1:21.62—the fastest of any second attempt. His combined time of 2:36.02 edged out France's Frederic Covili by .02 seconds and brought the United States its first giant slalom gold medal since Phil Mahre's at Furano, Japan, in March 1983.

The following day in Italy, Miller captured his second World Cup gold. The American led the slalom after both runs, and his combined time of 1:36.01 bettered Italy's Giorgio Rocca by a half second. His triumph marked the first World Cup slalom victory by a U.S. male since Steve Mahre's (Phil's twin) win at St. Anton, Austria, in 1983.

EXTRA POINT < < < < < < < < < < < < < < < < < < <

Bode Miller's chancy ski style also paid off in the 2002 Olympics. He skied to two silver medals, one in the giant slalom and one in the combined. Without his willingness to ski fearlessly, Miller would have always remained back in the pack.

The Bible talks about living without fear. Just like Miller pushed the edge with his skiing, God wants us to push ourselves and break out of our comfort zones. If we do this, God promises to be with us and help us.

GOAL! *Do something risky for the Lord. Some suggestions: Invite a friend to church who doesn't usually go, share about Jesus with someone who doesn't know him, participate in a ministry you've never done before like tutoring or feeding the homeless, or sign up for a mission trip. Ask God to help you live without fear.*

WHEN TWO HOT SCORERS go one-on-one, a shoot-out can occur. During the 2000 NBA basketball season, the Los Angeles Lakers' Kobe Bryant and the Golden State Warriors' Antawn Jamison matched shooting sprees.

The Lakers visited Golden State in Oakland. In his previous game, Jamison had totaled 51 points against the Seattle Supersonics, and Los Angeles was determined not to allow a repeat.

But Jamison's hot hand continued, hitting 8-of-12 shots in the first half as the Warriors took a 63–57 lead. Bryant answered with 17 third-quarter points to key a 21–6 run and put the Lakers in front 92–82. Trailing 104–95, Golden State closed with a 12–3 burst, leaving the game knotted 107–107 at the end of regulation.

With six seconds left in overtime and Los Angeles trailing 124–122, Horace Grant missed a layup, and Jamison ripped the rebound away from Bryant. Golden State's Bob Sura drew a foul and hit a single free throw. Bryant had a final opportunity, but his long three-pointer fell short as the Warriors won 125–122.

EXTRA < < < < < < < < < < < < < < < < < < < <
POINT Bryant and Jamison went basket for basket in overtime with Bryant scoring 12 of the Lakers' 15 points, and Jamison hitting 8 of the Warriors' 18. The duo each finished with 51 points, the first time opposing players totaled over 50 points each since December 14, 1962. In that Warrior-Laker matchup, Wilt Chamberlain netted 63 for Golden State and Elgin Baylor scored 50 for Los Angeles.

With the five-minute overtime added to the 48-minute game, the teams played a total of 53 minutes. A total of 51 points averages to nearly one point a minute. Bryant and Jamison both worked every moment of the game to try to earn their team a victory.

In athletics, we play to win. A good record means success. In our Christian life we also want to strive for victory, but winning means having a good name in God's eyes. When we win God's favor, then we're truly successful.

GOAL! *How do you think you can win God's favor? Write down some ideas.*

_____

_____

Read Proverbs 3:1-4. Ask God to help you follow his plan to win a good name.

Then you will win favor and a good name in the sight of God and man.
PROVERBS 3:4, NIV

05 DEC

WHAT DO YOU GET when you cross cycling and skiing?

No, this isn't a joke. The answer is *skibob*. This sport requires just a few things. First, you need a tight-fitting aerodynamic suit. Next, slip on a futuristic, slick helmet. Then find yourself a skibob, also known as a skibike. Strap on some miniskis, climb to the top of a mountain, straddle the bike, and let gravity take its course. Oh yeah, and you must also have nerves of steel and a need for speed . . . because in a matter of seconds you'll be zooming like a rocket.

How fast? you ask. Better let Romuald Bonvin answer that question. He's the best speedbike rider in the world. At the 2000 World Championships of Speed Skiing, Bonvin set a record by gliding 114 miles per hour. But after the race, he said that's only the beginning. Bonvin believes he can surpass 150 mph. In 2003, he took a step that way when he flew down a mountain at Les Arcs, France, at more than 125 mph—not bad for a guy who works as an account manager for a software company.

EXTRA POINT < < < < < < < < < < < < < < < < < < < < < Skibob, skibike, speedbike—whatever name you use—can't be called a traditional sport.

In a similar way, Jesus Christ can't be called a traditional leader. Many expected God's Son to crush the Romans and free his people. But Jesus combined passion and power. In the book of Matthew, Jesus' disciples broke a hand-washing tradition. When the Pharisees questioned Jesus about it, the Lord asked the religious leaders why they kept tradition rather than doing what was right.

During the holidays, most of our families enjoy established traditions— and we should. But sometimes we spend too much time and money on meaningless customs instead of celebrating God's Son's birth.

GOAL! *Sit down as a family to talk about your Christmas traditions. Which ones are worth keeping and which could be forgotten? Think about some new customs you want to try. The best way you can use your holiday time and money is to glorify him.*

THEN SOME
PHARISEES AND
TEACHERS OF
THE LAW CAME
TO JESUS FROM
JERUSALEM.
THEY ASKED HIM,
"WHY DON'T
YOUR FOLLOWERS
OBEY THE
UNWRITTEN
LAWS WHICH
HAVE BEEN
HANDED DOWN
TO US? THEY
DON'T WASH
THEIR HANDS
BEFORE THEY
EAT." JESUS
ANSWERED,
"AND WHY DO
YOU REFUSE
TO OBEY GOD'S
COMMAND SO
THAT YOU CAN
FOLLOW YOUR
OWN TEACHINGS?"
MATTHEW
15:1-3, NCV

HOCKEY GOALIES probably have the hardest job on the ice. Trying to keep a little puck out of a big net isn't easy, especially since NHL players can rifle the puck with precision. But years ago playing goalie was even harder.

In 1896, the Ontario Hockey Association stated: "The goalkeeper must not during play lie, sit, or kneel upon the ice; he may, when in goal, stop the puck with his hands, but shall not throw or hold it. He may wear pads, but must not wear a garment such as would give him undue assistance in keeping goal." In other words, the poor guy had no helmet, no glove, no leg pads, a regular stick, and had to stand the whole time. How times have changed.

Before the turn of the century, goalies started wearing cricket pads on their legs. Goalie gloves gained more padding in 1915—the same year two-sided goalie sticks were invented. Then in 1917, goalies were allowed to drop to the ice under National Hockey League rules. Goalie equipment continued to advance through the years as goalies began wearing masks in 1959. And today hockey goalies stay relatively safe from harm behind all their specialized padding—although blocking that puck can still be a pain.

> That is why you need to put on God's full armor. Then on the day of evil you will be able to stand strong. And when you have finished the whole fight, you will still be standing.
>
> EPHESIANS 6:13, NCV

EXTRA POINT < < < < < < < < < < < < < < < < < < < < Can you imagine trying to stop a puck traveling more than 100 mph without a helmet or padding? Early hockey goalies must have had a lot of guts . . . and perhaps little brains. They tried to do their job, but it was hard. Modern NHL goalies have an easier time defending the goal because of all their equipment.

As Christians, we should follow the goalies' example. We need to put on all the safety equipment we can to protect ourselves against Satan's schemes. In Ephesians, that protection is described as the armor of God. By equipping ourselves with the breastplate of righteousness, the shield of faith, and the helmet of salvation, we'll be better protected and able to play effectively for God.

GOAL! *Don't go through life without spiritual padding. Ask God to help equip you with the right protection to ward off the shots that you'll take on earth.*

WITH A STRANGE ARRAY of events that show off the power of the human body, strongman competitions can be amazing to watch. At the 2003 MHP X-treme Strongman Championship in Atlanta, the two-time defending world's strongest man, Mariusz Pudzianowski, muscled his way to the title.

The three-day competition began with the "Polish Power" taking an early lead by winning the Keg Load in 35.09 seconds. He took fourth in the Hercules Hold by gripping chains connected to two SUVs on ramps for 29.33 seconds. And he finished third in the Yoke Walk—an event where the athlete carries an 800-pound weight. Day two saw Pudzianowski all but wrap up the title. He earned fourth in the Truck Pull but took first in the Axle Press (by benching the 300-pound truck axle nine times), Conan's Wheel (which involves dragging a weighted cage in a circle), and the Medley (an event where athletes walk a distance with two heavy cans in their hands, push a weighted sled across the floor, and flip over a Ford Escort station wagon).

On the final day, the 29-year-old muscleman took fourth in a platform squat contest, first in the Tire Flip (with an 800-pound tire), and second in the Stones of Strength—which requires a competitor to lift stones of 265, 300, 330, 360, and 380 pounds onto 54-inch platforms.

EXTRA < < < < < < < < < < < < < < < < < < < <
POINT Mariusz Pudzianowski has dominated recent strongman competitions. Standing 6-foot-1-inch and weighing 288 pounds of pure muscle, Pudzianowski proves time after time that he has the speed and explosiveness to stay at the top.

While Pudzianowski's rock-hard body is impressive, only one person deserves to be called the *Rock*—and that's God. In the book of Samuel, David writes that God is the rock and the source of his strength. Pudzianowski may be able to stack some heavy stones in less than 30 seconds, but with God's power David killed a lion with his bare hands, defeated a giant, and became king of a great nation . . . and he didn't even go to the gym!

GOAL! *Do you rely on your muscles for strength? A strong body certainly helps in athletics. But remember that God is the source of true power.*

For who is God, except the Lord? And who is a rock, except our God? God is my strength and power, and He makes my way perfect.

2 SAMUEL 22:32-33, NKJV

08 DEC

God blesses you
who are hated
and excluded
and mocked
and cursed
because you
are identified
with me, the
Son of Man.
When that
happens,
rejoice! Yes,
leap for joy!
For a great
reward awaits
you in heaven.

LUKE 6:22-23

SPORTSWRITERS TABBED wide receiver R. C. Owens "Alley Oop" because of his leaping catches. But in 1962, Owens demonstrated his jumping ability also worked on defense.

For years, the 6-foot-3-inch athlete attempted to convince the San Francisco 49ers coaches he could block field goals using a unique method. Owens would stand beneath the goalpost, time his leap, and bat the ball aside like a basketball player blocking a shot. However, San Francisco's staff never permitted him to try his idea in a game.

Following a trade to the Baltimore Colts, Owens earned the opportunity to put his plan into practice. During the first quarter in a game against the Washington Redskins at Baltimore's Memorial Stadium, Bobby Khayat attempted a 43-yard field goal. Sensing the proper moment, Colts coach Weeb Ewbank stationed Owens under the goalposts. As Khayat's kick tapered downward, Owens eyed the ball, leaped above the ten-foot crossbar, and swatted the ball to the ground. Everyone sat in stunned disbelief.

The Colts went on to win the game 34–21 as Johnny Unitas completed a personal best 25-of-36 passes for 367 yards in the contest.

EXTRA POINT < < < < < < < < < < < < < < < < < < < < After the San Francisco coaches rejected R. C. Owens's field-goal–blocking idea, Alley Oop didn't give up and made his leaping pay off. Colts coach Weeb Ewbank gave the receiver an opportunity to succeed—and he did. And after his historic block, R. C. Owens leapt in celebration.

Like Owens, many of us find our ideas rejected. Some people may even poke fun at us. Jesus Christ told his followers to expect rejection, exclusion, and insults for their faith. But one day they would leap for joy.

Sometimes we're rejected, excluded, and insulted for our faith too. When that happens, we need to remember our reward will be in heaven if not on earth.

GOAL! *Think about what Christ did for you. Doesn't it make you want to leap and praise him? Remember to keep your eyes focused on him this Christmas season.*

EVEN GREAT TEAMS require rest to perform their best. In the 1998 NCAA women's soccer final, a weary University of North Carolina squad couldn't contain a well-rested opponent.

The Tar Heels faced the University of Florida Gators less than 48 hours after playing a four-overtime, 149-minute semifinal match against the University of Portland. The 1–0 decision gave UNC the opportunity to capture its third straight and 16th overall national women's soccer championship.

But the Gators scored early and played great defense. Florida's Danielle Fotopoulos broke toward the top of the North Carolina box and drew a foul from Lindsay Stoecker. On the ensuing free kick, the striker cleared UNC's defensive wall. The ball buzzed over the outstretched hands of goalie Siri Mullinix, hit the crossbar, and dropped into the net for a 1–0 Gators lead.

Two tremendous saves by Florida goalie Meredith Flaherty, a transfer from Clemson, preserved the shutout. Late in the first half, North Carolina's Lorrie Fair fired an 8-foot shot toward the net that Flaherty stopped with a two-handed save. In the closing minutes before halftime, Anne Remy booted an 18-footer that glanced off the shoulder of Florida's Erin Gilhart and caromed toward the upper left corner of the goal. But Flaherty dove and tipped the ball out-of-bounds. The Gators won the national championship 1–0 over an exhausted UNC squad.

EXTRA POINT < < < < < < < < < < < < < < < < < < < < < Even college students like the Tar Heels soccer stars need rest. Participating in lengthy, stress-filled games saps energy. Without adequate sleep and recovery time, players often don't play to their full potential. When that happens, winning becomes difficult or even impossible.

God created our body to refresh itself. Nutritious food such as fresh fruits and vegetables help. Drinking water rather than soda or caffeine is always a good idea. Exercising works out stress, and sleep restores energy.

Taking care of ourselves as our heavenly Father desires helps us win in athletics and in life.

GOAL! *A lack of sleep results in memory lapses, attention deficits, depressed moods, slowed reactions, and decreased motivation. Sleeping eight to nine hours a night is about right. Keep a record of your sleep for a week. Are you getting enough? Thank God for rest and rejuvenation.*

Even youths will become exhausted, and young men will give up.
ISAIAH 40:30

10 DEC

Pride leads to disgrace, but with humility comes wisdom.

PROVERBS 11:2

IN A PREGAME PRESS CONFERENCE in 1977, New Orleans Saints quarterback Archie Manning remarked that a loss to the winless Tampa Bay Buccaneers would be a disgrace. After their Sunday encounter, Manning's words rang true.

Since their formation the previous year, the Buccaneers had lost every single game in the team's history. Twelve weeks into their second season, Tampa Bay rode an NFL record 26-game losing streak.

But playing on the Saints' home turf at the Superdome, the Bucs struck early with two Dave Green field goals. Tampa Bay increased the lead to 13–0 before halftime when quarterback Gary Huff hit Morris Owens with a five-yard touchdown pass.

In the second half, the Buccaneers defense took out almost two years of frustration on the Saints. Mike Washington put Tampa Bay in front 20–0 with a 45-yard interception return for a touchdown in the third quarter. Richard Wood followed Washington's example by returning a second pass ten yards for a touchdown and a 26–0 lead.

New Orleans managed two touchdowns in the fourth quarter, a 2-yard run by Manning and an 11-yard Manning-to-John Gilliam pass. As the game wound down, Greg Johnson put the exclamation mark on the Bucs' first victory by catching a deflected Manning aerial in the end zone for six points. In all, the Saints threw six interceptions with three returned for touchdowns, which tied the NFL record.

EXTRA POINT < < < < < < < < < < < < < < < < < < < < < In the 12 games prior to the 33–14 win over the Saints that season, Tampa Bay had scored only 53 points—23 of those in its game against Seattle.

How did New Orleans allow a winless Tampa Bay squad to soundly defeat it? Some coaches might suggest overconfidence on the part of the Saints. New Orleans may have simply looked at the winless expansion team from Tampa Bay as an easy opponent.

While God wants us to feel positive about ourselves, excessive pride leads to disgrace. Being arrogant isn't a good trait. But humility brings realistic wisdom that allows us to build on our strengths and overcome our weaknesses.

GOAL! *Draw a line down the middle of a piece of paper. Label one column "Strengths" and the other one "Weaknesses." Make a realistic list of each. Ask God to help you maximize your strengths and minimize your weaknesses.*

STEEP. NASTY. ICY. BIG. BURLY.

Snowboarders often display a unique vocabulary in describing the superpipes where they perform amazing stunts. And at the 2002 Mountain Dew Pro Nationals in Breckenridge, Colorado, the winners of the men's and women's divisions both showed great respect for one of the toughest pipes in the world.

Norwegian Kjersti Oestgaard Buaas put together an awesome initial run to score 91.3 points. And it was a good thing she did, because in her third run, Buaas took a gnarly spill and smacked her head on the ice. But before being carted away to the emergency room, Buaas's huge frontside 540 melon grab and a massive air-to-fakey earned her the gold. France's Dorian Vidal tallied in the low 80s for second, while Anne Molin Kongsgaard of the United States finished third.

On the men's side, it was a clean sweep for the United States. Luke Wynen nailed his first run to score 88.3 points and hold on to first. Steve Fisher earned 88 points, and judges gave Rob Kingwell 87.8 to round out the top three. Wynen, who scored big with a McTwist indy grab, frontside cork 720 melon grab, and cab 540 stalefish, crashed on his final run but wasn't hurt.

EXTRA POINT

‹ ‹

After winning his superpipe gold, Luke Wynen said the huge pipe had worried him all week. His goal was to just land on his feet—instead of on his back or head.

Staying on your feet is a good idea in life, too. Sure, we all mess up and fall. But God can help keep us safe and standing tall. The Bible says God can make us pure and new, without any wrong in us. That means he cleans us up when we make mistakes. When we ask his forgiveness through Jesus Christ, God saves us from our sins and helps us stand before him like gold-medal winners.

GOAL!

Next time you snowboard, count how many times you fall. Multiply that number by a thousand and that's probably not even close to how many times you'll sin in your life. Thank God for his saving power that makes a Christian clean before him.

God is strong and can help you not to fall. He can bring you before his glory without any wrong in you and can give you great joy. He is the only God, the One who saves us. To him be glory, greatness, power, and authority through Jesus Christ our Lord for all time past, now, and forever. Amen.

JUDE 1:24-25, NCV

12 DEC

Jesus said,

"Don't let your

hearts be

troubled. Trust

in God, and

trust in me."

JOHN 14:1, NCV

AT FIRST GLANCE, curling might not look like a sport, yet it made quite an impression at the 2002 Winter Olympics in Salt Lake City.

Never heard of curling? That's okay. It's sort of like shuffleboard played on ice—except for the fact that curling's a team sport and shuffleboard is an individual endeavor. The key pieces of equipment in curling are a large, heavy object and brooms. That's right, *brooms*. One player skids the heavy object, called a stone, along the ice and lets it go toward the target. Then two athletes with brooms madly sweep in front of the stone . . . looking sort of like street cleaners stuck on fast-forward. But all this sweeping has a purpose: It speeds up, turns, and helps maneuver the stone toward its goal.

Enough history. At the 2002 Games, Canada was heavily favored to win the gold with skipper Kevin Martin at the helm. Martin earned his way to Salt Lake City by getting through the toughest qualification in the world. However, he entered the Games without ever winning a world-level event.

And that proved to be the case again. In the finals, Martin came up just short of Norway's Pal Trulsen. Martin had a chance to lead his team to victory with the final stone, but he threw it too hard and it knocked the Norwegian stone into the scoring circle and skidded away. Trulsen and his Norwegian teammates won 6–5 in a huge upset.

EXTRA POINT < < < < < < < < < < < < < < < < < < < < < <

Kevin Martin experienced great pressure in the curling finals. Pal Trulsen and his teammates weren't stressed at all. With the weight of his country on his shoulders, Martin made a key mistake with his last stone. He let it go with too much speed and his teammates couldn't slow it down.

A lot of times in life we want to slow down. The pressures mount up and we wonder how to cope. This time of year can be especially stressful with the holidays, concerts, family get-togethers, and school tests. But Jesus tells us not to be troubled.

GOAL! *When you start feeling like you're going to burst, turn to God. Ask for his calming presence to help you. By trusting in him, you can make it through the most stressful times you face.*

ASK ANY MOUNTAIN CLIMBER why he ascends the highest peaks, and you may get the answer, "Because it's there." But ask Todd Huston why he climbs mountains and he'd probably say, "Because I wanted to prove that with hard work and God's help, you can overcome any challenge."

When Todd was 14, climbing mountains was the furthest thing from his mind. He enjoyed football and waterskiing. But on a family vacation, his legs got caught in the propeller of a motorboat. Doctors initially saved his legs, but several years later his right leg had to be amputated below the knee. After graduating from college and getting a job in Los Angeles, Todd heard about the 50 Peaks Project—a group that was looking for a leg amputee to join its team in trying to break the record for climbing the 50 highest peaks in the nation—one in each state. Todd didn't think he was capable of the feat, but he trusted God and sent in his application. He was accepted and started training for the climb. But nothing could have prepared him for the grueling schedule. While some states, like Kansas, didn't pose much of a challenge, hiking up Mt. McKinley in Alaska pushed him to the limit. He dragged himself to the top of the 20,320-foot peak and knew the hardest part was behind him.

After conquering a few more mountains, Todd found himself standing on top of Hawaii's Mauna Kea—the final peak—in a record time of 66 days, 22 hours, and 47 minutes.

EXTRA POINT < < < < < < < < < < < < < < < < < < < Climbing the 50 highest points in each state wouldn't be easy with two legs . . . let alone one. But Todd Huston inspired others and showed them that anything is possible. His determination shone from the mountaintops.

God wants us to shine from the high places, too. Jesus Christ said we are a light to the world and that we should go to the high places so our light can be seen by other people.

You are the light that gives light to the world. A city that is built on a hill cannot be hidden. And people don't hide a light under a bowl. They put it on a lampstand so the light shines for all the people in the house.

MATTHEW 5:14-15, NCV

GOAL! *Don't hide your faith. Be bold for Jesus Christ. Ask God to help your light shine at home, church, school, and anywhere else you go.*

14 DEC

How I rejoice in
God my Savior!

LUKE 1:47

SELDOM CAN AN UNDERSIZED, undermanned squad defeat the nation's No. 1 college basketball team. But in 1999, the Xavier University Musketeers upset the Cincinnati Bearcats to set off a huge celebration.

Xavier hosted the game as the visitors struck quickly for a 5–0 lead. Then senior forward Darnell Williams keyed a 19–8 run for the Musketeers with a dunk, a three-pointer, and five free throws.

Relying on zone defense, foul shots, and daring tosses, Xavier kept the Bearcats off balance. With 13 seconds remaining and the game tied 62–62, Xavier's Lloyd Price stole the ball. Price called a time-out, and Kevin Frey hit a driving bank shot on the inbounds play. Four seconds later, Frey nailed two foul shots, upping the lead to 66–62.

Kenyon Martin scored inside for Cincinnati, but Price was fouled and went to the line with 3.3 seconds left. Although he missed both attempts, Alvin Brown slapped the rebound back to Price, who threw the ball toward the basket at the buzzer. Hundreds of Musketeers fans swarmed the court, rubbing blue body paint onto the players to celebrate the 66–64 victory.

EXTRA POINT < < < < < < < < < < < < < < < < < < < < Winning always brings celebration. Upsetting a No. 1-ranked crosstown rival moved the rejoicing to all-out jubilation. The cheering, singing, and shouting, combined with signs and body paint, turned the scene into a Musketeer-blue festival.

The Christmas holidays are a time of celebration too. Mary rejoiced when she knew she would give birth to God's Son. And we follow her example by singing, playing instruments, and praising God for his amazing gift of Jesus. We decorate, buy gifts, bake goodies, and listen to carols on the radio and in the shopping mall to get in the Christmas spirit.

But many who celebrate the season don't understand the reason. God wants us to rejoice, but he also wants us to tell others why.

GOAL! *Do you know a person or a family who doesn't know the true meaning of Christmas? Perhaps they've moved from another country or follow a different religion. Share the truth of Jesus' birth with them. Ask God to help you.*

ANGELS HAVE APPEARED since the beginning of creation. But in 1961, angels made their first appearance in American League outfields.

Major League Baseball reached southern California following the 1957 season when Walter O'Malley moved the National League's Dodgers from Brooklyn to Los Angeles. After averaging more than 2 million fans for three years, American League owners felt the need to establish their presence in the area too.

AL owners awarded a franchise to Los Angeles during the 1960 winter meetings. Former motion-picture star and ardent baseball fan Gene Autry headed the ownership group for the new club. To christen the new organization, Autry selected the name "Angels," which served a twofold purpose. The original Los Angeles Angels had been a charter franchise of the Pacific Coast League. And since *los angeles* translates from Spanish into English as "the angels," many refer to Los Angeles as "the city of angels."

The Angels finished the 1961 season with a 70–91 record—the best winning percentage of any expansion team in major league history. Years later, the Angels changed their name to the Anaheim Angels. And in 2002, the Angels won their first World Series title.

EXTRA POINT

‹ Joseph must have felt that he lived in a "city of angels" when he received God's word from a heavenly messenger. The young man surely knew Isaiah's prophecy about the Messiah's birth. Joseph could feel secure with his young wife. He would be Jesus' earthly father. Imagine his excitement, his awe, his honor!

The angel explained that God would send Jesus to save people from their sin. And that includes you.

GOAL! *Search the Bible for verses that include the word angels. (You might want to use a concordance or Bible computer program.) You'll find at least 100 references in most translations. Note how God uses the heavenly beings in the Bible and how he can use angels today. Praise the Lord for the message the angel gave Joseph.*

> But after he had considered this, an angel of the Lord appeared to him in a dream and said, "Joseph son of David, do not be afraid to take Mary home as your wife, because what is conceived in her is from the Holy Spirit. She will give birth to a son, and you are to give him the name Jesus, because he will save his people from their sins."
>
> MATTHEW 1:20-21, NIV

16 DEC

THE PERSON WHO INVENTED the elevator had the right idea. Walk into a box; press a button; watch the doors close. And when they re-open, you see you've been magically transported to another floor. It's a beautiful thing—but there's not much sport in it.

Running up stairs may not seem like much of a sport either. But sprinting up 86 flights of stairs at the Empire State Building certainly takes a lot of athletic ability. Every year runners gather at this New York City landmark to race to the top. And from 1999 to 2003, Paul Crake won five straight times.

Legs pumping, heart pounding, lungs burning, Crake cranked his way up 86 floors in 9 minutes and 53 seconds in his 2000 victory. With that win, he became the first person to break ten minutes in the competition. Since that time, he's broken his old record twice. His 2003 trek to the top took just 9 minutes and 33 seconds—his fastest time ever. Of course, race officials still beat him to the top . . . taking the elevator.

EXTRA POINT

< < < < < < < < < < < < < < < < < < < <

The race up the Empire State Building began in 1977. While running up 86 flights of stairs may not sound too difficult, it actually involves climbing up 1,576 stairs to make it to the top. As one of the world's best tower runners, Paul Crake pushes through the pain and sprints up the tight hallways, which are filled with stagnant air.

Some people think that once they accept Christ their life will become one long walk through a flowery field. But God never promised that. In fact, the apostle Peter said the opposite. He explained that Christ's followers shouldn't be surprised when they suffer. Sometimes life can feel like a never-ending stairway—it's tiring, hard to breathe, and difficult. At those times, we need to follow Crake's example of climbing toward the goal and keeping our eyes focused upward!

My friends, do not be surprised at the terrible trouble which now comes to test you. Do not think that something strange is happening to you. But be happy that you are sharing in Christ's sufferings so that you will be happy and full of joy when Christ comes again in glory.

1 PETER 4:12-13, NCV

GOAL! *What would you choose: a flat walk or an uphill climb? You might naturally like to take the easy way. When life becomes difficult, remember Jesus' suffering and thank him for helping you reach the top.*

HOURS AFTER HIGH SCHOOL graduation, Dorothy "Dot" Richardson flew from her Orlando, Florida, home to Colorado Springs, Colorado, to try out for the USA softball squad. The 17-year-old's surprise selection brought Richardson honor but meant hard work and years of travel.

After a summer of international competition, Richardson enrolled at Western Illinois University but later transferred to the University of California at Los Angeles. After receiving her degree in kinesiology from UCLA, she attended the University of Louisville Medical School. California became her home once again during an orthopedic surgical residency in Los Angeles.

As a collegiate shortstop, medical school student, and surgical resident, the 1996 and 2000 gold-medal Olympian trekked around the world to compete. Studies, softball, and medicine left Doctor Dot little time for family and friends. But every year for the holidays, Dot flew to her parents' Orlando home, usually arriving on Christmas Eve.

Richardson often used her holidays to squeeze in projects. One year, the All-American rallied her family to film two instructional softball videos at her first playing field. She also established the tradition of shopping on Christmas Eve for her father, mother, sisters, brothers, and grandparents. Years added ten nieces and nephews to the growing list. But whatever she purchased, Richardson remembered that thought—not cost—provided the true value of the gifts.

> And this is how you will recognize him: You will find a baby lying in a manger, wrapped snugly in strips of cloth!
>
> LUKE 2:12

EXTRA POINT

< < < < < < < < < < < < < < < < < < < <

Though short, the hours spent with family celebrating Christ's birth revived and sustained the busy physician-athlete. One holiday she and her grandfather found themselves riding alone together. Her beloved grandpa didn't look well and had difficulty breathing. In the car, he shared about his wonderful life and his faith in God. Dot felt surrounded by the glow of Christmas and the glow of his love.

Her grandfather died a few weeks later, but Dot knew they'd see each other once again in heaven. She believed that truth because of Jesus, the gift God gave at Christmastime. And that's what God wants us to celebrate this holiday season: the gift of salvation through his Son.

GOAL! *Is your Christmas shopping done? The best presents are more about meaning than money. Your Christmas celebration will be blessed the most as you focus on the baby born in a manger.*

18 DEC

And the child grew and became strong; he was filled with wisdom, and the grace of God was upon him.

LUKE 2:40, NIV

KURT WARNER BURST onto the NFL scene in a blaze of glory. In 1999, an injury to the St. Louis Rams starting quarterback gave Warner the chance to play. And he made the most of the opportunity by leading the Rams to a Super Bowl victory.

Warner's 4,353 passing yards for 41 touchdowns and 13 interceptions earned him the NFL's Most Valuable Player award that season. He also passed for a Super Bowl record 414 yards to claim MVP honors in football's biggest game.

But as fans in St. Louis know, Warner's an MVP off the field as well. His First Things First Foundation helps children and families.

Through the FUNdamental ticket program, Kurt provides 20 tickets to every Rams home game for those involved with Sunshine Ministries. The kids and parents attend a church service with Kurt and his wife, Brenda, on the Friday night before the game. Warner has also teamed up with Homes for the Holidays to help single mothers purchase houses. First Things First joins with local organizations and the St. Louis Rams for a winter coat drive called Warner's Warm-up. Each year Rams fans donate an average of 10,000 coats and $10,000, which is distributed to homeless shelters, schools, and social service centers. And through First Things First Scholars, Kurt awards $4,000 scholarships to high school graduates who are positively influencing others and want to continue their education.

EXTRA POINT < < < < < < < < < < < < < < < < < < < < Kurt knows he's blessed to play in the NFL. He gives God the glory for his skills and achievements every chance he gets. And he gives back to society as a demonstration of God's love. By helping the less fortunate, Kurt's doing exactly what God commands. He wants children to grow up with hope.

In the Bible, Luke wrote that Jesus grew in strength, wisdom, and grace. Jesus' family wasn't wealthy. He didn't live a life of privilege. God is concerned about our material needs, but that's not his main desire. He wants us to grow like Jesus—in strength and wisdom and grace.

GOAL! *Something that might be meaningful this season would be to give Christmas gifts to a child who needs your help. Consider Angel Tree, a ministry that provides presents for children whose parents are in jail. Or you could send a gift-filled shoe box to a needy child through Operation Christmas Child. Ask God to help the child grow in strength and wisdom and grace.*

CLIMBING TO THE TOP of Mt. Everest—the world's highest mountain—is one of the most difficult challenges on the planet. Not only is oxygen hard to come by, but high winds, flash storms, and falling ice often claim the life of climbers trying to make it to the 29,035-foot summit.

But in 2000, Slovenian mountaineer Davo Karnicar not only climbed to the peak of Mt. Everest, but once he got there he strapped on a pair of skis and carved his way down to base camp at 17,550 feet. While it took him days to climb to the summit with partner Franc Oderlap and Sherpas Ang Dorjee and Passang Tenzing, Karnicar skied the more than two vertical miles in just five hours.

Karnicar started his historic ascent at 10:30 p.m. With a beautiful full moon and clear skies, Karnicar and Oderlap made an uneventful climb to the summit. Views from the top were spectacular, but temperatures were freezing . . . as always. After taking photographs, preparing his equipment, and warming up, Karnicar snapped on his skis and started down. Treacherous conditions and the threat of avalanches kept Karnicar on his toes. But the experienced skier stayed focused and made it safely to an exuberant group at base camp.

> The wise people will shine like the brightness of the sky. Those who teach others to live right will shine like stars forever and ever.
>
> DANIEL 12:3, NCV

EXTRA POINT < < < < < < < < < < < < < < < < < < < < < < For years Davo Karnicar had dreamed of skiing down the world's tallest mountain. When a snowstorm halted his efforts in 1996, he regrouped, replanned, and climbed for the stars four years later. His 2000 ascent went perfectly as he skied into the record books—a shining example of what perseverance can accomplish.

God wants his followers to shine as examples to the world too. The prophet Daniel wrote that when we teach others how to live according to God's commands, we will shine like stars. Mt. Everest certainly towers in the sky, but the stars greatly surpass it by shining millions of miles away for all to see.

GOAL! *Imagine what it was like for Davo Karnicar to accomplish his dream. You can commit to God to make it one of your dreams to teach others about him. You can do it every day with your words and actions. God wants to help you shine for him.*

> I have seen the
> Savior you have
> given to all
> people. He is a
> light to reveal
> God to the
> nations, and he
> is the glory of
> your people
> Israel!
>
> LUKE 2:30-32

FEW SPORTS THRILL AUDIENCES like the bike vert competition. And in the 2003 Gravity Games, Dave Mirra proved once again that he can hit the big run when it counts.

Competing on the same ramp where he lost to Simon Tabron in the 2002 games, Mirra showed from the start that he was going for the gold. During his first run, Mirra fell after he attempted a tailwhip 540 followed by an opposite one footed X up flair over the channel. Mirra thrives on pushing the envelope—as well as his fellow competitors—by throwing the toughest tricks in seemingly impossible combinations.

Needing a huge score on his second run, Mirra attacked the ramp with total abandon. Feeding off the energy of the gigantic crowd and decked out on an old-school bike with graphics identical to those on the first freestyle BMX bike, Mirra hit every move flawlessly. His score of 95 locked up first place and $23,000 in prize money.

Tabron looked to challenge Mirra as he completed his 50th 900 in the competition but had to settle for third with 92.2 points. Kevin Robinson's 92.2 points were good enough for second place (he won in a tiebreaker against Tabron because he had a higher second-run score).

EXTRA POINT < < < < < < < < < < < < < < < < < < < < < With his high-flying aerials, mind-blowing spins, and bone-jarring flips, Dave Mirra has earned his nickname of "Miracle Boy." For years he dominated the bike vert and street bike competitions. And while Mirra has certainly performed and invented some miraculous stunts, he isn't qualified to even lube the chain of Jesus Christ, who was truly miraculous.

Jesus' birth was a real miracle. Not only was he born to a virgin, but his birth and life fulfilled numerous other Old Testament prophecies. Plus, he performed miracle after miracle as he healed the sick, walked on water, and taught about God. When Simeon saw Jesus, he knew immediately that he was looking at the Savior.

GOAL! *Next time you're marveling at your favorite athlete's endeavors, take a few moments to remember the real Miracle Child. Then thank God for sending his Son to earth.*

GREAT BRITAIN ISN'T KNOWN as a Winter Olympics powerhouse. Heading into the 2002 Games in Salt Lake City, the Brits hadn't brought home a gold medal in the Winter Games for 18 years. But the all-Scottish women's curling team ended that streak. By squeaking out a victory over Switzerland in the finals, Great Britain brought home an unlikely gold.

It's not that the Scottish team didn't know anything about curling—which looks like part shuffleboard and part horseshoes played on the ice. Curling is actually one of the core sports in the Scottish Institute of Sport. But experts didn't view the squad of Rhona Martin, Debbie Knox, Fiona MacDonald, Janice Rankin, and Margaret Morton as one of the favorites.

Martin skippered the team through two tight playoff victories in the qualifying round. Then in the semifinals, the Brits beat pre-Games favorite Canada to set up a match against Switzerland. Great Britain built a 3–1 edge in the finals before the Swiss fought back to tie things at 3–3. It appeared as if Switzerland would win the gold when its stone rested in the scoring zone with the Brits having only one stone left. Martin made the most of the attempt as she and her teammates piloted the stone into the Swiss stone and knocked it away. Great Britain's stone remained closest to the center as it won 4–3.

> Faith means being sure of the things we hope for and knowing that something is real even if we do not see it.
> HEBREWS 11:1, NCV

EXTRA POINT

< < < < < < < < < < < < < < < < < < <

Numerous times during the Salt Lake City Games, Great Britain teetered on the brink of defeat. But each time Rhona Martin remained calm and helped her team claim victory. When asked how she managed to win gold, Martin said she just had faith that she could do it.

Faith is a key ingredient in our Christian life too. Without faith it's impossible for us to believe in Jesus Christ. Sure, there's historical knowledge that Jesus Christ walked the earth. But we must have faith that Jesus is God's Son who came to save us from our sins. Having faith in ourselves is important and can help us achieve things on earth, but having faith in Jesus has eternal rewards.

GOAL! *Look up the definition of faith in the dictionary and write it down.*

Praise God for faith to believe in him.

22 DEC

SAY WITH YOUR MOUTH,

"JESUS IS LORD."

BELIEVE IN YOUR HEART THAT GOD RAISED HIM FROM THE DEAD. THEN YOU WILL BE SAVED.

ROMANS 10:9, NIrV

WORLD-CLASS TABLE TENNIS hardly resembles the game played in basements around the globe. Featuring smashes barely visible to the naked eye, curling spin shots, and amazing defensive blocks, the World Table Tennis Championships pits the best players in head-to-head competition. At the 2003 event, Austria's Werner Schlager rode the momentum of a surprising quarterfinals comeback victory to win the men's title.

In the quarters, Schlager faced defending world champ Wang Liqin of China. The powerful Chinese player quickly dispatched Schlager 11–5 in the first game. In the second, Schlager mixed up his spins and shot selection to knot things with his 11–5 victory. Four games were needed for either player to advance, and the third match stayed close. With the score tied 8–8, Liqin erupted for three straight points to win 11–8. Liqin built a 7–1 lead in the fourth, but Schlager stormed back with a few backhand winners and tied things 10–10. But with 15,000 fans cheering Liqin's name, he claimed the game 15–13—one away from victory. Schlager showed some fight by winning the fifth game 11–9. In the sixth game, it appeared as if the defending champ would continue as his topspin forehand earned him a 10–6 edge over Schlager. One point away from defeat, Schlager nailed three amazing shots—including a topspin winner on top of Liqin's topspin. When Liqin blocked a shot into the net, Schlager earned a 13–11 win to set up a deciding seventh game—which Schlager claimed 11–5.

EXTRA POINT < < < < < < < < < < < < < < < < < < < < After coming back from the brink of defeat to beat the defending world champion, Werner Schlager rolled to the championship. He defeated Linghui Kong of China in the semifinals, and then he bested Korea's Joo Se Hyuk in the finals.

Nothing beats a comeback win. And there's never been a sweeter come-from-behind victory than when Jesus Christ triumphed over death. Satan thought he'd won when God's Son was nailed to a cross. But Jesus rose from the dead to defeat sin and Satan for all time!

GOAL! *Next time you think there's no way you can win, think about Jesus' amazing victory. This Christmas thank God's Son for coming to earth and dying so you could have everlasting life.*

23 DEC

She gave birth
to her first
child, a son.
She wrapped
him snugly in
strips of cloth
and laid him
in a manger,
because there
was no room
for them in the
village inn.

LUKE 2:7

CLINCHING A PLAYOFF SPOT excites every fan in an NFL

city. But in 2000, when the Indianapolis Colts were striving for a postseason berth, it caused problems for a local church.

Because the Colts' final game of the season was broadcast on national television, the kickoff time switched from 1:00 to 4:15 on Christmas Eve. The pastor of St. John the Evangelist Church protested. For many years, St. John, located across the street from the RCA Dome, had been holding Christmas Eve family mass at 5:30 p.m. Religious leaders considered canceling the service due to parking concerns.

The Colts needed a victory over the Minnesota Vikings coupled with a New York Jets loss to capture their second straight playoff berth. With the Jets starting three hours earlier, Indianapolis learned of New York's defeat shortly after its game began. Millions watched the game on television due to the playoff implications.

Since Minnesota had already wrapped up first place in the central division, victory meant little to the Vikings. The contest turned into a rout, and Indianapolis waltzed to a 31–10 win. Peyton Manning completed 25 of 36 passes for 283 yards and four touchdowns, setting a new club record with 33 for the year. Edgerrin James ran for 128 yards, capturing the NFL rushing title with 1,709.

EXTRA POINT < < < < < < < < < < < < < < < < < < < < < <

As it turned out, both the game and the church service went well for Indianapolis. A group of local business leaders stepped in and paid for 400 reserved parking places to ensure the estimated 1,000 parishioners would find room to park and attend Christmas Eve services at St. John. And there was still plenty of room for Colts fans.

On the first Christmas Eve, Mary and Joseph had trouble finding room. The Roman emperor called for a census requiring every man to return to his family's hometown. With all the people in Bethlehem, innkeepers had no place for the expectant couple. They were finally offered shelter in a stable. Mary gave birth, wrapped the baby in strips of cloth, and laid him in a manger.

GOAL! *Attend a Christmas Eve service. As you think about the Savior's birth, ask God to help you always keep room in your heart for Jesus.*

PRACTICE SQUAD PLAYERS on NFL teams earn little recognition or reward. But at Christmastime in 2001, Washington Redskins wide receiver Justin Skaggs received the greatest gift of his career.

After Skaggs played collegiate football at Evangel University in Springfield, Missouri, few expected the 6-foot-4-inch, 205-pound speedster to sign an NFL contract. The All-Heart of America Athletic Conference flanker and sprinter first opted for the Tulsa Talons of the Arena Football League. But Skaggs pursued his NFL dream and produced a videotape of highlights. Three NFL teams contacted him. Although the New York Giants and the Seattle Seahawks lost interest, the Redskins inked the former flanker on his 22nd birthday.

A strong preseason showing with three receptions for 57 yards and a 31-yard kickoff return ensured Skaggs a practice squad slot. Although he remained inactive, he practiced with the team, received a modest salary, and waited for the day he would become a full-fledged Redskin.

On Christmas Day, the former Crusader learned his dream had come true. Washington promoted him to the active roster, and Skaggs suited up for the final regular season contest.

EXTRA POINT < < < < < < < < < < < < < < < < < < < < < < What wonderful words for Justin Skaggs! After months of practice, the unlikely player's perseverance paid dividends. Justin's birthday gift was a pro contract. His Christmas gift was a Washington Redskins uniform.

In the Bible, some unlikely people received good news too. God's angel appeared at night to shepherds guarding their sheep out in the countryside. But the angel's birth announcement included other people too. The heavenly being's words echoed throughout the world and throughout time: "A Savior has been born to you; he is Christ the Lord."

GOAL! *Did your parents send birth announcements when you arrived? What did they look like? Imagine an angel announcing the birth of God's Son. Praise God for the good news of the Savior.*

And there were shepherds living out in the fields nearby, keeping watch over their flocks at night. An angel of the Lord appeared to them, and the glory of the Lord shone around them, and they were terrified. But the angel said to them, "Do not be afraid. I bring you good news of great joy that will be for all people. Today in the town of David a Savior has been born to you; he is Christ the Lord."

LUKE 2:8-11, NIV

25 DEC

You heard
their cries for
help and saved
them. They
put their trust
in you and
were never
disappointed.

PSALM 22:5

PROFESSIONAL FOOTBALL OFFICIALS usually maintain tight control of a game. But in 2000, confusion reigned at the conclusion of the Miami Dolphins contest against the New England Patriots.

New England, sporting a lackluster 5–10 record, hosted the Dolphins in the season finale. Trailing 24–17 late in the fourth quarter, Miami mounted an 11-play, 65-yard drive with Lamar Smith plunging over from the 1-yard line.

Two plays later, the Dolphins regained possession on a Zach Thomas interception. Jay Fiedler directed Miami from its own 24 to the New England 31, and Olindo Mare kicked a 49-yard field goal with 15 seconds left to play to put the Dolphins in front 27–24.

Just eight seconds remained when the Patriots took over on offense. Drew Bledsoe appeared to fumble, Miami recovered, the clock ran out, and both teams shook hands and retreated to their locker room. But after a long delay, referee Johnny Grier ruled Bledsoe's pass as an incompletion and ordered three seconds to be put back on the clock.

By then, most players had removed their equipment and showered, so coaches scrambled to place full teams on the field. Michael Bishop took the final New England snap and threw an incompletion to end the game. Fewer than 100 fans witnessed the final play more than 30 minutes after most thought the contest over.

EXTRA POINT ‹ ‹ ‹ ‹ ‹ ‹ ‹ ‹ ‹ ‹ ‹ ‹ ‹ ‹ ‹ ‹ ‹ ‹ ‹ Can you think of a stranger way to end a game? Players, coaches, and fans thought the contest was over. No one expected another play, but confused officials changed a call. At least 22 players returned to the field. And even though that last snap could have changed the winner, the pass amounted to nothing.

The day after Christmas often offers a letdown too. Trees seem bare without packages. Gifts don't sparkle as brightly out of the wrappings. We disappear to the mall to exchange presents or hit the sales. Or we think about the things we didn't get.

Our relationship with Jesus is never a letdown. He fulfills all our needs and helps us when we call.

GOAL! *Plan a special family activity to help others during the week after Christmas. Praise God that his Son never leaves us disappointed.*

LONG STRETCHES WITHOUT A TRIP into the post-season cause teams to thirst for victory. In 2000, the Arizona Cardinals overcame one of the NFL's longest playoff droughts.

You have given me the shield of your salvation; your help has made me great.

2 SAMUEL 22:36

In the regular-season finale, the Cardinals entertained the San Diego Chargers at Sun Devil Stadium before 71,670 fans—the fourth largest crowd in franchise history. An Arizona victory would ensure the team a playoff game against the Dallas Cowboys.

At the end of the third quarter, the Cardinals led 13–3. But a 26-yard John Carney field goal closed San Diego's gap to 13–6. With under two minutes remaining, Chargers quarterback Craig Whelihan marched his team from its own 32 to the Cardinal 30. Facing fourth-and-20 with 22 seconds on the clock, the game appeared virtually over, but Whelihan rolled right, fired the football between two defenders, and connected with Ryan Tidwell for a 30-yard touchdown pass that knotted the score at 13–13.

Carney kicked off with 16 seconds left to play, and Eric Metcalf ignited Cardinal hopes by returning the ball to San Diego's 44-yard line. Arizona quarterback Jake Plummer drilled a ten-yard pass to Frank Sanders, and the Cardinals called a time-out with three ticks to go.

Chris Jacke, who had been signed in early December to replace an injured Joe Nedney, lined up for a 52-yard field goal attempt. His boot sailed true, and the Cardinals won 16–13 to earn a playoff berth for the first time since 1982 . . . and only the second time since 1975.

EXTRA POINT < < < < < < < < < < < < < < < < < < < < < < Finally, a key victory earned the Cardinals a spot in the playoffs. They claimed a place among the NFL's great teams for the first time in 18 seasons.

In the Bible, King David experienced many victories. But he also knew the feeling of having to wait for success. He longed for victory. And when he was raised up as king, he knew who made him great. After being rescued time after time by God, David sang a song of praise to him in 2 Samuel. We can live by David's inspiring words today.

GOAL! *Read 2 Samuel 22. Notice the words David used to describe God. See how the Lord answered his cries for help and gave him victory. Praise God that he still gives us victory today.*

They passed on
to the people
all the truth
they received
from me.
They did not
lie or cheat;
they walked
with me, living
good and
righteous lives,
and they turned
many from
lives of sin.

MALACHI 2:6

A LOPSIDED HALFTIME SCORE often predicts the final outcome of a football game. But those who relied on the point difference at the break in the 2001 GMAC Bowl wound up mistaken.

After two quarters, the Marshall Thundering Herd trailed the East Carolina Pirates, 38–8. Several hundred fans left, and thousands more switched the channel, thinking the Pirates would win easily.

But Marshall scored four third quarter touchdowns, including two by its defense on 25-yard interception returns by Ralph Street and Terrence Tarpley. East Carolina countered with a 32-yard Kevin Miller field goal, and the third period ended with the Pirates in front 41–36.

In the final two minutes, East Carolina led 51–45 and recovered an onside kick. Marshall held and took over the ball on the 20-yard line with 50 seconds remaining. Herd quarterback Byron Leftwich tied the score on an 11-yard touchdown pass to Darius Watts, but Curtis Head missed the extra point to force overtime.

Both teams tallied touchdowns in the first extra period, but Marshall held East Carolina to a 37-yard field goal in the second. With the Thundering Herd on offense, Leftwich connected with Josh Davis on an 8-yard touchdown reception for a 64–61 come-from-behind victory. The 125-point total represented the highest scoring postseason contest since Texas Tech defeated Air Force 55–41 in the 1995 Copper Bowl.

EXTRA POINT < < < < < < < < < < < < < < < < < < < Imagine the surprise of those who left the game early or changed the channel. Most couldn't believe the score they heard on the news or read in the paper. Their halftime predictions proved false.

The prophet Malachi encouraged God's priests to stay away from falsehood. The Lord specifically pointed to Levi as a person who always spoke the truth.

As Christians, we're God's priests today. We should follow Levi's example and live honestly. We should always tell the truth as God leads us. By doing these things, we can help lead many people to Christ.

GOAL! *Have you been tempted to say what others want to hear rather than the truth? Ask God to help you always tell the truth.*

TODAY'S NFL PLAYOFFS pit the best teams from the AFC and the NFC in a battle for the Super Bowl championship. Many years it's impossible to predict which team will win it all. But early on, the NFC (then called the NFL) dominated the Super Bowl. NFC teams won the first two contests. Heading into Super Bowl III in the Miami, Florida, Orange Bowl, most agreed that the Baltimore Colts were a lock.

The NFC Colts had lost only once in 16 games all season and were 17-point favorites against the AFC's (known as the AFL) New York Jets. But somebody must have forgotten to tell that to Jets quarterback Joe Namath. On the Thursday before Super Bowl Sunday, Namath boldly guaranteed that the Jets would win the game.

Many football fans laughed at Namath's prediction, but the brash quarterback backed up his words with his actions. Leading a balanced Jets attack, Namath passed for ten first downs. New York also rushed for ten first downs as they kept the Colts' defense off balance. New York built up a 16–0 lead early in the fourth quarter. And after Johnny Unitas came off the bench to lead Baltimore to a late touchdown, the game ended 16–7 in favor of the Jets. For his part, Namath completed 17 of 28 passes for 206 yards and was named the Super Bowl Most Valuable Player.

Dear children, don't just talk about love. Put your love into action. Then it will truly be love.

1 JOHN 3:18, NIrV

EXTRA POINT < < < < < < < < < < < < < < < < < < < Modern-day athletes often run their mouth and guarantee victory. But when Joe Namath guaranteed victory in 1969, his boast shocked the sports world. And when he backed up his prediction with his actions on the field, Namath proved that his words meant something.

God wants our words to mean something as well. If we say one thing and do another, people lose respect for us. People judge you by your actions. St. Francis of Assisi said, "Preach the gospel at all times and when necessary use words." That means our actions speak louder than our words. And if we happen to open our mouth and say something, we need to make sure our actions back it up.

GOAL! *Do your actions reflect your words? If you're not sure, ask your parents or a close friend. Pray for God to help you walk your talk.*

29 DEC

He is the head of the body, which is the church. Everything comes from him. He is the first one who was raised from the dead. So in all things Jesus has first place.

COLOSSIANS 1:18, NCV

JUGGLING A SOCCER BALL takes supreme concentration and skill. Using all parts of your body (except your arms and hands) to keep the ball from touching the ground is a key skill in the most popular sport in the world.

But some people aren't satisfied with juggling a soccer ball. They're looking for a greater challenge. Sweden's Tomas Lundman is one of those athletes. He takes the phrase "Now that's using your head" to a new extreme.

According to Guinness World Records, Lundman holds the record for bouncing a tennis ball on his head. He set the mark at the Royal Tennis Hall in Stockholm, Sweden, at the end of December 2002. Eyes looking up, back arched, and feet wide, Lundman used only his head to constantly juggle a tennis ball for 60 minutes. While that sounds impressive—and nearly impossible—he beat Luis Silva's old record by only seven seconds.

EXTRA POINT < < < < < < < < < < < < < < < < < < < < < < The human head is amazing. Experts say the average head weighs about eight pounds. Inside the skull, the brain runs the entire body . . . and we don't even need to think about it! Not only is the human head a medical marvel, it also comes in handy in sports. Whether they're thinking through a situation or heading the ball to a teammate, athletes often use their head.

Nobody could argue that Tomas Lundman has a nifty noggin. His heading skills are world famous. The Bible also talks about a famous head: Jesus Christ. God's Son is the head of the church. Jesus laid down God's law while he was alive, demonstrated how to live for God, and died and rose from the dead so we could join him in heaven. Now that's *truly* using his head!

GOAL! *Write down some ways that Jesus being the head of the church is like your head being over your body.*

_____

_____

_____

Remember to use your spiritual head—Jesus Christ—as you make decisions in life.

FANS HEAD TO A FOOTBALL STADIUM expecting to see a game. But a thick blanket of fog made it difficult for everybody to see during the 1988 NFL divisional playoffs.

Despite fears of biting winds and single-digit temperatures, the Soldier Field thermometer read 32 degrees when the Chicago Bears hosted the Philadelphia Eagles. The Bears struck early on a Dennis McKinnon 64-yard touchdown reception. Chicago padded the margin on a 4-yard Neal Anderson touchdown run and a 46-yard Kevin Butler field goal. Meanwhile, the Eagles scored three first-half field goals.

Just before the intermission, the unusually warm weather created a thick fog rolling off Lake Michigan. Referee Jim Tunney and NFL executive director Don Weiss conferred and agreed the game should continue.

But fans and television viewers witnessed little of the second half. Sideline cameras showed grainy images, while overhead shots revealed a gray mess. Reporters and television announcers received information relayed from roaming sideline officials with walkie-talkies.

Due to the fog and a shoulder injury to quarterback Mike Tomczak, the Bears attempted only seven passes in the second half. Although Philadelphia reached Bears territory on 9 of 13 possessions, Chicago's defense limited the Eagles to Luis Zendejas's four field goals, and the Bears advanced with a 20–12 triumph.

EXTRA POINT
< < < < < < < < < < < < < < < < < < < < < Poor visibility created difficulty for both teams. Long passes were impossible. Coaches couldn't read offenses or defenses. Players only saw a small part of what occurred on the field.

The Bible says that we know only part of God's wonders. We view a blurry image like a reflection in an old, cracked mirror. But when we get to heaven, we'll see God clearly . . . just as clearly as God sees us now.

Now we see things imperfectly as in a poor mirror, but then we will see everything with perfect clarity. All that I know now is partial and incomplete, but then I will know everything completely, just as God knows me now.
1 CORINTHIANS 13:12

GOAL! *Why not make a New Year's resolution to reflect God's love to everyone this year? Write down any other resolutions you may have.*

_____

_____

_____

Thank God for glimpses of heaven on earth, and praise him that he offers the opportunity for everyone to see him clearly in heaven.

31 DEC

INDEX

INDEX

KATHY HILLMAN AND JOHN HILLMAN, along with their now-grown children, Marshall, Michael, and Holly, have spent most of their family life enjoying athletic events at the youth, high school, college, and professional levels. Working with students ages six through sixteen led the Hillmans to combine their love of sports with their devotion to God through the writing of *Devos for Sports Fans* as well as two previous books. The Hillmans are currently involved with both the collegiate world and the sports world and live in Waco, Texas.

JESSE FLOREA has worked with Focus on the Family for more than ten years, where he's served as an editor for the youth magazines *Breakaway, Clubhouse,* and *Clubhouse Jr.* In addition, he has covered sports in newspapers for more than nineteen years. He works with kids at church and wants to equip them with the skills to live an exciting life for Jesus Christ. He lives with his wife and two children in Colorado Springs.

areUthirsty.com

well . . . are you?

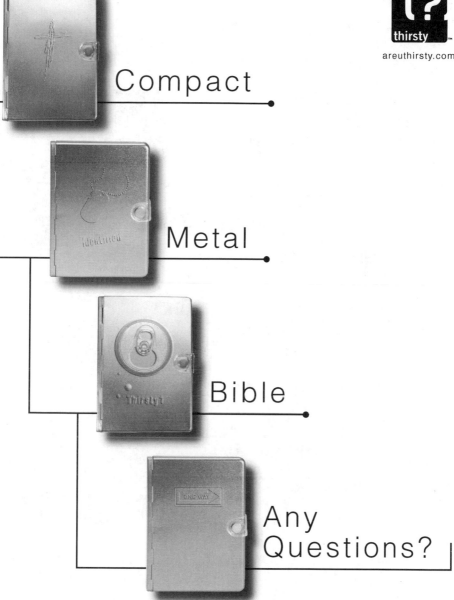

areuthirsty.com

Compact

Metal

Bible

Any Questions?

Available wherever Bibles are sold

Are you a Lord of the Rings junkie?

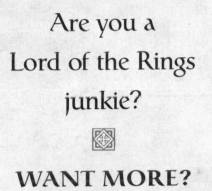

WANT MORE?

Check out *Walking with Frodo*...a devotional that uses Tolkien's stories to lead you through nine pairs of choices–darkness or light, betrayal or loyalty, deception or honesty, to name just a few–and reveals what the Bible has to say about each.

ARE YOU READY FOR THE CHALLENGE?

areUthirsty.com
ISBN 0-8423-8554-1